FROM AQUINO II TO DUTERTE
(2010–2018)

The **ISEAS – Yusof Ishak Institute** (formerly Institute of Southeast Asian Studies) is an autonomous organization established in 1968. It is a regional centre dedicated to the study of socio-political, security, and economic trends and developments in Southeast Asia and its wider geostrategic and economic environment. The Institute's research programmes are grouped under Regional Economic Studies (RES), Regional Strategic and Political Studies (RSPS), and Regional Social and Cultural Studies (RSCS). The Institute is also home to the ASEAN Studies Centre (ASC), the Nalanda-Sriwijaya Centre (NSC) and the Singapore APEC Study Centre.

ISEAS Publishing, an established academic press, has issued more than 2,000 books and journals. It is the largest scholarly publisher of research about Southeast Asia from within the region. ISEAS Publishing works with many other academic and trade publishers and distributors to disseminate important research and analyses from and about Southeast Asia to the rest of the world.

FROM AQUINO II TO DUTERTE (2010–2018)

Change, Continuity—and Rupture

EDITED BY
IMELDA DEINLA
BJÖRN DRESSEL

First published in Singapore in 2019 by
ISEAS Publishing
30 Heng Mui Keng Terrace
Singapore 119614
E-mail: publish@iseas.edu.sg
Website: http://bookshop.iseas.edu.sg

All rights reserved. No part of this publication may be reproduced, stored in a retrieval system, or transmitted in any form or by any means, electronic, mechanical, photocopying, recording or otherwise, without the prior permission of the ISEAS – Yusof Ishak Institute.

© 2019 ISEAS – Yusof Ishak Institute, Singapore

The responsibility for facts and opinions in this publication rests exclusively with the authors and their interpretations do not necessarily reflect the views or the policy of the publisher or its supporters.

ISEAS Library Cataloguing-in-Publication Data

From Aquino II to Duterte (2010–2018) : Change, Continuity—and Rupture / edited by Imelda Deinla & Björn Dressel.
1. Philippines—Politics and government—1986–
2. Philippines—Economic conditions—21st century.
3. Peace-building—Philippines.
4. Philippines—Foreign relations.
I. Deinla, Imelda, editor.
II. Dressel, Björn, editor.
III. Title: Change, Continuity—and Rupture
DS686.614 F931   2019

ISBN 978-981-4843-28-7 (soft cover)
ISBN 978-981-4843-29-4 (ebook, PDF)

Cover photo: Photo entry by Mylene Tiondo, for the 2018 IslamNotPhobia Photo Exhibit Project by Team Pakigsandurot of MSU-IIT.

Typeset by Superskill Graphics Pte Ltd

Contents

List of Tables	vii
List of Figures	viii
Acknowledgements	xi
Acronyms and Glossary	xiii
Contributors	xxv

Introduction: From Aquino II to Duterte (2010–2018):
Change, Continuity—and Rupture 1
Imelda Deinla and Björn Dressel

PART I: POLITICS AND GOVERNANCE

1. The Rise of Illiberal Democracy in the Philippines:
Duterte's Early Presidency 39
Mark R. Thompson

2. Finding Federalism in the Philippines: Federalism—
"The Centerpiece of My Campaign" 62
Steven Rood

3. On Crooked Ways and Straight Paths:
Assessing Anticorruption Governance of the Arroyo
and Aquino Governments 99
Kidjie Saguin

PART II: ECONOMIC GOVERNANCE

4. How Has the Economy Fared under the Duterte
Administration So Far? 127
Maria Socorro Gochoco-Bautista

5. The Philippine Economy: Renewed Dynamism,
   Old Challenges   145
   Christopher Cabuay and Hal Hill

6. Competition Law and Policy in the Philippines:
   A Role in Sustained and Inclusive Economic Growth   186
   Rachel Burgess

PART III: PEACE PROCESS IN MINDANAO

7. Prospects for Lasting Peace in Mindanao:
   Peacemaking and Peacebuilding under the Aquino and
   Duterte Administrations   207
   Matthew Stephens

8. Prospects for the Normalization Process in the Southern
   Philippines: An Architecture of Uncertainty?   239
   Georgi Engelbrecht

PART IV: INTERNATIONAL ENVIRONMENT

9. The Philippines and the South China Sea/West Philippine Sea
   Conflict: Challenges and Prospects for Peace, Diplomacy and
   External Defence Capability   265
   Noel M. Morada

10. Fall from Grace, Descent from Power? Civil Society after
    Philippine Democracy's Lost Decade   285
    Aries A. Arugay

Index   309

List of Tables

I.1	Percentage Distribution of Families and Incomes, by Modified Socioeconomic Class, 2009	17
2.1	Constitutional Provisions That Need Amending	69
2.2	Agreement on Federating the Regional Governments, 17 May–3 June 2002	69
2.3	Agreement on Changing to Federalism as Soon as Possible, by Area, January 2004	70
2.4	Post-Election Party Switching in the House of Representatives	76
2.5	Opinion Polls on Amending the Philippine Constitution in 2014 and 2016	77
2.6	Opinion Polls on Federalism in 2009 and 2016	78
3.1	Critical Capacities for Corruption Control	104
5.1	Philippine Regional GDP, at Constant 2000 Prices in PhP	168
5.2	Top and Bottom Income Shares, the Philippines and Neighbours	171
5.3	Education Enrolment and Survival Rates, the Philippines and Neighbours	174

List of Figures

I.1	Net Satisfaction Ratings, Presidents since 1984	14
I.2	Net Satisfaction Ratings for Rodrigo Duterte by Age: September 2016–June 2018	19
I.3	Net Satisfaction Ratings for Rodrigo Duterte by Class: September 2016–June 2018	20
I.4	Net Satisfaction Ratings for Rodrigo Duterte by Education: September 2016–June 2018	21
2.1	The Anti-Charter Change Rally in 1997	66
2.2	Economic Density in the Philippines, 2007	81
2.3	Peace and Development Roadmap of the Duterte Administration	87
5.1	Economic Growth, the Philippines and Neighbours, 2000–16	148
5.2	Agricultural Growth, the Philippines and Neighbours, 2000–16	149
5.3	Industrial Growth, the Philippines and Neighbours, 2000–16	150
5.4	Services Growth, the Philippines and Neighbours, 2000–16	151
5.5	Inflation, the Philippines and Neighbours, 2000–17	154
5.6	Exchange Rates, the Philippines and Neighbours, 2000–17	156
5.7	Stock Market Indices, the Philippines and Neighbours, 2013–17	157
5.8	Current Account Balances, the Philippines and Neighbours, 2000–16	159
5.9	Government Revenue, the Philippines and Neighbours, 2000–16	161
5.10	Fiscal Balances, the Philippines and Neighbours, 2000–16	162

5.11	Remittances and BPO Revenues, 2000–17	163
5.12	Poverty Incidence, the Philippines and Neighbours, 1985–2016	170
5.13	Unemployed Rates, the Philippines and Neighbours, 2000–17	173
5.14	Ease of Doing Business, the Philippines and Neighbours, 2004–17	177
5.15	Logistics Performance Index, the Philippines and Neighbours, 2007–16	179
5.16	Corruption Perception Index, the Philippines and Neighbours, 2000–16	180
7.1	MILF Vertical and Horizontal Conflict Incidents, 2011–16	212
7.2	Annual Budget for PAMANA	214
7.3	Private Sector Investments in ARMM, 2012–16	218
7.4	Poverty Incidents among Population in ARMM, 2006–15	219
7.5	Violent Conflict Incidents and Deaths in the Proposed Bangsamoro Territory, 2011–16	222
8.1	MILF Decommissioning in Context	258

Acknowledgements

Undoubtedly, "change" has been a recurring theme in Philippine political, economic and social landscape—one recently pronounced under the controversial Duterte presidency. While the politics of change has also intensified in many other parts of the world as shown in the surge of populist movements and leadership, what is peculiar in the Philippine case is the frequency and intensity of narratives of change—and change rhetoric—that have animated political discourse and the everyday lives of ordinary Filipinos since post-colonial statehood.

It is against this background that this volume asks: How different is Duterte's programme of change from the past governments, particularly from its predecessor, the Aquino II administration? Is there a shift in regime orientation and policy preferences from Aquino II to Duterte? What will this mean to the future direction of Philippine democracy, its economic development, peace and security, and relations with other countries?

This volume focuses on four critical areas—Politics and Governance; Economic Governance; Mindanao and the Peace Process; and International Relations—to illustrate continuities or discontinuities in policies and governance of institutions to explain the dynamics of change in the Philippines. It pays particular attention to the crucial period between Aquino II and the early years of Duterte. The reason is that Aquino II represents an important period for rebuilding and consolidating institutions of governance and accountability after two previous tumultuous administrations (Estrada and Macapagal Arroyo). Aquino II also demonstrates the inherent flaws of Philippine democracy and unravels the contradictory forces vying for state power that sets the scene for Duterte's rise to the presidency.

An assemblage of expertise from the academic, practitioner and policy community came together to share their ideas for this volume. The seed towards this intellectual endeavour has come, however, from the Philippines Update Conference on 5–6 August 2016 hosted at the College of Asia and the Pacific of the Australian National University (ANU) with the theme, "Sustaining the Momentum for Change Beyond 2016". Special thanks are therefore in order for the conference convenors: Teresa Jopson, Nicole Curato, Imelda Deinla, and Björn Dressel. We also wish to express our deepest gratitude to various organizations at the ANU, ANU Filipino Association (ANUFA), School of Regulation and Global Governance (RegNet), the Filipino-Australian community in Canberra, volunteers, presenters and audience who came from all over Australia and the Philippines for the Philippines Update 2016. We thank our friends—Sora Lee, Janice Li, Margie Hequilan, and Mana Takahishi—who devoted valuable time in helping us prepare for the conference.

We are grateful for the generous funding support of the Department of Foreign Affairs and Trade (DFAT) of Australia and the ANU Southeast Asia Institute. The Update was made more special as it coincided with the seventieth anniversary of the Philippines-Australia bilateral relations.

We thank the ANU Philippines Project and its staff, past and present—Allinettes Adigue, Amy Hamilton, Rory MacNeil, and Kent Marjun Primor—who all have contributed towards the conference and completion of this publication, and Tanya Mark for excellent copy-editing work. We also acknowledge the continuing support of Professors Hal Hill, Veronica Taylor, Arsenio Balisacan, Paul Hutchcroft and Mina Roces. Finally, we are sincerely grateful to the ISEAS – Yusof Ishak Institute in Singapore and Ng Kok Kiong, Head of ISEAS Publishing, for the trust on this collection and making this publication a reality.

Imelda Deinla and Björn Dressel

Acronyms and Glossary

AdCom	Advocacy Commission 2006; was chaired by Lito Lorenzana, President of the Centrist Democracy Political Institute (CDPI), a political, non-profit organization, in partnership with Konrad-Adenauer-Stiftung (KAS) Philippines. Lorenzana is also Chair of the Centrist Democratic Party of the Philippines (CDP), was Chairman of the AdCom, and Secretary-General of the 2005 ConCom. Under President Gloria Macapagal Arroyo, the ConCom was tasked to revise the 1987 Constitution of the Philippines.
AFP	Armed Forces of the Philippines
AmBisyon 2040	The Philippine Development Plan (PDP) 2017–2022, the blueprint for the country's development under the Duterte administration, launched by NEDA. The PDP 2017–2022 stems from the 10-point Socioeconomic Agenda and is the first of four medium-term plans towards *AmBisyon Natin 2040*, the collective vision of Filipinos over the next 25 years.
ARF	ASEAN Regional Forum
ARMM	Autonomous Region in Muslim Mindanao; enshrined in the 1987 Constitution and established by Republic Act 9054, now comprises the provinces of Basilan, Lanao del Sur, Maguindanao, Sulu and Tawi-Tawi, and the cities of Marawi and Lamitan.

archipelagic state	Any internationally recognized state or country comprising a series of islands that form an archipelago—defined by the UN Convention on the Law of the Sea in order to define what borders such states should be allowed to claim.
ASEAN	Association of Southeast Asian Nations; formed in 1967 by Indonesia, Malaysia, the Philippines, Singapore, and Thailand to promote political and economic cooperation and regional stability. Its membership now includes Brunei, Cambodia, Laos, Myanmar and Vietnam.
AU$	Australian dollar
BBL	Bangsamoro Basic Law
BCF	Bangsamoro Coordination Forum
BDA	Bangsamoro Development Agency
BIAF	Bangsamoro Islamic Armed Forces
BIFF	Bangsamoro Islamic Freedom Fighters
BIR	Bureau of Internal Revenue
BOL	Bangsamoro Organic Law
BPO	business process outsourcing
BSP	Bangko Sentral ng Pilipinas; central bank of the Philippines, established 3 July 1993.
BTC	Bangsamoro Transition Commission
CAB	Comprehensive Agreement on the Bangsamoro
cacique	*cacique* democracy; a term originally used by Benedict Anderson to describe the feudal political system in many parts of the Philippines where strong local leaders have almost warlord-type powers. *Cacique* is from a Taíno word *kassiquan* (to keep house)—in Taíno culture *cacique* rank was apparently established via democratic means.
CAFGUs	Civilian Armed Forces Geographical Units
CCS	Competition Commission of Singapore
CCT	Conditional Cash Transfer; a poverty alleviation targeted transfer programme where cash is directly provided to beneficiary families (usually

	mothers) on the condition that children attend school regularly and family members visit health centres regularly. CCT is locally known as *Pantawid Pamilya Pilipino Program* (or 4Ps) in the Philippines.
CDP	Centrist Democratic Party
CDPI	Centrist Democratic Party Institute; founded in 2010 to support centrist (Christian-Muslim value-oriented) democratic movements and political parties in the Philippines in their efforts to help shape policy to create major reforms. The CDPI has been a partner of the KAS since 2011.
CFO	Commission on Filipinos Overseas
Charter Change	Shortened to *Cha-Cha*; is also known as Constitutional reform and refers to amendments or revisions in the 1987 Philippine Constitution. See *Rappler.com*, https://www.rappler.com/newsbreak/iq/193718-charter-change-explainer-philippine-constitution.
CLMV	Cambodia, Laos, Myanmar and Vietnam; the CLMV countries
CMFP	Citizens' Movement for a Federal Philippines
CNN	Communist Party of the Philippines/New People's Army/National Democratic Front
COA	Commission on Audit
COC	Code of Conduct
COMELEC	Commission on Elections
ConCom	Consultative Commission (on charter change); on 25 July 2005, in her State of the Nation Address, President Gloria Macapagal Arroyo announced the creation of the Consultative Commission on Charter Change, tasked to revise the 1987 Constitution. An Executive Order signed by President Rodrigo Duterte 7 December 2016 (re)formed ConCom on 19 February 2018, to draft a charter for shifting to a federal form of government—one of President Duterte's campaign promises.

CONFED MINDANAO	Confederation of Provincial Governors, City Mayors and Municipal Mayors and Municipal League Presidents of Mindanao
Congress	Commonly referred to as Congress, the House of Representatives of the Philippines is the lower house of the Congress of the Philippines.
Cory Constitution	Refers to the 1987 Philippine Constitution.
CPI	Corruption Perceptions Index; *see also* TI (Transparency International)
CPLA	Cordillera People's Liberation Army
CPP	Communist Party of the Philippines; the CPP-NPA-NDF rebellion refers to the ongoing conflict between the Government of the Philippines and the communist coalition of the CPP, the New People's Army (NPA), and the National Democratic Front (NDF).
CPP-NPA	Communist Party of the Philippines–New People's Army
CSC	Civil Service Commission
CSOs	civil society organizations
DAP	Disbursement Acceleration Program
DDR	Disarmament, Demobilization and Reintegration
deep democracy	Term developed by Arny Mindell in 1988. Unlike "classical" democracy, which focuses on majority rule, "deep" democracy suggests all voices, awareness, and frameworks of reality are important.
DILG	Department of the Interior and Local Government
DOC	Declaration of the Conduct of Parties in the South China Sea
DSWD	Department of Social Welfare and Development
EDCA	Enhanced Defense Cooperation Agreement; between the US and the Philippines.
EDSA	*Epifanio de los Santos Avenue*; Philippine's People Power Revolution—over four days in February 1986, culminating in a US-sponsored flight carrying Ferdinand Marcos and his family out

Acronyms and Glossary xvii

	of the country and ending a dictatorship of more than twenty years.
EEZ	exclusive economic zone
EODB	Ease of Doing Business Index; ranking business regulation created by the World Bank.
ERC	Energy Regulatory Commission
EU	European Union
FAB	Framework Agreement on the Bangsamoro
FDI	foreign direct investment
FIES	Family Income and Expenditure Surveys
FPA	Final Peace Agreement
FUNDANGOs	fund-driven NGOs
GDP	gross domestic product
GONGOs	government-owned NGOs
GPH	Government of the Philippines
GRINGOs	government-run or -initiated NGOs
GRP	gross regional product
GSP	Generalised System of Preferences; a preferential tariff system which provides for a formal system of exemption from the more general rules of the World Trade Organization (WTO). Formerly the General Agreement on Tariffs and Trade (GATT).
GSP+	General System of Preferences Plus; a special incentive arrangement for sustainable development and good governance, GSP+ grants full removal of tariffs on over 66 per cent of EU tariff lines allowing vulnerable developing countries vital access to the EU market and contributing to their growth.
Hyatt 10	In 2005 during the "Hello Garci" controversy, 7 Cabinet members and 3 bureau heads resigned and called on President Gloria Macapagal Arroyo to also resign. The group announced their resignation in a press conference at the Hyatt Hotel in Pasay City.
ICJ	International Court of Justice
ICP	Independent Commission on Policing

ICT	information and communications technology (or technologies)
IDAP	Integrity Development Action Plan
IDB	International Decommissioning Body
IDR	Integrity Development Review
IEG	Independent Evaluation Group; evaluates development effectiveness of the World Bank Group.
IMP	Integrity Management Program
IMT	International Monitoring Team
IPAC	Institute for Policy Analysis of Conflict
IRA	Internal Revenue Allotment
ISO	International Organization for Standardization; an international body founded on 23 February 1947 promoting worldwide proprietary, industrial and commercial standards.
IT	information technology
JNC	Joint Normalization Committee
JPSC	Joint Peace and Security Committee
JPST	Joint Peace and Security Teams
LGU	Local Government Unit
LPI	Logistics Performance Index; an interactive tool for trade logistics created by the World Bank that scores and compares countries on efficient movement of goods.
KAS	Konrad-Adenaur-Stiftung; a German political foundation which promotes political education initiatives worldwide.
LP	Liberal Party
MAMFI	*Masaganang Ani para sa Magsasaka* Foundation Inc.
MAO	Mergers and Acquisitions Office
MAO-AD	Memorandum of Agreement on Ancestral Domain
Medium Run	A period of about 12 years during which capital stock adjusts gradually to bring the economy to long-run equilibrium, underpinned by macroeconomic principles. The Short Run is a

	period of about 3 years during which prices (and wages) adjust gradually to bring the economy to medium-run equilibrium.
MILF	Moro Islamic Liberation Front; based in Mindanao
MINCODE	Mindanao Coalition of Development NGO Networks
MNLF	Moro National Liberation Front
Moro	A member of predominantly Muslim peoples of the southern Philippines; word origin is via Spanish derived from Latin *Mauritius* (Moorish), a derivative of *Maurus* (a Moor).
MOU	Memorandum of Understanding
MRAP	Moral Renewal Action Plan
MSMEs	micro, small and medium-sized enterprises
NACPA	National Anti-Corruption Program of Action
NBN	National Broadband Network
NCR	National Capital Region; Metropolitan Manila (*Kalakhang Maynila, Kamaynilaan*) is the seat of government, one of three defined metropolitan areas of the Philippines.
NCS	National Security Council; the principal advisory body on the proper coordination and integration of plans and policies affecting national security.
NEDA	National Economic and Development Authority
NDF/P	National Democratic Front/of the Philippines; *see also* CPP
NIE	*Número de identidad de extranjero*; Non-interest expense(?); a tax identification number
NFA	National Food Authority
NGO	non-government organization
NPA	New People's Army; *see also* CPP
NTF-DPAGs	National Task Force for the Disbandment of the Private Armed Groups
OECD	Organisation for Economic Co-operation and Development
OFW	Overseas Filipino Worker/Overseas Foreign Worker

OPAPP	Office of the Presidential Adviser on the Peace Process
OPEC	Organization of Petroleum Exporting Countries; a group of 12 of the world's major oil-exporting nations. OPEC was founded in 1960 to coordinate petroleum policies of its members, and provide member states with technical and economic aid.
PAGC	Presidential Anti-Graft Commission
PAGs	Private Armed Groups
PAMANA	*Payapa at Masaganang Pamayanan*; a programme established in 2010 for peacebuilding and development in areas affected by and vulnerable to conflict.
Pang-FI	*Pangkabuhayan* Foundation Inc.
PCA	Permanent Court of Arbitration; an inter-governmental organization established by treaty in 1899, located at the Hague; PCA is an official UN observer, not a UN agency.
PCC	Philippines Competition Commission
PDP	Philippines Development Plan
PDP-Laban	Partido Demokratiko Pilipino–Lakas ng Bayan; the ruling political party in the Philippines
PEZA	Philippine Export Zone Authority
PhilGEPS	Philippine Government Electronic Procurement System
PhP	Philippine peso; since 2017, the ISO 4217 standard refers to the currency by the Filipino term "piso". Other ways of writing the peso sign are "PHP", "Php", "P$", or "P".
PIRMA	People's Initiative for Reform, Modernization and Action; *pirma* is "signature" in Tagalog.
Plurality vote	or "relative majority"; describes the circumstance when a candidate polls more votes than any other, but does not receive a majority.
PNP	Philippine National Police
POs	People's Organizations
PPP	public-private partnership

Acronyms and Glossary

PISA	Programme for International Student Assessment; an initiative of the OECD intended to evaluate educational systems by measuring 15-year-old school pupils' understandings and skills in science, reading and mathematics to everyday situations.
PSA	Philippine Statistical Authority
PSEI	Philippine Stock Exchange Index
quo warranto	legal term for a writ (order) used to challenge the right to public or corporate office.
RH	Reproductive Health
RPA-ABB	Revolutionary Proletarian Army – Alex Boncayo Brigade
SCS	South China Sea
SALWS	small arms and light weapons
SDPFFI	Social Development Program for Farmers Development
SMEs	small and medium enterprises
SONA	State of the Nation Address
SWS	Social Weather Stations; a private non-profit, non-stock research institution established in 1985 with members called Fellows who are social scientists in economics, political science, sociology, statistics, market research, and other fields
TAG	Transparent Accountable Governance
TESDA	Technical Education and Skills Development Authority
TI	Transparency International; an international non-government organization based in Berlin, Germany.
TI CPI	Transparency International Corruption Perceptions Index; TI has published the CPI since 1995, ranking countries each year "by their perceived levels of corruption, as determined by expert assessments and opinion surveys". The CPI generally defines corruption as "the misuse of public power for private benefit".

	The Philippines was ranked 111/180 and scored 34/100 in the 2017 CPI.
TIMSS	Trends in International Mathematics and Science Study; an initiative of the International Association for the Evaluation of Educational Achievement (IEA); examines how well Year 4 and Year 8 students have mastered factual and procedural knowledge taught in school mathematics and science curricula.
TJRC	Transitional Justice and Reconciliation Commission
TRAIN	Tax Reform for Acceleration and Inclusion
UAE	United Arab Emirates
UBJP	United Bangsamoro Justice Party
UK	United Kingdom
ULAP	Union of Local Authorities of the Philippines
UN	United Nations
UNCAC	United Nations Convention Against Corruption
UNCTAD	United Nations Conference on Trade and Development; the main UN body dealing with trade, investment and development issues.
UNCLOS	United Nations Convention on the Law of the Sea; also called the Law of the Sea Convention or the Law of the Sea treaty—an international agreement from the third UN Conference on the Law of the Sea (UNCLOS III), that took place between 1973 and 1982.
UP	University of the Philippines
US	United States
USAID	United States Agency for International Development
US$	United States dollar
UXOs	unexploded ordnances
VACC	Volunteers Against Crime and Corruption
VAT	value-added tax; a consumption tax placed on a product whenever value is added at each stage of the supply chain, from production to point of sale.

Acronyms and Glossary xxiii

VoPI	Volume of Production Index
WDR	World Development Report
WGI	Worldwide Governance Indicators; a set of composite indicators covering six dimensions of governance for over 200 countries from 1996 to 2016.
WJP	World Justice Project Rule of Law Index; world's leading source for original, independent data on the rule of law.
WPS	West Philippine Sea
WTO	World Trade Organization
ZTE	ZTE Corporation is a Chinese multinational telecommunications equipment and systems company.

Contributors

Aries A. Arugay is Associate Professor of Political Science in the University of the Philippines-Diliman. He is also Co-convenor of the Strategic Studies Program of the University of the Philippines Center for Integrative and Development Studies and Research Fellow at the Asia Pacific Pathways to Progress Foundation, Inc. He has done research and published on topics such as civil society, contentious politics, democratic erosion, and performative populism using cases from Southeast Asia and Latin America.

Rachel Burgess is a lecturer in competition and consumer law at the University of Southern Queensland and a research fellow at the Deakin University IPA-Deakin SME Research Centre. She holds a Bachelor of Laws (Hons) from the Queensland University of Technology and a Master of Laws in Public International Law (with Merit) from the University of London.

Christopher Cabuay is an Australia Awards Scholar taking his PhD in Economics at the Crawford School of Public Policy, Australian National University. He finished his Bachelor of Science in Applied Economics and Masters of Science in Economics at the De La Salle University School of Economics.

Imelda Deinla is Research Fellow at the School of Regulation and Global Governance at the Australian National University (ANU), and Director of the ANU Philippines Project, a policy-engaged research initiative on economics, trade, politics and governance on the Philippines.

Björn Dressel is Associate Professor at the Crawford School of Public Policy at the Australian National University, and previously held an Australian Research Council Early Career Researcher Award (2013–2018).

Georgi Engelbrecht has been working in the Southern Philippines for the last seven years primarily on civilian protection and human rights/ humanitarian law and is having a legal and political science perspective on the conflict in Mindanao, as well as the peace process. He is a German national and currently assisting the European Union's peacebuilding programmes in Mindanao.

Maria Socorro Gochoco-Bautista is the Bangko Sentral ng Pilipinas Sterling Chair Professor of Monetary Economics at the University of the Philippines School of Economics. She is a member and former Chair of the Asian Shadow Financial Regulatory Committee and an Associate Editor of Asian Economic Papers.

Hal Hill is the H.W. Arndt Professor Emeritus of Southeast Asian Economies in the Arndt Corden Department of Economics, Crawford School of Public Policy, ANU College of Asia and the Pacific, the Australian National University. His main research interest is the economic development of Southeast Asia.

Noel M. Morada is Director (Regional Diplomacy and Capacity Building) Asia Pacific Centre for the Responsibility to Protect (R2P), School of Political Science and International Studies, The University of Queensland.

Steven Rood was formerly the Asia Foundation's country representative for the Philippines and Pacific Island Nations. In his concurrent role as regional advisor for Local Governance, he helped build local government, decentralization, and municipal government programmes throughout the region.

Kidjie Saguin is a PhD student at the Lee Kuan Yew School of Public Policy, National University of Singapore (NUS). He holds a Master in Public Policy (Social Policy) from NUS and a BA in Public Administration (cum laude) from the University of the Philippines.

Matthew Stephens is a senior social development specialist at the World Bank in Washington, D.C. He was formerly assigned in the Philippines working on conflict, security, and development.

Mark R. Thompson is professor of politics at the City University of Hong Kong, where he is head of the Department of Asian and International Studies (AIS) and also director of the Southeast Asia Research Centre.

Introduction
From Aquino II to Duterte: Change, Continuity—and Rupture

Imelda Deinla and Björn Dressel

Democratic practices of the Philippines, Asia's oldest democracy and the second most populous country in the ASEAN region, have been a puzzle to many scholars and observers of democracy. While vibrant in terms of voter turnout, civic engagement, and institutional protections, there are widespread flaws in Philippine democratic processes—illustrated by persistent pernicious elite politics, continued institutional weakness, and widespread abuse of public office.[1]

The country's economic record is as patchy as its democracy. The long-standing description of the Philippines as the "sick man of Asia" has been rebutted by the country's rapid economic growth over the last decade (2007–17). However, with regular boom and bust cycles, and persistent deep-seated poverty and inequality, concerns remain about the equity and sustainability of this type of growth in the Philippines.[2] Built on the legacies of Spanish and United States colonial rule, the Philippine state remains confronted by constant challenges to its legitimacy—including Asia's longest communist rebellion, Muslim separatist insurgencies in Mindanao, and large-scale public protests such as the first and second *Epifanio de los Santos Avenue* (EDSA 1 and 2), Philippine's People Power Revolution that forced changes in leadership through extra-constitutional processes.[3]

"Change" has therefore been a recurring theme in Philippine political, economic, and social discourses. The discourse of change holds considerable appeal and permeates the everyday lives of ordinary Filipinos with remarkable intensity and frequency. The discourse informs the thinking of political observers who identify competing reformist and populist narratives of change in Philippine politics.[4] Change seems to characterize the transition from the administration of Aquino II (2010–16) to the administration of current president Rodrigo Roa Duterte (2016–). Aquino II was elected on a technocratic "straight path" (*daang matuwid*) reform platform that challenged the widespread abuse of public office under the presidency of Gloria Macapagal Arroyo (2001–10). Duterte—a maverick former mayor of Davao city in Mindanao—rode high on a campaign promise in the 2016 presidential election of bringing about law and order in a swift and decisive manner, embodied in his slogan "Change Is Coming".

But how much change has actually taken place? What kind of change is unfolding and for whom? Are we simply witnessing business-as-usual, fragmented Filipino elite politics, as a feature of discordant democracy in the Philippines? Or has there indeed been change—a rupture in the transition to illiberal, undemocratic practices?

Since the People Power Revolution (EDSA 1) that toppled the Marcos dictatorship in 1986, the Philippines has frequently cycled through recurrent reforms and populism. But changes being introduced by the Duterte administration seem unusually deep and far-reaching—suggesting a concerted attempt to reorganize, or indeed replace, the liberal state-society relations that previously characterized the post-1986 political settlement. Academic observers have therefore described the election of Duterte as a point of historical rupture, rather than merely another instance of populism sweeping the world.[5]

After more than two years in office, Duterte seems to be leading the Philippines towards illiberalism. First and foremost, violence has defined his rule. While the Philippines has experienced political violence and extrajudicial killings, Duterte's war on drugs since assuming office in June 2017 has claimed more than 20,000 lives. Most of these deaths happened as a result of police operations or were perpetrated by unknown assailants. Dubbed as a "war against the poor", most of the victims have come from poor villages or squatter areas in Manila and nearby provinces.[6] Extrajudicial killings of suspected communist rebels, journalists and local politicians continue to dominate headlines.

Another concerning development under Duterte has been sustained and concerted attacks on independent constitutional bodies. Examples of these attacks include the filing of impeachment procedures and subsequent removal of the Chief Justice of the Supreme Court, Maria Lourdes Sereno, based on a *quo warranto* proceeding, a legal procedure for removing public officials on the grounds that the officials have no legal right to continue holding office.[7] Impeachment complaints have also been filed against the Ombudsman and the vice president based on scant and trivial evidence. Legislative threats and harassment were also directed against the Commission on Human Rights and its officials, one example being when the lower house voted to give the Commission a budget of PhP1,000 (approximately AUD20).

The Philippine Supreme Court, regarded as the bastion of democracy, is now embroiled in contentious elite politics—undermining its independence and further weakening constitutional checks and balances. The participation of five members of the bench in the impeachment proceedings against Chief Justice Sereno—pre-empting the Senate decision by ruling on the *quo warranto* proceeding—has put a spotlight on the deep politicization of the judiciary and the impact of this on constitutional principles and the rule of law. Decisions of the Court involving important political issues show a pattern of "judicial docility"[8] that favours executive preferences or deferment to political decision making. Examples of such cases include the burial of the late authoritarian ruler Ferdinand Marcos, and the imposition and further extension of martial law in Mindanao.

An ongoing constitutional reform initiative is in progress to facilitate a shift from a unitary presidential to a federal parliamentary system. This initiative—despite the absence of public support towards a federal form of government[9]—is backed by the political rhetoric that federalism offers the solution to oligarchic control by "imperial Manila" of the country's politics and the economy. A draft federal constitution formulated by the Consultative Committee (Con-Com)—the body created by the president to study and propose amendments to the 1987 Constitution—was submitted in 2018 to the legislature and the president.

Martial law was imposed across Mindanao in response to the Marawi City siege in 2017, with threats from the Duterte administration to declare a revolutionary form of government and place the entire country under martial law. Freedom of the press—except publications that favour the Duterte administration—is under assault, as illustrated by revocation of the licence of the critical media platform Rappler.com. Many mainstream media outlets, meanwhile, such as *CNN, Philippines Daily Inquirer, Philippines Star*, etc.—although traditionally considered the most vibrant in Asia—are now often seen as practising self-censorship.[10]

Despite arbitrary, coercive, or overt violent actions by the Duterte administration, many of the developments eroding Philippine democracy have been met with surprisingly little resistance from either political elites or civil society actors. A majority of Filipinos have expressed continuing approval of, and trust in, President Duterte and his administration.[11]

Contributing authors in this volume thus address the following questions: What has allowed the Duterte administration to dismantle the post-Marcos political settlement so rapidly and with little opposition? Have Philippine elites abandoned their support for grounding the political system in liberal-constitutional democracy and institutions? Or is this political settlement not about agreement on liberal democracy per se but merely a casual arrangement among the elites to facilitate transfer of power and maintain their political salience? And why has the country's broad and vibrant civil society—previously a compelling force in any efforts to weaken democracy and its institutions—failed to respond effectively to Duterte's attacks on the rule of law and human rights?

As further highlighted by the contributions to this volume, we believe that some of the remarkable economic and political gains made under the Aquino II administration had unintended consequences that laid the foundation for Duterte's illiberal democracy. The paradoxes of elite democracy and unequal development brought to the fore latent illiberal features that had previously surfaced in the form of authoritarianism during the Marcos years. We thus argue that growing social and economic insecurity in middle-class constituencies—rather than elite fragmentation—has undermined the ability of civil society to act collectively, thus accelerating the trend towards illiberalism.[12]

To explain the resurgence of anti-liberal forces in the Philippine political landscape, this chapter begins by mapping the fault-lines in the failures of the Aquino II administration. We then discuss the assault on liberal institutions before focusing on the elite and civil society dynamics that made this assault possible. Proceeding in this manner does not simply fulfil an academic purpose. It also seeks to identify existing societal spaces with the strength and capacity to resist—and even stand up against—the debilitating impact of the new and dangerous monopoly of power.

I. A SHORT MARCH INTO ILLIBERAL DEMOCRACY: FROM AQUINO II TO DUTERTE

Since the late 1990s, assumptions that economic development and liberal democracy go hand in hand in Asia can no longer be sustained. As one of the most diverse regions in the world in terms of governance—socialist, democratic, semi-authoritarian and authoritarian—the region has seen authoritarian and illiberal democracies emerge alongside rapid capitalist development. While both modes of democracy may recognize the vibrancy of a capitalist economy, authoritarian regimes generally deny free and fair electoral processes. Illiberal democracies, on the other hand—although adorned with the institutional and procedural trappings of democracy—have low levels of participation and inclusiveness.[13] Dominated by elites—or controlled by an oligarchy—illiberal democracies also tend to demonstrate persistent patterns of violence, gross human rights violations, and a culture of impunity—which narrows and ultimately eliminates avenues for political dissent and reconfiguring state and institutional arrangements. While in many countries this scenario has led to outright authoritarianism, there has been a trend in some Southeast Asian nations—particularly Singapore and Malaysia—to combine features of liberalism and authoritarianism, by segregating politics from economics and pursuing some social and economic redistributive projects.[14] This type of regime is, however, not unique to the Southeast Asian region. Countries in this region have undergone alternating phases of authoritarian and liberal governments, or coexistence of the two types of regime[15]—vulnerable, however, to further authoritarian backsliding, particularly when institutions are weak and civil society is divided, as in the case of Cambodia.[16]

The situation in the Philippines exemplifies the phenomenon of illiberal democracy. Duterte disavows being an authoritarian as do his throngs of supporters who continue to profess allegiance to "democratic" values.[17] Democracy with a liberal democratic constitution on paper does not preclude the emergence of an illiberal or authoritarian order. In fact, in the last quarter century, democratic practices are increasingly flourishing side-by-side with illiberal regimes in the region.[18] A rearticulation of the meaning of democracy is evident in the Philippines—neither an idealized version, nor merely part of a "populist tide". As political, economic and social processes have become more dynamic and interwoven in the region, it is necessary to revisit binary conceptions of liberal versus authoritarian regimes.

Except for the Marcos dictatorship from 1965 to 1986, the Philippines seems to have shunned attempts at absolute authoritarian or illiberal governments—with several unsuccessful military-led *coup d'etats* since Aquino I. The Philippines has been described as *"cacique* democracy"[19] or "low-quality democracy"[20]—notions based on the disproportionate influence of traditional political elites and dynasties on political institutions. Effective participation and true representation are therefore largely illusory with elites taking turns in power nationally and locally. Political structures that emerged from US colonial rule are characterized by disenfranchisement of the masses, unstable patronage-infested political parties, dominance of political dynasties, and a spoils system that has eroded bureaucratic autonomy.[21]

These patterns of dynastic democracy and systemic institutional weakness have proven remarkably stable. Despite the occasional emergence of elite fractures—triggering new institutional arrangements as in the post-Marcos 1987 Constitution—political elites in the Philippines have remained consistent in their social composition and in their control over state institutions. The political elites have proven resilient—colluding when necessary—and emerging unscathed through political fractures. In the 2013 elections, it has been suggested that 74 per cent of the elected members of the House of Representatives came from political dynasties.[22]

The dominance of dynastic families has been so pervasive that the Philippines has been cited to have one of the highest concentrations of political dynasties in Asia.[23] In a landmark 2012 study, Mendoza et al. found districts controlled by political dynasties tended to have significantly higher incidences of poverty.[24] In our view, this happens because these families have been adroitly capable at reaching accommodation amongst themselves and with other political actors, despite electoral competition and growing demands from civil society. Moreover, liberal features of the post-1987 political settlement are maintained because most elites have more or less equal access to legal and political institutions to generate economic rents—thus lessening genuine elite conflicts.

Are these descriptions still accurate? Recent developments suggest Duterte has actively erected an illiberal democracy by taking advantage of weaknesses in the post-1987 liberal reformist order.[25] Duterte also flirts openly with a populist form of authoritarianism—examples such as his suggestion of a revolutionary government or his recent statement prioritizing "human lives over human rights"[26] reminding some observers of past-fascist patterns in Europe.[27]

Consideration of elite–civil society dynamics are thus central to understanding the current dynamics under the Duterte regime—whether civil society is cohesive or fragmented often determines regime stability or change.[28] For instance, the cohesion of civil society and alliances formed among segments of the elite generated regime change and resistance to authoritarian tendencies in the Philippines such as EDSA 1 and 2. From this vantage point, the divisions within civil society generated by Duterte's broader appeal for change seem problematic as his use of rhetoric particularly resonates among the Filipino middle class, the traditional backbone of civil society activism in the Philippines.[29]

Duterte was not, however, the first president to challenge the liberal post-EDSA political settlement. There have been regular coup attempts by conservative factions particularly during the administration of the first post-Marcos democratic leader, Corazon Aquino (1986–92). Although Fidel Ramos (1993–99) is generally credited with having presided over a stable and progressive political and economic administration, his administration did launch—albeit unsuccessfully—the Charter Change initiative to revise the 1986 "Freedom Constitution".

Challenges have also emerged from flagrant abuses of public office. The second People Power revolution (EDSA 2) was mounted against the government of President Joseph Estrada (1999–2001), whose moral authority to govern was questioned based on massive corruption. Similarly, hopes for Estrada's successor—President Macapagal Arroyo (2001–10), a former civil society and democracy champion—were quickly dashed by accusations of large-scale corruption and allegations of rigged presidential elections to which she responded by declaring a state of emergency and attempted to curtail rights of assembly.[30] Macapagal Arroyo was accused of committing plunder or large-scale corruption in 2012 after she stepped down from power but was acquitted in 2017 of the charge by the Supreme Court.

During the period of strong clamour for change in governance, a relatively inexperienced Benigno Aquino Jr., son of democracy icon Cory Aquino, was elected president in 2010 on a reformist platform to bring *daang matuwid* to government. Benigno Aquino is widely credited with restoring economic growth and political stability in the Philippines. During Aquino II's administration, the country averaged 6.5 per cent annual GDP growth, and reforms were initiated in budgeting, delivery of services to the poor, and disaster preparedness.[31] Aquino II enabled independent oversight institutions such as the Ombudsman and the Supreme Court to have larger roles—with both institutions forcefully holding public officials to account on many occasions. The Supreme Court in particular—riding on a wave of strong public support—combatted the main source of political patronage, the congressional pork barrel much to the irritation of President Benigno Aquino II.[32]

Yet the reformist drive of the Aquino II administration was also beset with failures, neglect, and miscalculation—failures that culminated in Duterte's presidency. Filipinos are known to elect presidents who do not belong to the incumbent's party, with the exception of the Marcos presidency. One of the Aquino II administration's critical failures was its inability to pass the Bangsamoro Basic Law (BBL) following peace negotiations with the Muslim secessionist Moro Islamic Liberation Front (MILF). This failure to pass the BBL was in large part due to Congress' refusal to prioritize the bill after forty-four policemen were killed in the Mamasapano clash in Maguindanao that was criticized by the public nationwide.[33] Public perception that economic growth had not improved the situation of low-income groups—and that oligarchs continued to monopolize power and wealth throughout the country—was rife.[34] Poor delivery of basic services most obviously in transport and communications, high cost of living, and concerns over personal safety contributed to the perception that the Aquino II administration had failed. Such issues resonated deeply with not only the poor, but perhaps even more so with the urban middle classes who have been particularly receptive to Duterte's strong-man rhetoric on "rapid change".

II. THE DUTERTE PRESIDENCY: ERODING RULE OF LAW MECHANISMS?

With so much attention focused on Duterte's shadowy "war on drugs", a far more worrying trend unfolded before the public's eye—a systematic assault on and erosion of the salience of independent institutions and institutions of the rule of law. Rule of law has been perennially weak in the Philippines, with episodic periods of displays of independence by the Supreme Court. A survey by a business organization in 2014 and 2015 revealed that lower courts and the appellate court, the Court of Appeals, are perceived as one of the weakest performing government institutions in the Philippines.³⁵ The rule of law index by the World Justice Project illustrates the continuous deterioration of many aspects of the rule of law since Duterte's assumption to power.³⁶

The Supreme Court—the highest court in the Philippines—has become the particular object of vicious politics and politicization. In the first two years of his presidency, Duterte's allies within and outside Congress have moved to remove, through impeachment, four high-ranking officials—Vice President Leni Robredo, Commission on Elections Chair Andres Bautista, Chief Justice Lourdes Sereno, and Ombudsman Conchita Carpio Morales. These public officials stood firmly while performing their functions and criticizing government policies. These impeachment initiatives are commonly being used, or abused, to target critical voices within the government and to dismantle accountability mechanisms of the post-Marcos liberal constitutional architecture.³⁷

Aggressive use of impeachment proceedings did not originate with the Duterte administration. The Philippine Constitution—adopted in 1987 after the 1986 revolution that ousted Ferdinand Marcos—provided for a stronger tripartite system of checks and balances while creating independent Constitutional Commissions and the Office of the Ombudsman (Section 2, Art IX, 1987 Constitution). The President and Vice President, members of the Constitutional Commissions, the Ombudsman, Chief Justice, and Justices of the Supreme Court can only be removed by impeachment under this provision. This instrument has been formally used a number of times. The Philippine House of Representatives impeached former president Joseph Estrada (1998–2001) in 2000 though procedural matters ended his trial prematurely. Impeachment charges were filed against Estrada's successor, Gloria Macapagal Arroyo (2001–10) in 2005, 2006, 2007, and 2008, though none prospered. In 2011, the House impeached both Ombudsman Merceditas Gutierrez and Chief Justice Renato Corona. Gutierrez resigned before the Senate convened the impeachment court, so Corona's 2012 conviction by the Senate for the betrayal of public trust is the only successful impeachment case under the 1987 Constitution.

History illuminates the extraordinary nature of impeachment, the primary function of which is to prevent those who hold power from abusing their authority and subverting constitutional order. Criteria for successful prosecution are deliberately set high as impeachment overturns the electoral and appointive procedures that brought the highest officials to power. The 1987 Constitution limits the grounds for impeachment to "high crimes and misdemeanours" (Art. IX)—that is, culpable violation of the Constitution, graft and corruption, and betrayal of public trust. While the definition in the 1987 Constitution does not obscure the fact that impeachment is inherently political, adherence to strict legal standards has prevented or short-circuited many previous attempts at impeachment.

In the Philippine context, impeachment was precisely directed against the resurgence of authoritarian rule and arbitrary use of government powers by high officials. It is not intended to remove officials because they disagree with the executive leadership. Due to this anti-authoritarian rationale for impeachment, Bueza opined that procedures at the lower house, the House of Representatives, were set so low even citizens could set in motion proceedings for impeachment.[38] This is now the crux of how this procedure became a weapon to remove critics and, ironically, to institute unimpeded state power.

Increasing politicization of the process and a deliberate lowering of legal standards—illustrated by cases filed in 2017—are therefore obvious. Impeachment complaints filed against Vice President Leni Robredo in March 2017 charged betrayal of public trust and culpable violation of the constitution, based on Robredo's video message to the United Nations criticizing the administration's war on drugs, especially extrajudicial killings. The complaint against Commission on Elections Chair Andres Bautista filed in September 2017 by the Volunteers Against Crime and Corruption (VACC)—allied with Duterte—charged with failure to declare certain properties in his statements of assets and measures put in place to prevent hacking of the Commission on Elections website in 2016. Although the House Committee on Justice dismissed the complaint—and Bautista had by then announced his resignation—the House voted 137–75 to overturn the Committee dismissal and transmitted articles of impeachment to the Senate for trial. In the same month, a case was also prepared against Ombudsman Conchita Carpio Morales—shortly after the Ombudsman's Office announced it was investigating the Duterte family's alleged multibillion-peso wealth—and the president threatened an impeachment complaint, charging Morales with selective justice and use of falsified documents.

The most significant effort of impeachment to date has been the removal of Chief Justice Maria Lourdes Sereno from office—by her own colleagues—through a *quo warranto* proceeding. The *quo warranto,* a legal instrument to remove a public official from office, is predicated on the illegality of the office holder to hold office in the first instance. The *quo warranto* proceeding against Sereno, filed by the Office of the Solicitor General, the government's chief legal counsel, sidestepped the pending impeachment proceeding against the Chief Justice before the House of Representatives while using some of the grounds in the impeachment. In an unprecedented ruling, the vote of 8–6 in the Supreme Court made a distinction between impeachment and *quo warranto* proceeding, thus paving the way for the Chief Justice's removal by reason of non-declaration of her statement of assets and liabilities.[39]

Looking at the impeachment proceeding initiated against Sereno—in conjunction with the *quo warranto* suit—it is clear the aim was to remove a government critic and ensure a pliant judiciary. In two separate complaints, Sereno is accused of culpable violation of the Constitution, corruption, and other high crimes. Charges include: failure to disclose assets truthfully, delay in acting on retirement benefits for judges, falsifying Supreme Court resolutions, manipulating the Judicial and Bar Council, and extravagant use of public funds on a vehicle and official travel.

Chief Justice Sereno is also charged with betrayal of public trust for her public reply to President Duterte's allegations linking judges to the drug trade. Other charges include: (a) criticizing the imposition of martial law; (b) preventing Court of Appeals Justices from making courtesy calls on the president; and (c) favouring some judicial personnel over others. While Duterte disavows any hand in the proceedings, he has ordered speeding up the impeachment process[40]—and filing of a new complaint for Sereno's failure to declare her earnings prior to entering government service.

Working at the intersection between law and politics, ouster efforts draw critical attention to Duterte's agenda for a political reordering of the post-Marcos liberal architecture. What might first appear to be simply a personal impulse of the president is instead calculated and strategic—Duterte's allies are using legal processes such as impeachment and *quo warranto* proceedings to silence critics and dismantle critical veto gates in the institutional system. Removal of the Chief Justice, for instance, would clear a path for control of the Supreme Court in order to diminish both the possibility that it would derail political plans for constitutional change and its opposition to controversial policies such as the war on drugs and martial law in Mindanao. The removal of an independent Ombudsman and

Election Commissioner tampers with horizontal accountability mechanisms that could control excessive presidential powers. The disproportionate power of the president is a result of weak party politics and presidential control of discretionary funds that can be allocated to favoured politicians. Moreover, the removal of the vice president would eliminate the possibility of an agenda-threatening leadership change should President Duterte's ill health deteriorate further.

The Sereno ouster highlighted the fragile state of the institution of the rule of law that is the bulwark against illiberal rule. It exposed the deep politicization and division within the judiciary, with five justices even testifying against Sereno in the impeachment proceeding in Congress. The fragmentation in the bench can be seen as a rift between those who are more accepting of claimed executive prerogatives and those who seek to subject government actions to greater constitutional scrutiny—as shown in the cases on martial law, the burial of Marcos and dismissal of plunder charges against Duterte's allies. The retirement of several justices has meanwhile exacerbated concerns about a court stacked with Duterte nominees as, during his term, the president will most likely appoint eleven out of fifteen justices. At stake is therefore nothing less than the independence of the judiciary, which has been the main safeguard against executive abuse in the post-Marcos era.

III. EXPLAINING CHANGE: THE CURRENT FRAGMENTATION OF ELITES AND CIVIL SOCIETY

Philippine democracy lacks the essential mechanisms of institutional and social controls necessary to curb elite appetites for perpetuating power. The constitutional safeguards of checks and balances are largely unreliable because of structural and institutional infirmities. Civil society previously filled this gap by pushing liberal agenda from the bottom up and acting as a form of vertical accountability through elections and extraconstitutional means. During the campaign and since Duterte's election, civil society has, however, become deeply divided—with voices from the left initially in tactical alliance with the president's party during the campaign and up to Duterte's first year in office.

At present, there is no voice loud enough to effectively resist Duterte's illiberal policies. Looking at the impact of Sereno's ouster as a measure of the influence of civil society in political decision making, it is evident that protest actions and opposition are still too weak to affect the actions of political—and judicial—actors. Sereno's removal, however, engendered a common ground and a platform, the Coalition for Justice, through which various splintered groups, lawyers, students, churches and non-government organizations (NGOs), come together as a single voice to denounce erosion of the rule of law and democratic institutions.

The 1987 Constitution put in place a system of separation of powers with checks and balances, yet the executive always held the balance of power because of control over the national budget and finance. Julio Teehankee observed that a president who enjoys public support will also enjoy the backing of a malleable Congress.[41] As a populist leader, Duterte relies on a high popularity rating, backed by a propaganda machine—promoting his achievements, defending him, and disparaging or threatening critics through social media. The huge popularity that Duterte enjoys allows him to count on temporary loyalties of members of Congress and enable congressional allies to push his agenda with little opposition. See Figure I.1.

There is also a mass movement being created called "Dutertismo" embodying Duterte's so-called vision of a "final solution" to the country's ills through drastic measures.[42] According to Randy David, Dutertismo is a contingent product of a culture that views leadership as the domain of a few, rather than a leadership of shared responsibility—a belief bred by a hierarchical system that "separates the powerful elites from the impoverished masses". The Dutertismo brand of leadership translates to governance with little or no regard for the rule of law and constitutional processes.

The lack of strong institutional and regulatory controls in Philippine politics is demonstrated by the inability of Congress to pass anti-dynasty legislation or provide a penalty for party-switching, which is the current norm rather than the exception.[43] Political dynasties are barred under the 1987 Constitution[44] thus, politicians who were members of or identified with the party of former president Aquino—the Liberal Party—readily shifted allegiance to the new power-brokers, the *Partido Demokratiko Pilipino–Lakas ng Bayan* (PDP-Laban). In the May 2016 elections, there were originally only three legislators who were members of the PDP-Laban. Once Duterte assumed office in July 2016, 105 more members switched to PDP-Laban, 71 of them from the Liberal Party.[45] Duterte's coalition comprised a "supermajority" in the lower house, placing him in a position of great

FIGURE I.1
Net Satisfaction Ratings, Presidents since 1984

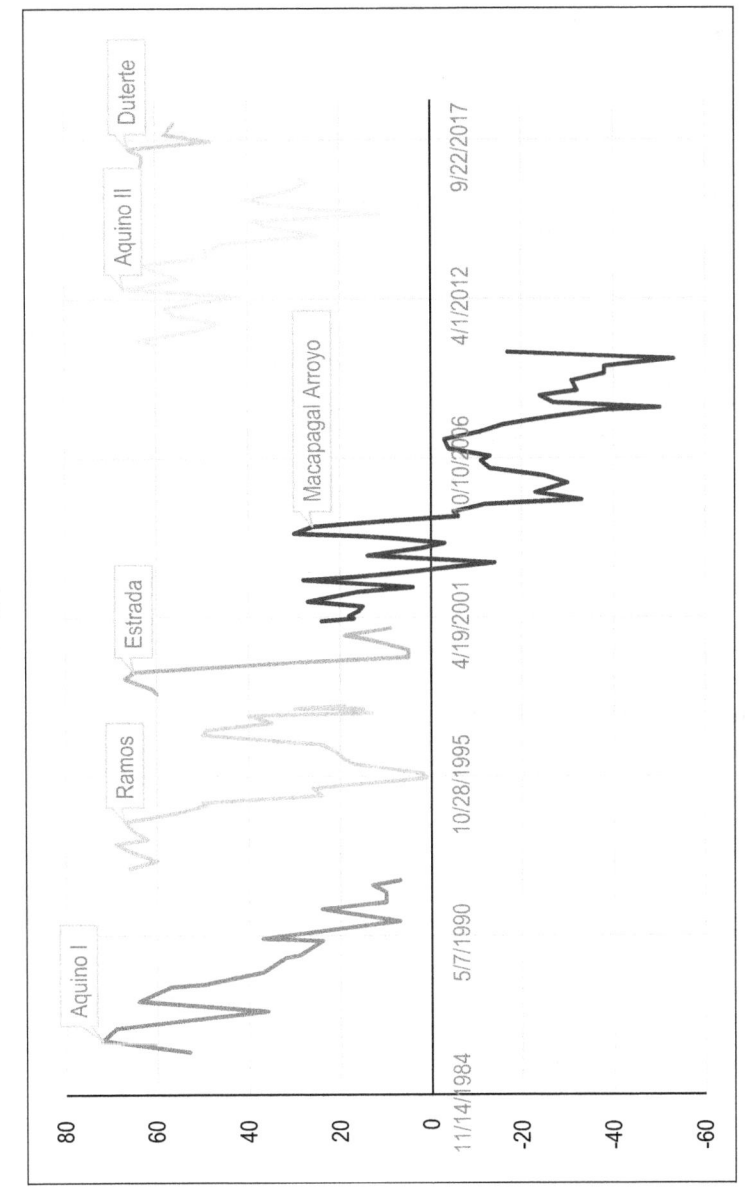

Source: SWS Net Satisfaction Surveys (1984–2018).

strength and allowing martial law to be imposed without the legislature and Supreme Court undertaking a stringent review, plus basing the conduct of impeachment proceedings against Sereno on lower legal standards. In September 2017, 119 members—against 32 opposed—voted to slash the Commission on Human Rights budget to just PhP1,000 (approximately AU$20) although the budget was restored after a major public outcry.[46]

Even so-called "left" politicians joined the PDP-Laban coalition, especially those with the National Democratic Front (NDF) purportedly in the hope that Duterte would make good on his promises to undermine the oligarchs, adopt substantive redistributive programmes, and pursue a peace agreement with the Communist Party of the Philippines–New People's Army (CPP-NPA).[47] The NDF and PDP-Laban alliance has since evaporated—as have negotiations with the CPP-NPA for a peace settlement.[48] The Duterte administration has in fact moved to declare the CPP-NPA a terrorist organization. As a result, since mid-2017, a string of suspected leftist rebels or supporters have been killed by unknown assailants, and criminal charges are being revived against well-known political left leaders.[49]

The continued dominance of political dynasties has been a fixture of the Philippine Congress post-EDSA.[50] Many political dynasties were built by members of the opposition in the Marcos years, with some newer members erecting their own dynasties during the later resurgence of liberal democracy. The Marcos family and their allies have been undertaking a political renaissance—aligning themselves with other marginalized elites of the post-Marcos period—the same elites cast aside after the Estrada impeachment, and those from Gloria Macapagal Arroyo's exit from power. This latter group and the elites that coalesced around Duterte in his run for the presidency are seen by the public as populating Duterte's new elite coalition.

The 17th Congress under Duterte is composed of political dynasties. Of the 293 House members, 153 (52 per cent) are serving their second or third term, and only 140 (47 per cent) are first-time representatives.[51] Many of the first-time representatives have experience in local government and relatives who are politicians. An estimated 190 representatives have links to political dynasties by either blood or marriage—at least 131 with relatives actively serving in a political position and another 25 with relatives who previously served. In the Senate, 13 of 24 members have links to political dynasties—8 of these have relatives currently occupying another political seat, and 5 succeeded a relative as senator. There is also a "minority bloc" in the House whose members are mostly party-list representatives.[52] Unsurprisingly, those in the "majority bloc" are solid supporters of Duterte's agenda. Former president Gloria Macapagal Arroyo—now Duterte's key ally—recently wrested control of the Congress on 23 July 2018 on the occasion of the president's second State of the Nation Address (SONA) by being elected Speaker after a brief power struggle.

The Senate, however, remains diverse, as PDP-Laban accounts for only five of twenty-three members. Consequently, the Senate elections in 2019 will be critical in determining whether Duterte will control the whole Congress.

Civil society in the Philippines is not monolithic—tending to be ideologically diverse.[53] Civil society groups have in the past been willing to come together on major political issues to advocate for or oppose important government policies particularly initiatives that risk undermining constitutional democracy. Civil society has also been influential in shaping public opinion—contributing to the government in reconsidering policies—or the courts invalidating policy measures.

To manage civil society, Duterte has adopted a divide-and-rule strategy that relies heavily on co-optation, for example, appointing civil society activists to the Cabinet.[54] Duterte has also devoted considerable time espousing issues advocated by civil society groups, for example, speaking out publicly on the importance of environmental protection and the eradication of illicit drugs and crimes.[55] The effect has been to widen existing divisions in civil society. The former presidential spokesperson, Harry Roque, was a well-known human rights lawyer and university professor—expelled by his own party-list organization, Kabayan, for pronouncements contradicting party principles.[56]

The wedge between those who support Duterte and those critical of him has become very wide—reflecting polarization in civil society. Duterte's supporters call his detractors *"dilawan"*, for supporters of the previous administration and the Liberal Party.[57] Duterte's critics call his supporters *Dutertards* and accusing Duterte supporters of being dumb.[58] Social media has become the battleground of competing ideas and norms among civil society and within groups and families. The little space available for safe and robust discourse has made it even more difficult for embattled institutions and officials to harness support from the public—critical in influencing or mitigating the Duterte administration's policies.

Civil society fragmentation, however, reflects deep-rooted structural issues. The period between Aquino II and Duterte created more opportunity for poor and middle-class Filipinos to express their political views. Strong economic growth during the Aquino II presidency resulted in an explosion of jobs and income, which helped to expand the country's base of middle-income earners—many of them young, technologically adept, and seeking a good life.[59] Many Filipinos who now have considerable disposable incomes are in their late twenties to early forties.[60] This demographic is most open in expressing opinions and their dissatisfaction with poor delivery of services, painful traffic problems in Manila, anomalies at airports, and slow and expensive internet connectivity.[61] This group also blames the failure of the law and the rule of law when there are no effective government services, in the face of rampant corruption, and privileging the influential and rich.[62]

Income disparities in the Philippines are extremely wide. Standard practice for market and opinion researchers is to classify respondents into socioeconomic classes of A, B, C, D, and E—a classification based on proxy measures for income, wealth and assets—such as conditions in the community where homes are located, materials used in construction of the home, furnishings, and whether respondents own or rent.[63] In 2009 Social Weather Stations (SWS) released a report, "Family Income Distribution in the Philippines from 1985 to 2009", with percentages of the Filipino population by class in 1985 and in 2009.[64] Key results of the SWS report are included in Table I.1, demonstrating stark income inequality problems in the Philippines.

TABLE I.1
Percentage Distribution of Families and Incomes,
by Modified Socioeconomic Class, 2009

Class	Population Percentage	Average Annual Income	Proportion of National Income
AB	1%	PhP1,857,000 (US$38,579)	9%
C	9%	PhP603,000 (US$12,527)	26%
D	60%	PhP191,000 (US$3,968)	56%
E	30%	PhP62,000 (US$1,288)	9%

A new survey by the National Economic and Development Authority (NEDA) in 2016 found that the typical Filipino had "middle-class aspirations" to live a "simple and comfortable life".[65] In practical terms, this means owning a medium-sized home and a car, enough money to cover daily needs, and being able to afford a good education for their children. According to NEDA, to achieve this dream per capita annual income must be at least US$11,000—roughly the same as the middle-income earners in Class C. However, those in this category are still "at risk" and in an unstable position because of the high cost of living and the constant uncertainty about economic conditions in the Philippines. This group of Filipinos are typically concerned about crime and corruption, ineffective government services, systemic justice and serious flaws in the administration of justice. The fragility of this class is expressed in their desire to lead a deep-rooted, comfortable, and secure life.

Duterte has considerable support from the middle class and more educated Filipinos. As Julio Teehankee remarked: "The Duterte phenomenon is elite-driven. It is not the revolt of the poor. It is the angry protest of the new middle class: BPO workers, Uber drivers, and OFWs."[66] The exit polls in 2016 presidential elections showed Duterte was elected by voters from a variety of socioeconomic backgrounds—but the majority of votes for him were from larger percentages of more affluent and educated people.[67] Since Duterte took office, this group has continued to support him and his policies clearly demonstrated by his trust and satisfaction ratings over time. Figures I.2 to I.4 illustrate that Duterte has enjoyed particularly strong support from Filipinos aged twenty-five to forty-five, the high-middle-income earners, and college graduates.

The division in civil society can also be inferred from examining Duterte's supporters. Members of this group—although not formally organized—demonstrate collective aspirations through social media that is effectively harnessed by the government to support its policies and measures. Duterte admitted that his presidential campaign utilized social media campaigners,[68] but denied the government currently employs an army of social media bloggers and "trolls".[69] However, several enthusiastic bloggers—such as Mocha Uson and Trixie de Guzman—have been appointed to the government.[70] Many Duterte supporters are very active in social media, particularly Facebook—known for trolling and vilifying Duterte's critics, and sometimes aggressively threatening people with violence.

Introduction: From Aquino II to Duterte (2010–2018)

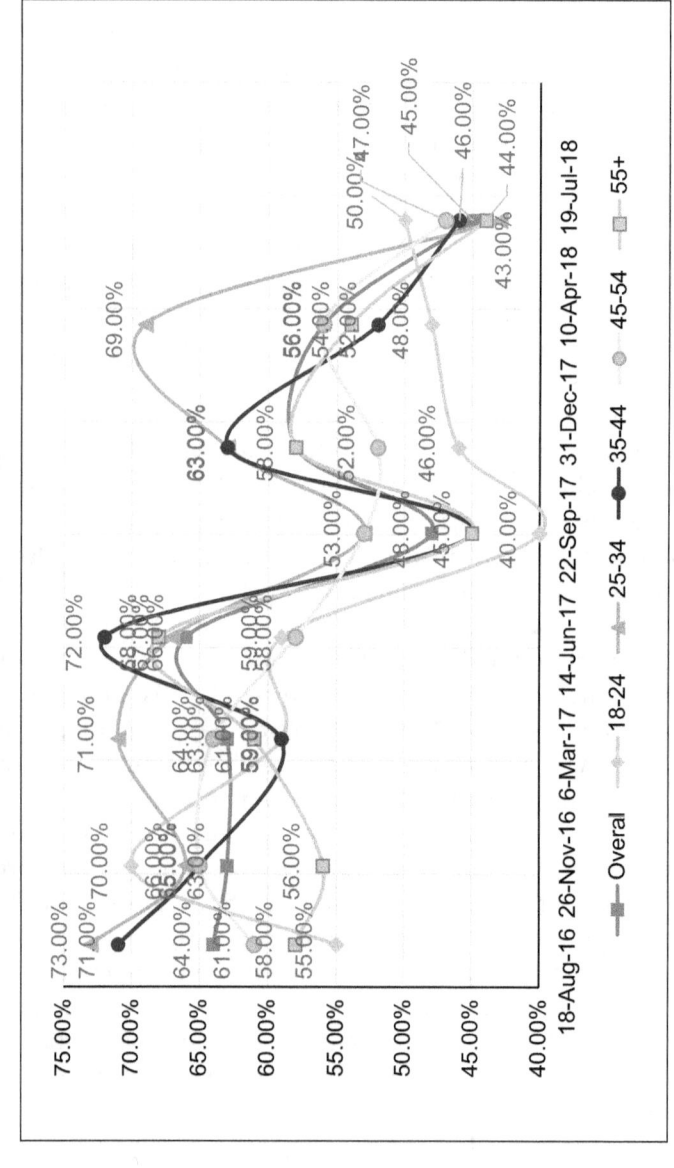

FIGURE I.2
Net Satisfaction Ratings for Rodrigo Duterte by Age: September 2016 – June 2018

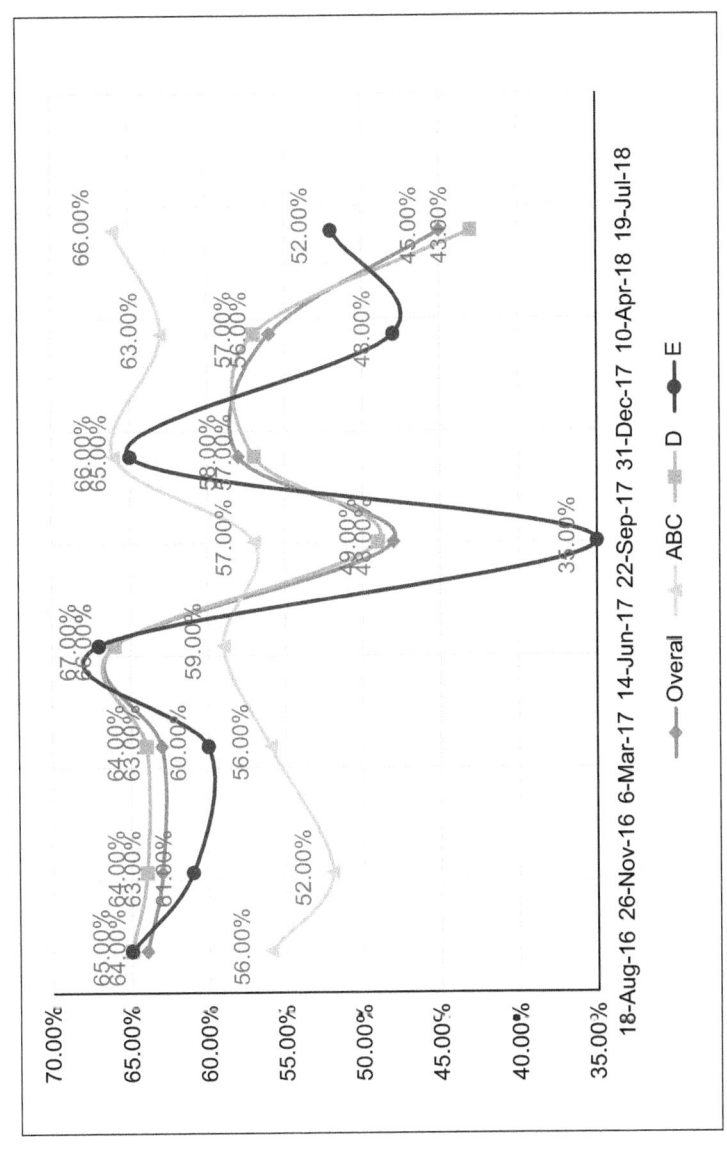

FIGURE I.3
Net Satisfaction Ratings for Rodrigo Duterte by Class: September 2016 – June 2018

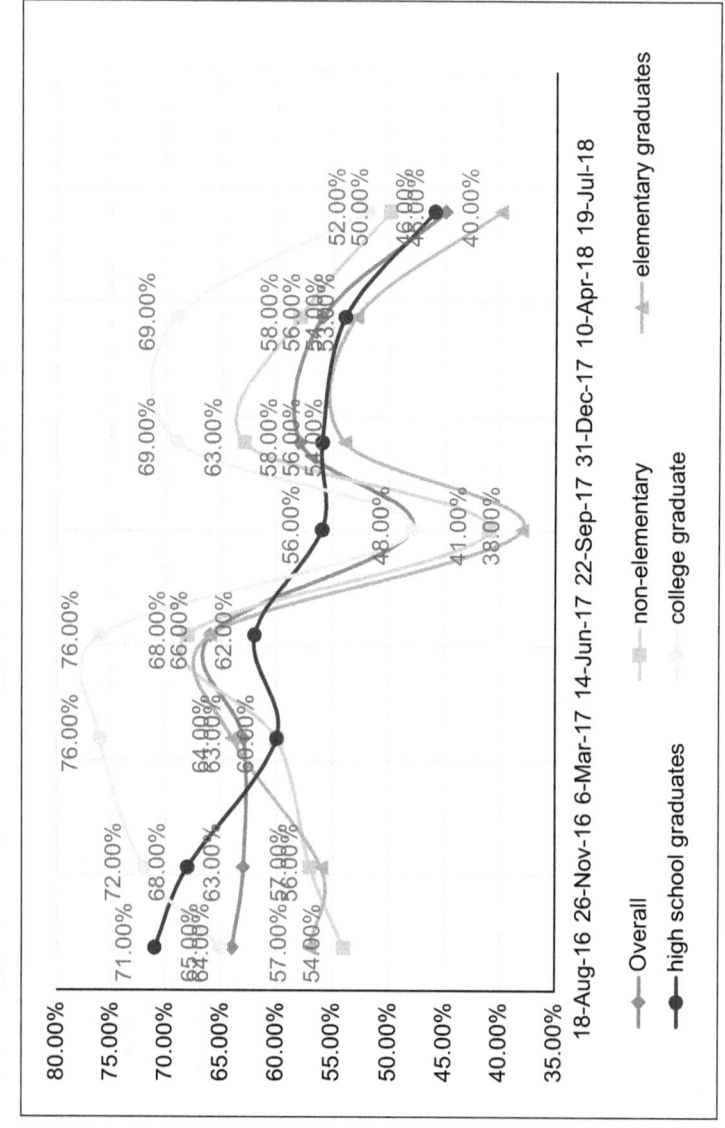

FIGURE I.4
Net Satisfaction Ratings for Rodrigo Duterte by Education: September 2016 – June 2018

IV. STRUCTURE OF THE BOOK

The introductory chapter draws attention to patterns of continuity and rupture as the Philippines transitioned from Aquino II to the Duterte administration. The goal of the contributors of this book is to enrich debates on Philippine politics and society with much-needed recognition of the unfolding of an uncertain political trajectory. With the unravelling of the post-1986 political settlement and seeming illiberal turn of the Duterte government—and consolidation of a new elite coalition—there is much food for thought. What is of concern is the growing fragmentation of civil society that has traditionally been the champion of liberal values and democratic institutions. This is in part because of the Philippines middle class' divided stance of the president's law and order agenda and his declarations in eradicating the oligarchy. Since the dismantling of the Marcos dictatorship in 1986, the Philippine Supreme Court—hailed as the "bulwark of democracy" for its previous records of resisting constitutional encroachments and attempts at eroding protection of civil liberties—is now at its weakest point.

With all this in mind, what do individual contributions in this volume offer? Authors were invited for their informative insights into issues identified in four critical areas.

Part I brings together contributions on *politics and governance*:

- *Mark R. Thompson* discusses recent developments in the Philippines from a comparative perspective, and draws attention to how the rise of illiberal democracy is embodied in President Rodrigo Duterte's "right" populism—using Duterte's violent war on drugs as the central case study. Comparing contemporary Hungary with the Philippines, Thompson suggests why and how Duterte has been able to establish illiberal democracy in the Philippines, and considers this illiberalism in the context of formally democratic institutions. The chapter concludes with a forecast and proviso that, despite some setbacks—given Duterte's continued popularity and new "friends" abroad (closer relations with China and Donald Trump's approaches to his fellow "populist")—violent strongman rule is likely to continue in the Philippines for some time.

- *Steven Rood's* contribution further explores recent political and institutional changes in the Philippines based on in-depth study of the federalism debate that has dominated recent public discussions on constitutional reform. Rood argues that the politics of the move to federalism should be understood in terms of three main issues: (1) the concerns of the national (= Manila-centric) elites who have long blocked political-institutional change; (2) the perspective of democracy advocates worried that change will merely entrench local elites; and (3) the concerns of business people about the uncertainty of increased local regulation. Rood concludes by discussing the potentially complex relationship between the thrust for federalism and the Bangsamoro peace process.

- *Kidjie Saguin* offers insights into the capacity to combat corruption of the administrations of Gloria Macapagal Arroyo and Benigno S. Aquino III. Saguin argues that what is most critical in controlling corruption is the legitimacy of political leaders and leaders of anticorruption agencies. Saguin's chapter invites critical reflection on the Duterte administration's recent attacks on oversight agencies despite its formal commitment to eradicating corruption.

Part II analyses *economic governance*:

- *Maria Socorro Gochoco-Bautista* examines the Duterte administration's 10-Point Socioeconomic Agenda, intended to promote inclusive growth. Gochoco-Bautista presents her analysis in the context of the push towards federalism—Duterte intends to use federalism to promote regional development, and as a means to decentralize political and economic power away from "Imperial Manila". Noting major policy changes are underway, Gochoco-Bautista questions whether the move towards federalism will deliver on the inclusive growth agenda any better than a unitary government.

- *Christopher Cabuay and Hal Hill's* chapter with a narrative of the country's recent economic performance complements Gochoco-Bautista's critical analysis. Hill looks at the Philippine's rapid economic growth during the Aquino II administration and the continuing dynamism under Duterte—the country having now outgrown its description as the "sick man of Asia". Cabuay and Hill explore some of the main development challenges for the Philippine in particular the need to map a path to more inclusive and peaceful growth.

- Part II ends with a detailed case study by *Rachel Burgess* on competition law and inclusive growth. In force since 2017, the Philippine Competition Act was envisioned to break down cartels and reduce the price of goods and services to consumers especially the millions of Filipinos living below the poverty line. Yet, as Burgess makes clear, whether the law succeeds in promoting inclusive growth will ultimately depend on uncertain exogenous factors. Burgess specifies the importance of technical expertise, acceptance by Filipino business, and the actual and perceived success of the regulator—the Philippines Competition Commission (PCC)—in applying the law fairly and transparently.

Part III focuses on the unfolding *peace process in Mindanao*:

- *Matthew Stephens* draws attention to aspects of the Duterte administration's approach to building peace in Mindanao—including convergence between the two major Moro fronts, putting constitutional change on the table, and offering the prospect of federalism. Stephens expresses concern that these approaches fail to address deficits in local governance and the role of local governments perpetuating a status quo of instability and poverty. Stephens considers the situation in Mindanao has been worsened by the lack of a credible plan for socioeconomic recovery—requiring fifteen to twenty years of dedicated financial and technical assistance—and concludes the root causes of conflict in Mindanao cannot be resolved during the term of this government.

- *Georgi Engelbrecht* complements Stephens's perspective with a detailed study of the peace agreement between the government and the Moro Islamic Liberation Front (MILF) signed in 2014, seeking to establish a meaningful form of self-governance in the "autonomous" region of the Bangsamoro. Engelbrecht points out serious failures that led to the current situation. Central to these failures is the Aquino II administration not passing the Bangsamoro Basic Law (BBL), resulting in MILF forces not having been decommissioned. As a consequence, the national military was not redeployed. In essence, the critical security component of "normalization" never occurred—nor is it likely. Engelbrecht then raises questions about the best way forward as Duterte charts a new path for the peace process based on ambitious goals of the recently passed Bangsamoro Organic Law and inclusivity.

Part IV concludes the contributions by drawing attention to the *international environment*:

- *Noel M. Morada* explores the prospects for Philippine-China relations under Duterte, noting the Philippines has traditionally used bilateral and multilateral (mainly ASEAN) mechanisms to deal with China on issues arising in the South China Sea (SCS) and the West Philippines Sea (WPS). Morada also considers the implications of the Permanent Court of Arbitration's decision favourable to the Philippines. After drawing attention to internal and external factors that could influence policy on the SCS/WPS, Morada examines the challenges the Philippines confronts in attempting to effectively enforce the decision of the international court and defend its maritime claims.

- *Aries A. Arugay* provides a sober analysis on the potential of civil society in the Philippines. Looking at the period 2001–10—otherwise known as Philippine democracy's lost decade—Arugay argues several events further fragmented civil society, decreased legitimacy to challenge state authority and embody popular interests, and weakened the position of civil society to influence policy. Filipino civil society has been significantly weakened since 2010—and unable to influence key political outcomes during the Aquino II administration as seen in cases such as the pork-barrel scandal, the Reproductive Health Law debate, and the 2013 mid-term elections. Arugay ends his chapter by discussing prospects of civil society action and resistance against the current erosion of liberal democracy in the Philippines under the Duterte administration.

CONCLUSION

The contributions of this volume demonstrate the Philippines has entered a critical period—one of continuity and rupture in significant policy areas. Now in its third year, the Duterte administration is shaking up the entire spectrum of Philippine society with "unconventional" approaches to solving what Duterte perceives as the nation's ills. An illiberal democratic regime is being fashioned in a systematic way under the façade of anti-Manila, anti-oligarchy, and anti-church rhetoric—facilitated in part by Duterte's populist appeal and well-oiled propaganda machine—and encouraged by a rising insecure middle class that continues to give high support to his administration's policies.

Illiberal democracy and liberal capitalism are not mutually exclusive and indeed can coexist. These terms have been used by many strongmen and illiberal regimes in their "playbooks"—to induce the public into giving up fundamental rights and dignity—in return for promised prosperity and security. This also explains the disjuncture between economics and politics that sees continuity and expansion of liberal economic policymaking yet drastic shifts and breaks in the political arena. As history has shown, most populist—or authoritarian leaderships—have failed in both political participation and economic redistribution.[71] Worse, these types of governments have compromised legal and institutional constraints on executive power. The Philippines only need look back at the time of Marcos when his family and cronies plundered the Philippines, curtailed human rights and emasculated the rule of law.

As the authors have shown, we are witnessing continuity of Aquino II policies that stimulated economic growth and directed government agencies to deliver more inclusive, pro-poor growth. Duterte's first two years sustained robust economic growth—6.9 per cent in 2016 and 6.7 per cent in 2017. Management of the economy was largely left to technocrats, thus ensuring continuity with the previous administration. The same can be said for high-profile pro-poor social development programmes like the 4Ps—*Pantawid Pamilya Pilipino Program*—conditional cash transfer and the *AmBisyon 2040* agenda. There have been, however, criticisms over slow and disjointed progress on the agenda which are growing—particularly with regard to health and education.[72] A major infrastructure programme, *Build Build Build*, has been announced in 2018 to fast track big infrastructure projects and spur growth. Significant tax reform legislation, and the Tax

Reform for Acceleration and Inclusion (TRAIN) law, have also been passed to enhance and increase tax collection while exempting low-income groups. However, this new tax initiative has been blamed for the rapid acceleration of inflation now affecting prices of major commodities such as rice and petroleum.[73]

On the other hand, there has been a distinct break in the political narrative—almost a rupture with the past. The president has made a deliberate, sweeping effort to replace the liberal constitutional order with an illiberal model. "Dutertismo" targets dissent in independent media and the opposition and shows little regard for the rule of law and institutional checks and balances. The politicized use of impeachment procedures and other legal processes against the Chief Justice of the Supreme Court and members of constitutional bodies has undermined the system of checks and balances and mechanisms of accountability. This politicization has also eroded the professionalism—and even the functioning—of critical independent oversight agencies at a time when the country is confronted by unrestrained use of power—demonstrated by the war on drugs and the ever-growing number of related extrajudicial killings.

These developments are not new per se. In the past, there have been presidential assaults on institutions, declarations of martial law, and allegations of corruption such as those of Fidel Ramos (1992–98), Joseph Estrada (1999–2001) and Gloria Macapagal Arroyo (2001–10). Current political developments however, show a more decisive push towards illiberal rule that started with the bloody war on drugs. What sets Duterte apart from his populist predecessor Joseph Estrada is his unapologetic endorsement of violence and—as with Marcos—his unabashed contempt for institutions and legal processes.

While the draft federal constitution calls for institutional strengthening—including political parties—the political policies and actions of the Duterte administration demonstrate dismal regard for institutions and legal processes. Added to these developments is the restoration to power of those accused of large-scale corruption, whose cases against them were dismissed. Following the retirement of Ombudsman Conchita Carpio-Morales in July 2018—highly regarded for her integrity and independence—the newly appointed Ombudsman Samuel Martires moved to remove personnel who investigated Duterte for allegedly holding bank accounts not declared in his assets,[74] despite the Duterte government's bold campaign promises to end corruption. The appointment of Ombudsman Samuel Martires on 26 July

2018 raises concerns about the future of democracy in the Philippines and its current development trajectory.

Perhaps it is too early to evaluate long-term damage to legal institutions. However, undermining the courts has obviously created politicization—and divisions among members of the bench and the legal profession. The decision of the Supreme Court in *quo warranto* is perceived by many to be politically motivated rather than a reasoned independent legal judgement.[75] Such a ruling could have severe consequences for an independent judiciary and salience of the rule of law in securing liberal democracy.

Broad dissatisfaction with systematic injustice bred discontent with the previous political system—thus propelling Duterte to power in the first place. The politicization—or as some Philippine commentators would term "weaponizing"[76]—of legal mechanisms is counter-intuitive. Politicization of legal mechanisms might also jeopardize the sustainability of the current trajectory of policy and growth over the next few years which depends on stability and effectiveness of legal rules and regulation. As the Philippine government mounts regular assaults on critical institutions of independent oversight and justice, the Philippines' ranking on the 2017 Corruption Perceptions Index (CPI), Transparency International (TI) has fallen from 101st in 2016 to 111th in 2017.[77]

The divisions within civil society that have made collective action largely ineffectual are of particular concern. Although civil society did foment a public uproar over proposed cuts to the budget of the Human Rights Commission and the Sereno ouster initiative, more sustained and broad opposition seems unlikely at this point in time. This lack of opposition is due in large part to waning participation of traditional middle class in civil society advocacies, and implicit endorsement of Duterte policies that could promote "safety" and economic well-being for the middle class in more ways than a liberal democracy. There is little indication that the broader political reordering now underway might be opposed by political elites—who seem committed to accommodation as long as Duterte's approval ratings stay high and the economy continues to expand.

The lack of opposition by political elites does not necessarily mean that authoritarian backsliding is unstoppable. Heated public debates about the impeachment of the Chief Justice and proposed far-reaching constitutional changes also suggest there may be limits to the potential for illiberal excesses. Since the Marcos regime, both the middle class and the elites supported independent institutions like the Supreme Court (though not necessarily for the same reasons), allowing the judiciary to rise above "politics", particularly when constitutional stability was threatened. This did not happen, however, in the Sereno ouster even when the issue provoked a constitutional confrontation with the Senate.

With a deeply divided civil society—including the legal profession—the Senate adopted restraint in so far as it only called the Supreme Court to reconsider its decision on the Sereno ouster. The Court, confident there will be no effective repercussions against their action, stayed firm on their ruling. This issue, however, has revitalized the civil society and brought new alliances. The Coalition for Justice was loosely formed around "justice and rule of law" to denounce the impeachment and subsequent removal of Sereno. Whether this can be sustained and potentially expand into broad-based activism or opposition is something that is uncertain—given the Filipino tendency for forgetting vital issues and penchant for salacious controversies.

The Philippine Congress—like most opportunistic political dynasties—has been known to follow the direction of power. However, the Congress has been known to resist—or turn against—executive power when the president's popularity declines (as in Joseph Estrada's fall from power) or when public opinion is strong (as in the non-passage of the BBL during Aquino II). Duterte's illiberal turn is contingent on the continued support of the Congress—and the public. Similarly, the post-1987 consensus on building up oversight and justice institutions, for example, independent budgets, more transparent appointment processes, collegiality, and the post-EDSA legacy, was due to benefits on offer for resolving elite conflict as well as addressing middle-class concerns about abuse by powerful interests. If the process of deinstitutionalization further deteriorates, these two constituencies—the Congress and the people—might reunite to combat illiberalism—although by then the damage to important constitutional institutions may be irreversible.

The Philippines is now at a critical juncture of continuity and change having seen continuity of economic growth. Whether such growth will translate into equitable and redistributive development depends, however, on how politics is shaped in pursuit of this goal. The popular appeal of illiberal or authoritarian regimes has depended on the leader's promises to deliver on economic redistribution and greater political participation. With methodical circulation of fake news and ingenious use of social media, present-day authoritarian leaders may attain more longevity than their predecessors—and not deliver on their promises. As currently witnessed in the Philippines, institutional and legal safeguards can easily be dismantled with an ill-informed citizenry who value "quick fixes" rather than the building of stable and effective institutions.

Much is at stake for the Philippines as the Duterte presidency unfolds. External changes are also unravelling—as documented in the compilation of these chapters. A realignment in the Philippine's foreign relations policy—aimed at fostering closer relations with non-traditional allies such as China and Russia—is also causing internal unease among the general population. Duterte's constant praise of China and seeming lack of interest to enforce the Philippine's legal victory in the international court of arbitration case involving the South China Sea (see Morada in Chapter 9), is of particular concern. External powers (e.g., United States, Japan, Australia) are watching this development with great interest and are aware of the high stakes involved—regional peace and stability, freedom of navigation, and the international rule of law.

ACKNOWLEDGMENTS

The authors would like to thank Rory MacNeil and Kent Marjun Primor for providing research and editing assistance.

Notes

1. Paul Hutchcroft and Joel Rocamora, "Strong Demands and Weak Institutions: The Origins and Evolution of the Democratic Deficit in the Philippines", *Journal of East Asian Studies* 3 (2003): 259–92; Bjorn Dressel, "The Philippines: How Much Real Democracy", *International Political Science Review* 32, issue 5 (2011): 529–45.
2. Arsenio Balisacan and Hal Hill, "The Philippine Development Puzzle", in *Southeast Asian Affairs 2002*, edited by Daljit Singh and Anthony L. Smith, pp. 237–52 (Singapore: Institute of Southeast Asian Studies, 2002); Emmanuel de Dios and Paul Hutchcroft, "The Philippine Political Economy: Development, Policies, and Challenges", in *Political Economy*, edited by E. de Dios and P. Hutchcroft, pp. 45–75 (Oxford University Press, 2003).
3. Imelda Deinla, *The Development of the Rule of Law in ASEAN: The State and Regional Integration* (Cambridge: Cambridge University Press, 2017); Dante Gatmaytan, "The State of Liberal Democracy", *Global Review of Constitutional Law* (University of the Philippines, 2018).

4. Mark Thompson, "Reformism vs. Populism in the Philippines", *Journal of Democracy* 21, issue 4 (2010): 154–68.
5. Mark Thompson, "Populism and the Revival of Reform: Competing Political Narratives in the Philippines", *Contemporary Southeast Asia* 32, no. 1 (2010): 1–28.
6. Matt Wells, "Philippines: Duterte's 'War on Drug' Is a War on the Poor", *Amnesty International*, 4 February 2017, https://www.amnesty.org/en/latest/news/2017/02/war-on-drugs-war-on-poor/ (accessed 7 September 2018).
7. Imelda Deinla, Veronica Taylor, and Steven Rood, "Philippines: Justice Removed, Justice Denied", *Lowy Institute online*, 17 May 2018, https://www.lowyinstitute.org/the-interpreter/philippines-justice-removed-justice-denied (accessed 14 August 2018).
8. Gatmaytan, "The State of Liberal Democracy".
9. Gaea Katreena Cabico, "Pulse Asia: 6 out of 10 Filipinos Oppose Charter Change", *PhilStar Online*, 2 May 2018, https://www.philstar.com/headlines/2018/05/02/1811466/pulse-asia-6-out-10-filipinos-oppose-charter-change (accessed 7 September 2018).
10. Euan McKirdy, "Philippines Revokes License of Rappler, News Site Critical of Duterte Administration", *CNN Online*, 16 January 2018, https://edition.cnn.com/2018/01/15/asia/philippines-rappler-sec-license-revoked/index.html (accessed 7 September 2018).
11. Ellalyn de Vera-Ruiz, "SWS Survey: Net Satisfaction Rating of Duterte Administration Still Very Good", *Manila Bulletin*, 5 August 2018, https://news.mb.com.ph/2018/08/05/sws-survey-net-satisfaction-rating-of-duterte-administration-still-very-good/ (accessed 18 October 2018).
12. Imelda Deinla, "Duterte and the Insecurity of the Philippine Middle Class", seminar series on Governance and the Power of Fear, School of Regulation and Global Governance, Australian National University, 30 November 2017, http://regnet.anu.edu.au/news-events/news/7036/duterte-and-insecurity-philippine-middle-class (accessed 7 September 2018).
13. Fareed Zakaria, "The Rise of Illiberal Democracy", *Foreign Affairs* 76, no. 6 (1997): 22–43, http://www.jstor.org/stable/20048274 (accessed 24 April 2018).
14. Deinla, *The Development of the Rule of Law in ASEAN*.
15. Sheri Berman, "The Pipe Dream of Undemocratic Liberalism", *Journal of Democracy* 28, no. 3 (2017): 29–38.
16. Young Sokphea, "Transnational Advocacy Networks in Global Supply Chains: A Study of Civil Society Organizations' Sugar Movements in Cambodia," *Journal of Civil Society* 13, no. 1 (2017): 35–53.
17. Miguel Syjuco, "I Thought Democracy Had Failed Filipinos. But it Is We Who Have Failed It", *The Guardian*, 22 October 2017, https://www.theguardian.

com/commentisfree/2017/oct/22/i-thought-democracy-had-failed-filipinos-but-it-is-we-who-have-failed-it (accessed 27 April 2018).
18. Zakaria, "The Rise of Illiberal Democracy".
19. Benedict Anderson, "Cacique Democracy and the Philippines: Origins and Dreams", *New Left Review*, no. 169 (1988): 3–31.
20. William Case, *Politics in Southeast Asia: Democracy or Less* (Richmond: Curzon, 2002).
21. David Wurfel, *Filipino Politics: Development and Decay* (Ithaca: Cornell University Press, 1988); Patricio Abinales and Donna Amoroso, *State Society in the Philippines* (Lanham: Rowman and Littlefield, 2005); Walden Bello, *Deglobalization: Ideas for a New World Economy* (London and New York: Zed Books, 2004).
22. Teresa S. Encarnacion Tadem and Eduardo C. Tadem, "Political Dynasties in the Philippines: Persistent Patterns, Perennial Problems", *South East Asia Research* 24, no. 3 (2016): 328–40, http://journals.sagepub.com/doi/pdf/10.1177/0967828X16659730 (accessed 27 April 2018).
23. Ronald Mendoza et al., "Inequality in Democracy: Insights from an Empirical Analysis of Political Dynasties in the 15th Philippine Congress", *Philippine Political Science Journal* 33, no. 2 (2012): 132–45, https://www.tandfonline.com/doi/pdf/10.1080/01154451.2012.734094?needAccess=true (accessed 27 April 2018).
24. Ibid.
25. Mark Thompson, "Duterte's Illiberal Democracy", *East Asia Forum*, 7 August 2017, http://www.eastasiaforum.org/2017/08/07/80706/ (accessed 6 September 2018).
26. Rodrigo Duterte, "State of the Nation Address 2018", *PhilStar Online*, 23 July 2018, https://www.philstar.com/headlines/2018/07/23/1836195/full-text-dutertes-2018-sona-speech (accessed 6 September 2018).
27. Walden Bello, "Rodrigo Duterte: A Fascist Original", *Foreign Policy in Focus*, 6 January 2017, https://fpif.org/rodrigo-duterte-fascist-original/ (accessed 6 September 2018).
28. Eva-lotta Hedman, *In the Name of Civil Society: From Free Election Movements to People Power in the Philippines* (Honolulu: University of Hawaii Press, 2006).
29. Eva-lotta Hedman, "The Philippines in 2005: Old Dynamics, New Conjecture", *Asian Survey* XLVI, no. 1 (2006): 187–93; Jose Magadia, "Contemporary Civil Society in the Philippines", in *Southeast Asian Affairs 1999*, edited by Daljit Singh and John Funston, pp. 253–68 (Singapore: Institute of Southeast Asian Studies, 1999); Sidney Silliman and Lela Garner Noble, *Organizing for Democracy: NGOs, Civil Society, and the Philippine State* (Honolulu: University of Hawaii Press, 1998).
30. Benjamin Muego, "The Philippines in 2004: A Gathering Storm", *Southeast Asian*

Affairs 2005, edited by Chin Kin Wah and Daljit Singh, pp. 293–312 (Singapore: Institute of Southeast Asian Studies, 2005).
31. Chris Schnabel, "Beyond the Numbers: How Aquino Fuelled the Economy", *Rappler Online*, 18 June 2016, https://www.rappler.com/business/economy-watch/136536-president-aquino-economy-legacy (accessed 6 September 2018).
32. Imelda Deinla, "Public Support and Judicial Empowerment of the Philippine Supreme Court", *Contemporary Southeast Asia* 36, no. 1 (2014): 128–58.
33. Marc Jayson Cayabyab, "House Panel to Stall BBL Passage Pending Mamasapano Incident Reports", *Inquirer.Net Online*, 2 February 2015, http://newsinfo.inquirer.net/669936/house-panel-to-stall-bbl-passage-pending-mamasapano-incident-reports (accessed 6 September 2018).
34. Keren Blankfeld, "Philippines' 50 Richest 2016: President Rodrigo Duterte's War on Oligarchs", *Forbes Online*, 24 August 2016, https://www.forbes.com/sites/kerenblankfeld/2016/08/24/philippines-50-richest-2016-president-rodrigo-duterte-wages-war-on-oligarchs/#2e1484b22cbd (accessed 6 September 2018).
35. Makati Business Club, "MBC Executive Outlook Survey Second Semester 2014", Makati Business Club, https://mbc.com.ph/2014/08/29/mbc-executive-outlook-survey-second-semester-2014/ (accessed 6 September 2018).
36. World Bank, "World Justice Project Rule Of Law Index 2017–2018", World Bank, https://worldjusticeproject.org/sites/default/files/documents/WJP_ROLI_2017-18_Online-Edition.pdf (accessed 6 September 2018).
37. Cristina Regina Bonoan and Björn Dressel, "Dismantling a Liberal Constitution, One Institution at a Time", *New Mandala*, 24 May 2018, http://www.newmandala.org/dismantling-liberal-constitution-one-institution-time/ (accessed 2 October 2018).
38. Michael Bueza, "Fast Facts: How Does Impeachment Work?", *Rappler Online*, 20 May 2017, https://www.rappler.com/newsbreak/iq/164340-fast-facts-impeachment-process (accessed 6 September 2018).
39. Republic of the Philippines vs. Maria Lourdes P.A. Sereno in G.R. No. 237428, http://sc.judiciary.gov.ph/pdf/web/viewer.html?file=/jurisprudence/2018/may2018/237428.pdf (accessed 14 August 2018).
40. Dane Angelo M. Enerio, "Duterte: 'Fast-Track' Sereno's Impeachment", *Business World Online*, 9 April 2018, http://www.bworldonline.com/duterte-fast-track-serenos-impeachment/ (accessed 14 August 2018).
41. Julio C. Teehankee, "Electoral Politics in the Philippines", in *Electoral Politics in Southeast and East Asia*, edited by Aurel Croissant, Marei John, and Gabriel Bruns, pp. 149–202 (Singapore and Bonn: Friedrich Ebert Stiftung, S., 2002), http://library.fes.de/pdf-files/iez/01361006.pdf (accessed 27 April 2018).
42. Randy David, "Dutertismo: The First 100 days", *Inquirer.net Online*, 8 October 2016, http://newsinfo.inquirer.net/823086/dutertismo-the-first-100-days (accessed 14 August 2018).

43. ABS-CBN News, "Why the Philippines Needs an Anti-Dynasty Law", *ABS-CBN News Online*, 21 August 2015, http://news.abs-cbn.com/nation/08/20/15/why-philippines-needs-anti-dynasty-law (accessed 14 August 2018).
44. See Art. II, sec. 26 of the 1987 Philippine constitution, http://hrlibrary.umn.edu/research/Philippines/PHILIPPINE%20CONSTITUTION.pdf (accessed 14 August 2018).
45. CNN Philippines, "More LP Members, Political Parties Vow Alliance with Duterte", *CNN Philippines Online*, 23 May 2016, http://cnnphilippines.com/news/2016/05/23/liberal-party-LP-members-lakas-cmd-nup-vow-alliance-duterte-alvarez.html (accessed 14 August 2018).
46. Audrey Morallo, "House Gives CHR a P1,000 budget", *PhilStar Global Online*, 12 September 2017, https://www.philstar.com/headlines/2017/09/12/1738419/house-gives-chr-p1000-budget (accessed 14 August 2018).
47. Eimor P. Santos, "Duterte Gov't, NDF Set Peace Talks for July", *CNN Philippines Online*, 17 June 2016, http://cnnphilippines.com/news/2016/06/16/GPH-NDF-peace-talks-set-for-July.html (accessed 14 August 2018).
48. Presidential Communications Operations Office, News Release, 24 November 2017, https://pcoo.gov.ph/news_releases/duterte-formally-ends-peace-talks-reds/ (accessed 14 August 2018).
49. Edu Punay, "DOJ Wants NDF, CPP Leaders Back in Jail", *PhilStar Global Online*, 2 July 2018, https://pcoo.gov.ph/news_releases/duterte-formally-ends-peace-talks-reds/ (accessed 14 August 2018).
50. Tadem and Tadem, "Political Dynasties in the Philippines".
51. Carmel Abao, "Pluralism, Populism and Their Perversions: Congress in the Time of Duterte", *Rappler Online*, 17 September 2017, https://www.rappler.com/thought-leaders/182416-pluralism-populism-perversions-congress-duterte-part-1 (accessed 7 September 2018).
52. The party-list system was included in the 1987 Constitution to give representation to marginalized groups. In practice, most of those on the lists are professional politicians and members of elites "representing" marginalized groups.
53. Silliman and Noble, *Organizing for Democracy*.
54. Nestor Corrales, "Duterte Offers DENR Post to Gina Lopez of ABS-CBN Foundation", *Inquirer.Net Online*, 20 June 2016, http://newsinfo.inquirer.net/791532/duterte-offers-denr-post-to-gina-lopez-of-abs-cbn-foundation (accessed 14 August 2018).
55. Ali Ian Marcelino Biong, "Duterte Declares Environmental Protection as Priority, Slams Mining Industry", *PhilStar Global Online*, 23 July 2018, https://www.philstar.com/headlines/2018/07/23/1836168/duterte-declares-environmental-protection-top-priority-slams-mining-industry (accessed 16 August 2018).
56. CNN Philippines, "Kabayan Partylist removes Harry Roque as Member, Representative", *CNN Philippines Online*, 24 January 2017, http://

cnnphilippines.com/news/2017/01/24/kabayan-partylist-removes-harry-roque.html (accessed 16 August 2018).
57. Frances Mangosing, "Now an Army Resource Speaker, Mocha Gets Back at Critics", *Inquirer.net Online*, 15 March 2017, http://newsinfo.inquirer.net/880909/now-an-army-resource-speaker-mocha-gets-back-at-critics (accessed 15 August 2018).
58. Mong Palatino, "Beware Duterte's Troll Army in the Philippines", *Diplomat Online*, 18 November 2017, https://thediplomat.com/2017/11/beware-dutertes-troll-army-in-the-philippines/ (accessed 15 August 2018).
59. Dennis F. Quilala, "The Philippines in 2014: Unmasking the *daang matuwid*". *Philippine Political Science Journal* 36, no. 1 (2015): 94–109, https://www.tandfonline.com/doi/full/10.1080/01154451.2015.1026389 (accessed 27 April 2018).
60. Chrisee Dela Paz, "How the Millennial Consumer Is Reshaping the PH Economy", *Rappler Online*, 26 August 2015, https://www.rappler.com/business/economy-watch/103716-maybank-ph-miilennials-drive-ph-economy-maybank (accessed 15 August 2018).
61. Eimor P. Santos, "Millennials Speak Up on What EDSA Means to Them", *CNN Philippines Online*, 25 February 2016, http://cnnphilippines.com/news/2016/02/25/Millenials-1986-EDSA-Revolution.html (accessed 15 August 2018).
62. Imelda Deinla, "Rule of Law Deficit Behind Voter Dismay in the Philippines", *East Asia Forum Online*, 4 May 2016, http://www.eastasiaforum.org/2016/05/04/rule-of-law-deficit-behind-voter-dismay-in-philippines/ (accessed 7 September 2018); Imelda Deinla, "What Is Australia's Stake in Philippines Chaos", *Diplomat Online*, 24 August 2017, https://thediplomat.com/2017/08/what-is-australias-stake-in-philippine-chaos/ (accessed 7 September 2018).
63. See, for example, Nielsen's explanation of ABCDE categories. http://www.nielsen-admosphere.bg/files/2014/06/ABCDE-socio-economic-classification-MEDIARESEARCH-specification-2015.pdf (accessed 15 August 2018).
64. Tomas Africa, "Family Income Distribution in the Philippines, 1985–2009: Essentially the Same", *Social Weather Stations*, 18 March 2011, https://www.sws.org.ph/downloads/publications/pr20110321%20-%20Family%20Income%20Distribution%20by%20Mr%20Tomas%20Africa_FINAL.pdf (accessed 27 April 2018).
65. National Economic and Development Authority, "Highlights of the National Survey on the Aspirations of the Filipino People", *Ambisyon Natin 2040*, October 2016, http://2040.neda.gov.ph/wp-content/uploads/2016/10/AmbisyonHighlightsBrochure-rev2.pdf (accessed 17 April 2018).
66. R.G. Cruz, "Why Duterte is Popular Among Wealthy, Middle-Class Voters", *ABS-CBN News*, 1 May 2016, http://news.abs-cbn.com/halalan2016/

focus/04/30/16/why-duterte-is-popular-among-wealthy-middle-class-voters (accessed 27 April 2018).
67. ABS-CBN News, "More Millennials Voted for Duterte, Exit Poll Shows", *ABS-CBN News Online*, 14 May 2016, http://news.abs-cbn.com/halalan2016/focus/05/14/16/more-millennials-voted-for-duterte-exit-poll-shows (accessed 15 August 2018).
68. Catherine S. Valente, "Dutere on Use of 'Troll' Army: I Have Followers", *Manila Times Online*, 25 July 2017, https://www.manilatimes.net/duterte-on-use-of-troll-army-i-have-followers/340560/ (accessed 15 August 2018).
69. Ibid.
70. Jessica Bartolome, "Mocha Uson appointed as assistant secretary at Duterte's comms office", *GMA News Online*, 9 May 2017, http://www.gmanetwork.com/news/news/nation/610076/mocha-uson-appointed-assistant-secretary-at-duterte-s-comms-office/story/ (accessed 15 August 2018).
71. Christian Houle and Paul D. Kenny, "The Political and Economic Consequences of Populist Rule in Latin America", *Government and Opposition* 53, no. 2 (2018): 256–87.
72. Rahael Baladad, "Duterte's Social Development Agenda: Radical Change or Business as Usual?", *Global South Online*, 9 June 2017, https://focusweb.org/content/duterte-s-social-development-agenda-radical-change-or-business-usual (accessed 15 August 2018).
73. Jess Diaz, "Consumer Prices up due to TRAIN", *Philstar Global Online*, 28 February 2018, https://www.philstar.com/headlines/2018/02/28/1792093/consumer-prices-due-train (accessed 15 August 2018).
74. Rey E. Requejo and Rio N. Araja, "Ombudsman to Enforce Dismissal Order vs Carandang", *Manilastandard.net Online*, 6 August 2018, http://thestandard.com.ph/mobile/article/272376 (accessed 15 August 2018).
75. Elmor P. Santos, "Sereno Ouster Shows SC Bowing to 'Aggressive' SolGen—Justice Leonen", *CNN Philippines Online*, 16 May 2018, http://cnnphilippines.com/news/2018/05/11/Sereno-ouster-dissenting-Justice-Leonen-Solicitor-General-Calida.html (accessed 15 August 2018).
76. Rey Panaligan, Ben Rosario, and Jeffrey Damicog, "IBP cautions Congress on misuse of impeachment", *Manila Bulletin Online*, 6 September 2017, https://news.mb.com.ph/2017/09/06/ibp-cautions-congress-on-misuse-of-impeachment/ (accessed 15 August 2018).
77. See 2017 Corruption Perception Index results conducted by Transparency International, https://www.transparency.org/news/feature/corruption_perceptions_index_2017#table (accessed 15 August 2018).

PART I

Politics and Governance

1

The Rise of Illiberal Democracy in the Philippines:
Duterte's Early Presidency

Mark R. Thompson

INTRODUCTION

Hungarian Prime Minister Viktor Orbán, a right populist, espouses what he calls "illiberal democracy". Orbán has weakened media independence, clamped down on the judiciary, intimidated non-government organizations (NGOs) and shown open preference for ethnic Hungarians while targetting minority groups and migrants.[1] He is creating a Hungarian version of the regimes of Vladimir Putin of Russia and Recep Tayyip Erdoğan of Turkey.[2] Orbán has rejected criticism from the European Union that he has weakened civil liberties and eliminated most constitutional checks on his executive authority, claiming he is only acting in the interests of his people who gave his party a super-majority in the legislature.[3]

This chapter attempts to apply the concept of "illiberal democracy" to the Philippines under the presidency of Rodrigo R. Duterte. If illiberal democracy can be understood as having a legitimately elected leader who has not (yet) formally curbed freedom of speech or limited powers of branches of government—yet whose rule is marked by systematic violations of civil liberties—then this term arguably applies to the Duterte administration in the Philippines more so than Orbán's rule in Hungary. The latter regime has become a "Potemkin democracy" since the 2014 (and the recent 2018) elections in which the ruling party enjoyed unfair advantages, leaving it with only a "democratic façade" in what is in fact "quasi 'one-party rule'".[4] With his super-majority in parliament, Orbán had laws passed that target the press, independent government agencies, NGOs, and even the prestigious Central European University (CEU)—the most recent subject of Orbán's ire threatened with closure through so-called "lex CEU" legislation.[5] By contrast, although Duterte has cowed the courts, won control of Congress, and had his chief opponent Leila de Lima jailed on dubious charges—while putting another leading critic, Vice President Maria Leonor "Leni" Robredo under significant pressure—he has not manipulated elections. Duterte was elected in free and fair polls in May 2016 and has formally upheld most democratic rules. The press is not formally censored (although several news outlets have been subject to presidential intimidation) and Congress and the courts have not been subject to legal restrictions (but the Supreme Court Chief Justice and a Duterte critic was removed in an irregular fashion). It is "only" the substance of what he has done that is obviously illiberal—in particular orchestrating and encouraging the killing of thousands of supposed drug dealers and addicts. Thus, while Duterte acts illiberally, he is democratically legitimate and, to a large extent, rules constitutionally.

It is beyond the scope of this chapter to offer an elaborate theoretical exposition of "illiberal democracy". The arguments put forward will, however, help to clarify the concept by referring to ideal typical counterpoints. On the one hand—because illiberal democracy in the Philippines under Duterte involves free and fair elections—it differs from electoral authoritarianism, a concept which covers "authoritarian regimes [that] play the game of multiparty elections" yet "violate the liberal-democratic principles of freedom and fairness so profoundly and systematically as to render elections instruments of authoritarian rule".[6] Examples of authoritarian regimes in East Asia include Malaysia (until the recent opposition victory in May 2018) and Singapore. On the other hand, illiberal democracy in the Philippines under Duterte differs from "liberal oligarchy"—in which regimes abide by liberal principles but the leadership is either not elected or only partially elected. Examples of liberal oligarchy include the Austro-Hungarian Empire before World War I and Hong Kong in East Asia today. Illiberal democracy upholds participation rights while violating personal liberties, which loosely follows the distinction used by Freedom House between civil (personal) liberties and political (participation) rights. The former "allow for the freedoms of expression and belief, associational and organizational rights, rule of law, and personal autonomy without interference from the state" while the latter enable people to participate freely in the political process, including the right to vote freely for distinct alternatives in legitimate elections, compete for public office, join political parties and organizations, and elect representatives who have a decisive impact on public policies and are accountable to the electorate.[7]

The most important aspect of Duterte's illiberal rule had been his monomaniacal pursuit of a violent crackdown on drug pushers and users which has resulted in thousands of deaths in less than a year in office.[8] The most serious effort to count the number of those killed in what Duterte calls "a war on drugs" has been undertaken by the respected internet news outlet Rappler which estimates over 7,000 Filipinos were killed during the "drug war" in the first ten months of Duterte's presidency.[9] Other estimates are as high as 9,000 as of mid-April 2017.[10] By February 2018, an opposition senator, citing police data, claimed up to 20,000 people had been killed in the violent drug crackdown.[11] The Philippine Commission on Human Rights (CHR) claims the anti-drug campaign involves "summary executions, corruption, and abuse of power" with widespread extrajudicial killings[12]—a finding backed by reports from Amnesty International,[13] Human Rights Watch[14] and a tell-all report compiled by two senior police insiders.[15]

This chapter will attempt to explain why and how illiberal democracy could be established in the Philippines under Duterte and what exactly this illiberalism consists of in still formal democratic institutions. The first part of this chapter will argue that although Duterte's predecessor, Benigno "Noynoy" S. Aquino III, was widely perceived to be personally honest, "liberal reformism" became vulnerable to being replaced by violent illiberalism because its narrative of "good governance" had been undermined, strategic allies were discredited, and liberal institutions weakened. In other words, Aquino III's personal popularity could not keep liberal reformism from becoming disjunctive as a form of political order.

In fact, because Aquino III was popular, voters blamed "the system", not him, for these failures.

The second part of this chapter will discuss how Duterte was able to construct an illiberal democracy despite supposed widespread support among Filipinos for democratic institutions and a limited concern about drugs and criminality. Duterte is an illiberal "right" populist who mobilized a mass constituency through the media—particularly social media—portraying a corrupt elite who coddle drug dealers and addicts. Duterte had first constructed this strongman political model at the local level before "nationalizing" it after his election as president.

The final section examines the nature of the crackdown on drugs which is at the heart of the Duterte administration's illiberalism. How the drug war has been carried out will be examined briefly and also how widespread abuses—including mass killing of drug "criminals"—have become increasingly well documented. Why Duterte had to "pause" his drug war due to revelations of the kidnapping and killing of a South Korean businessmen by police in the anti-drug squad will also be examined. Duterte remains committed to the drug war, "reloading" it—albeit at a slower pace of killing—despite signs of growing domestic opposition.

WHY? THE DECLINE OF LIBERAL REFORMISM

The violently illiberal turn of Philippine politics since Duterte's election in the 9 May 2016 presidential elections is puzzling when one considers it was preceded by six years of political stability and high growth (averaging nearly 6 per cent) under the (relatively) liberal and (supposedly) reformist administration of Benigno "Noynoy" Aquino III. Under Aquino's administration, the economic acceleration from his predecessor Gloria Macapagal Arroyo continued without political destabilization as her administration had faced mass demonstrations and several coup attempts. Benigno Aquino III was widely seen as honest—with no revelations about major scandals involving his relatives or close friends. By contrast, Arroyo was the most unpopular post-Marcos president with key scandals linked to her husband, son and "cronies". This allowed Aquino to claim that it was not the reformist political order that was to blame but Arroyo's poor leadership. Distinguishing himself from his scandal-plagued predecessor, Aquino promised to take the "straight path" (*daang matuwid*) to clean up corruption which he claimed would also eradicate poverty. Economic growth was among the highest among the Association of Southeast Asian Nations (ASEAN). Corrupt politicians finally seemed to be held accountable. More people paid their taxes after a Bureau of International Revenue crackdown. On the coat-tails of Aquino's high opinion poll ratings, pro-administration candidates dominated mid-term congressional elections in 2013. International credit rating agencies such as Fitch also gave Aquino's administration a vote of confidence, upping the country's rating to investment grade. The Philippines steadily improved its ranking in Transparency International's Corruption Perception Index, moving in 2011 from 129th most corrupt—of 177 countries—to 105th in 2012, then to 95th in 2015.[16] Given how fast Aquino seemed to be moving along the "straight path", it is not surprising he had the highest popularity levels over his term than any president since Ferdinand Marcos.[17]

Why then did liberal reformist-oriented electoral democracy in the Philippines prove vulnerable to Duterte's bloody political challenge? In the post-Marcos Philippines, the discourse of liberal reformism—the claim that re-establishing democracy, fighting corruption, and improving the efficiency of governance should be the country's top priorities—has been used by most presidents as their chief campaign narrative and subsequent "regime script". Liberal reformism can be understood as a "bourgeois" political storyline that promises "I will not steal from you." It skirts questions about high inequality, much less redistribution, avoiding direct class-based appeals. It can appear uncaring and morally self-righteous, particularly as poverty rates and unemployment have remained high during the post-Marcos era.[18]

In its final three years in power the Aquino administration's reformist credentials were eroded by a pork-barrel scandal, rampant smuggling and unaddressed structural problems. There were high rates of unemployment and poverty despite economic growth—with only marginal improvement in education and healthcare for the masses. The Aquino administration's inability to deal quickly and effectively with the devastation caused by the supertyphoon Haiyan (known as "Yolanda" in the Philippines) in large parts of the Western Visayas in 2013 was another indication of its failure. Liberal reformism had hit a "dead end".[19]

Particularly damaging to the Aquino administration's good governance narrative were revelations about the Priority Development Assistance Fund (PDAF), the main vehicle for government pork barrelling. The PDAF scandal's impact was wide ranging. It was revealed that doling out patronage to legislators had been crucial to getting them to pass reformist legislation or to remove supposedly corrupt officials— with revelations about pork-barrel funds for "soft projects" going to Senators who voted in favour of Supreme Court Chief Justice Corona's removal from office after impeachment on corruption charges which drew particular scorn.[20] It was also revealed that pork-barrel funds often ended up in legislators' pockets instead of slated projects. Only anti-Aquino legislators were targeted in the follow-up investigation, which raised suspicions that Aquino was using the scandal as a chance to strike back at political enemies rather than making a serious effort to eliminate pork-barrel abuses.[21]

The Aquino government was also widely seen to have failed in delivering efficient public services because of underspending on infrastructure, allowing public transportation in Manila to decay with its traffic becoming among the worst in Asia—dubbed "carmageddon" by Philippine netizens. Moreover, there was a major military debacle when forty-four members of the Special Armed Forces sent to arrest a wanted Islamic terrorist were massacred in a bungled operation in southern Mindanao in January 2016—the so-called Mamasapano incident. A mere three months later, several farmers protesting the delay in the delivery of relief goods to a drought-hit part of Mindanao were killed and over one hundred injured in a violent police crackdown. There was also a growing sense that the illegal drug problem was spiralling out of control and that criminality was generally on the rise during Aquino's time in office, even if the statistical evidence for this proved to be dubious.[22] Aquino himself admitted his pledge to clean up the Bureau of Customs had failed miserably, with three customs commissioners quitting due to purported political pressure exercised by smugglers during Aquino's six-year term.

Not only had graft persisted while government competence in key areas was low, but the fundamental structure of Philippines society had also not changed—symbolized by the Aquino-Cojuangco family's tenacious resistance to court-ordered land redistribution of its huge sugar plantation Hacienda Luisita. The communist left was generally excluded from policy making. Social issues—including land reform—were not prioritized. The Philippines' impressive macroeconomic growth during the Aquino presidency had largely been fuelled by remittances from the 10 per cent of the country's population working abroad—often in menial jobs—and business process outsourcing—primarily call centres mainly foreign-owned and easily moved to another country. Antoinette R. Raquiza has shown that a new group of tycoons has emerged, overshadowing the old landed oligarchy and also demonstrates that their wealth is not primarily based in industry but in a rapidly growing service sector and speculative real estate investments.[23]

Furthermore, economic growth remains profoundly unequal. Cielito Habito calculated that the growth in the aggregate wealth of the country's forty richest families in 2011 was equivalent to over three-quarters of the increase in the country's gross domestic product (GDP) in that year.[24] Unemployment rose during Aquino's presidency, while poverty hardly dipped and self-reported poverty actually increased. Aquino did increase government funding of an anti-poverty programme, a Brazilian-style conditional cash transfer (CCT) scheme. Critics, such as Maria Victoria R. Raquiza, however, argue the increase in CCT benefits motivated by the ruling Liberal Party's desire for more patronage resources for elections would have been better spent on providing universal social services and boosting industrial policy to create more jobs.[25]

Given Aquino's personal popularity, the problems of liberal reformism could no longer be blamed on an individual, but were now attributed to the nature of the political order itself. This systemic vulnerability set the stage for liberal reformism to be replaced by an illiberal alternative. With liberal reformism tarnished irreparably during the second half of the Aquino presidency, Aquino's handpicked successor, Mar Roxas—who promised to continue the policies of the Aquino administration—always trailed in the polls, finishing a distant second to Duterte in the 2016 presidential election.[26] Earlier attempts to pre-empt liberalism by "left" populists who made appeals to help the much-neglected poor had been effectively marginalized by self-proclaimed reformers. The weaknesses of the "good governance" narrative might not have led to violent, illiberal populism had pro-poor populist leaders been allowed to serve out their term in office—and not been cheated in elections, or undermined through selective investigations.[27]

The Catholic Church hierarchy—despite being very powerful for a long time in Philippine society—became a particularly important strategic group after it was politicized under Marcos' rule[28]—then embraced its self-anointed "role as a guardian of democracy".[29] But after the death of the powerful Manila Archbishop Jaime Cardinal Sin in 2005, Church leadership became fragmented and revelations of sexual abuses in the Roman Catholic Church further weakened the Church.[30] During Noynoy

Aquino's presidency, the Catholic Church hierarchy led a high-profile campaign against a moderate reproductive health bill that focused on making contraception more widely available to the poor yet did not mention abortion—despite the large number of dangerous "back alley" abortions in the Philippines. The women's movement strongly supported this bill.[31] Although the bill was passed in late 2013, the Church led efforts to have the Supreme Court partially block it and the Church's Congressional allies defund it. Duterte easily outmanoeuvred the Church by threatening to expose sex scandals—claiming himself to have been abused by a priest as a child—and also claimed the Church's involvement in corruption and hardline stance against all forms of reproductive health as a hazard to Filipinas' well-being. The Church had been a bastion of liberal critiques of human rights abuses during the Marcos period and to a lesser extent during the post-Marcos period. But placed on the defensive, the Catholic Bishops' Conference of the Philippines only issued its first statement against extrajudicial killings in mid-September 2016—two and a half-months after Duterte took office and after almost 3,000 people had been killed in his "war on drugs".[32]

Civil society activists have been the most volatile and easily mobilized elite strategic group in the post-Marcos Philippines. Vulnerable to co-optation by political elites,[33] so-called social democrats—linked to intellectuals and activists close to the Jesuits in the Catholic Church—were dominant among civil society activists during the Aquino administration, taking a lion's share of government social welfare positions. These moderate left elements, were however, gradually disillusioned and discredited by the PDAF pork-barrel scandal, poor management of reconstruction following the Haiyan typhoon and other natural disasters, and continued high levels of social inequality, unemployment and poverty—despite high growth. Once Duterte was elected, this once-powerful group of social democrats found itself quickly marginalized.

Few major institutional reforms had been made during the Aquino administration—with the serious problems of the Philippine justice system obviously unresolved. The trial of those accused of committing the 2009 Maguindanao massacre that killed fifty-seven people, including thirty-two journalists and media workers—which Aquino had vowed would be concluded, and the perpetrators brought to justice before his term ended—was symbolic of the phenomenon of "justice delayed".[34] Even more embarrassing was a police raid of the biggest jail in the Philippines in late 2014—the national Bilibid prison—which revealed imprisoned drug lords "living like kings".[35] While crime statistics show major crimes declined during the Aquino administration,[36] such incidents reinforced the *perception* of the Aquino administration as weak on crime and incapable of enforcing the law. Moreover, the selective prosecution of legislators found to have diverted pork-barrel funds increased cynicism about Aquino's commitment to the rule of law—as cases filed by the Department of Justice were confined to Aquino's enemies.[37] The weaknesses of the justice system and supposed neglect of criminality and drug abuse by the Aquino administration provided Duterte with the opportunity to promise and then carry out a violent war on drugs.

One could assume the judiciary would be at the forefront of efforts to curb extrajudicial killings under Duterte. However, the removal of Chief Justice Renato Corona by the Aquino administration for transparent political motives made the Supreme Court wary of confronting a president. In addition, a number of judges, including Supreme Court justices, faced accusations of political influence peddling and even plagiarism. Unlike in the United States where the judiciary played a major role in stopping a number of Trump's more illiberal actions by overruling controversial executive orders, Duterte has faced little judicial constraint in the Philippines.

Although coming to power with only a handful of party mates, Duterte soon enjoyed a supermajority in both houses of congress through a familiar process of defections to the winning president's side—known as "political butterflies" or *balimbings* in the Philippines (after the multipronged star fruit). This mass political defection, also known as "turncoatism", occurred despite Liberal Party warnings during the preceding campaign that Duterte planned to establish a dictatorship.[38] Mass defections also indicated how hollow the Liberal Party's promise to become a "programmatic" party with a clear political doctrine and membership loyalty had been. Rather, it proved, like all other major political parties in the country, to be a loose association of traditional politicians (*trapos*) striving to gain power to access pork barrel.[39]

HOW? DUTERTE'S "RIGHT POPULISM"

What was it about Duterte's message that voters found so appealing—given that drugs and criminality were not a major concern of voters according to polls until Duterte launched his candidacy for president?[40] Data show that overall crime has been declining for several years and serious crime was also decreasing at the end of the Aquino administration.[41] Yet a plurality of voters chose Duterte, who threatened to declare martial law if the drug problem could not be brought under control—despite a survey at the end of 2015 which found more than three-quarters of Filipinos were satisfied with the way democracy worked in the country, an increase from a low 28 per cent during Aquino's predecessor Gloria Macapagal Arroyo.[42]

Duterte managed to "perform a crisis", striking a chord with a "frustrated public" with his promise to crackdown on drugs.[43] Rather than criticize the Aquino regime for its social neglect—as Jejomar Binay, the vice president under Noynoy Aquino and another presidential candidate in 2016, did with his pro-poor message during the presidential campaign—Duterte's "dystopian narrative shifted the discussion to a more urgent solution, the arrest and/or killing of drug dealers and users until the problem is eradicated." But this "comes at a price" Duterte warned, "the price of liberal rights".[44] This targeting of drug criminals was crucial to Duterte winning the 2016 presidential election and his skyrocketing popularity after taking office.[45]

Most of today's populists around the globe are not explicitly anti-democratic, but their "principled anti-pluralist" conception of "the people"—simple and good—means they are only "impersonators" of democrats.[46] There are different ideological directions in populism. A distinction can be made between "left populism" (the US's Bernie Sanders, the UK's Jeremy Corbyn, Spain's Podemos party and, in the Philippines, former president Joseph E. Estrada, presidential candidate Fernando Poe, Jr, known as FPJ, and Binay in the Philippines) which "taps into people's anger by appealing to their sense of social justice and calling for the regulation of capitalism" and "right populism" (Donald Trump in the US and Marie Le Pen in France) that "appeals to people's fears and prejudices".[47] Jan-Werner Müller[48] argues that for right populists "elites are often immoral in the specific sense that they actually work only for themselves (as opposed to the common good) and for essentially undeserving minorities who do not truly belong to the demos".[49]

Thousands were killed by extrajudicial killings of suspected drug dealers and users during Duterte's first few months in office which were denounced by the United Nations, many Western countries, and international and domestic human rights groups. Nicole Curato, following

Pratt, speaks of the "fantasy" of "penal populism": a "virtuous public" set apart from "degenerates who do not deserve due process".[50] Despite Duterte's nationalist discourse and ties to the communist left,[51] his political discourse can be classified as illiberal "right" populism. This populism enabled Duterte to mobilize a mass constituency through the media—particularly social media—using radical rhetoric to portray a corrupt elite coddling drug dealers and addicts. Duterte's discursive demonology does not focus on abstract, structural factors such as "globalization" and "capitalism"—like that of "left" populists—but rather on drug addicts whom he considers "beyond redemption" because, "once you're addicted to *shabu* [the term used for crystal meth in the Philippines], rehabilitation is no longer a viable option".[52]

Duterte's popularity soared with the launch of his "war on drugs", peaking at over 90 per cent after his first 100 days in office. It is no surprise that Duterte's strongman image resonated so strongly with many Filipinos when one considers nearly two-thirds of Filipino respondents answered in wave 4 and 6 of the World Values survey they favoured "strong leaders", and nearly half preferring military to civilian rule.[53] Eric Vincent C. Batalla has pointed out that while Filipinos may claim they want "a democratic system, many also entertain the idea of a strong leader and autocratic rule".[54]

Unlike the "left" populist president, Joseph E. Estrada (1998–2001)—Duterte's strongest support came from elite and so-called middle class "ABC" voters—not the poorest voters.[55] Those inclined to believe that Duterte's rise is part of a global outrage against growing inequality overlook the fact that core supporters during his campaign were among the country's most prosperous, even if his support base expanded across class lines after his election. "Dutertismo"—as the Philippine sociologist Randy David has termed it—has generally been driven by middle-class worries about drugs and crime—as well as crumbling infrastructure and continued corruption.[56] Duterte's aggressive electoral campaign played to the deep resentments of those voters who were marginally better off after a couple of decades of solid growth. The "politics of anger"[57] leaves little room for treating drugs as a health problem, and using the rule of law to deal with it, thereby avoiding the criminalization of the poor.[58]

A distinctive feature of right populism in the Philippines was that Duterte crafted and honed his skills for nearly three decades at the local level before he became president. Duterte was either mayor or the power-behind-the-throne—first with his one-time political ally and later his daughter, standing in for him after he had to step aside due to term limits—of the large city of Davao located in the southern island of Mindanao. John Sidel's notion of local "bossism"[59] captures Duterte's leadership style well. But, in addition, Duterte was part of a subset of warlords who did not focus on fighting his political enemies, but rather focused his wrath and firepower on drug criminals—allowing him to cut deals with communist insurgents and make peace with surrounding political bosses to fight "the bad guys". As Danilo Reyes has shown, several mayors in the Philippines have pursued similar strategies of "eliminating" criminals through extrajudicial killings, not only to deter crime but also to win popularity that has aided their re-election campaigns.[60] In an environment of lawlessness, where institutions are weak, the strongman who protects the good common *tao* (people) against the evil criminals is not only able to legitimize his ruthless *modus operandi* but also to insure his long-term hold on office. It was during his time as mayor that Duterte constructed a tough-guy (*siga*) image, proclaiming himself the saviour of communist-infiltrated and crime-infested Davao.[61] The people of Davao "allowed him to rule with an iron fist in exchange for social peace and personal security".[62] Besides his regional voting strengths in Mindanao Island[63] and among fellow Cebuano speakers generally, Duterte polled strongly in the May 2016 elections in urban areas where worries about crime are greatest and media-based political narratives are most crucial to attracting votes.[64]

Another aspect of Duterte's right populist appeal that has received little systematic attention is his "informal" (read cuss-filled) political speech.[65] Duterte's discursive style, vulgar and often offensive, has helped him connect to voters through its informality, known in the literature as "style switching"—political actors in public situations employing an inappropriately informal style.[66] Duterte was a charismatic campaigner with his "colourful" language perceived as an indication of his "refreshing authenticity".[67]

WHAT? THE BLOODY WAR ON DRUGS

In Duterte's so-called "war on drugs", suspects have died "fighting back" (*nalaban*) against the police, after being shot by motorcycle-riding vigilante gunmen or kidnapped by quasi-official death squads, their tortured and taped up bodies left with a cardboard confessional sign strapped around their necks saying "pusher" or "drug lord" and dumped under a bridge or in a neighbouring town. The guilt of victims has been assumed—never proven, seriously investigated, or even questioned. Duterte unleashed police vigilantes in a nationally directed but locally conducted killing spree. During the first 100 days of Duterte's administration, an average of thirty-six Filipinos were killed daily, about half of these extrajudicial killings in the country's capital Manila with most others also in major urban centres.[68]

Given Duterte and his supporters' efforts to defend his record through an old political ruse of the "principle of deniability"—particularly widespread in a political class dominated by lawyers of which Duterte is one, also being a former prosecutor—it is difficult to tie Duterte to particular deaths during the anti-drug campaign. But such a deniability strategy is implausible in terms of seeing Duterte as orchestrating and encouraging the campaign given his repeated threats to kill drug dealers and users, telling Filipinos to "forget the laws on human rights" in his final presidential campaign speech.[69]

According to a report by Amnesty International, the war on drugs in the Philippines has created "an economy of murder" among the police tasked with carrying out the campaign.[70] An investigation by the human rights group revealed that police are paid hundreds of US dollars for each extrajudicial killing, but not for arrests. The investigation also revealed that the murders are staged to make them seem like legitimate police operations, as evidence is planted and reports falsified. As well as often stealing from the homes of the murder victims, police also have links to funeral homes, who pay to get a corpse delivered to them, causing the usually destitute families of the victims' additional hardship. Police lock down poor neighbourhoods under a policy known as Oplan TokHang—a portmanteau combining the Cebuano words *tuktok* (knock) and *hangyo* (plead)—to get drug dealers and users to surrender. This is in stark contrast to their polite treatment of people in rich neighbourhoods, where they go from house to house investigating people for possible drug use. Most victims of police and vigilante "hits" are poor and defenceless people, making the war against the drugs appear more like a war against the poor.[71] A recent study of coercive anti-drug campaigns around the world concluded after surveying the literature that "the failures of the 'war on drugs' have been well documented".[72] Rather there is a need for "sustainable development" to be prioritized over "eradication ... militarization, widespread criminalization or any other 'pigheaded' anti-drug policies".[73] Criticizing Duterte's drug crackdown, Collins predicted that, based on evidence from similar coercive anti-drug efforts around the world, "the Philippines' new 'war' will fail and society will emerge worse off from it".[74]

After slow-drip revelations in January 2017 that several members of the Philippine National Police Anti-Illegal Drugs Group had kidnapped and killed Jee Ick-joo—a South Korean businessman—in October 2016, a reluctant Duterte temporarily called off his "war on drugs" at the end of January 2017.[75] It was particularly embarrassing for the government that these criminal cops had taken Jee Ick-joo to police headquarters in Metro Manila where they strangled him before demanding a large ransom from his wife, who was led to believe he was still alive. Critics claimed that Jee's killing was further proof that corrupt police had been using the war on drugs to commit crimes of their own—particularly against those involved in the drug trade—in order to cover their tracks.[76] There is also growing evidence that many of those killed in the drug war were innocent—of course, all of those murdered either in "police encounters" or by motorcycle assassins were denied any sort of due process. A number of stories have also emerged that suggest mistakes were being made or scores settled under the cover of the drug crackdown.

CONCLUSION

In mid-2018, the Philippines was entering a political crossroads—with worries mounting that the country's liberal institutions were being further eroded. Supreme Court Chief Justice Maria Lourdes Sereno, whom Duterte called "an enemy", was removed in what most legal experts consider an irregular fashion without congressional impeachment proceedings by her fellow Supreme Court Justices who were emboldened by Duterte's criticisms. Vice President and presidential critic Maria Leonor "Leni" Robredo is facing an electoral challenge by her challenger and dictator's son Ferdinand "Bong Bong" Marcos that could lead the former's removal and replacement by the latter. A Consultative Committee has proposed a new federal constitution which, while including major political reforms (an anti-dynasty provision and measures to strengthen political parties), has been criticized for creating an unwieldy and expensive federal structure at a time Philippine economy is experiencing difficulties, particularly rising inflation, a depreciating peso, and a decline in promised external investment as foreign firms have apparently been scared off by the drug war and general political uncertainty. In the meantime, the drug war remains unrelenting, despite continued human rights outrages including the well-documented killing of a minor Kian de los Santos which was caught on CCTV in August 2018, with Duterte reaffirming in his third State of the Nation address in July 2018 that "the illegal drugs war will not be sidelined ... it will be as relentless and chilling, if you will, as on the day it began".[77]

It has been argued in this chapter that Duterte has quickly erected an "illiberal democracy" in the Philippines since his election as president in May 2016 by immediately launching a violent anti-drug crackdown which had already killed thousands within the first ten months of his presidency. Duterte was able to take advantage of the systemic crisis of this once-dominant liberal reformist political order despite the personal popularity of his predecessor Noynoy Aquino due to the undermining of the good governance narrative, the discrediting of key elite strategic groups backing it (particularly the Church and social democrats) and the weakening of liberal institutions. Deploying an illiberal populist "order *over* law"[78] narrative during his presidential campaign, which has become the "governing script" of his early presidency, any remaining institutional barriers to this illiberalism were quickly sidelined with mass defections to his once-tiny political party and the timidity of the Supreme Court. Although a nascent elite and female-led opposition to Duterte has emerged, it remains largely powerless and much mocked as of this writing.[79] Under Duterte, democracy has been bloodied through the systematic violation of human rights in the name of a crackdown on drugs through the impunity of the police who have been encouraged and supported by Duterte. Walden Bello points out that Duterte has not "feared to transgress liberal discourse [which] not only does ... not trouble a significant part of the population, they've even clapped for it!"[80] Criticized by the Obama administration for massive human rights violations during the drug war, Duterte seems to have found a new political friend in US President Donald Trump who has praised the crackdown.[81] Still popular at home and finding new allies abroad, Duterte has drawn on techniques common to illiberal democracies around the world to which he added his own violent interpretation. But while his rule is highly illiberal, he continues to point to his democratic legitimacy. Duterte promises national political salvation by claiming that only a violent strongman rule can bring political order to the country with weak institutions.

Notes

Research for this chapter was supported by the Hong Kong Research Grants Council, University Grants Committee [grant no. 9042600]. The author would like to express his appreciation to the organizers and participants of the Philippine Update Conference at the Australian National University on 2–3 September 2016 and to the following institutions for hosting talks where earlier versions of this paper were presented: the Saw Swee-Hock Southeast Asia Centre of the London School of Economics, 25 October 2017; the Weatherhead East Asian Institute, 15 February 2017; the Center for Southeast Asian Studies, University of California Berkeley, 4 April 2017; and the Philippine Political Science Association conference, Cebu, 11–12 May 2017. Portions of this paper were previously published in a special issue of the *Journal of Current Southeast Asian Affairs*, https://journals.sub.uni-hamburg.de/giga/jsaa/article/view/1007/1014 and https://journals.sub.uni-hamburg.de/giga/jsaa/article/view/1009/1021.

1. Paul Taylor, "Confronting 'Illiberal Democracy' in Central Europe", *New York Times*, 8 June 2015, https://www.nytimes.com/2015/06/09/business/international/central-europe-confronts-illiberal-democracy.html?_r=0; Andrew MacDowall., "Illiberal Democracy: How Hungary's Orbán Is Testing Europe", *World Politics Review*, 18 December 2014, http://www.worldpoliticsreview.com/articles/14699/illiberal-democracy-how-hungary-s-orban-is-testing-europe.
2. Michael Stewart, "Losing the Central European University Would be a Tragedy for Hungarian Public Life", *Europp*, 10 April 2017, http://blogs.lse.ac.uk/europpblog/2017/04/10/central-european-university-closure-orban/.
3. Taylor, "Confronting 'Illiberal Democracy'"; MacDowall, "Illiberal Democracy".
4. Attila Ágh, "De-Europeanization and De-democratization Trends in ICE: From the Potemkin Democracy to the Elected Autocracy in Hungary", *Journal of Comparative Politics* 8, no. 2 (July 2015): 4–26.
5. Stewart, "Losing the Central European University".
6. Andreas Schedler, ed., *Electoral Authoritarianism: The Dynamics of Unfree Competition* (Boulder: Lynne Rienner, 2006), p. 3.
7. Freedom House, "Freedom in the World: Methodology—Introduction", Freedom in the World report, 2009, https://freedomhouse.org/report/countries-crossroads-2011/methodology-0.
8. The term "monomania" is most commonly associated with Ahab, Herman Melville's anti-hero in *Moby Dick*, who is fixated on killing the white whale, convincing his crew to go along with his quixotic and dangerous search for it.

9. Michael Bueza, "In Numbers: The Philippines' 'War on Drugs'", *Rappler*, 7 November 2016, 18th update, http://www.rappler.com/newsbreak/iq/145814-numbers-statistics-philippines-war-drugs.
10. Manuel Mogato and Clare Baldwin, "Special Report: Police Describe Kill Rewards, Staged Crime Scenes in Duterte's Drug War", Reuters, 18 April 2017, http://www.reuters.com/article/us-philippines-duterte-police-specialrep-idUSKBN17K1F4; Rappler uses numbers of those killed that the Philippine National Police (PNP) tagged "deaths under investigation" (DUI)—a term not used until Duterte came to power. The Duterte administration and its supporters have attacked this method of counting the number of deaths as "fake news", saying the real figure is closer to 1,400 killed (Asian Correspondent Staff 2017). Yet it is the police themselves who provided these statistics in the course of crackdown, but have not provided follow-up information about investigations (Rappler 2017). The Duterte administration is acting disingenuously by not providing the information that would be needed to make a more credible count and then blaming those who try, despite the sparse information available.
11. Ted Regencia, "Senator: Rodrigo Duterte's Drug War Has Killed 20,000", *Aljazeera*, 22 February 2018, https://www.aljazeera.com/news/2018/02/senator-rodrigo-duterte-drug-war-killed-20000-180221134139202.html.
12. Yuji Vincent Gonzales, "Drug War Fraught with Abuses—CHR", *Philippine Daily Inquirer*, 31 January 2017, http://newsinfo.inquirer.net/866916/drug-war-halt-a-recognition-of-gaps-abuses-chr.
13. Steve Mollman, "Murder by Numbers: Duterte's War on Drugs Has Created 'an Economy of Murder' in the Philippines, Says Amnesty International", *Quartz*, 1 February 2017, https://qz.com/900039/dutertes-war-on-drugs-has-created-an-economy-of-murder-in-the-philippines-says-amnesty-international/.
14. Associated Press, "Philippines Police Plant Evidence to Justify Killings in Drug War, Says Report", *The Guardian*, 2 March 2017, https://www.theguardian.com/world/2017/mar/02/philippines-police-plant-evidence-to-justify-killings-in-drug-war-says-report.
15. Mogato and Baldwin, "Special Report: Police in Duterte's Drug War"; The Philippine president has even compared his violent campaign with Hitler's Holocaust against the Jews, with Duterte saying he would gladly murder three million drug dealers and users. This showed Duterte to be a poor political mathematician. It is estimated Hitler killed twice as many Jews as Duterte claimed (6 million) while a 2015 survey by the major drug research and policy agency, the president's Dangerous Drugs Board (DDB), showed the Philippines has fewer than half the number of drug users Duterte asserted (1.8 million, with only a third of taking illegal substances in the past year). On this, see: Clare Baldwin and Andrew R.C. Marshall, "2 Dead Cops Daily and Other 'Dubious'

Data in Du30's Drug War", ABS-CBN News, 24 October 2016, http://news.abs-cbn.com/focus/10/24/16/2-dead-cops-daily-and-other-dubious-data-in-du30s-war-on-drugs.
16. Tradingeconomics, "Philippines Corruption Rank: 1995–2016", *Tradingeconomics*, 2016, http://www.tradingeconomics.com/philippines/corruption-rank.
17. Social Weather Stations (SWS), "Third Quarter 2016 Social Weather Survey: 'Very Good' +64 Net Satisfaction Rating for President Rodrigo R. Duterte", *Social Weather Stations*, 10 October 2016, http://www.sws.org.ph/swsmain/artcldisppage/?artcsyscode=ART-20161006061108.
18. Mark R. Thompson, "Reformism versus Populism in the Philippines", *Journal of Democracy* 21, no. 4 (October 2010): 154–68.
19. Mark R. Thompson, "Aquino's Reformism Hits a Dead End", *East Asia Forum*, 30 September 2014, http://www.eastasiaforum.org/2014/09/30/aquinos-reformism-hits-a-dead-end/.
20. Rigoberto Tiglao, "DBM Data Confirm P100M 'Bribe' to 16 Senators Each", *RigobertoTiglao.com*, 3 October 2013, http://www.rigobertotiglao.com/2013/10/03/dbm-data-confirm-p100m-bribe-to-16-senators-each/.
21. Ronald D. Holmes, "Pork Transmogrified: The Unending Story of Particularistic Spending in the Philippines", in *Handbook of the Contemporary Philippines*, edited by Eric C. Batalla and Mark R. Thompson (London: Routledge, 2018).
22. Baldwin and Marshall, "2 Dead Cops Daily".
23. Antoinette R. Raquiza, "Changing Configuration of Philippine Capitalism", *Philippine Political Science Journal* 35, no. 2 (2014): 225–50.
24. Cielito F. Habito, "Inequity, Initiative and Inclusive Growth", *Philippine Daily Inquirer*, 11 March 2013, http://opinion.inquirer.net/48623/inequity-initiative-and-inclusive-growth (accessed 14 March 2013).
25. Ma. Victoria R. Raquiza, "Elusive Inclusive Growth: The Manufacturing Resurgence Programme, the Conditional Cash Transfer Scheme, and Neoliberalism in the Philippines" (PhD dissertation, City University of Hong Kong, 2016).
26. Julio C. Teehankee and Mark R. Thompson, "Mar Roxas as Default Candidate of the Elite", *Rappler*, 19 September 2015, http://www.rappler.com/thought-leaders/106340-mar-roxas-default-candidate-of-the-elite.
27. Despite being in office less than half of his presidential term, Joseph E. Estrada, the former movie star elected president in 1998, did much more for the poor than he is commonly credited for, particularly in the realm of land reform and the introduction of inexpensive government treasury bills to offer safe investments to the less well-off. On this, see: Saturnino M. Borras, *Pro-poor Land Reform: A Critique* (Ottawa: University of Ottawa Press, 2007), pp. 249–52; Domini M. Torrevillas, "Leonor Briones, Silliman's Eminent Person", *Philippine Star*, 27 August 2013, http://www.philstar.com/opinion/2013/08/27/1138261/

leonor-brionessillimans-eminent-person. Accused of corruption, Estrada was overthrown in an elite-led insurrection in early 2001 although he remained very popular among the country's disadvantaged. On this, see: Julio C. Teehankee and Mark R. Thompson, "Duterte and the Politics of Anger in the Philippines", *East Asia Forum*, 8 May 2016, http://www.eastasiaforum.org/2016/05/08/duterte-and-the-politics-of-anger-in-the-philippines/. Estrada's successor, his vice-president Gloria Macapagal Arroyo, manipulated the 2004 presidential election to "defeat" Estrada's friend and fellow movie star-politician Fernando Poe, Jr., widely known as FPJ and also much loved by poor Filipino voters. The most recent episode of elite efforts to defeat populism involved the targeted discrediting through a senate investigation of Aquino's vice president and 2016 presidential candidate Jejomar "Jojo" Binay who had adopted a pro-poor populist narrative similar to Estrada and FPJ's but finished only fourth in the 2016 presidential election.
28. Robert L. Youngblood, *Marcos against the Church: Economic Development and Political Repression in the Philippines* (Ithaca: Cornell University Press, 1990).
29. Coeli M. Barry, "The Limits of Conservative Church Reformism in the Democratic Philippines", in *Religious Organizations and Democratization: Case Studies from Contemporary Asia*, edited by Tun-jen Cheng and Deborah A. Brown (New York: M.E. Sharpe, 2006), p. 157.
30. Aries C. Rufo, *Altar of Secrets: Sex, Politics, and Money in the Philippine Catholic Church* (Manila: Journalism for Nationbuilding Foundation, 2013).
31. Diana Mendoza, "Engaging the State, Challenging the Church: The Women's Movement and Policy Reforms in the Philippines" (PhD dissertation, City University of Hong Kong, 2013).
32. Clare Baldwin and Manolo Serapio Jr., "Once-powerful Philippines Church Divided, Subdued over Drug Killings", Reuters, 11 October 2016, http://www.reuters.com/article/us-philippines-duterte-church-insight-idUSKCN12A07Y.
33. Ben Reid, "Development NGOs, Semiclientelism, and the State in the Philippines: From 'Crossover' to Double-crossed", *Kasarinlan: Philippine Journal of Third World Studies* 23, no. 1 (2008): 4–42; David Lewis, "Sideways Strategies: Civil Society–State Reformist Crossover Activities in the Philippines 1986–2010", *Contemporary Southeast Asia* 35, no. 1 (2013): 27–55.
34. Coleen Jose, "Justice Delayed Is Justice Denied in Philippines' Maguindanao Massacre", *Committee to Project Journalists*, 31 July 2015, https://cpj.org/x/651d.
35. *ABC* (Australia), "Prisoners 'Living Like Kings' in Philippines' Bilibid Jail with Secret Luxury Cells, Raid Reveals", 15 December 2014, http://www.abc.net.au/news/2014-12-16/strip-bars-and-drugs-uncovered-in-philippine-bilibid-jail-raid/5969234.
36. Baldwin and Marshall, "2 Dead Cops Daily".
37. Joel R. San Juan, "Legal Experts Confirm 'Selective Justice' under Aquino",

Business Mirror, 26 June 2015, http://www.businessmirror.com.ph/legal-experts-confirm-selective-justice-under-aquino/.
38. Nikko Dizon, "Aquino Expected LP Members' Defection to PDP-Laban", *Philippine Daily Inquirer*, 24 May 2016, http://newsinfo.inquirer.net/787355/aquino-expected-lp-members-defection-to-pdp-laban.
39. Allen Hicken, "Party and Party System Institutionalization in the Philippines," in *Routledge Handbook of the Contemporary Philippines*, edited by Eric C. Batalla and Mark R. Thompson (London: Routledge, 2018); Holmes, "Pork Transmogrified".
40. Pulse Asia, "Ulat Ng Bayan, Nationwide Survey on Urgent National and Local Concerns", September 2014 – September 2016, http://www.pulseasia.ph/. In December 2015, according to Pulse Asia data (2015–16), at 25 per cent "crime" was only the sixth "most urgent national concern" behind controlling inflation, workers' pay, corruption, creating more jobs, and reducing poverty. But once Duterte's campaign began in earnest, public opinion changed, with crime the number one concern in June 2016 at 52 per cent ahead of these other worries. But by September 2016 crime had again become only the sixth most urgent concern at 31 per cent.
41. Baldwin and Marshall, "2 Dead Cops Daily".
42. Kathryn Mae P. Tubadeza, "Majority of Filipinos Satisfied with How Democracy Works: SWS", *Business World*, 25 February 2016, http://www.bworldonline.com/content.php?section=.
43. Nicole Curato. "Flirting with Authoritarian Fantasies? Rodrigo Duterte and the New Terms of Philippine Populism", *Journal of Contemporary Asia* 47, no. 1 (2016): 7.
44. Ibid.
45. Teehankee and Thompson, "Duterte and the Politics of Anger in the Philippines".
46. Jan-Werner Müller, *What Is Populism?* (Philadelphia: University of Pennsylvania Press, 2016).
47. James Putzel, "Can Duterte 'Populism' Bring Lasting Peace, Development?", *Philippine Daily Inquirer*, 28 August 2016, http://opinion.inquirer.net/96846/can-it-bring-lasting-peace-development.
48. Müller, *What Is Populism?*
49. Ibid.
50. Curato, "Flirting with Authoritarian Fantasies?".
51. Julio C. Teehankee, "Duterte's Resurgent Nationalism in the Philippines: A Discursive Institutionalist Analysis", *Journal of Current Southeast Asian Affairs* 35 no. 3 (2016): 69–89; Duterte appointed several key militant leaders linked to the communists to Cabinet positions related to social issues (labour, welfare and agrarian reform). Although business leaders complained about efforts to raise the minimum wage as well as discussions about ending short-

term contractualization that deprives workers of benefits (known as *endo*, as in end of contract), it is unclear how much business leaders really have to fear. While claiming he is the Philippines' "first left-leaning president", Duterte's economic agenda has thus far not veered far from the neoliberal orthodoxy of his predecessors. On this, see: Eric Vincent C. Batalla, "Divided Politics and Economic Growth in the Philippines", *Journal of Current Southeast Asian Affairs* 35, no. 3 (2016): 161–86. Yet apparently as a quid pro quo for its government appointments, the far left, with a few important exceptions (e.g., see: Teddy Casiño, "Confronting extrajudicial killings under Duterte", *Rappler*, 19 September 2011, http://www.rappler.com/thought-leaders/146642-confronting-extrajudicial-killings-duterte), has been silent or even supportive of Duterte despite his administration's human rights violations, an issue that used to be at the top of their agenda when they were targeted for extrajudicial killings by the military under past post-Marcos administrations.

52. Paterno Esmaquel II, "Cardinal Tagle on Christmas: Why No Hope for Those Astray?", *Rappler*, 23 December 2016, http://www.rappler.com/nation/156434-cardinal-tagle-christmas-message-hope-astray.
53. World Value Survey, "World Value Survey 1981–2015 official aggregate v.20150418, 2015. World Values Survey Association", *World Values Survey*, http://www.worldvaluessurvey.org/WVSContents.jsp? CMSID=intinfo.
54. Personal communication.
55. Julio C. Teehankee and Mark R. Thompson, "The Vote in the Philippines: Electing a Strongman", *Journal of Democracy* 27, no. 4 (2016): 124–34.
56. Randy David, "Dutertismo", *Philippine Daily Inquirer*, 1 May 2016, http://opinion.inquirer.net/94530/dutertismo.
57. Teehankee and Thompson, "Duterte and the Politics of Anger in the Philippines".
58. Rose-an Dioquino, "Walden Bello Tells Duterte: Addressing Poverty, Not Killings, the Way to Solve Drug Problem", *GMA News*, 12 August 2016, http://www.gmanetwork.com/news/story/ 577394/news/nation/walden-bello-tells-duterte-addressing-poverty-not-killings-the-way-to-solve-drug-problem.
59. John Sidel, "Bossism and Democracy in the Philippines, Thailand, and Indonesia: Towards an Alternative Framework for the Study of 'Local Strongmen'", in *Politicising Democracy: The New Local Politics of Democratisation*, edited by John Harriss, Kristin Stokke, and Olle Tornquist (Basingstoke: Palgrave Macmillan, 2014), pp. 51–74; John Sidel, *Capital, Coercion, and Crime: Bossism in the Philippines* (Stanford: Stanford University Press, 1999).
60. Danilo Andres Reyes, "The Spectacle of Violence in Duterte's 'War on Drugs'", *Journal of Current Southeast Asian Affairs* 35, no. 3 (2016): 111–37.
61. Teehankee and Thompson, "Electing a Strongman".
62. Francis Isaac and Joy Aceron, "Making Sense of Digong Duterte", *Rappler*,

30 January 2016, https://www.rappler.com/thought-leaders/120239-rodrigo-duterte-elections-2016.
63. Among Duterte's loyalist voters in Mindanao were those concentrated in Eastern Mindanao around his regional stronghold of Davao but also in Western Mindanao among Muslim voters. As the only president from Mindanao, Duterte has advocated the interests of the southern Philippines, and Muslims in particular, as the "first president of the Moro people". In July 2018, Rodrigo Duterte signed the Bangsamoro Organic Law, a major step towards creating a Muslim-majority substate although it still awaits final approval in a local referendum.
64. Putzel, "Can Duterte 'Populism' Bring Lasting Peace?".
65. Anna Szilágyi and Mark Thompson, "Digong and Donald: The Indiscreet Charm of Informality in Politics", *Rappler*, 30 November 2016, https://www.rappler.com/thought-leaders/154066-digong-donald-trump-informality-language.
66. William Labov, *Sociolinguistic Patterns* (Philadelphia: University of Pennsylvania Press, 1973).
67. Ana P. Santos, "Why is Duterte so Popular in the Philippines", *Deutsche Welle*, 9 September 2016, http://www.dw.com/en/why-is-duterte-so-popular-in-the-philippines/a-19540056.
68. Peter Kreuzer, "'If They Resist, Kill Them All': Police Vigilantism in the Philippines", *PRIF Report*, No. 142. Peace Research Institute Frankfurt, 2016, https://www.hsfk.de/fileadmin/HSFK/hsfk_publikationen/prif142.pdf.
69. Quoted in Manny Mogato, Karen Lema, David Lague, and Jerome Morales, "Blood and Benefits: Duterte Imposes His Hometown Formula on the Philippines", Reuters, 26 December 2016, http://www.reuters.com/investigates/special-report/philippines-davao-model/.
70. Mollman, "Murder by Numbers".
71. Dioquino, "Walden Bello Tells Duterte"; Teehankee and Thompson, "Electing a Strongman".
72. John Collins, "Development First: Multilateralism in the Post-'War on Drugs' Era", in *After the Drug Wars: Report of the LSE Expert Group on the Economics of Drug Policy*, LSE Ideas (London: London School of Economics, 2016).
73. Ibid.
74. John Collins, "Why the Philippines' New War on Drug Users Will Fail", *Business World Online*, 2 August 2016, http://www.bworldonline.com/content.php?section=Opinion&title=why-the-philippines-new-war-on-drug-users-will-fail&id=131265.
75. Mark R Thompson, "Philippine Opposition Finds Its Voice as Duterte Pauses His Bloody Drug War", *The Conversation*, 14 February 2017, https://theconversation.com/philippine-opposition-finds-its-voice-as-duterte-pauses-his-bloody-drug-war-72731.

76. Erik De Castro, "Special Report: Police Describe Kill Rewards, Staged Crime Scenes in Duterte's Drug War", Reuters, 18 April 2017, http://www.reuters.com/article/us-philippines-duterte-police-specialrep-idUSKBN17K1F4.
77. Rambo Talabong, "Drug War Will Be 'as Chilling as the Day It Began'—Duterte", *Rappler*, 23 July 2018, https://www.rappler.com/nation/208009-duterte-war-on-drugs-chilling.
78. Thomas Pepinsky, "Democracy against Disorder in Southeast Asia", *Journal of Democracy* 28, no. 2 (April 2017): 120–31.
79. For their supporters the "three Ls", Vice President Maria Leonor "Leni" Santo Tomas Robredo, Senator Leila de Lima, and Loida Nicholas Lewis, a leading Philippine-American activist, are promising new faces of the opposition. But they are the object of (typically misogynist) scorn from "Dutertards" as "the three stooges", the "three leading 'Ls' of the Liberal Party's League of Loathsome Ladies. On this, see: "The Three Stooges—Leila, Leni, Loida", *The Volatician*, 11 December 2016, http://www.thevolatilian.com/three-stooges-leila-leni-loida/. De Lima has been jailed on dubious charges of contacts with drug dealers while Robredo has been pressured by Duterte and his supporters, charged with supporting a secret plot to overthrow the president. Former president Fidel V. Ramos, long the *eminence grise* of Filipino politics (who played a role in the overthrow of Estrada, saving Arroyo from being toppled, and encouraging Duterte to run for the presidency) has become a kind of "semi-oppositionist" who, while continuing to support his administration, has called Duterte's presidency a "huge disappointment and letdown" by focusing on the drug crackdown instead of on job creation and investment. On this, see: David Sim, "Is Duterte's War on Drugs Really a War on the Poor?", *International Business Times*, 14 October 2016, http://www.ibtimes.co.uk/dutertes-war-drugs-really-war-poor-graphic-images-1586262.
80. Walden Bello, "The Left under Duterte", *Jacobin*, 7 August 2016, https://www.jacobinmag.com/2016/06/walden-bello-philippines-duterte-dignidad-coalition-akbayan/.
81. Mark R. Thompson, "Donald Trump and Rodrigo Duterte: A Not-So-Surprising Political Friendship", *Huffington Post*, 5 May 2017, http://www.huffingtonpost.com/entry/donald-trump-and-rodrigo-duterte-a-not-so-surprising_us_590d0c49e4b046ea176aeb56.

2

Finding Federalism in the Philippines:
Federalism—"the Centerpiece of My Campaign"[1]

Steven Rood

INTRODUCTION

Under the presidency of Rodrigo Roa Duterte, 2017 could have been the year when the Philippines began a shift from a unitary system of government—which has been in operation under colonial rule and since independence post-1946—to a federal form of government. In point of fact, the administration's mechanism for kick-starting the process, the Consultative Committee, only started work in January 2018 and handed its product (a completely new draft constitution) to the Philippine Congress in July 2018. With less than a year before the May 2019 mid-term elections, quick action by Congress on federalizing the Philippines seems unlikely.

The unitary system often sits uncomfortably on top of considerable political and social localism—elected officials with their own power bases, and ethnic groups who feel different from the dominant elite in Manila. While the 1991 Local Government Code did try to address the need to move power and resources further out to the periphery, impetus for broader change remains. For some twenty years there have been consistent calls to amend various provisions of the 1987 Constitution, and this time the effort is being undertaken in the first part of the term of a popular President—so constitutional revision might materialize.

That constitutional amendment might happen may seem surprising, given the failure of previous attempts and the fact that the "status quo regarding decentralization [under the 1991 Local Government Code] appears to satisfy both sub-national and central elites".[2] However, the status quo does not satisfy President Duterte—the most influential political actor in the Philippines. This chapter traces the advocacy for federalism and concludes that any possibility of federalizing depends on the attitude of the current president regarding constitutional change. President Gloria Macapagal Arroyo, for example, toyed with the idea, but was fundamentally only interested in instituting a parliamentary system. President Benigno S. Aquino III, on the other hand, was opposed to any change in the constitution instituted under his mother's administration. Federalism is currently possible due to the particular advocacy of President Duterte. Many elites are dubious, and public opinion is certainly not driving this prospect. The President, who launched his preliminary campaign by traversing the country talking about federalism, is clear in his insistence for federalism.

However, President Duterte is not clear on details of what such a change in governance would entail. An official consultative committee to draw up recommendations for constitutional changes was finally named in early 2018, and issued a report in July 2018, but many details are lacking and in any case the recommendations have still to be acted upon by Congress before any changes are instituted. In the meantime, innumerable efforts have been made to canvass possible federal structures—draft constitutions in principle and detail—and to comment both positively and negatively on the possibility of federalism. In this short chapter it is not possible to chronicle exhaustively the rapidly expanding public discourse. Rather, previous efforts to advocate federalism are discussed, along with the efforts of candidate and President Duterte to promote federalism. Some of the most important practicalities and effects of federalism are examined, with particular reference to considerations of fiscal federalism, fears of the strengthening dominance by local clans, and efforts to grant Muslims in the southern Philippines increased autonomy over their own affairs.

FEDERALISM AND CONSTITUTIONAL CHANGE PRIOR TO 2001

A number of authors trace an advocacy of federalism back to Jose Rizal in his 1890 essay, "The Philippines a Century Hence" as a way of introducing the idea that federalism has deep roots in Philippine history.[3] As Randy David points out however:

> Rizal was certainly aware of the persistence of strong regional identities in the country. But, instead of building a political system along the existing fault lines of ethnic segmentation, he was more concerned with "unit[ing] the whole Archipelago into one compact, vigorous, and homogenous body." This is the first line under statement of purpose in the draft constitution he wrote for the Liga Filipina [1892], a political organization that anticipated the broad structures of a Filipino government.[4]

Rizal therefore opted for a unitary state—like the Spanish and American colonial regimes and all subsequent constitutions of the Republic of the Philippine. Perhaps Rizal did indeed believe that in the future—a century hence—there would be a Federal Philippines. If this were so, it would be some twenty-five years overdue from Rizal's perspective.

This is not to say that all notions of federalism were absent from Philippine history. In fact, during the 1898 thrust for independence, the "Federal State of the Visayas" was represented in the Malolos Congress. However, Bohol, Negros and the "District of Visayas" (Panay) had their own governments that had some reservations about the Malolos government's authority. This federal state was dissolved in April 1899.[5] Another proposal was made to the 1971 Constitutional Commission by Salvador Araneta, for a five-state federal republic, but this was not seriously considered.[6]

After the 1986 *Epifanio de los Santos Avenue* (EDSA) or People's Power Revolution, there was a general feeling in the appointed Constitutional Commission that the problems of insurgency, economic malaise and political unrest facing the Philippines were such that a federalist system was out of the question. To avoid overcentralization, the University of the Philippines draft of the constitution enfranchised any region to petition to become "autonomous". The Commission rejected this approach as a risk to fragmenting the nation. Thus, the privilege of "autonomy" was restricted to the two regions seen as actively requesting such a status: Muslim Mindanao, by dint of the 1976 Tripoli Agreement with the Moro National Liberation Front; and the Cordillera, due to active lobbying led most prominently by the Cordillera Peoples Alliance. Each of these two regions were seen to be sharing "common and distinctive historical and cultural heritage, economic and social structures and other relevant characteristics".[7]

A new Local Government Code—devolving more authority and revenue to provinces, cities, municipalities, and *barangays* (villages)—was passed in October 1991 at the end of the first post-EDSA presidency of Corazon C. Aquino. Implementation began in 1992, and has continued since without wholesale amendment despite a mandate to consider changes after five years. Despite considerable attention to governance reform having been lavished on the decentralized system, the general consensus is that overall "the quality of governance and public services remains low" yet (as noted, above) "few decision-makers [are] invested in real reform of the system".[8]

Towards the scheduled end of Ramos' 1992–98 term, efforts to amend the constitution centred on lifting term limits for the presidency—and shift to a parliamentary system at the same time—rather than on federalism. The People's Initiative for Reform, Modernization and Action, PIRMA (*signature* in Tagalog) submitted millions of signatures gathered for such a change. The Supreme Court ruled that inasmuch as there was not yet a law implementing the provision in the 1987 Constitution for a people's initiative, the petition itself was deficient.[9] Considerable opposition to this change to the "Cory Constitution" was mobilized, led by many from the coalition of the EDSA revolution.[10] That this first attempt to change the constitution failed set the pattern for subsequent attempts.

Figure 2.1 shows then Senator Gloria Macapagal Arroyo at the anti-Charter Change rally in 1997 with Jaime Cardinal Sin, former President Corazon Aquino and then Vice President Joseph Estrada, among others. They were opposing the charter change moves by supporters of then President Fidel Ramos.[11]

FEDERALISM PROJECT UNDER PRESIDENT GLORIA MACAPAGAL ARROYO (2001–10)

In his short tenure as President, Joseph Estrada did float the idea of constitutional change, mostly to loosen the economically restrictive

FIGURE 2.1
The Anti-Charter Change Rally in 1997

Source: Photo courtesy of Archdiocesan Office of Communications / Noli I. Yamsuan.

provisions of the 1987 constitution. However, he dropped the idea by early 2000. Within a year Estrada had been ousted by "People Power II" and replaced by Vice President Gloria Macapagal Arroyo. President Macapagal Arroyo was not initially invested in charter change, saying it was a "distraction". By the time she had (controversially) won the May 2004 election, she was finally quoted in July as saying that "Charter reform is our strategic hope for change."[12] By that time, intellectual and political arguments for federalism were beginning to become more widespread, though popular demand from the citizenry was absent.

In the 2000s, former University of the Philippines (UP) President Jose V. Abueva had begun to publish a long series of articles and books that form part of the substrate of any effort for federalism. He went on to chair the 2005 Constitutional Commission appointed by President Macapagal Arroyo, and when President-elect Duterte was asked by his party mates after the 2016 election how they should go about designing federalism, his response was "Go talk to UP President Abueva." Not only did Abueva articulate the general case for increased decentralization in the Philippines through federalism, but he also worked out a complete draft for a federal republic with a parliamentary system.[13]

These ideas were independently taken up by elected legislators from Mindanao, in the south and the Visayas, in the central Philippines—regions where the elites often feel that the Philippines is too Manila-centric. Senators "Nene" Pimentel and "Kit" Tatad, from Mindanao and John Osmeña from Cebu introduced proposals to change to a federal system in 2000. However, nothing came of this as the Senate was consumed by December 2000 with the impeachment trial of President Joseph "Erap" Estrada that ended inconclusively in January 2001, with the ensuing "People Power II".

Advocacy for federalism was taken up by civil society organizations, particularly from Mindanao. The Citizens' Movement for a Federal Philippines (CMFP) took up the cudgels for a federal republic, often with support from the Konrad-Adenauer-Stiftung (KAS) Foundation.[14] A prominent figure in the efforts for federalism was Rey Magno Teves, the Secretary-General of *Kusog Mindanaw* (Strong Mindanaw)—a Mindanao-wide forum, which brought together: civil society (Mindanao Coalition of Development NGO Networks, or MINCODE)); the private sector (Mindanao Business Council); and elected local officials (Confederation of Provincial Governors, City Mayors and Municipal Mayors and Municipal League Presidents of Mindanao, or CONFED MINDANAO). Mindanao-wide discussions of the federalism issue had therefore begun at the turn of the twenty-first century.

The KAS Foundation steadily supported Philippine scholars and stakeholders in studies, conferences, and publications over at least a fifteen-year period.[15] Continuity of support over such a long period was provided by a series of intellectually committed KAS Country Representatives, with care taken by KAS to provide exposure to international experiences without dictating any particular model. For his part, thought-leader Abueva insisted on a model relevant to the Philippines, including basic terms drawn from Filipino rather than English, such as *Federasyon* and *Estados* (states) in his draft constitution.[16]

In the run-up to the 2004 election, President Arroyo was particularly concerned about the strength of her main opponent in Mindanao, Fernando Poe, Jr. Arroyo made numerous trips to the island, and local stakeholders presented various proposed policy agenda items.[17] Arroyo was persuaded by the CMFP, and others in Mindanao, to include federalism in her platform for the 2004 election with constitutional change.[18] She mentioned the issue both in the campaign, and in her subsequent July 2004 State of the Nation Address[19]—the first after she won a full term in May 2004. However, no concrete action was taken until 2005, after the so-called "Hello Garci" crisis. In June 2005 recordings surfaced purportedly containing phone conversations between the President and Commission on Elections (COMELEC) Commissioner Virgilio Garcillano. These recordings were said to prove electoral fraud by Gloria Macapagal Arroyo. In late June 2005 President Macapagal Arroyo apologized[20] for a "lapse in judgement", but on 8 July 2005, seven Cabinet members and three heads of government agencies resigned in protest over the scandal. They were known as the "Hyatt 10"—named after the hotel where they held their press conference.

Much of the rest of President Arroyo's administration—she served her full term until the 30 June 2010 inauguration of her successor, Benigno S. Aquino III—can be seen as a struggle for political survival in light of her unpopularity and many controversies. The CMFP felt that moves Arroyo made to fulfil her campaign promise of constitutional reform were her way of reaching out to a significant constituency. In the State of the Nation Address July 2005, President Arroyo announced that it was time to start "the great debate on Charter Change" and in August 2005 she issued an executive order creating a Consultative Commission (ConCom) to propose constitutional changes.

One of the observations made in this chapter is the extent to which moves to amend the 1987 Constitution are not driven by popular demand. Social Weather Stations (SWS) data illustrated this, from the period 1999—when it was being bruited about by the Estrada administration—to May 2005, just before the establishment of the ConCom. At the beginning of this period, only 14 per cent of respondents thought the Constitution needed changing, rising to 30 per cent by 2005.[21]

In 2005, even at the height of the proposal to change the constitution, respondents were vague when asked what they thought. Table 2.1 shows follow-up responses about which provisions needed amending.

The vast majority of those who answered the Constitution needed to be changed did not offer any examples of provisions that needed changing. All categories provided did not require constitutional amendment except, arguably, allowing divorce.

The situation is similar with respect to specific opinions on federalism. In 2002, a direct question on federalism was posed by Social Weather Stations, with results displayed in Table 2.2.

It is hard to imagine a more perfect illustration of public indifference and lack of knowledge on a particular topic: 20 per cent agree, 20 per cent

Finding Federalism in the Philippines

TABLE 2.1
Constitutional Provisions That Need Amending

Lower prices	3.1%
Corruption	2.0%
"Many"	1.9%
How government is run—whatever about it; rights of poor	1.7%
They don't allow divorce in the Philippines—they should	1.0%
About VAT—Tax	0.6%
Don't know/Can't say	18%

Source: Social Weather Stations, 2nd Quarter 2005 Social Weather Survey, 14–23 May 2005 (computer file); Social Weather Stations results are typically based on probability samples of 1,200 respondents—300 each from Metro Manila, the rest of Luzon, the Visayas, and Mindanao.

TABLE 2.2
Agreement on Federating the Regional Governments, 17 May–3 June 2002

PR, Q104. In case there would be regional governments throughout the country, do you ... (Strongly agree, Somewhat agree, Undecided if agree or disagree, Somewhat disagree, Strongly disagree)... that the system of government in the Philippines should be made FEDERAL, or don't you know enough about the FEDERAL system?

Agree	**20%**
Strongly agree	6
Somewhat agree	14
Undecided if agree or disagree	**20**
Disagree	**20**
Somewhat disagree	7
Strongly disagree	14
* *Net agree*	*+1*
Don't know enough about the Federal System	**40**

Note: *For greater precision, % Agree minus % Disagree are first computed before being rounded off.
Source: Social Weather Stations, 2nd Quarter Social Weather Survey, 17 May–3 June 2002 (computer file).

disagree, 20 per cent are undecided, and 40 per cent admit that they do not know enough about the federal system.

Table 2.3 represents results to a slightly different question almost two years later—with almost equally divided opinions from undecided respondents compared to those who agree with the proposition that there should be a change to a federal system of government. What stands out,

TABLE 2.3
Agreement on Changing to Federalism as Soon as Possible, by Area, January 2004

	RP	NCR	BAL. LUZON	VISAYAS	MINDANAO
AGREE	33%	30%	32%	28%	43%
Strongly agree	11	11	10	8	16
Somewhat agree	22	19	22	20	28
UNDECIDED	33	36	32	37	28
DISAGREE	27	26	26	30	26
Somewhat disagree	14	17	14	15	12
Strongly disagree	13	10	12	15	14
NET*	+7	+4	+6	–2	+17

Q46. Dapat gawin Federal ang sistema ng gobyerno sa lalong madaling panahon. [LUBOS NA SUMASANG-AYON, MEDYO SUMASANG-AYON, HINDI TIYAK KUNG SUMASANG-AYON O HINDI, MEDYO HINDI SUMASANG-AYON, LUBOS NA HINDI SUMASANG-AYON, O HINDI SAPAT ANG KAALAMAN TUNGKOL DITO]

Note: *NET equals % Agree minus % Disagree correctly rounded.
Don't Know and Refused figures are not shown.
Source: Social Weather Stations, SWS January 2004 Pre-Election Survey, 16–22 January 2004 (computer file).

however, is distinctly more favourable opinions in Mindanao where specific advocacy for federalism was more prevalent. A net difference of 17 per cent more respondents in Mindanao were in favour of the proposition. Since the start of advocacy for federalism, by far the largest number of proponents have been in Mindanao.

The Consultative Commission (ConCom) was eventually formed in August 2005 with fifty-five members. Despite their heavy involvement in the conceptualization of the thrust for constitutional change, only three members of the Citizens Movement for a Federal Philippines were appointed. The three members were Jose V. Abueva as Chair of the ConCom, Rey Magno Teves as Chair of the Committee on the Structure of the Republic, and Lito Lorenzana as Secretary-General—a veteran political operative with long-standing ties to Nene Pimentel and member of the CMFP.

The resulting December 2005 report advocated parliamentarianism, but did not recommend a shift to a federal system. Instead, the report included a proposal similar to the "enfranchisement" of all regions similar to that proposed by the University of the Philippines in 1986 (as noted above). Areas as small as one province[22] could petition for autonomy—similar to the 1987 Constitution for the Autonomous Region in Muslim Mindanao and the failed region for the Cordillera. If 60 per cent of regions and provinces in the entire country became "autonomous" then a move to federalism would be triggered. As Lorenzana states, the ConCom decided for the move to a federal government: "to equate it at first to regional governance then to autonomous territories and eventually to the creation of federal states.... The former local governors and the business persons sitting in the ConCom compelled the compromise."[23]

Moves to amend the 1987 Constitution, including the formation of an Advocacy Commission (AdCom) in 2006 chaired by Lorenzana, received opposition from several quarters, due to a general feeling that a constitutional amendment would establish a parliamentary form of government enabling President Macapagal Arroyo to remain as the head of government—as Prime Minister. Ultimately, moves to amend the constitution did not succeed. Lorenzana admitted that during hundreds of consultations by the AdCom it was obvious the concept of federalism was not clear to "the ordinary Filipino and the leaders nearest to them—the *barangay* officials and the local executives [mayors]".[24] In December 2006, congressional allies of President Macapagal Arroyo finally gave up all hope for constitutional changes for the duration of her administration.

Thus, in both the Ramos and Macapagal Arroyo administrations there were large-scale efforts for constitutional change which did not succeed. Under President Ramos there was certainty for substantive constitutional issues. In the case of President Macapagal Arroyo there was widespread suspicion that talk of improving constitutional governance was merely a cover to maintain the chief executive in office through a shift to a parliamentary system. Federalism was not the main thrust under either the Ramos or Macapagal Arroyo administration.

During the 2010–16 administration of President Benigno S. "Noynoy" Aquino III there was also some discussion of amending the constitution, focusing on the economic protectionist provisions of the 1987 Constitution. Proponents tried to avoid suspicions of ulterior motives—such as perpetuation in office—by suggesting merely the insertion of phraseology like "except as may be provided by law". In that case, proponents argued, each economic restriction could subsequently be debated in a transparent fashion by Congress without the possibility that the process could be hijacked for other purposes. President "Noynoy" Aquino was, however, adamant that no constitutional change was needed for the Philippines to thrive economically—and pointed to sustained economic growth numbers under his watch as proof. Without Presidential approval, no change was possible.

President Rodrigo Roa Duterte, on the other hand, has consistently advocated for constitutional change to a federal system of government even before being declared a candidate. The Philippines finally has a chief executive who supports a shift to federalism to allow more power to localities. We now discuss Duterte's efforts.

THE FEDERALISM PROJECT UNDER DUTERTE

When Rodrigo Roa Duterte—then Mayor of Davao City—was asked in early 2014 whether he would run for president, his response was clear: "You must be crazy. I said I am not interested to be president. I am not qualified to be president. I cannot dream of what I cannot be but I can only aspire for what I can be."[25] There were several potential candidates, called "presidentiables" in the Philippines, with national exposure. The most prominent candidates were: Vice President Jejomar Binay; Senator Grace Poe; and DILG Secretary Roxas—the designated successor of President "Noynoy" Aquino. Conventional wisdom was that to move directly from a local position to a nationwide one was very rare.[26] Mayor Duterte did have a certain notoriety as the tough-guy leader of a city—a long-standing reputation.[27]

By September 2014, talk began to heat up. When Mayor Duterte hosted Mindanao leaders in Davao, however, they downplayed any talk of the presidency although he was enlisted to begin talking about federalism throughout the country.[28] In that 2014 meeting, it was announced that there would be a follow-up larger meeting in Cebu. On 5 October 2014, Mayor Duterte inducted officers into a group called "Federal Advocates for a Better Philippines". By December 2014 he was described as the "new poster boy of federalism" and vowed at a Mindanao leaders' summit for federalism: "Once they open it (Constitution [to change economic provisions]), we'll start (a determined push for federalism)."[29]

As 2015 dawned, a "Listening Tour of Mayor Rody Roa Duterte to promote Federalism" was born, and the long discussion of "will he or won't he"—regarding his running for the presidency—began. As Duterte travelled the country with events highlighting federalism, albeit without much detail, the Facebook page[30] of the "operations centre" posted pictures from January with banners calling for him to run. As early as February 2015 he was saying—in Dagupan, Luzon—that he might run "to save the republic", although he generally insisted he was only the spokesman for those promoting federalism. For nearly all of 2015 the "will he or won't he" discourse continued—conveniently keeping the possibility of Duterte running for the presidency in the headlines and allowing him to gauge support. When the 16 October deadline for filing candidacies had passed, the PDP-Laban candidate was Martin Diño. On 8 December 2015, with the endorsement of PDP-Laban and Diño, Duterte filed a certificate of candidacy as a substitute. In the proclamation meeting held by the PDP-Laban, Duterte explicitly pledged to work for federalism, linking it to peace in Mindanao: "I am telling you now, nothing short of a federal structure would give Mindanao peace. Believe me, because I come from that place."[31]

Duterte decisively won the election on 9 May 2016, helped in considerable part by the series of three televised debates among presidential candidates—the first since 1998—that allowed the mayor of a southern city to be presented to the nation as a whole. Duterte did mention federalism during the campaign, but such advocacy was generally overshadowed by his anti-crime rhetoric—promising to fatten the fish in Manila Bay with the bodies of dead criminals.

Immediately after the election federalism advocates—particularly the Centrist Democratic Party whose Chair Lito Lorenzana is a long-time ally of Nene Pimentel, and central to the 2005–6 efforts under President Arroyo—moved to accelerate efforts.[32] The Centrist Democratic Party Institute (CDPI) brought members of the 2005 Consultative Commission—including Jose Abueva—to meet on 1 June 2016 with the presumptive Speaker of the House of Representatives, Pantaleon Alvarez, who told them that he was once again considering the formation of a constitutional commission to recommend changes.[33]

The PDP-Laban party then held a conference on Federalism and Constitutional Change at the end of June 2016—subsequently innumerable conferences, workshops, seminars, lectures, studies, and similar events were hosted by different organizations. One such event was titled "If Federalism is the answer, what is the question?" which played with the view that unspecified "federalism" was on offer and had been offered for more than a decade—without a clear view of how federalism will solve problems being adduced. The most elaborate title was the "Global Autonomy, Governance, and Federalism Forum" held on 19–20 October 2016 with more than thirty-five presentations.[34]

Once in office, President Duterte did indeed continue to advocate federalism. In his first State of the Nation Address on 25 July 2016, for example, he urged a change within four or five years, offering to step down prior to the end of his term—comparing this to the French system and a president who takes quick action in given situations as required. The Department of Interior and Local Government (DILG) created a Task Team on Federalism headed by Undersecretary Emily Padilla to conduct consultations and orientations nationwide.[35] The DILG used mandated semi-annual *barangay* (village) assemblies on the last Saturday of March to campaign for federalism—as had happened during the advocacy campaign for charter change in 2006.[36] Constitutional amendment requires action by the Philippine Congress—either to call for a constitutional convention to propose amendments to be ratified in a plebiscite—or to convene as a constituent assembly to propose amendments.[37] The history of popular suspicion on motives for congressional amendments led many to advocate for an elected constitutional convention—as in 1970, before martial law. However, estimates for the cost of a specialized body ran into billions of pesos, so President Duterte opted for constituent assembly—which in the Philippines has the unfortunate acronym Con-Ass.[38] House Speaker Alvarez tried to allay suspicion by drafting an order to be issued by the president to have a "consultative committee" of citizens to recommend amendments to the constitution. Duterte duly issued Executive Order 10 for such a body on 7 December 2016 to make recommendations within six months. By May 2017 appointments had not been issued for this body, and President Duterte announced[39] he would not issue such appointments until after the draft Bangsamoro Basic Law (BBL) was submitted to Congress mid-year. In the event, the draft BBL was submitted to Congress in September 2017, and a final version signed into law as the Bangsamoro Organic Law (BOL) in July 2018.[40] In the meantime, Duterte named the members of the Consultative Committee in January 2018 and it submitted its draft constitution to the President two weeks before the BOL was finalized.[41]

In the narration of increased momentum for federalism witnessed since Rodrigo Duterte bestirred himself in late 2014, it is important to note what this is not about: a party platform, public demand, or a specific model of federalism.

Decentralization and federalism have, however, long been on the platform of the PDP-Laban political party, and father and son Senators Pimentel are long-time advocates. President Duterte was also a PDP-Laban member as far back as 1998, when he was the only PDP-Laban member of the House of Representatives. A PDP Federalism Institute now exists, helping to coordinate research and advocacy on the issue. One needs to emphasize, however, that any chance of federalism becoming a reality in the Philippines arises from the personal advocacy of Rodrigo Duterte—not from elected officials keeping a promise put forth in a party platform during an election.

In fact, it is generally understood that "parties" in the Philippines are largely agglomerations of convenience for the purpose of running in elections and are malleable and/or disposable post elections, when it is clear who has won—particularly, the presidency. Candidates can then switch parties to the winning side. In the May 2016 elections, for example, only three PDP-Laban congressional candidates were elected to the House of Representatives at the same time that PDP-Laban presidential candidate Duterte won (see Table 2.4). By the time congress met there were ninety-seven members of the president's party due to switching. One of the three elected in May—Pantaleon Alvarez (who had not been a member of PDP-Laban during his one previous 1998–2001 term in the House)—was elected Speaker of the House. This fits the previous pattern of party switching (see Table 2.4), though it is in some contrast to the PDP-Laban's long-time attempt to be a more ideologically coherent party. Many longer term members of PDP-Laban resent the newcomers flooding into their party.[42]

Table 2.4 demonstrates how, after a presidential election, members of the House of Representatives promptly abandon the party label used in the election and jump to the party of the candidate that won the presidency. The 2004 election cycle is not included since unusually for the Philippines a candidate for president was the incumbent, Gloria Macapagal Arroyo, and since she won there was no need for those who had switched to her party after she ascended into office in January 2001 to switch again.

A second and surprising characteristic is that—just as in the previous decade—the possibility of constitutional amendment to institute federalism

TABLE 2.4
Post-Election Party Switching in the House of Representatives

House of Representatives: What's "Party" got to do with it?		
Two Main Party Groupings	Election Results	Congress Organized
	May 1998	July 1998
LAKAS-NUCD-UMDP	110	39
LAMMP (Estrada)	56	142
	May 2010	July 2010*
Lakas	105	89
Liberal Party (Aquino)	45	73
	May 2016	August 2016
Liberal Party	115	35
PDP-Laban (Duterte)	3	97

Note: *By the time of the next elections (May 2013), LAKAS members were down to 27 and LP were up to 90.
Source: Author's presentation.

is not being driven by popular demand. Candidate Duterte had, of course, made his approval of constitutional change to implement federalism very clear—at least to analysts. In July 2016, as Duterte was inaugurated, a Pulse Asia survey showed only 41 per cent of voters were aware of proposals to amend the constitution.[43] The increase in approval of constitutional change in recent years was greatest in the two regions Duterte won strongly—Metro Manila and Mindanao—so that a plurality in those areas were in favour (see Table 2.5). As President Duterte took office, changing the constitution was not even a plurality vote preference for the nation.

A plurality of the citizenry was now in favour of federalism, compared to a decade earlier under the presidency of Gloria Macapagal Arroyo in 2009, where there was a majority against federalism (see Table 2.6). Support grew most in Mindanao and Metro Manila where Duterte's vote was strongest. However, at the beginning of Duterte's term, support for his federalism project was barely a plurality vote among the citizenry as a whole.

Despite President Duterte's advocacy over the years, and since taking office, the average voter is still not seized with necessity to change the

TABLE 2.5
Opinion Polls on Amending the Philippine Constitution in 2014 and 2016
WHETHER OR NOT IT IS APPROPRIATE TO AMEND THE PRESENT PHILIPPINE CONSTITUTION AT THIS TIME
November 2014 and July 2016 / Philippines
(In Percent)

Base: Total Interviews, 100%

In your opinion, should the Constitution be amended or not amended at this time?		RP	NCR	LOCATION BL	VIS	MIN
YES, the Constitution SHOULD BE amended now	Jul '16	37	47	33	29	47
	Nov '14	27	23	24	28	32
	Change*	+10	+24	+9	+1	+15
NO, SHOULD NOT BE AMENDED NOW	Jul '16	44	42	42	58	36
	Nov '14	49	62	47	47	49
	Change*	–5	–20	–5	+11	–13
NO, the Constitution SHOULD NOT BE amended now, but it may be amended sometime in the future	Jul '16	29	29	31	28	25
	Nov '14	26	27	26	19	31
	Change*	+3	+2	+5	+9	–6
NO, the Constitution SHOULD NOT BE amended now nor any other time	Jul '16	15	13	11	30	11
	Nov '14	23	35	21	28	18
	Change*	–8	–22	–10	+2	–7
Don't Know/Can't say	Jul '16	19	11	24	14	17
	Nov '14	24	15	29	25	19
	Change*	–5	–4	–5	–11	–2

Note: * Change = Figures of July 2016 minus Figures of November 2014.
Pulse Asia surveys are typically based on probability samples of 1,200 respondents—300 each from the National Capital Region, the rest of Luzon, the Visayas, and Mindanao.
Source: Pulse Asia Research Inc., "July 2016 Nationwide Survey on Charter Change", n.d., http://www.pulseasia.ph/july-2016-nationwide-survey-on-charter-change/ (accessed 12 November 2016).

TABLE 2.6
Opinion Polls on Federalism in 2009 and 2016
WHETHER OR NOT IN FAVOUR OF CHANGING THE PRESENT UNITARY SYSTEM OF GOVERNMENT AND HAVING A FEDERAL SYSTEM OF GOVERNMENT
February 2009 and July 2016 / Philippines
(In Percent)

Are you in favour or not in favour of changing the present unitary system of government and having a federal system of government for the nation?	Base: Total Interviews, 100%	RP	NCR	LOCATION BL	VIS	MIN
IN FAVOUR	Jul '16	39	45	33	30	54
	Feb '09	22	17	19	31	22
	Change*	+17	+28	+14	–1	+32
UNDECIDED	Jul '16	28	23	29	32	25
	Feb '09	19	20	20	3	31
	Change*	+9	+3	+9	+29	–6
NOT IN FAVOUR	Jul '16	33	32	39	38	20
	Feb '09	59	63	61	66	47
	Change*	–26	–31	–22	–28	–27

Source: Pulse Asia Research Inc., "July 2016 Nationwide Survey on Charter Change", n.d., http://www.pulseasia.ph/july-2016-nationwide-survey-on-charter-change/ (accessed 12 November 2016).

1987 Constitution. In March 2018, Pulse Asia found only 3 per cent of respondents nationwide, and 5 per cent in Mindanao, cited changing the Constitution as one of the top three national concerns—tied last among fifteen issues presented. Pay, inflation, and poverty reduction were the top three issues, at 50 per cent, 45 per cent, and 35 per cent, respectively.[44]

We should note finally that President Duterte is not articulating the case for any particular form of federalism. As he said:

> There are plenty of models to choose from. It could be the US Electoral College, or like in France, where only the president is nationally elected and everyone else represents a local or limited territory. Indonesia is a federal parliament, Australia and New Zealand too. Singapore, Japan, and Malaysia are likewise federal parliaments.[45]

The President's statement on the federalism model he favours has the problem that, on this list, only the United States, Australia, and Malaysia are federal states. To his credit, Duterte has allowed think-tanks, political parties—particularly the PDP-Laban[46]—and the Consultative Commission to specify what is being proposed as federalism. In this manner Duterte is acting as a populist, as populist ideologies generally "do not provide answers to all major socio-political questions".[47]

INTERROGATING FEDERALISM

As noted by Ron May more than a decade ago—after the previous push for constitutional change during the administration of President Gloria Macapagal Arroyo—"the advantages claimed for federal over unitary systems read more like statements of faith than reasoned arguments".[48]

While specific constitutional proposals have been put forth—by former Senator Nene Pimentel[49] and Dr Jose Abueva,[50] for example—these have not been costed out, or explanations given as to the bases for their provisions. Three aspects that need to be taken into consideration will now be briefly discussed: the cost of federalism, the influence of political clans in decentralized politics, and the effect on peace efforts for Muslim Mindanao after the March 2014 Comprehensive Agreement on the Bangsamoro.

Financing Federalism

One estimate of the amount that should go to local and federal state governments after a change is 70 per cent of revenue, with only 30 per cent for the central government.⁵¹ Yet estimates of current spending for nationwide needs—such as debt service, defence, foreign affairs, pensions, for example—range from 47 to 53 per cent of the central government's budget, clearly above the 30 per cent proposed by some federalism advocates.⁵² Proponents of federalism sometimes list powers that will be given to the federal states, those powers that will be shared, and those reserved for the central government without addressing budgetary details. The latest proposal from the Consultative Committee puts the ratio at a more realistic 53 per cent (including an Equalization Fund) for the regions.⁵³

A common refrain from those who favour federalism is that localities will no longer have to remit taxes to the centre, but will be able to keep their revenues and spend them as they see fit, meaning local priorities can be funded by local resources. Resentment has long been expressed that major corporations with nationwide operations pay their taxes in Metro Manila, and other localities have to wait to get their share under the 1991 Local Government Code. While this is an accurate depiction of fiscal flows, the implication that localities could merely retain taxes locally and be self-sufficient is untrue as most parts of the Philippines do not generate enough activities for locally-raised taxes to enable self-sufficient local governance.

Figure 2.2 depicts the economic geography of the Philippines, giving the different gross regional domestic product per square kilometre in 2007.⁵⁴ The tall peak over Metro Manila and adjoining regions reflects the fact that this is where more than 60 per cent of Philippines GDP is generated, of which even the PDP-Laban is aware.⁵⁵ The small mound in the central Philippines is Cebu, and the slight shading in southern Mindanao is Davao City. In this scenario, to therefore speak of federal states—outside of central Luzon—financing themselves from their own tax revenue is clearly fanciful. The centralization of underlying economic activity in Metro Manila—not the diversion of taxes to the centre—is the true cause of fiscal imbalances.

Former Undersecretary of the Department of Finance Milwilda Guevara attempted to cost out a move to a federal system, and feels there is sufficient funding in the current budgetary mix.⁵⁶ Guevara calculated each state would require roughly PhP91 billion to function. Taking the current Philippine administrative regions as potential states,⁵⁷ and estimating potential taxable capacity as 10 per cent of gross regional domestic product,⁵⁸ only the National Capital Region and Regions III and IVA (the high peak in

FIGURE 2.2
Economic Density in the Philippines, 2007

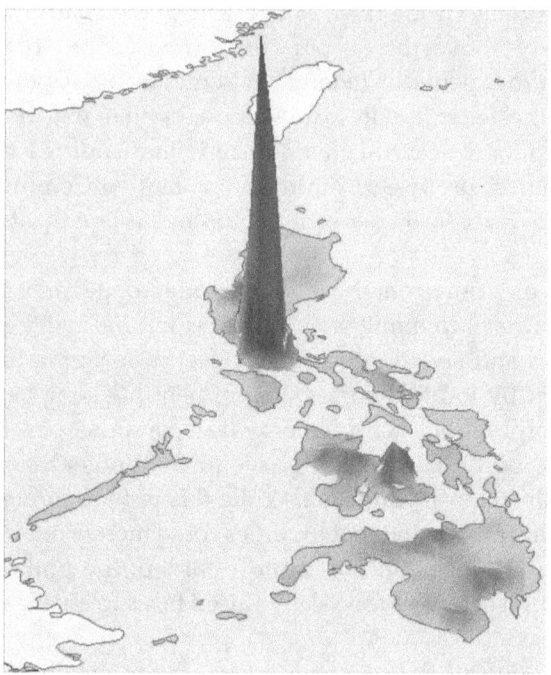

Source: World Bank, *Behind the Veil of Conflict: Moving Toward Economic Integration for Sustained Development and Peace in Mindanao* (Washington, D.C.: World Bank, 2010), p. 2. Reproduced with permission.

Figure 2.2) would be self-sustaining. Region VII, which includes Cebu City, also comes close to being self-sustaining. Even if 100 per cent of taxes from regions were retained, this would not be sufficient for a federal state government for most of the country.

The PDP-Laban advocacy primer speaks of "more equitable sharing of revenues and resources":

> Under our current unitary system, a lion share of government revenue and resources are allocated to the NCR [National Capital Region] and Luzon, whereas under a federal system all regions and provinces will get their commensurate share of taxes and fees collected in their respective jurisdictions in addition to fiscal transfers and grants from the federal government.[59]

Economic reality is that "commensurate share taxes and fees collected in their respective jurisdictions" will—for most prospective states—be dwarfed by "fiscal transfers and grants from the federal government [as above]", as is the case with the Internal Revenue Allotment (IRA) under the Local Government Code. Only one province in 2015 collected more local revenues than received in IRA, 28 per cent of the total number of cities for cities, and less than 5 per cent for municipalities.[60] Automatic allocation of the IRA creates a moral hazard, where local units do not exert much effort to raise local revenue. As transfers and grants can be intensely political, it is not clear how more than doubling the flow of resources from federal to local levels will change the situation.

Political Dynasties

We now turn to the issue of clans, the interaction between an "anarchy of families" and the prospect of federalism.[61] The Philippines is widely known to be ruled by clans, being a weak state and—as already noted—non-existent political parties. Local notables, families, and clans tend to be the building blocks of Philippine politics, with electoral networks of convenience at election time.[62] This underlying socio-political reality results in party-switching as depicted in Table 2.4—where the organizing principle of politics is kinship with "party" a label for temporary convenience.

Considerable attention has been paid to patron-clientelism, bossism, and the influence of family. This is part of popular lore as well as scholarship, which the 1987 Philippine Constitution tried to address: "The State shall … prohibit political dynasties as may be defined by law".[63] Unsurprisingly, the Philippine Congress—in which more than half of the members come from such dynasties—has failed to pass an anti-dynasty law.

Beyond colourful anecdotes, considerable effort has been made to tease out the extent of this phenomenon and its effects. Ronald Mendoza and associates have shown, for instance, that through 2016 the share of political dynasties in local government leadership was increasing, reaching 50 per cent in the latest elections.[64] The presence of political dynasties in provinces outside of Luzon—in Mindanao and the Visayas—further increases poverty.[65]

In the words of Christian Monsod, one of the framers of the 1987 Constitution, regarding a shift to federalism: "My bet is that the clans, political clans and dynasties will hijack those powers and keep them to themselves."[66] One analyst has stated that patronage practices, exchanges of particular goods—such as cash for immediate needs, recommendations and connections for employment—in exchange for political support, that underlie the success of dynasties, must be addressed by abandoning populism. Whether a switch away from populist clientelism is possible in the socio-political reality of the Philippines, it is certainly not the instincts of the Duterte administration.[67]

Federalism would establish a new layer of government, besides possibly endowing local strongmen with more powers and resources. Apart from the question of whether provinces, cities, and municipalities will continue to exist below the state level, which seems likely—as it would be politically unrealistic to propose to abolish the positions of most of the political class—there will be a new arena for political contestation. Elected officials are aware of the advantages of incumbency—one of the drivers for increasing dynastic control over the years—and tend to be leery of starting *de novo* in a new contest for head of a federal state. Any arrangement of "states" will throw several successful clans into the same contest, with unpredictable results. As noted by Lorenzana, governors were among those most leery of federalism during the 2005 Constitutional Commission[68]—and scepticism continues. Oriental Mindoro Governor Alfonso Umali, Jr.—in a discussion convened by the Union of Local Authorities of the Philippines (ULAP)—pointed to the need for a larger campaign funds to cover a larger area than a province with attendant dangers of increased corruption. ULAP's "LGU Roadmap to Genuine Local Autonomy through Federalism" did not contain one recommendation pertinent to federalism.[69]

Proponents of federalism have long had to address concerns around political clans and strongmen. In 2002, Jose Abueva's "Response to the Usual Objections" claimed that "by reforming political parties, strengthening the rule of law, empowering the people, improving governance, and holding leaders accountable" constitutional change will "displace local warlords".[70] The PDP-Laban's proposed amendments for constitutional change characterize federalism as "the grand bargain" and list a "Package of Reforms to Make Federalism Succeed":[71]

1. Make the anti-dynasty provision in the Constitution self-executing.
2. Support the development of strong and cohesive political parties by penalizing political butterflies.

3. Provide budget support to political parties just like in mature democracies.
4. Institute a system of proportional representation.
5. Lift the cap on the number of seats a political party can hold.
6. Raise the qualification requirements for presidential candidates.
7. Strengthen the powers of the COMELEC, CSC, COA, Ombudsman and Sandiganbayan and ensure their strong presence in every region.

This is a radical overhaul of the political system to encourage programmatic parties, discourage clans from politics, and reduce the influence of private money in elections. This is a leap in the dark with no reason to believe it will succeed.

Unfortunately, the consultative committee established by Executive Order 10, in July 2018, failed to provide details of a transition.[72] Ron May's earlier comment about "statements of faith" continued to apply in the current push for federalism.

Peace in Mindanao

We turn now to the role of federalism in promoting peace in Mindanao. Proponents of federalism—particularly if they come from the perspective of public administration—often tend to talk of federalism as the "next step" or "culmination" of the process of decentralization implemented under the Local Government Code (the Code).[73] It is taken for granted that the nation's ethnic diversity and archipelagic nature implies that decision-making should be moved towards the localities. While performance problems are noted under the Code, advocates call for further capacity-building, more funding, and greater accountability of local governments.

Some federalism advocates—particularly those from Mindanao—have felt that addressing long-standing grievances of Muslims in the southern Philippines is basic motivation for a shift in government structure. Despite peace agreements with the Moro National Liberation Front (MNLF) in 1976 and 1996, and the Moro Islamic Liberation Front (MILF) in 2014—implementation of those agreements via autonomy under the 1987 Constitution has proven unsatisfactory and incomplete.[74] In 2001, Senator Nene Pimentel said: "The proposal to adopt the federal system of government is meant primarily to provide the foundation for a just and lasting peace ... and secondarily to provide an equal opportunity for the development of the regions of the country ...."[75]

Rey Magno Teves similarly wrote that federalism "covers the primary demands of the MILF and other serious Moro groups for self-determination or effective self-governance short of secession".[76] Muslims who agree with this view of federalism, and had joined in the advocacy for federalism during the Arroyo Administration,[77] now certainly support President Duterte's thrust for federalism.[78]

From the inception of his listening tour in 2014, Rodrigo Duterte linked his advocacy for federalism with prospects for peace: "Mayor Duterte added that they see the implementation of a federal system of government as the only solution to the Mindanao insurgency problem."[79] Duterte's credibility on the issue of peace with the Bangsamoro is increased by a number of factors—such as his partial Moro ancestry, his long experience in Mindanao, his mentioning of injustices committed against the Moro people, and his personal acquaintance with leaders such as MNLF Founding Chair Nur Misuari, who endorsed Duterte in a video from his lair in Sulu. In a meeting at the MILF's Camp Darapanan during the presidential campaign Duterte said "Through federalism, we will correct the injustice committed against the Moro people, against Mindanao."[80]

The peace agreements with both the MNLF and the MILF have obvious bearings on debates about the powers of federal unit. The 1996 agreement with the MNLF was designed to be implemented within the confines of the 1987 Constitution—thus efforts to fully implement that agreement through legislation ought not to require amendments. On the other hand, the MILF and the government had a long-standing agreement that allowed negotiations to proceed beginning in 1997—the MILF would not talk about independence and the government would not talk about the constitution. Under the administration of Benigno S. Aquino III, government negotiators were instructed to explore the "flexibilities of the constitution" and managed to craft the Comprehensive Agreement on the Bangsamoro with the MILF in March 2014. Both the Aquino administration and the MILF argued that there were no unconstitutional provisions in the implementing bill—the draft Bangsamoro Basic Law (BBL)—submitted to Congress in September 2014. In April 2015 a "Peace Commission" of eminent citizens, appointed by President Aquino, affirmed that the draft BBL was constitutional. Many legislators felt, however, that some aspects of the bill under discussion were indeed unconstitutional and insisted on amending those portions. This dispute became moot when—in the aftermath of the January 2015 incident in Mamasapano, Maguindanao, when a police operation against a terrorism suspect went terribly wrong—Congress did not pass the BBL before the end of the term of President Noynoy Aquino.[81]

With discussion of constitutional change under a Duterte administration, there arises the question of the relation between constitutional change and implementation of peace agreements.[82] Immediately after the election, Pantaleon Alvarez—touted to become, and indeed became, Speaker of the House of Representatives—said the BBL would be downplayed. "The BBL will be absorbed by the federal form of government, because they are the same."[83] The MILF naturally objected, saying the BBL needed to be passed, as per the signed peace agreement, and that the problems of the Bangsamoro were not the same as those of other regions of the country.[84]

In order to solve this sequencing problem, the Office of the Presidential Assistant on the Peace Process, led by Jesus Dureza, in July 2016 developed a "roadmap" that had the two processes running simultaneously (see Figure 2.3). The "Legislative Track" would be touched off by a Bangsamoro Transition Commission—as per the March 2014 agreement—which would draft a new version of the enabling law that would not include provisions with constitutional issues. Those excluded provisions would be submitted for inclusion in constitutional change.

President Duterte endorsed this strategy, and referred to it in his first State of the Nation Address to Congress (translation):

> We can have this BBL, we give it minus the things that you [Congress] do not want, the constitutional issues we take out first.... So I ask you, pass it minus the constitutional issues that are contentious. We'll give it when the federal system comes....[85]

There are two fundamental problems with this "two track" approach—how is it decided what issues are constitutional—thus "parked"—and how the Philippine government can credibly commit to including both in a constitutional revision.

As noted, those from the MILF and the Aquino administration who drafted the original bill did not feel any part of it was unconstitutional, while many of the amendments later proposed in Congress under the Aquino

FIGURE 2.3
Peace and Development Roadmap of the Duterte Administration

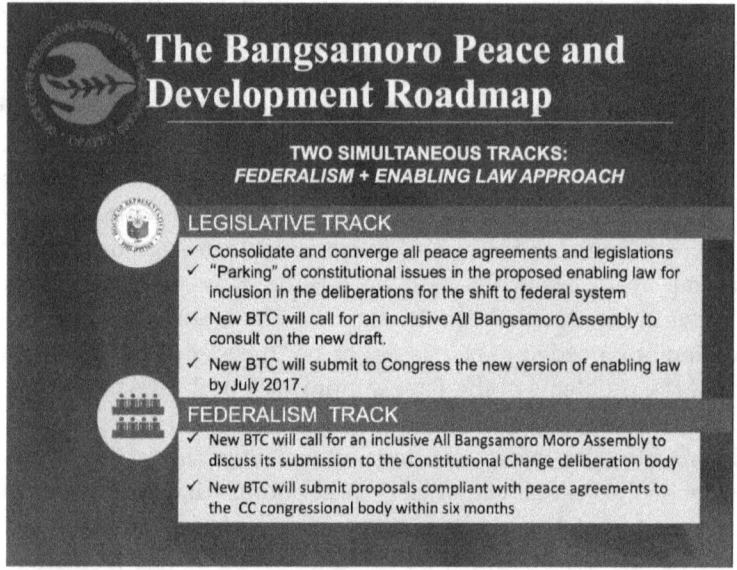

Source: Office of the Presidential Assistant on the Peace Process, *Peace and Development Roadmap of the Duterte Administration*, 2016, p. 17, http://www2.hss.de/fileadmin/suedostasien/philippines/downloads/2016/160805-Peace-and-Development-Agenda-and-Roadmap-Policy-Dialogue.pdf (accessed 3 July 2017). Reproduced with permission.

administration were not really about the constitution. An example of this conundrum comes from Duterte himself, as he has mentioned previously that he objects to the powers proposed for the head of the Bangsamoro (the chief minister) over the Bangsamoro police force—to "exercise operational control and supervision and disciplinary powers over the Bangsamoro Police".[86] Duterte identified this as one thing he finds unconstitutional[87] notwithstanding that these are exactly the same powers he exercised as city mayor—and as do all mayors throughout the Philippines.[88] President Duterte is well known for his desire for control over the police—even floating the idea of re-establishing the national Philippine Constabulary which was abolished by the 1987 Constitution—so it is understandable that he objects to others having "operational control and supervision". The fact remains that this authority has been exercised for decades under the current constitution. A similar problem would arise for any other provision: who is to judge which provisions must be set aside for later constitutional action.[89]

This brings us to the second problem as to what assurances the MILF, and other stakeholders working with them, have that such provisions would indeed be taken up in the process of instituting federalism? The body charged with doing this—the Philippine Congress—proved reluctant during the previous administration to include everything in the Comprehensive Agreement on the Bangsamoro agreed upon by the Executive Branch in legislation. Once again, the MILF will have to trust to the political will of a Philippine president.

The MILF is well aware of the political dynamics at play. Peace Panel Chair Mohagher Iqbal has stated that the MILF does not oppose federalism if the BBL becomes the template of Federal Government for the country.[90] House Speaker Alvarez said that the Congress would prioritize the BBL when it receives a draft, and that it might be a model for all other states in a federal system, and also that President Duterte was waiting for the draft from the Bangsamoro Transition Commission before appointing the members of the Consultative Committee for constitutional change (under Executive Order 10).

The draft BBL was presented by the Bangsamoro Transition Commission to Duterte on 17 July 2017. Interestingly, the next day Duterte met with MNLF Founding Chair Misuari, who had refused to participate in the Bangsamoro Transition Commission process. After the meeting, it was announced that Misuari's MNLF would no longer pursue their own legislative agenda—they would participate in the push for federalism which Misuari had promoted in the past (and Misuari did have a representative on the Consultative Committee, Randolph Parcasio).[91] The proposed sequence therefore seemed clear to all—Bangsamoro first, federalism next (though now that the Bangsamoro Law has been passed, the chances of success in the federalism endeavour are unclear).

This arrangement allowed the President to fulfil his promise to reach a lasting settlement with regard to the Bangsamoro while progress on federalism could start through the work of the Consultative Committee. Treating the draft Bangsamoro basic law as a "template" might have been useful—as provisions found controversial in the previous draft BBL could be discussed with a view to understanding how federal states might, for instance, handle tax matters or public order and safety.[92] In the event, there was little interaction between Congressional consideration of the BBL and

Consultative Committee deliberations on provisions of a new constitution, so this possibility was not realized.

CONCLUSION

The extraordinary focus on the president in the Philippine political system has allowed federalism back on the agenda despite any clear popular demand, specification of what will transpire, or serious study of the effects of such a change—and in the face of widespread scepticism based on the current landscape of political clans. As Davao City mayor, Rodrigo Roa Duterte had long chafed under what he felt was excessive centralization in Manila, and insufficient resources for the city that he governed. Duterte found a sympathetic ear from some federalism advocates, and has been consistent in his support of federalism—with a small core of the PDP-Laban political party—although this change is low on citizens' priorities.

Since taking office on 30 June 2016, President Duterte has had a profound effect on Philippine politics. Despite party-switching seemingly in the same pattern as post-martial law politics (see Table 2.4)—the general tenor of politics has shifted in a populist fashion. From the outset Duterte promised a bloody war on drugs, which he certainly delivered. His distaste for limits on his freedom of action—such as fixed terms for appointive officials, independent courts, and a free media—is of a different order than anything before. It has been characterized as "order over law".[93]

Duterte's rhetorical emphasis on federalism may be less consistent and clear than the war on drugs, but federalism would have more wide-ranging implications for governance and politics. There have long been federalism advocates who have not captured the imagination of the public or significant elites. Any chance of improving governance under federalism would require fundamental changes in the way the Philippines works—reducing the role of campaign finance, strengthening political parties, undermining the role of family and clans in politics—with no signs that any of this will happen. That federalism is being seriously considered in the Philippines is a demonstration of the power of faith in an idea.

Notes

1. Rodrigo Roa Duterte, on the campaign trail in Pangasinan, 2 March 2016. Pia Ranada, "Duterte's Pitch for Federalism: Centralized System Holds Back

PH", *Rappler*, 3 March 2016, http://www.rappler.com/nation/politics/elections/2016/124423-duterte-federalism-central-system-holding-regions-back (accessed 4 July 2017).
2. Sarah Shair-Rosenfield, "The Causes and Effects of the Local Government Code of the Philippines: Locked in a Status Quo of Weakly Decentralized Authority?", *Journal of Southeast Asian Economies* 33, no. 2 (2016): 166.
3. Pablo S. Trillana III, "Rizal, a Century and a Federal Republic Hence", *Philippine Daily Inquirer*, 5 June 2016, http://newsinfo.inquirer.net/789195/rizal-a-century-and-a-federal-republic-hence (accessed 25 March 2017).
4. Randy David, "Would Rizal Have Chosen Federalism?", *Philippine Daily Inquirer*, 19 June 2016, http://opinion.inquirer.net/95272/would-rizal-have-chosen-federalism (accessed 25 March 2017). David himself is a sceptic. He continues in the same column, "Federalism will not solve poverty and inequality, simply because it does not touch the real center. It only redraws the periphery."
5. Presidential Museum and Palace, "Evolution of the Revolution", http://malacanang.gov.ph/7824-evolution-of-the-revolution/ (accessed 25 March 2017).
6. Virgilio C. Galvez, "Federalist Papers: Part II", 30 October 2016, http://manilastandard.net/opinion/columns/220108/the-federalist-papers.html (accessed 9 August 2018).
7. (from Article X, section 15 of the 1987 Constitution); Adolfo Azcuna, "The View of the Constitutional Commission", in *Issues on Cordillera Autonomy: Conference Proceedings*, edited by Steven Rood (Baguio City: University of the Philippines College Baguio, Cordillera Studies Center, 1987), pp. 37–41. The Autonomous Region in Muslim Mindanao was established after ratification by plebiscite in 1989, and was revised in 2001 after the 1996 final agreement on the implementation of the 1976 Tripoli Agreement between the Government of the Republic of the Philippines (GRP) and the Moro National Liberation Front (MNLF). The Cordillera Autonomous Region has not been established since plebiscites failed in 1990 and 1998.
8. Shair-Rosenfield, "The Causes and Effects of the Local Government Code".
9. Alastair Dingwall, "Charter Change, Ramos and Aquino", *Rappler*, 15 August 2014, http://www.rappler.com/thought-leaders/66269-charter-change-ramos-aquino (accessed 25 March 2017).
10. Ronald D. Holmes, "Changing the Rules of the Game", *Inside Story*, 15 September 2014, http://insidestory.org.au/changing-the-rules-of-the-game (accessed 25 March 2017).
11. GMA News, "Gloria and Cha-Cha", *GMA News Online*, 13 August 2008, http://www.gmanetwork.com/news/story/113427/news/gloria-and-cha-cha (accessed 25 March 2017).

12. GMA News, "Charter Change Timeline", *GMA News Online*, 19 December 2006 (accessed 25 March 2017).
13. Jose V. Abueva, *Charter Change for Good Governance: Towards a Federal Republic of the Philippines with a Parliamentary Government* (Marikina: Center for Social Policy and Governance, Kalayaan College, 2005). As we will see, proposals to amend the unitary constitution often also proposed to change from a presidential to a parliamentary form of government. While it will be noted when relevant, detailed examination of parliamentary proposals requires a separate study.
14. Jose V. Abueva, "Response to the Usual Objections to Federalization and Parliamentary Government", in *Towards a Federal Republic of the Philippines with a Parliamentary Government: A Reader*, edited by Jose V. Abueva et al. (Manila: Center for Social Policy and Governance, Kalayaan College and Local Government Development Foundation, 2002), pp. 159–65.
15. Abueva, "Response to the Usual Objections"; Abueva, *Charter Change for Good Governance*; Institute for Autonomy and Governance, "Charter Change, Federalism and the Mindanao Peace Process", *Autonomy and Peace Review* 3, no. 4 (October–December 2007); Klaus Preschle and Edmund Tayao, eds., *Envisioning a Federal Philippines* (Manila: The Local Development Foundation LOGODEF, 2009); Alex Brillantes Jr., Simeon A. Ilago, and Raphael N. Montes Jr, eds., *The Future of Local Autonomy: Decentralization and Federalism* (Quezon City: Konrad Adenauer Stiftung & Center for Local and Regional Governance, National College of Public Administration and Governance, University of the Philippines, 2009); S.M. Santos, *Federalism and Cha-Cha for Peace: Critical Papers on Federalism and Charter Change for the Mindanao Peace Process*. (Cotabato City: Institute for Autonomy and Governace & Konrad Adenaur-Stiftung, 2016).
16. Abueva, *Charter Change for Good Governance*.
17. James Faustino and David Booth, "Development Entrepreneurship: How Donors and Leaders Can Foster Institutional Change", *Working Politically in Practice Series, Case Study No. 2* (San Francisco & London: Asia Foundation and Overseas Development Institute, 2014).
18. Jesus F. Llanto, "Charter Change Pet Issue of GMA [Gloria Macapagal-Arroyo] since 2004", *ABS-CBN News*, 15 August 2008, http://news.abs-cbn.com/nation/08/15/08/charter-change-pet-issue-gma-2004 (accessed 2 April 2017).
19. State of the Nation Address, 26 July 2004, *RTV Malacanang*, Youtube, https://youtu.be/0UFRvXO5kIU (accessed 7 August 2018).
20. Aurea Calica and Paolo Romero, "GMA: I'm Sorry, It's Me on Tape", *Philippine Star*, 28 June 2005, https://www.philstar.com/headlines/2005/06/28/283808/gma-i146m-sorry-it146s-me-tape (accessed 7 August 2018).
21. Social Weather Stations, "The 2nd Quarter SWS Social Weather Report: 30% Favor Amending Constitution; 64% Oppose Allowing GMA to be

Prime Minister", 2 August 2005, https://www.sws.org.ph/swsmain/artcldisppage/?artcsyscode=ART-20151217155226 (accessed 7 August 2018).

22. Under the 1987 Constitution, the Philippines Supreme Court has ruled that one province is insufficient to form an autonomous region (in cases arising from the 1990 and 1998 plebiscites in the Cordillera). The proposal to have single province autonomy is new.

23. Lito Monico Lorenzana, "Reflecting on Charter Change Initiatives: The Consultative Commission of 2005 and the Advocacy Commission of 2006", in *The Future of Local Autonomy: Decentralization and Federalism*, edited by Alex Brillantes Jr., Simeon A. Ilago, and Raphael N. Montes Jr (Quezon City: Konrad Adenauer Stiftung & Center for Local and Regional Governance, National College of Public Administration and Governance, University of the Philippines, 2009), p. 32.

24. Ibid., p. 37. https://pcoo.gov.ph/press-briefing/press-briefing-assistant-secretary-kris-ablan-presidential-communications-office-president-chairman-board-lito-monico-lorenzana-centrist-democracy-political-institute-cdpi/ (accessed 25 March 2017).

25. Karlos Manlupig, "Duterte for President? Supporters hold rally", *Rappler*, 2 April 2014, http://www.rappler.com/nation/54245-rally-duterte-for-president-2016 (accessed 5 April 2017).

26. Steven Rood, "Aspiring for National Office in the Philippines: Don't Start Local", *Asia Foundation*, 4 April 2012, http://asiafoundation.org/2012/04/04/aspiring-for-national-office-in-the-philippines-dont-start-local/ (accessed 6 April 2017); Vice President Binay being the only real example—going in 2010 from being mayor of Makati to Vice President. Joseph Estrada had gone from being mayor of San Juan to the Senate (elected nationwide)—but he was an extremely popular movie star.

27. Phil Zabriskie, "The Punisher", *Time Magazine*, 19 July 2002, http://content.time.com/time/subscriber/article/0,33009,265480-1,00.html (accessed 6 April 2017).

28. "5 Mindanao leaders meet with Duterte", *Davao Breaking*, 2014, http://davaobreakingnews.com/5-mindanao-leaders-meet-duterte/ (accessed 7 April 2017); One of the themes of the discussion was how the Bangsamoro Basic Law (BBL) being proposed to Congress as part of the peace process with the Moro Islamic Liberation Front (MILF) could be enhanced or modified by a move to federalism. This thread of discourse will be separately analysed, below.

29. Germelina Lacorte, "Federalism Dreamers Eye BBL, Charter Change", *Philippine Daily Inquirer*, 3 December 2014, http://newsinfo.inquirer.net/654242/federalism-dreamers-eye-bbl-charter-change#ixzz4ID6oxqyM (accessed 6 April 2017).

30. Listening Tour Operations Center's Facebook page, https://www.facebook.com/DuterteListeningTour/ (accessed 6 April 2017).
31. Mike Frialde, "PDP-Laban Names Duterte as 2016 Bet", *Philippine Star*, 30 November 2015, http://www.philstar.com/headlines/2015/12/01/1527741/pdp-laban-names-duterte-2016-bet (accessed 13 April 2017).
32. J.M. Ochave, "PDP-Laban – CDP Huge Talks on Alliance", *Centrist Democratic Party*, 2016, http://cdp.ph/index.php/component/k2/item/1-pdp-laban-cdp-huge-talks-on-alliance?start=8250 (accessed 12 April 2017).
33. Centrist Democracy Party Political Institute, "Speaker Bebot Alvarez meets with CDPI President on Constitutional Initiative", in *Centrist Democracy Party Political Institute*, 1 June 2016, http://www.cdpi.asia/index.php/2016-02-05-03-09-27/news/item/127-speaker-bebot-alvarez-meets-with-cdpi-president-on-constitutional-initiative (accessed 12 April 2017).
34. Institute for Autonomy and Governance, *#GAGF2016 E-Library*, in *Institute for Autonomy and* Governance, 2016, http://www.iag.org.ph/index.php?option=com_content&view=article&id=1402:gagf2016-e-library&catid=2:uncategorised (accessed 17 February 2017).
35. Cecille Suerte Felipe, "DILG Intensifies federalism campaign", *Philippine Star*, 12 January 2017, http://beta.philstar.com/headlines/2017/01/12/1661690/dilg-intensifies-federalism-campaign (accessed 13 April 2017).
36. Miriam Grace A. Go, "DILG mobilizes 42,000 barangays for federalism campaign", *Rappler*, 25 March 2017, http://www.rappler.com/nation/165139-dilg-march-25-barangay-assemblies-support-federalism (accessed 26 March 2017).
37. Because the 1986 Constitutional Commission wrote the procedures for amendment during a period when it was assumed that the Philippines would have a unicameral legislature, the wording is somewhat confusing when applied to a bicameral legislature. If, however, both the House of Representatives and the Senate separately achieve a three-fourths majority for amending the constitution, the ambiguity is moot.
38. J. Diaz, "Rody drops con-con in federalism bid", *Philippine Star*, 29 July 2016, http://www.philstar.com/headlines/2016/07/29/1607783/rody-drops-con-con-federalism-bid (accessed 14 April 2017).
39. Carolyn O. Arguillas, "Duterte to name 25 members of ConCom for Charter Change when...", *MindaNews*, 12 April 2017, http://www.mindanews.com/peace-process/2017/04/duterte-to-name-25-members-of-concom-for-charter-change-when/ (accessed 8 August 2017).
40. Nestor Coralles, "Duterte signs Bangsamoro Organic Law", *Philippine Daily Inquirer*, 26 July 2018, http://newsinfo.inquirer.net/1014757/duterte-signs-bangsamoro-organic-law (accessed 9 August 2018).

41. Pia Ranada, "Duterte Receives Consultative Committee's Draft Constitution", *Rappler*, 9 July 2018, https://www.rappler.com/nation/206824-duterte-receives-consultative-committee-draft-constitution (accessed 9 August 2018).
42. Perseus Echeminada, "Power Struggle Brewing in Ruling PDP-Laban Party", *Philippine Star*, 30 January 2017, https://www.philstar.com/headlines/2017/01/30/1666865/power-struggle-brewing-ruling-pdp-laban-party (accessed 9 August 2018).
43. Pulse Asia Research Inc., "July 2016 Nationwide Survey on Charter Change", n.d., http://www.pulseasia.ph/july-2016-nationwide-survey-on-charter-change/ (accessed 12 November 2016).
44. Pulse Asia Research Inc., "Pulse Asia Research's March 2018 Nationwide Survey on National Urgent Concerns and the National Administration Performance Ratings on Selected Issues", n.d., http://www.pulseasia.ph/march-2018-nationwide-survey-on-urgent-national-concerns-and-national-administration-performance-ratings-on-selected-issues/ (accessed 9 August 2018).
45. Olivia Limpe-Aw, "Can Duterte "The Punisher" Be This Country's Savior?", *Asian Dragon Magazine*, 27 November 2015, https://lifestyle.asiandragonmagazine.com/2015/11/27/can-duterte-the-punisher-be-this-countrys-savior/ (accessed 10 April 2017). This misunderstanding of the nature of governments was echoed in a controversial August 2018 video featuring Assistant Secretary Mocha Uson of the Presidential Communications Operations Office that cited France and Singapore as having federalist forms of government. http://opinion.inquirer.net/104012/mocha-usons-influencer-report-card#ixzz5NeaRuReP (accessed 9 August 2018).
46. In a primer, the PDP-Laban Federalism Institute discusses models from many countries, and anywhere from three to eleven states (plus the Federal Administrative Region of Metro Manila). See: PDP-Laban Federalism Institute, *Federalism 101* (Makati City: PDP-Laban Federalism Institute, 2016). In an advocacy presentation, they plump for eleven states, and a semi-presidential system of government. On this, see: PDP-Laban, PDP Laban's Model of Federalism: Semi-Presidential Federal System of Government for the Philippines (Powerpoint), *PDP-Laban*, March 2017, http://ncpag.upd.edu.ph/wp-content/uploads/2017/05/PDP-Labans-Model-of-Federalism-April-2017-2.pdf (accessed 12 July 2017).
47. Noam Gidron and Bart Bonikowski, "Varieties of Populism: Literature Review and Research Agenda", Working Paper Series No. 13-0004 (Cambridge, Massachusetts: Harvard University Weatherhead Center for International Affairs, 2013).
48. Ronald J. May, "Federalism Versus Autonomy: Debate and Practice in the Philippines", *Autonomy & Peace Review* 3 (October–December 2007), p. 49.

49. Aquilino Pimentel, Jr., *Federalizing the Philippines: A Primer* (Manila: Philippine Normal University, 2008).
50. Abueva, *Charter Change for Good Governance*.
51. Aquilino Pimentel Jr., "Federalizing the Philippines: The Final Solution within Reason", in *The Future of Local Autonomy: Decentralization and Federalism*, edited by Alex Brillantes Jr., Simeon A. Ilago, and Raphael N. Montes Jr (Quezon City: Konrad Adenauer Stiftung & Center for Local and Regional Governance, National College of Public Administration and Governance, University of the Philippines, 2009), p. 11.
52. M.M. Guevara and J.P. Gracia, *Financing Federalism: A Look at the Numbers* (Manila: Public Finance Institute of the Philippines, 2009); T.J. Palanca, "On Imperial Manila, Modernization Failure, and Comparative Advantage: A Close Look at Regional Accounts", 2014, http://www.tjpalanca.com/2014/09/regional-accounts-2013.html (accessed 13 October 2016).
53. http://newsinfo.inquirer.net/files/2018/07/INQ_Proposed-Draft_Constitution_Consultative-Committee_.pdf (accessed 9 August 2018). Article XIII, Sections 4 and 5.
54. World Bank, *Behind the Veil of Conflict: Moving Toward Economic Integration for Sustained Development and Peace in Mindanao* (Washington, D.C.: World Bank, 2010), p. 2.
55. PDP-Laban Federalism Institute, *Federalism 101*, p. 25.
56. Milwida M. Guevara, "How Much Does It Cost to Go Federal?", *Manila Bulletin*, 8 June 2016, http://2016.mb.com.ph/2016/06/07/how-much-does-it-cost-to-go-federal/ (accessed 14 February 2017).
57. An entirely separate discussion of what would the states be is not taken up in this chapter. For instance, the PDP-Laban's *Federalism 101* lists three different schemes—3, 7, or 11 states—with no criteria for choosing among them. PDP-Laban Federalism Institute, *Federalism 101*, pp. 42, 43, 45. The point about fiscal transfers would obtain whatever the configuration.
58. As a comparison, the national Bureau of Internal Revenue in 2016 managed to collect 13.7 per cent of GDP. "Tax Effort" (Department of Finance, 2017) http://www.dof.gov.ph/index.php/data/taxeffort/ (accessed 15 May 2017).
59. PDP-Laban Federalism Institute, *Federalism 101*, p. 49.
60. Ronald U. Mendoza and Jude Ocampo, *Caught between Imperial Manila and Provincial Dynasties: Towards a New Fiscal Federalism* (Quezon City: Ateneo School of Government, 2016), p. 10.
61. Alfred W. McCoy, *An Anarchy of Families: State and Family in the Philippines* (Madison, Wisconsin: University of Wisconsin Center for Southeast Asian Studies, 1994).
62. Paul D. Hutchcroft and Joel Rocamora, "Strong Demands and Weak Institutions:

The Origins and Evolution of the Democratic Deficit in the Philippines", *Journal of East Asian Studies* 3, no. 2 (August 2003): 259–92.
63. 1987 Philippine Constitution, Article II Section 26.
64. Ronald U. Mendoza and Miann Banaag, *Dynasties Thrive under Decentralization in the Philippines* (Quezon City: Ateneo School of Government, 2017), p. 1.
65. Ronald U. Mendoza, Edsel L. Beja Jr., Victor S. Venida, and David B. Yap, "Political Dynasties and Poverty: Measurement and Evidence of Linkages in the Philippines", *Oxford Development Studies* 44, no. 2 (2016): 189–201.
66. Trishia Billones, "Monsod Prefers Change in LGU Code over Federalism", *ABS-CBN News*, 3 June 2016, http://news.abs-cbn.com/nation/06/03/16/monsod-prefers-change-in-lgu-code-over-federalism (accessed 20 April 2017).
67. Michael Henry Ll. Yusingco, "Toxic Brew: Federalism and Political Dynasties", *Philippine Daily Inquirer*, 22 August 2015, http://opinion.inquirer.net/87820/toxic-brew-federalism-and-political-dynasties (accessed 20 April 2017).
68. Lorenzana, "Reflecting on Charter Change Initiatives", p. 32.
69. Union of Local Authorities of the Philippines (ULAP), *Critical Issues and Queries of Local Governments on Federalism* (Mandaluyong: Union of Local Authorities of the Philippines, 2016).
70. Jose V. Abueva et al., eds., *Towards a Federal Republic of the Philippines with a Parliamentary Government* (Manila: Center for Social Policy and Governance, Kalayaan College and Local Government Development Foundation, 2002), p. 161.
71. PDP-Laban, "PDP Laban's Model of Federalism: Semi-Presidential System of Government for the Philippines", March 2017, http://ncpag.upd.edu.ph/wp-content/uploads/2017/05/PDP-Labans-Model-of-Federalism-April-2017-2.pdf.
72. https://www.rappler.com/thought-leaders/207852-duterte-federalism-consultative-committee-missed-homework-part-1 (accessed 9 August 2018).
73. A.B.J. Brillantes and D.O. Moscare, "Federalism: The Culmination of Decentralization and Devolution in the Philippines", in *Towards a Federal Republic of the Philippines with a Parliamentary Government: A Reader*, edited by Jose V. Abueva et al., p. 45.
74. Steven Rood, "The Role of International Actors in the Search for Peace in Mindanao", in *Mindanao: The Long Journey to Peace and Prosperity*, edited by Paul Hutchcroft (Mandaluyong City, Philippines: Anvil, 2016), pp. 63–95.
75. Aquilino Pimentel Jr., "Federalizing the Republic: The Ultimate Basis for a Just and Lasting Peace in Central and Southern Mindanao", in *Federalizing the Philippines: A Primer*, edited by Aquilino Pimentel Jr. (Manila: Philippine Normal University Press, 2008), p. 476.
76. R.M. Teves, "Federalism: An Idea Whose Time Has Come", in *Towards a Federal*

Republic of the Philippines with a Parliamentary Government: A Reader, edited by Jose V. Abueva et al., pp. 187–92.
77. Rexcel Sorza, "Muslims Gather Million Signatures for Federal Philippines", *IslamicOnline.net*, 28 August 2005, http://www.islamicboard.com/archive/index.php/t-4707.html (accessed 1 May 2017).
78. Sukarno D. Tanggol, *Regional Autonomy and Federalism: Concepts and Issues for the Bangsamoro Government* (Iligan: MSU-Iligan Institute of Technology, 2002); "Muslim leaders promote federalism", *Manila Standard*, 17 December 2016, http://thestandard.com.ph/news/-main-stories/top-stories/224392/muslim-leaders-promote-federalism.html (accessed 20 April 2017).
79. *Davao Breaking*, "5 Mindanao leaders meet with Duterte", 2014, http://davaobreakingnews.com/5-mindanao-leaders-meet-duterte/ (accessed 7 April 2017). Note that the website's archives cover up to January 2017 only, 2014 articles may no longer be available.
80. E. Regalado, "Duterte, MILF want to bring peace in Mindanao", *Philippine Star*, 28 February 2016, http://www.philstar.com:8080/headlines/2016/02/29/1557993/duterte-milf-want-bring-peace-mindanao (accessed 8 October 2016).
81. Third-Party Monitoring Team, "Third Public Report, January 2015 to February 2016", p. 12, http://archive.peace.gov.ph/sites/default/files/160226%20TPMT%20PR-3%20Pt%201%20Report%20final.pdf (accessed 13 February 2017).
82. This, of course, applies also to the peace process with the National Democratic Front of the Philippines, but the question is considerably more abstract since there is not even yet a bilateral ceasefire in place in those negotiations.
83. Trishia Billones, "Monsod Prefers Change in LGU Code over Federalism", *ABS-CBN News*, 3 June 2016, http://news.abs-cbn.com/nation/06/03/16/monsod-prefers-change-in-lgu-code-over-federalism (accessed 20 April 2017).
84. A. Romero, "MILF: Pass BBL First Before Shifting to Federalism", *Philippine Star*, 15 June 2016, http://www.philstar.com/headlines/2016/06/15/1593162/milf-pass-bbl-first-shifting-federalism (accessed 4 May 2017).
85. Official Gazette of the Republic of the Philippines, *The 2016 State of the Nation Address*, http://www.gov.ph/2016/07/26/the-2016-state-of-the-nation-address/ (accessed 12 November 2016).
86. House Bill No. 4994, Article XI, Section 8.cv.
87. Nestor Corrales, "Duterte 'Ready to Concede' BBL sans Unconstitutional Provisions", *Philippine Daily Inquirer*, 22 July 2016, http://newsinfo.inquirer.net/798329/duterte-ready-to-concede-bbl-sans-unconstitutional-provisions (accessed 24 July 2016).
88. Republic Act 6975, Section 51 and Republic Act 8551, Section 62.

89. The Supreme Court, asked to rule on the constitutionality of the Comprehensive Agreement on the Bangsamoro, ruled that without an implementing law it is premature. Tech Torres-Tupas, "SC Junks Petitions vs Bangsamoro Agreements—It's Premature", 2016, http://newsinfo.inquirer.net/849006/sc-junks-petitions-vs-bangsamoro-agreements-says-its-premature (accessed 18 May 2017).
90. Luwaran Moidz, "FBCSO Conducts Orientation-Dialogue on Federalism and BBL in Maguindanao", *Luwaran.net*, 15 December 2016, http://www.luwaran.net/home/index.php/news/20-central-mindanao/998-fbcso-conducts-orientation-dialogue-on-federalism-and-bbl-in-maguindanao (accessed 13 February 2017).
91. Carolyn O. Arguillas, "Nur's MNLF Will No Longer Submit Proposed ARMM Amendatory Law; Will Push for Federalism Instead", MindaNews, 19 July 2017, http://www.mindanews.com/peace-process/2017/07/nurs-mnlf-will-no-longer-submit-proposed-armm-amendatory-law-will-push-for-federalism-instead/ (accessed 20 July 2017).
92. Third-Party Monitoring Team, *Third Public Report, January 2015 to February 2016*, p. 7.
93. Ronald D. Holmes and Mark R. Thompson, "Duterte's Year of Sound and Fury", *The Diplomat*, 30 June 2017, http://thediplomat.com/2017/06/dutertes-year-of-sound-and-fury/ (accessed 12 July 2017).

3

On Crooked Ways and Straight Paths:
Assessing Anticorruption Governance Capacity of the Arroyo and Aquino Governments

Kidjie Saguin

INTRODUCTION

Little progress has been made globally towards eliminating corruption. Former World Bank President Jim Yong Kim called public corruption—defined as misuse and abuse of public office for private gain—as "public enemy number one" owing to the profound impact on development and persistence of corruption despite resources channelled towards corruption control for decades. Developing countries still contend with pervasive corruption, and even governments of highly advanced economies are not spared from major corruption scandals. Transparency International reported in 2014 that corruption remains a major public policy issue in all regions of the world.[1]

Frustrations over anticorruption strategies are captured by admissions of failure in the international anticorruption agenda. Based on an evaluation of the World Bank's public sector and governance reforms, Director General of the World Bank's Independent Evaluation Group, Vinod Thomas, lamented that "[d]irect measures to reduce corruption ... rarely succeeded, as they often lacked the necessary support from political elites and the judicial system."[2] Technical approaches adopted in the past following the idea of corruption as a principal-agent problem shied away from addressing the highly political nature of corruption—reducing the effectiveness of such approaches to rhetoric. In response to inadequacies in theories of corruption and corruption control, some scholars started to conceptualize corruption as a collective action problem—whereby "everyone" will act corruptly if corruption is expected to be the norm. Alina Mungiu contends that traditional control of corruption fails because of a faulty assumption about the benevolence of principals to take up duties to control corruption. Institutionalists have fallen short of proposing possible solutions to the collective action problem by recommending losers of the "corrupt game" to come together to form an "insurrection army"—ignoring that corruption may be equally pervasive among civil society.[3]

Empirical studies also do not offer directions for resolving the conceptualization debate. Some scholars support the assertion that political competition,[4] economic prosperity and political leadership[5] have attenuating effects on corruption. There is also evidence reinforcing the roles of professional and meritocratic bureaucracy,[6] and administrative structure[7] in controlling corruption. What appears to be lacking is a well-defined mechanism that determines the efficacy of these contextual factors against the incidence of corruption. Approaches conceptualizing corruption have often been placed at two opposing ends of the spectrum with little systematic effort at integration. Most scholarly work has inevitably supported one of the two approaches but since each approach has its own merits, choosing one over the other discounts the contribution of the other.

I aim to fill this gap and conceptualize governance capacity as the mechanism behind factors identified by the different theories of corruption and how these factors moderate effective control of corruption. Governance capacity is defined as the set of systemic and organizational resources necessary in managing public affairs.[8] I contend that the notion of capacity underpins complementarity between the two competing anticorruption theories. The capacity to bridge information asymmetry is central for principal-agent theorists. Institutionalists find the capacity to steer actors for collective action as vital to corruption control. Although these theories attempt to explain individual corrupt transactions, the unit of analysis—where the theories are most powerful in explaining corruption—fundamentally differs. The principal-agent problem can be primarily viewed in the context of public organizations with multiple principals—including the general public at the broader level and elected officials at the bureaucracy level. On the other hand, the problem of collective action pertains to failure of coordination at the systemic level. Institutions act against the enforcement of the principle of universalism and in favour of competitive particularism.[9] By identifying governance capacity as the underlying mechanism in corruption control, this chapter hopes to contribute to the global anticorruption discourse by proposing an alternative theoretical framework in identifying and assessing corruption control strategies.

The Philippine experience with corruption control is used as a case in point. A qualitative comparative analysis of two administrations' anticorruption governance capacity was employed to examine critical capacities of corruption control. Clear moments of variation between the two administrations were exploited to establish a causal inference based on process tracing.[10] The comparative case study follows what Gerring would call a "most-similar" case study but the cases were chosen to tease out differences in an otherwise similar policy system to ascertain causes for the diverging outcomes.[11]

This chapter is organized as follows. The following section lays out the analytical framework derived from two competing conceptualizations of corruption and corruption control. Six critical capacities vital to the success of corruption control are identified at systemic and organizational levels. Based on a normative framework for anticorruption governance capacity, I conclude that legitimacy of political leaders is critical in corruption control. Getting the politics right and setting universalism as a norm contribute to preventing and minimizing corruption. Success of the "straight path to governance" agenda happened without significant alteration to anticorruption governance architecture—particularly since flagship accountability measures did not eventuate.

CRITICAL CAPACITIES FOR CORRUPTION CONTROL

Policymakers and academics are in consensus on the definition of corruption as the misuse and abuse of public office for private gain.[12] This definition is derived from Joseph Nye's conceptualization of corruption as the "behavior which deviates from the formal duties of a public role because of private regarding (personal, close family, private clique) pecuniary or status gains".[13] Compared to other definitions, such as "privatization of public policy",[14] Nye's definition is the convention as it encapsulates the dyadic nature of corruption. Corruption comprises an action that violates a normative framework (misuse/abuse), and the perverse outcome of the action (private gain). Such a conceptualization of why corrupt acts occur inevitably influences the problems of corruption control.

Advocates who treat corruption as a principal-agent problem—or when agents have delegated authority to act on behalf of the principals—attribute the action to an incentive structure suitable for self-interested agents to veer away from delegated tasks. The low likelihood of getting caught, low magnitude of penalties, and high returns of actions make up the right mix of incentives for corruption.[15] Some view such incentives as a function of the political system and bureaucratic culture.[16] Others identify missing systems to bridge the asymmetry of information as the correct means to minimize corruption. Control of corruption under the principal-agent model follows the heuristic formula of Klitgaard—a systems-based approach to control corruption by minimizing monopoly, reducing power and increasing accountability.[17] These strategies have largely been ruled out as naive for their failure to recognize larger power relations at play or in other words, political corruption. Several studies point to potential effective solutions to organizational corruption such as systematization of information management.[18] Maesschalck and Bertók suggest to build on the compliance-based approach by adding values-based interventions like codes of conduct—arguing corruption will not occur as long as there are sufficient internal controls or individual values and moral character, and external controls or regulations and accountability mechanisms.[19]

Individual corrupt actions are also due to a failure of institutions to prevent such occurrences. The "good governance regime" attempts to bring institutions into discourses on corruption and is espoused for developing countries under the framework of foreign aid. Under this framework, corruption in government is defined as a "symptom" of failed governance where governance refers to "the traditions and institutions by which authority in a country is exercised".[20] Shah and Schachter follow the principal-agent problem as the root cause of corruption and suggest refocusing anticorruption efforts at the systemic level by addressing clientelism, selective justice, ineffective checks and balances, and weak political leadership. Corruption control is fundamental to stopping the governance system from failing—not only by strengthening rule of law but also by resolving any doubts about the legitimacy of the state as a "guardian of public interest".[21]

The framing of corruption based on these definitions has not been satisfactory, as revealed by the Independent Evaluation Group (IEG) evaluation.[22] The poor conceptualization of corruption motivated institutionalists to frame corruption as a collective action problem. The assumption that corruption is the breakdown of principal-agent relationship is problematic because it overestimates the desire of a benevolent principal or principals to minimize corruption.[23] These principals would in fact benefit the majority, even in a democratic system.[24] Incentive-based corruption control interventions will prove ineffective because everyone expects everyone to be corrupt. As stated by Rothstein, "why would agents that either stand to gain from corrupt practices or who can only [lose] by refraining from corruption at all be interested in creating such 'efficient' institutions?"[25] The institutionalists' shortcoming is in developing nuanced corruption control strategies. At best, institutionalists suggest creating an "insurrection army" of losers of a corrupt system to transform corrupt shared expectations of societal actors for all to play fair.[26] However, this becomes infeasible when corruption is equally pervasive among non-state actors, or captured by the state.[27]

The way forward is to bring together these different definitions into a cohesive framework[28]—a unifying mechanism which continues to elude most scholars. Despite the absence of systematic conceptualization and measurement, the notion of capacity can be used to integrate otherwise conflicting accounts of corruption. Scholars of the principal-agent problem discuss the capacity to bridge information asymmetry between principals and agents by formulating and enforcing legal and policy frameworks that reduce incentives for corruption, and mobilizing actors who serve as checks and balances to government.[29] From the perspective of collective action, corruption essentially points to the incapacity of actors and institutions to bear the cost of being non-corrupt.[30] As a consequence, corruption control is the capability of "controlling [society's] most violent or selfish tendencies".[31] Any attempt at controlling corruption is therefore contingent upon the possession of critical capacities enabling societal actors to set up institutions of corruption control. Anticorruption governance capacities are essential resources at systemic and organizational levels.[32] Resources at the systemic level are demonstrations of political power that regulate parameters of decision making, agenda setting and preference shaping.[33] Organizational capacity includes assets, systems, procedures, information and knowledge that enable organizational performance.[34]

Critical capacities for corruption control (Table 3.1) pertain to: analytical capacities in assessing problems and identifying solutions; managerial capacities for implementing the decisions; and political capacities to navigate complex social relationships.[35] Analytical capacity pertains to making and assessing strategies for corruption, involving efficient and appropriate matching of corruption control strategies with specific corruption vulnerabilities. Inevitably, national anticorruption plans play a major role in coalescing actors towards identified problems and proposed solutions.[36] Managerial capacity—as a function of coherence and complementarity between societal actors—can foster greater investments on political bargaining in institutionalized, formal spaces such as the parliament and elections.[37] What this means is that actors are able to negotiate for institutionalization of norms of universal provision of resources—moving away from competitive particularism.[38] Corruption control entails high levels of political capacity, defined here as the capacity to steer actors—particularly those that possess competing interests—to act collectively.[39] To ensure anticorruption machinery is

TABLE 3.1
Critical Capacities for Corruption Control

Dimensions	Systemic	Organizational
Political	Legitimacy of the state	Organizational legitimacy of anticorruption bodies
Managerial	Coherence of societal actors	Coordination of processes within anticorruption bodies
Analytical	National anticorruption planning	System to identify organizational vulnerabilities to corruption

operating, mobilization of financial and political resources is vital. At the systemic level, anticorruption studies have put emphasis on the importance of the legitimacy of the state as the guardian of public interest.[40] Political legitimacy is typically measured by capturing citizens' attitudes and perceptions—often including questions about trust[41]—especially as the state is expected to negotiate between competing interests in an environment with high levels of distrust.[42]

Critical capacities for anticorruption agencies refer to external and internal control mechanisms as well as coordination of internal processes. Watchdog agencies like auditor-generals and the ombudsman are pillars of a national integrity system as they determine what organizations can and cannot do but require public trust and confidence to be able to act.[43] Well-coordinated internal processes refer to wider dissemination of information about goals, plans and operating procedures within an organization and across other organizations, minimizing information asymmetry.[44] A functioning internal control system can also identify organizational vulnerabilities to corruption. These critical capacities set the underpinnings of an anticorruption governance effective in corruption control.

THE CASE OF PHILIPPINE ANTICORRUPTION GOVERNANCE CAPACITY

The Philippines has long been a basket case of deep-rooted corruption and failed anticorruption reforms. The Spanish colonial legacy of particularism combined with incomplete modernization of the bureaucracy under American occupation resulted in institutionalization of unethical practices in government.[45] Anticorruption agencies—introduced as early as the 1950s—were persistently short-lived and ineffective.[46] Corruption reached its peak during the Marcos dictatorship characterized by widespread cronyism—which partially drove the economy into crisis.[47] Despite optimism following the People Power Revolution, "corruption in the public and private sectors in the Philippines"—as noted in a 2000 World Bank report—remains "pervasive and deep-rooted, touching even the judiciary and the media".[48] While certain gains were observed on market reforms under the Ramos administration being able to challenge cartels and oligopolies persistent throughout the country's history[49]—the reinstatement of many Marcos cronies in the Estrada cabinet was detrimental to sustaining the reform momentum.[50]

Recent strides in Transparency International's Corruption Perception Index (TI CPI) are therefore a remarkable achievement for any government administration.[51] Under the helm of President Benigno S. Aquino, the country moved up CPI rankings from 134th in 2010 to 95th out of 168 countries in 2014. The Philippines' ranking progressively improved since 2010—only deteriorating in 2015 due to budget realignment scandals. Arroyo's government, mired by controversies, saw a worsening level of corruption perception since 2004 after a highly contested election amidst allegations of fraud.

Arroyo's Anticorruption Governance Capacity

Gloria Macapagal Arroyo was thrown into the presidency following the removal of the popular but corrupt Joseph Estrada. Then vice-president, Arroyo was sworn into power after a four-day peaceful people power demonstration after a much-televised bitter impeachment trial of Estrada. From the very beginning, Arroyo's ascendancy was in question since Estrada claimed he left the presidential palace temporarily. A violent pro-Estrada rally against the arrest of Estrada and his son, Jinggoy, forced Arroyo to declare a state of rebellion, eventually issuing orders for the arrest of Estrada's key supporters.[52] The mid-term legislative elections in May 2001 would have been the right time to settle any doubts about the legitimacy of Arroyo's government. While Arroyo's People Power Coalition secured eight out of thirteen Senate seats, the election results were not the most credible. The automation of election in May 2001 miserably failed and the election turned out to be one of the bloodiest in the post-Marcos era.[53]

Arroyo's erratic trust ratings punctuated by an election scandal are evidence of her contested legitimacy as president. While Arroyo's assumption of the presidency generated positive trust ratings above 50 per cent in March 2001, her trust ratings measured by Pulse Asia dipped to 45 per cent in almost the same period in April 2002. Arroyo continually struggled to keep her legitimacy afloat. The May 2004 elections did little to improve the situation when Arroyo narrowly won against Fernando Poe Jr.—a popular movie actor—by about 3.5 percentage points. Poe filed an electoral protest citing evidence of electoral fraud but died in December 2004 without resolution. Despite the death of Poe, allegation of fraud continued and culminated in the release of "Hello Garci" tapes—an alleged recording of a conversation between Arroyo and Election Commissioner Virgillio Garcillano. The scandal forced Arroyo to admit to having conversations with the commissioner. No impeachment trials were initiated despite numerous attempts by the minority in Congress.

Arroyo emerged scarred from the scandal and never regained the trust of the wider public. Her trust ratings went below 20 per cent since after the 2004 election. The president of the poll firm Social Weather Station called Arroyo the "least popular" of the four presidents since 1986 because of her negative satisfaction ratings.[54] Not only was Arroyo beleaguered by persistently low approval ratings, she also faced several tests of her ability to retain power. She had to contend with military uprisings by junior officers in both of her terms as president. Even before the presidential elections, she faced a *coup d'état* attempt in 2003 with junior military officers citing corruption in the military as the prime reason for their rebellion. In 2006, another coup attempt was foiled and led to orders for the arrest of nationalist legislators thought to have supported the coup. The same mutineers also took hostage of a luxury hotel in Makati City in 2007 to call for the resignation of Arroyo. She also suffered from a major falling out of reform-oriented members of the cabinet. In 2005, ten cabinet members—subsequently called "Hyatt 10"—including six department secretaries resigned in protest to the 2004 alleged electoral rigging. There is a sharply defined incoherence among societal actors in their support for Arroyo's alleged crooked ways. Civil society from both sides of the political spectrum regularly mobilized against Arroyo's government. High-ranking military officials and politicians—particularly in the House of Representatives—rallied behind Arroyo, even during attempts to overthrow her.

With legitimacy in question, Arroyo turned to political rhetoric—part of which was to clamp down on corruption—and gained a proclivity for authoritarianism.[55] Not only did Arroyo pledge support towards "good governance" initiatives, anticorruption reforms began to be incorporated in the medium-term plans of the government. The Medium-Term Philippine Development Plan (MTPDP) 2004–2010 has a dedicated chapter on anticorruption and good governance—a remarkable policy pronouncement towards prioritizing "punitive and preventive measures to address corruption incidences and vulnerabilities and promoting zero corruption tolerance" through societal values formation, with government working closely with civil society and the private sector.[56] The inclusion of anticorruption into the national plan ensured societal actors were brought together to implement the measures. A multisectoral anticorruption council was established and comprised national government anticorruption agencies as well as local government units, civil society, academes, religious groups, media and professional organizations, among others.

The Arroyo administration embodied an organized well-equipped government with the right instruments for corruption control.[57] Over eighteen anticorruption agencies comprise a sophisticated administrative framework for anticorruption including constitutionally mandated independent commissions like the Office of the Ombudsman, Civil Service Commission and Commission on Audit. International development agencies such as the World Bank[58] recommended policy responses to corruption and Arroyo pushed for the strengthening and creation of anticorruption agencies. Arroyo also created the Presidential Anti-Graft and Corruption Commission in 2001 as the preventive arm of the executive—focusing on lifestyle checks of appointed officials and educational programmes. Other agencies were also formalized to cater to specific corruption control strategies such as the Presidential Committee on Effective Governance—a cabinet-level coordinating body spearheading the signature reduction campaign. Another agency is the Presidential Commission on Values Formation, a government entity created through an executive order with a mandate to establish "a strong foundation for moral value formation in the government bureaucracy".[59] High levels of private sector and civil society participation marked Arroyo's term—through critical alliances such as the Transparent Accountable Governance (TAG) Project of Asia Foundation, Government and Budget Watch Projects and a Transparency and Accountability Network—to serve as checks and partners against corruption.

Just like Arroyo, the leadership of key corruption control agencies has also been taken to task. In 2005, Merceditas Gutierrez became the Ombudsman and proved to be a polarizing figure, particularly due to her affinity to the First Gentleman Mike Arroyo. Gutierrez also did not enjoy high levels of public trust as shown by her subsequent negative SWS satisfaction ratings: –17 in March 2008, –22 June in 2009, –9 in September 2010 and –9 in March 2011.[60] The independence of Gutierrez from the Arroyo family did not escape questioning when the Ombudsman failed to act on several corruption scandals that erupted during her term. Legislative hearings on National Broadband Network deals with the Chinese firm ZTE Corporation (NBN/ZTE deals), MegaPacific scandal, fertilizer scam and "Euro generals" cloaked Gutierrez' independence with a veil of uncertainty. Motivated by inaction on these scandals, two impeachment complaints were filed against Gutierrez. The first impeachment complaint failed to progress due to dismissal of the case in the House of Representatives in 2009. In 2010, however, once Aquino assumed the role of President, impeachment cases continued to be filed in the House which advanced to holding trials in the Senate. In April 2011, Gutierrez resigned as Ombudsman even before the trial commenced, calling her resignation a win-win solution.

Notwithstanding the question of legitimacy of the political and bureaucratic leadership, anticorruption agencies continue to coordinate efforts outside the national planning initiative. Set up in 1997, the Inter-Agency Anti-Graft Coordinating Council is a cabinet-level coordinating body between the anticorruption agencies including the Commission on Audit (COA), Civil Service Commission (CSC), National Bureau of Investigation, Presidential Council Against Crime and Corruption—which became the Presidential Anti-Graft Commission (PAGC)—the Ombudsman and Department of Justice. Then President Estrada formalized the partnership between the agencies and mandated the council with the "implementation of their programs and projects as well as in the prevention, detection, investigation, and prosecution of graft cases, with the end in view of promoting a more efficient, economical, and effective government".[61] In 2000, a national anticorruption plan was drawn up to converge corruption control strategies into one cohesive strategy. In 2003, the government pushed for the ratification of the United Nations Convention Against Corruption (UNCAC). A 2006 National Anti-Corruption Program of Action (NACPA) was also prepared in an endeavour to coordinate the government's anticorruption activities.

The political battle for legitimacy affords an opportunity to introduce wide-scale programmes that boost the analytical capacity of anticorruption agencies. Under the Integrity Development Review (IDR), sixteen graft-prone agencies were systematically examined on the capacity of their internal systems to prevent corruption and weak points or vulnerabilities of mission-critical services to corruption. The IDR involved development of an action plan on how to address vulnerabilities and weak points in internal systems of organizations. The United States Agency for International Development (USAID) and the European Commission (EC) funded the conduct of the IDR—indicating that, despite the political turmoil, anticorruption agencies continued to enhance their analytical capacities. The resident ombudsman programme rolled over into Arroyo's term where dedicated staff funded by the Office of the Ombudsman seconded to "graft-prone" agencies served advisory roles in improving organizational policies and programmes to prevent corruption—including the IDR.[62] Non-state actors were equally engaged. Social Weather Station began their Enterprise Survey, funded by the TAG project—to obtain public perception about corruption—including satisfaction with anticorruption initiatives and perceived losses from corruption.

The crafting of the Integrity Development Action Plan (IDAP) served as the government's national anticorruption framework from 2004 onwards, further strengthening the analytical capacity of the Arroyo administration. The IDAP is composed of twenty-two "doables" categorized into four approaches to corruption control—prevention, education, investigation and detection, and strategic partnership. PAGC advocated for the implementation of the IDAP in over a hundred government agencies and provided incentives such as awards for compliance to the "doables". In 2009, implementation of IDAP was made mandatory along with the development of a Moral Renewal Action Plan (MRAP). While the IDAP featured compliance-based interventions, MRAP is fundamentally values-based—seeking to institutionalize "values formation and ethical behavior for government officers and employees, as well as the strengthening of people's values to achieve zero tolerance for corruption".[63] These initiatives generated a deeper corruption control embedded in government processes. For example, the Department of Social Welfare and Development incorporated adherence to IDAP into individual employee performance.[64]

Despite these efforts to bring in societal actors to work on good governance initiatives, perceptions of corruption remained high, indicating that public confidence is particularly important in anticorruption initiatives.[65] Corruption was still considered to be a main problem despite strong and sophisticated anticorruption organizational power. The higher level of analytical capacity in identifying vulnerable areas to corruption and formulating corresponding solutions is muted by the highly contested legitimacy of the state as a guardian of public interest. Coordination between anticorruption agencies was rendered moot because of evident and growing demands for Arroyo's resignation—due to her perceived corrupt hold of power from civil society, junior military officers and even her cabinet. The case of Arroyo's anticorruption governance capacity provides evidence to the argument that apolitical anticorruption measures are bound to fail.[66] The "tone from the top" or "leadership by example" becomes relevant in this context—as shown by the experience of Asian cities like Hong Kong and countries like Singapore.[67]

The fact that Arroyo failed to make any gains in reducing corruption despite a strong governance architecture—while Aquino achieved the almost impossible even without a strong lead anticorruption agency—affirms that political legitimacy is a critical capacity for effective corruption control. This assertion is partially corroborated by evidence that politics matter in anticorruption.[68] This chapter forwards this assertion and argues that successful anticorruption measures are predicated on huge public support and trust for political leadership and may only require integrity systems to function with a minimal degree of sophistication. In other words, administrative reforms to align values of self-interested agents are necessary, but insufficient, to generate significant drivers for successful anticorruption campaigns. As Bukovansky noted, "[s]tandards that lack legitimacy [the ethical problem] are less likely than legitimate standards to be effectively enforced [the pragmatic problem]".[69]

What appears to be evident in Arroyo's anticorruption governance is the use of attempts to improve analytical and operational capacities to derive political legitimacy. Arroyo compensated for her deficit in legitimacy at the systemic level by creating focal points to send signals that the virtues of universalism were being protected. This required adopting structures of coordination and anticorruption approaches that were advocated and financed by international organizations.[70] Such an isomorphic response is viewed as a way to generate legitimacy—particularly germane in anticorruption initiatives.[71] It can thus be argued that a complex architecture of anticorruption institutions is indicative of large-scale efforts to legitimize an otherwise corrupt government.

By bringing to the surface the idea of anticorruption governance capacity, it is important for anticorruption agencies to contextualize strategies on the political environment. Earlier efforts were made to categorize strategies based on levels of trust and incidence of corruption[72]—suggesting self-interests of rational actors in various contexts.[73] Collective action theories assert sub-optimal social outcomes materialize because of the inability to act towards a common goal of resisting corruption. The criticality of all capacities identified in this chapter are brought together to show alignment of self-interests of various actors. Political leaders have the power to redirect resources towards generating legitimacy. Resources flow on one level of governance to compensate for capacity deficits in others—as shown in the case of Arroyo. Similarly, a government that enjoys political legitimacy enables an environment where anticorruption agencies can genuinely deliver results without being preoccupied with generating their own organizational legitimacy. Such an understanding of how resources should flow can unlock the black box of anticorruption effectiveness.

Aquino's Anticorruption Governance Capacity

Aquino came into power with a rhetoric of change following a defining campaign slogan against corruption: *Kung walang corrupt, walang mahirap* (If there are no corrupt, no one will be poor). His platform for political change resonated with a large number of voters—paving the way for a landslide victory by almost 17 percentage points against Joseph Estrada standing for re-election. This win also gave Aquino resounding legitimacy—particularly as the elections were not mired with controversies like Arroyo's 2004 victory. This legitimacy becomes salient in Aquino's trust ratings of about 80 per cent in October 2010—one of the highest ratings of a president since 1999. Aquino's legitimacy and popularity were built on a critique of the corruption-laden administration of Arroyo. In his first State of the Nation Address, Aquino laid out his promise of bringing public interest into the core of government programmes and committed to an honest public service through the so-called "straight path to good governance" (*daang matuwid*). The *daang matuwid* rhetoric proved effective in setting the tone of Aquino's presidency—further advanced by his pronouncement of *walang wang-wang* or prohibition of the use of sirens to clear the streets for government officials. Aquino continued to be popular even half-way through his six-year presidential term—a feat for any democratically elected political leader. While most former presidents started equally with high SWS satisfaction ratings, Aquino's ratings remained in the +50 range until 2014 when his administration was affected by the Disbursement Acceleration Program (DAP) issue. Despite this setback, Aquino ended his term with +27 satisfaction rating—higher than his mother, Corazon Aquino, and Fidel Ramos.

One of the unique features of the Aquino administration was the huge social movement behind his ascent to the presidency. The death of Aquino's mother in August 2009—former President Corazon Aquino—exponentially translated to a call for him to run for president, like his mother. Rocamora called this movement a "reform constituency" wherein the initial "organizational expression to the political resolve" of transformation among NGO leaders was redirected towards gaining traction for Aquino's candidacy.[74] Aquino emerged as the reluctant presidential candidate after the withdrawal of the Liberal Party (LP) stalwart, Senator Mar Roxas, who conceded that "[t]he passing of our beloved former President Aquino has reawakened a passion among us. I acknowledge this as fuel to bring us to the realization of our dream: Good will triumph over evil."[75] Strong civil society support was manifested in the composition of the senatorial ticket and eventually the cabinet. Risa Hontiveros, who represented the progressive Akbayan Citizen's Action Party, ran for a senate seat under Aquino's party. Although she lost, Hontiveros' venture into national politics with the LP marked the beginning of the inclusion of progressive groups into mainstream political parties and the blossoming of a "perceived sense of complementarity in the identity, directions, and actions of the LP and Akbayan".[76] Joel Rocamora joined the cabinet as the antipoverty minister. Aquino's cabinet also enjoyed the return of most of the Hyatt 10, a lauded act of bringing experience and integrity into a government publicly perceived to lack competence. Aquino, as De Jesus noted, "comes to the presidency with much more political and government experience and a wider network than Cory Aquino started with. Aquino made use of Cory's network in his campaign and in his administration"—including the Hyatt 10.[77] The apparent complementarity of societal actors, and inclusion of progressive groups into public governance—which remained throughout the rest of Aquino's term—have shaped the ability of the government to get things done.

Most will argue that Aquino's term was largely built on vindictive politics, but the legacy of Arroyo's misgivings influenced the framing of vision and planning anticorruption strategies. The Social Contract with the Filipino People introduced improving legitimacy of the state as an expressed element of the social contract. Aquino identified ideals of transformative leadership, integrity and professionalization of the bureaucracy to change how things were being done in the government. The chapter on "Good Governance and Rule of Law" of the Philippine

Development Plan 2011–2016 aimed to improve public service delivery, curb bureaucratic and political corruption, strengthen rule of law and enhance citizen's participation and access to information.[78] While much of the system's reforms were carried over from the Arroyo government—such as the financial management system and procurement—the pursuit of the passage of the Freedom of Information Act, budget transparency and wider citizen engagement in local governance are seen to be innovative additions by the Aquino government. Aquino also revived the cabinet clusters—a way to promote horizontal coherence in delivering programmes such as anticorruption reforms. The Good Governance and Anticorruption Cabinet Cluster was specifically mandated to "regain the trust and confidence of the public in government" in addition to duties of promoting transparency, accountability and participatory governance. The Good Governance and Anticorruption Cabinet Cluster eventually released a plan that pledged initiatives on:

1. regular disclosure of information on official acts and services;
2. availability of mechanisms for public access to information;
3. punitive and preventive anticorruption measures;
4. results-oriented management;
5. citizen's participation in governance; and
6. partnerships and constituency-building.

Unlike Arroyo's appointments, Aquino's delegated authority in the independent anticorruption bodies benefitted from positive perception from the public. The Office of the Ombudsman—headed by former Associate Justice Conchita Carpio-Morales—proved to have unquestionable levels of integrity. Satisfaction levels for Carpio-Morales at the Office of the Ombudsman were better than for her predecessor and she maintained positive levels since assuming office: +49 in April 2016. Net sincerity ratings of anticorruption agencies also remained "good" based on a survey of enterprises. According to the survey, the Ombudsman is considered sincere in 2012 (+38), 2013 (+23) and 2015 (+36) from a negative sincerity rating in 2009 (–8).[79] The public also positively perceive COA—due to speedy investigations of corruption scandals and high-profile cases like the *Pantawid Pamilyang Pilipino* Program (the country's conditional cash transfer programme), and disbursement of disaster funds for cyclone Yolanda, for example.

However, the high levels of political legitimacy were not met with an equivalent deployment of multi-actor anticorruption machinery. Aquino abolished PAGC in the first days of his administration on the perceived functional overlap between the Ombudsman and PAGC. Aquino replaced PAGC through his first executive order, creating the Truth Commission with a mandate to investigate "reports of graft and corruption of such scale and magnitude that shock and offend the moral and ethical sensibilities of the people ... during the previous administration".[80] Despite consistency with the *daang matuwid* rhetoric of making Arroyo accountable, the Truth Commission's constitutionality was challenged by several lawmakers at the Supreme Court, citing violation of the equal protection clause of the Philippine Constitution. The Supreme Court declared the Truth Commission unconstitutional after less than a year of operation. This ruling was a setback to Aquino's roadmap of exacting accountability as a cornerstone of corruption control. A Discipline Office was established under the Office of President to absorb the prevention function of PAGC through the Integrity Development Unit and investigative function of presidential appointees and elected officials through the Administrative Discipline Unit. The ability of the Discipline Office to shape anticorruption governance remains unclear—particularly when compared to the accomplishments of PAGC.

The absence of a lead anticorruption agency resulted in the relegation of a decentralized identification of anticorruption measures to the backburner indefinitely. Public sector organizations continue to implement some aspects of IDR, IDAP and MRAP but have refocused their energy towards complying with centrally mandated provision. Aquino's government opted for "soft" constraints on national agencies through a performance-based incentive system. In 2011, a results-based performance management system was established by harmonizing existing performance measurement systems in the government and linking actual performance to miscellaneous pay of government workers. Eligibility for the pay-for-performance scheme is contingent on achieving presidential directives, organizational objectives, and good governance conditions. These conditions are:

1. establishment of a transparency seal;
2. posting of bid notices and awards on the website of Philippine Government Electronic Procurement System (PhilGEPS);
3. liquidation of all cash advances to officials and employees; and
4. establishment of a citizen's charter or its equivalent.

Such a highly centralized and compliance-based approach restricts innovation in identifying specific anticorruption strategies at the organizational level. Although the Aquino government replaced the IDAP with the Integrity Management Program (IMP) in 2015, the programme hardly gained traction among government agencies—as agencies were only encouraged to comply. IMP calls for the creation of an agency-specific, contextualized integrity management policy but most agencies only seemed to "rehash" their IDAP to comply.

Compared to Arroyo's term, Aquino's success in improving corruption perceptions can be associated with high levels of political legitimacy he enjoyed. Aquino's political legitimacy was built on a kind of politics that showed a marked departure from that of his predecessor through the *daang matuwid* rhetoric. Aquino's "straight path to governance" initiative was not without setbacks. The ill-fate of the Truth Commission and lack of influence of the Discipline Office created a void in the lead agency role among anticorruption bodies. Despite this, the anticorruption governance architecture managed to achieve what other presidential administrations have not. The political leadership's legitimate hold of power pushed for wider adoption of the principle of universalism—for example, *walang wang-wang*—allowing for anticorruption agencies, typically preoccupied in fighting for their own legitimacy, to channel resources towards enforcing their agencies' roles in the integrity system.

CONCLUSION AND IMPLICATIONS

Through a comparative case study, this chapter contributes to theoretical and practical aspects of anticorruption governance. The utility of anticorruption governance capacity as an underlying mechanism for examining corruption control strategies was presented. The case study has shown the concept of governance capacity can bring together two different theories of corruption into an integrated framework. Aquino can be seen as better able in bridging information asymmetry as indicated by coherence among societal actors, particularly made salient by the reform constituency.[81] The value of universalism was an underpinning principle of Aquino's government as shown in the straight path rhetoric and also how the idea of "inclusive growth" was framed—severely lacking in Arroyo's government. The framework suggests focusing on critical governance capacities to advance theories of corruption and corruption control.

The puzzle over the performance of Aquino compared to Arroyo's government in terms of outcomes in preventing and minimizing corruption has been explained. Using the Philippine experience, there is a lesson to be learned from emphasizing the political nature of anticorruption work. For any government to launch an anticorruption programme it fundamentally needs to be perceived by the public as legitimate, sincere and honest. Arroyo's focus on good governance and building up anticorruption machinery did not reap positive gains because of her contested legitimacy. Aquino's easy attainment of better corruption perception outcomes can be attributed to his high levels of political legitimacy ushered in by the rhetoric of "straight path to governance". The public credibly believed Aquino's hold on power to be legitimate and correct for initiatives to clean the bureaucracy.

The chapter's findings have important implications for anticorruption planning. The current president, Rodrigo Duterte, derives his legitimacy from a landslide victory in 2016 built on a promise of dismantling elite liberal institutions.[82] Duterte's propagation of universalism represents correcting an imbalance in power to influence the government and respond to the "protest of the wealthy, newly rich, well off, and the modestly successful new middle class"[83]—the segment of the population thought to be losers of Aquino's "inclusive growth" and politics. Duterte is essentially centralizing anticorruption governance, relying on his widespread political support to implement corruption control measures while side-lining the existing complex system of agencies. In his first State of the Nation Address, Duterte declared "for those who have valid reasons to complain about graft and corruption, the gates of Malacañang will be open."[84] Although the new Philippine Development Plan still features a set of strategies for effective governance and fair administration of justice, the ability of such reliance on systemic anticorruption capacity to drive anticorruption performance remains unclear. Despite immense popular support for the president, it will only be a matter of time before the public take to task Duterte's apparent commitment to inclusion. As Curato states: "[p]art of [Duterte's] populism's capacity of including previously marginalised voices is its corollary logic of exclusion."[85]

This chapter also proposes a novel contribution towards anticorruption research, which is constrained by the use of a single country where macro-institutions remained largely stable over the course of the two governments. Future research could consider applying this integrative framework in other countries at various levels of development. A cross-country comparison could further advance the framework by controlling for variables like social trust and civil service pay, for example—important for the two differing theories of corruption.

Notes

1. Transparency International, "Corruption Perceptions Index 2014: Regional Analysis", 2014, http://www.transparency.org/cpi2014/regional_analysis.
2. IEG, *Public Sector Reform: What Works and Why? An IEG Evaluation of World Bank Support* (Washington, D.C.: World Bank, 2008), p. xi.
3. Alina Mungiu, "Corruption: Diagnosis and Treatment", *Journal of Democracy* 17, no. 3 (2006): 86–99.
4. Gabriella R. Montinola and Robert W. Jackman, "Sources of Corruption: A Cross-Country Study", *British Journal of Political Science* 32, no. 1 (2002): 147–70.
5. Vito Tanzi, "Corruption around the World: Causes, Consequences, Scope, and Cures", *Staff Papers-International Monetary Fund* (1998): 559–94.
6. Carl Dahlström, Victor Lapuente, and Jan Teorell, "The Merit of Meritocratization: Politics, Bureaucracy, and the Institutional Deterrents of Corruption", *Political Research Quarterly* 65, no. 3 (2012): 656–68; James E. Rauch and Peter B. Evans, "Bureaucratic Structure and Bureaucratic Performance in Less Developed Countries", *Journal of Public Economics* 75, no. 1 (2000): 49–71; Jeffrey Henderson et al., "Bureaucratic Effects: Weberian' State Agencies and Poverty Reduction", *Sociology* 41, no. 3 (2007): 515–32.
7. Daniel Treisman, "The Causes of Corruption: A Cross-National Study", *Journal of Public Economics* 76, no. 3 (2000): 399–457.
8. X. Wu, M. Ramesh, and M. Howlett, "Policy Capacity: A Conceptual Framework for Understanding Policy Competences and Capabilities", *Policy and Society* 34, no. 3 (2015): 165–71; M. Ramesh, Kidjie Saguin, Michael P. Howlett, and Xun Wu, "Rethinking Governance Capacity as Organizational and Systemic Resources", Lee Kuan Yew School of Public Policy Research Paper, no. 16-12 (Singapore: Lee Kuan Yew School of Public Policy, 2016).
9. Mungiu, "Corruption: Diagnosis and Treatment".
10. Evan S. Lieberman, "Causal Inference in Historical Institutional Analysis: A Specification of Periodization Strategies", *Comparative Political Studies* 34, no. 9 (2001): 1011–35; Alexander L. George and Andrew Bennett, *Case Studies and Theory Development in the Social Sciences* (Cambridge, MA: MIT Press, 2005).
11. John Gerring, *Case Study Research: Principles and Practices* (Cambridge: Cambridge University Press, 2006).
12. Pranab Bardhan, "Corruption and Development: A Review of Issues", *Journal of Economic Literature* 35, no. 3 (1997): 1320–46.

13. Joseph Samuel Nye, "Corruption and Political Development: A Cost-Benefit Analysis", *American Political Science Review* 61, no. 2 (1967): 419.
14. Daniel Kaufmann, "Myths and Realities of Governance and Corruption", in *The Global Competitiveness Report 2005–2006* (World Economic Forum, 2005).
15. Gary S. Becker and George J. Stigler, "Law Enforcement, Malfeasance, and Compensation of Enforcers", *Journal of Legal Studies* 3, no. 1 (1974).
16. Susan Rose-Ackerman, *Corruption and Government* (Cambridge: Cambridge University Press, 1999).
17. Robert Klitgaard, *Controlling Corruption* (Berkeley, CA: University of California Press, 1988).
18. Jin-Wook Choi, "Institutional Structures and Effectiveness of Anticorruption Agencies: A Comparative Analysis of South Korea and Hong Kong", *Asian Journal of Political Science* 17, no. 2 (2009); Jon S.T. Quah, "Preventing Police Corruption in Singapore: The Role of Recruitment, Training and Socialisation", *Asia Pacific Journal of Public Administration* 28, no. 1 (2006).
19. Jeroen Maesschalck and János Bertók, "Towards a Sound Integrity Framework: Instruments, Processes, Structures and Conditions for Implementation", in *Global Forum on Public Governance* (Paris: Organisation for Economic Co-operation and Development, 2009).
20. Anwar Shah and Mark Schacter, "Combating Corruption: Look before You Leap", *Finance and Development* 41, no. 4 (2004).
21. Anwar Shah, "Tailoring the Fight against Corruption to Country Circumstances", *Performance Accountability And Combating Corruption* (Washington, D.C.: World Bank, 2007).
22. IEG, *Public Sector Reform*.
23. Jan Teorell, "Corruption as an Institution: Rethinking the Nature and Origins of the Grabbing Hand" (Göteborg, Sweden: Göteborg University, 2007).
24. Michael Johnston, "Corruption and Democratic Consolidation", in *Democracy and Corruption* (New Jersey: Princeton University, 1999).
25. Bo Rothstein, "Anti-Corruption: The Indirect 'Big Bang' Approach", *Review of International Political Economy* 18, no. 2 (2011): 234.
26. Mungiu, "Corruption: Diagnosis and Treatment"; Anna Persson, Bo Rothstein, and Jan Teorell, "Why Anticorruption Reforms Fail—Systemic Corruption as a Collective Action Problem", *Governance* 26, no. 3 (2013).
27. James H. Mittelman and Robert Johnston, "The Globalization of Organized Crime, the Courtesan State, and the Corruption of Civil Society", *Global Governance* 5, no. 1 (1999); Timothy Besley and Andrea Prat, "Handcuffs for the Grabbing Hand? Media Capture and Government Accountability", *American Economic Review* 96, no. 3 (2006).
28. Robert Williams, "New Concepts for Old?", *Third World Quarterly* 20, no. 3 (1999); Paul D. Hutchcroft, "The Politics of Privilege: Assessing the Impact of

Rents, Corruption, and Clientelism on Third World Development", *Political Studies* 45, no. 3 (1997).
29. Shah and Schacter, "Combating Corruption", pp. 40–43; Michael Johnston and Sahr J. Kpundeh, "Building a Clean Machine: Anti-Corruption Coalitions and Sustainable Reform", *World Bank Policy Research Working Paper*, no. 3466 (2004); Mark Robinson, "Corruption and Development: An Introduction", *European Journal of Development Research* 10, no. 1 (1998).
30. Rothstein, "Anti-Corruption"; Margaret Levi, *Of Rule and Revenue*, vol. 13 (Berkeley: University of California Press, 1988).
31. Alina Mungiu-Pippidi, "Controlling Corruption through Collective Action", *Journal of Democracy* 24, no. 1 (2013): 106.
32. Ramesh et al., "Rethinking Governance Capacity".
33. Colin Hay, *Political Analysis: A Critical Introduction* (Basingstoke: Palgrave Macmillan, 2002).
34. Jay Barney, "Firm Resources and Sustained Competitive Advantage", *Journal of Management* 17, no. 1 (1991); Richard L. Daft, *Organizational Theory and Design* (New York: West, 1983).
35. Wu, Ramesh, and Howlett, "Policy Capacity".
36. UNODC, "National Anti-Corruption Strategies: A Practical Guide for Development and Implementation", in *The United Nations Convention against Corruption* (Vienna: United Nations Office on Drugs and Crime, 2015).
37. Carlos Scartascini and Mariano Tommasi, "The Making of Policy: Institutionalized or Not?", *American Journal of Political Science* 56, no. 4 (2012).
38. Mungiu, "Corruption: Diagnosis and Treatment".
39. Ibid.
40. Shah and Schacter, "Combating Corruption", pp. 40–43.
41. M. Stephen Weatherford, "Measuring Political Legitimacy", *American Political Science Review* 86, no. 1 (1992).
42. Susan Rose-Ackerman, "Trust, Honesty and Corruption: Reflection on the State-Building Process", *European Journal of Sociology* 42, no. 3 (2001).
43. Jeremy Pope, *Confronting Corruption: The Elements of a National Integrity System* (London: Transparency International, 2000).
44. Ben S. Kuipers et al., "The Management of Change in Public Organizations: A Literature Review", *Public Administration* 92, no. 1 (2014); Richard E. Matland, "Synthesizing the Implementation Literature: The Ambiguity-Conflict Model of Policy Implementation", *Journal of Public Administration Research and Theory* 5, no. 2 (1995).
45. Jenny Balboa and Erlinda M. Medalla, "Anti-Corruption and Governance: The Philippine Experience" (paper presented at the APEC Study Center Consortium Conference, Ho Chi Minh City, Vietnam, 2006).
46. Eric C. Batalla, "De-Institutionalizing Corruption in the Philippines: Identifying

Strategic Requirements for Reinventing Institutions" (paper for conference on Institutionalizing Strategies to Combat Corruption: Lessons from East Asia, sponsored by the KAS and DLSU-YCEA, Makati, Philippines, 12–13 August 2000).
47. Joel Rocamora, "Corruption in the Philippines: A Beginner's Guide", in *Pork and Other Perks: Corruption and Governance in the Philippines*, edited by Sheila Coronel (Quezon City: Philippine Center for Investigative Journalism, 1998).
48. Vinay Bhargava, "Combating Corruption in the Philippines", World Bank Report No. 20369-PH (Manila: Philippine Country Management Unit, World Bank, 2000), p. ii.
49. Alex Magno, "The Market Consensus", *Far Eastern Economic Review* 158 (1995).
50. Paul Hutchcroft, "Obstructive Corruption: The Politics of Privilege in the Philippines", *Rents, Rent-Seeking and Economic Development: Theory and Evidence in Asia*, edited by Mushtaq H. Khan and K.S. Jomo (Cambridge: Cambridge University Press, 2000), pp. 207–47.
51. Transparency International's Corruption Perception Index (CPI).
52. Mel C. Labrador, "The Philippines in 2001: High Drama, a New President, and Setting the Stage for Recovery", *Asian Survey* 42, no. 1 (2002).
53. Ibid.
54. GMANews.TV, "Arroyo Now Most Unpopular President in 20 Years—SWS", *GMA News Online*, 4 April 2006.
55. Paul D. Hutchcroft, "The Arroyo Imbroglio in the Philippines", *Journal of Democracy* 19, no. 1 (2008): 141–55.
56. National Economic Development Authority, *Medium Term Philippine Development Plan 2004–2010* (2004), p. 251.
57. Nathan Gilbert Quimpo, "Philippines", in *Countries at the Crossroads: An Analysis of Democratic Governance*, edited by Jake Dizard CW and Vanessa Tucker (New York, Washington, D.C., Lanham, Boulder, Toronto, Oxford: Freedom House; Rowman & Littlefield, 2012).
58. World Bank, "Combating Corruption in the Philippines: An Update", World Bank Report No. 23687 (Washington, D.C.: World Bank, 2001).
59. Executive Order No. 317, s. 2004 Creating the Presidential Commission On Values Formation.
60. SWS, "First Quarter 2011 Social Weather Survey: 52% Agree with SC Decision to Let Gutierrez Impeachment Proceed; 83% Want Garcia Charged with Plunder; Gutierrez's Net Satisfaction Rating Stays at −9", *BusinessWorld*, 2011.
61. Administrative Order No. 79, s. 1999 Recognizing the Establishment of the Inter-Agency Anti-Graft Coordinating Council and Directing Government Agencies to Extend Support and Assistance to It.
62. Nelson Nogot Moratalla, "Graft and Corruption: The Philippine Experience", *Resource Materials Series*, no. 56 (1999).

63. Administrative Order 255, Directing the Heads of the Executive Department to Lead Moral Renewal in Their Agencies.
64. PIA, "DSWD Remains Number 1 in Fight against Corruption," *PIA Archive News Reader*, 13 October 2009.
65. Eiji Oyamada, "President Gloria Macapagal-Arroyo's Anti-Corruption Strategy in the Philippines an Evaluation", *Asian Journal of Political Science* 13, no. 1 (2005); Quimpo, "Philippines", pp. 533–60.
66. Rose-Ackerman, *Corruption and Government*; Rothstein, "Anti-Corruption"; Mungiu, "Corruption: Diagnosis and Treatment".
67. Hilton L. Root, *Small Countries, Big Lessons: Governance and the Rise of East Asia* (Oxford: Oxford University Press, 1996).
68. Montinola and Jackman, "Sources of Corruption"; Tanzi, "Corruption around the World".
69. Mlada Bukovansky, "The Hollowness of Anti-Corruption Discourse", *Review of International Political Economy* 13, no. 2 (2006): 184.
70. Peter Larmour, "Civilizing Techniques: Transparency International and the Spread of Anti-Corruption", Asia Pacific School of Economics and Government Discussion Papers (Canberra: Crawford School of Economics and Government, Australian National University, 2005).
71. Luís De Sousa, "Anti-Corruption Agencies: Between Empowerment and Irrelevance", *Crime, Law and Social Change* 53, no. 1 (2010); Seongcheol Kim, Hyun Jeong Kim, and Heejin Lee, "An Institutional Analysis of an E-Government System for Anti-Corruption: The Case of Open", *Government Information Quarterly* 26, no. 1 (2009).
72. Shah and Schacter, "Combating Corruption".
73. Monika Bauhr and Naghmeh Nasiritousi, "Why Pay Bribes? Collective Action and Anticorruption Efforts", *QoG Working Paper Series* 18 (2011).
74. Joel Rocamora, "Partisanship and Reform: The Making of a Presidential Campaign", in *The Politics of Change in the Philippines*, edited by Yuko Kasuya and Nathan Gilbert Quimpo (Manila: Anvil Publishing Inc., 2010), p. 82.
75. ABS-CBN News, "Mar Roxas Withdraws from 2010 Race", 2 September 2009, https://news.abs-cbn.com/nation/09/01/09/mar-roxas-withdraws-2010-race.
76. Hansley A. Juliano, "Tensions and Developments in Akbayan's Alliance with the Aquino Administration", *Kasarinlan: Philippine Journal of Third World Studies* 30, no. 1 (2016): 24.
77. Edilberto C. De Jesus, "The Philippines in 2010: Reclaiming Hope", in *Southeast Asian Affairs 2011*, edited by Daljit Singh (Singapore: Institute of Southeast Asian Studies, 2011), p. 229.
78. National Economic and Development Authority, Philippine Development Plan 2011–2016 (2011).
79. Social Weather Station, Surveys of Enterprise on Corruption (2009–2015).

80. Executive Order No. 1, s. 2010, Creating the Philippine Truth Commission of 2010 (2010).
81. Rocamora, "Partisanship and Reform".
82. Mark R. Thompson, "Bloodied Democracy: Duterte and the Death of Liberal Reformism in the Philippines", *Journal of Current Southeast Asian Affairs* 35, no. 3 (2016): 39–68.
83. Julio C. Teehankee, "Duterte's Resurgent Nationalism in the Philippines: A Discursive Institutionalist Analysis", *Journal of Current Southeast Asian Affairs* 35, no. 3 (2016): 73.
84. Rodrigo Duterte, "2016 State of the Nation Address", *Official Gazette*, http://www.officialgazette.gov.ph/2016/07/26/the-2016-state-of-the-nation-address/.
85. Nicole Curato, "Flirting with Authoritarian Fantasies? Rodrigo Duterte and the New Terms of Philippine Populism", *Journal of Contemporary Asia* 47, no. 1 (2017): 151.

PART II

Economic Governance

4

How Has the Economy Fared under the Duterte Administration So Far?

Maria Socorro Gochoco-Bautista

INTRODUCTION

President Duterte inherited an economy from the Aquino administration that had grown at a yearly average rate of 6.2 per cent over the previous five years—the highest average rate of growth the economy had achieved since the 1970s. By end 2016, the economy had had seventy-one quarters of positive growth, which was remarkable in that it occurred against the backdrop of the Global Financial Crisis in 2008–9. Fiscal and monetary policies were responsibly conducted, increased spending occurred while fiscal space was also being created so the country managed to achieve investment-grade status after a long time of being below this. Inflation was under 2 per cent, well within the Bangko Sentral ng Pilipinas (BSP)'s target of 2–4 per cent.

Under President Duterte's watch, growth continued and the economy expanded by 6.6 per cent in the fourth quarter of 2016. Although this was the slowest quarterly growth rate in 2016, it was higher than the 6.3 per cent in the same quarter in 2015. According to Director General Ernesto Pernia of the National Economic and Development Authority (NEDA), "For the full year of 2016, we are so far the fastest growing economy with China at 6.7 per cent and Vietnam's 6.7 per cent".[1]

Nevertheless, it is clear that daunting challenges remain. Despite growth, poverty remains a long-standing and pervasive problem. By the end of the Aquino administration in 2016, poverty incidence did decline —to 21.6 per cent—from about 25 per cent over several decades.

There is no denying the economy needs to grow robustly in order to significantly reduce poverty. The greater challenge is how to make growth more inclusive and reduce poverty and income inequality. NEDA Director General Pernia has stated "the target of 6.5–7.5 per cent growth for 2017 is highly likely" to be achieved. In the medium term, we expect growth to strengthen further towards 7 or 8 per cent, with the economy expanding by about 50 per cent in real terms and per capita income rising by over 40 per cent over the next six years".[2] These growth rates would put the Philippines in the upper-middle income category by 2022 and reduce poverty incidence from 21.6 per cent to 14 per cent—lifting about 6 million Filipinos out of poverty.[3]

On 20 June 2016, President Duterte's economic team presented his administration's 10-point socioeconomic agenda in Davao to members of the business community. The socioeconomic agenda laid out by Duterte's economic team is sound and recognizes more has to be done to make growth inclusive, raise the productivity of resources, and the efficiency within which the economy operates. The 10-point Socioeconomic Plan also acknowledges that the fiscal, monetary and trade economic policies of the Aquino administration should be maintained—implying they were sound and indeed had delivered positive growth rates. The 10-point plan includes:

- the institution of progressive tax reform;
- increasing competitiveness and easing the cost of doing business;
- accelerating annual infrastructure spending;
- increasing agricultural productivity and rural tourism;
- encouraging investments by ensuring security of land tenure and addressing bottlenecks in land management and titling agencies;

- investing in human capital development including health and education systems;
- promoting science, technology and the creative arts to enhance innovation;
- improving social protection programmes, including the Conditional Cash Transfer Program; and
- strengthening the implementation of the Responsible Parenthood and Reproductive Health Law.

In the beginning, President Duterte did not really expend much political capital to push for the passage of important and difficult laws to implement his administration's socioeconomic agenda, leaving economic matters to be dealt with by his economic team. The exception to this is the president's issuance of Executive Order 12 to implement the Responsible Parenthood and Reproductive Health Act of 2012. The implementation of this Reproductive Health Law was blocked by a temporary restraining order issued by the Supreme Court. The president deserves much praise and support for Executive Order (EO) 12 signed in January 2017. Of 6 million women with unmet family planning needs, 2 million live in poverty.[4] With the population growing at 1.7 per cent per year, family planning and reproductive health need to be addressed, especially among the poor. President Duterte did not present the 10-point socioeconomic agenda to the public. Almost all of his pronouncements since the start of his administration have been about the "war on drugs"—perhaps indicative of his focus on what he perceives to be the most important problem facing the country. Duterte's approach to the drug problem may be based on his experience in dealing with the drug problem in Davao. Duterte's other public pronouncements thus far have been about eliminating corruption, and charting an "independent" foreign policy and "economic and political separation from the United States".

There is a real danger that people—especially those in Congress—may take President Duterte's relative silence on socioeconomic reforms to mean these reforms are not of top priority to him or the people—and these reforms can therefore be put on the back burner, either because the economy will continue to grow well and/or his economic team can handle economic reforms. Should this occur, it would be a pity and a mistake as the president continues to have strong public support, his party controls

Congress, and difficult reforms will not be easy to pass in Congress. Duterte needs to expend some political capital to get these important reforms passed.

Department of Finance Secretary Dominguez touted robust growth in 2016 as "clear proof that no amount of political chatter from certain quarters could undermine the upward trajectory of a domestic economy that is in pretty good shape under a Duterte presidency that is fully committed to sustaining its growth momentum".[5] While the economy has an internal growth engine that has kept it going—mainly reliant on private consumption demand and public spending—this does not mean the economy will continue its upward trajectory as if on autopilot. There are risks to sustaining robust growth and to making growth inclusive.

MANUFACTURING GROWTH

According to the NEDA, manufacturing posted double-digit growth in both December 2016 and for the full year 2016 due to an increase in production of petroleum products, food manufactures, and transport equipment. Philippine Statistical Authority's (PSA) monthly survey of selected industries for December 2016 showed the Volume of Production Index (VoPI) for manufacturing increased from 5 per cent to 23 per cent in the same period in 2015. The VoPI for manufacturing grew by 19.2 per cent from a 2.7 per cent decline recorded in December 2015. The 2016 full year VoPI manufacturing grew 14.1 per cent from 2.5 per cent growth recorded in 2015. Construction manufacturing sustained an upward trend in response to the increase in demand for residential (19.2 per cent) and non-residential buildings (27.3 per cent) during the third quarter of 2016. Food manufacturing grew 25.1 per cent in December 2016, the highest production volumes recorded since 2013. Secretary of Budget and Management Diokno was quoted as saying that "there appears to be a structural shift: industry, especially manufacturing, has outpaced services. This has significant impact on the creation of decent jobs".[6]

For the full year 2016, PSA data show that manufacturing employment grew by 5.4 per cent from 2.6 per cent in 2015— impressive, considering employment growth in manufacturing actually contracted by 1.16 per cent in 2013. Services employment is the fastest growing sector, registering 7.14 per cent employment growth in 2016 from 5.37 per cent in 2015.

Despite the growth in the manufacturing sector, the share of manufacturing employment remained low at 8.3 per cent in 2016—a percentage that had not changed much since 8.4 per cent in 2010. It is important to note that this is not jobless growth because employment increased.

UNEMPLOYMENT

Unemployment declined to a new record low of 4.7 per cent at the end of October 2016.[7] This brought the number of jobless Filipinos down from 2.37 million in 2015 to 2.04 million in 2016—a drop of 332,000 workers in the ranks of the unemployed. Even more remarkable, this drop in unemployment happened with an even higher labour force participation rate—1.88 million net new jobs were created in the same period despite an increase in the labour force of 1.54 million workers.[8] Clearly, this is not jobless growth.

Overall, the jobless rate declined to 5.5 per cent in 2016 from 6.3 per cent in 2015.[9] The PSA stated that of 68.1 million Filipinos in the labour force, 43.2 million were "economically active"—either employed or unemployed. The employment rate translates to 40.8 million Filipinos with jobs. More than half—55.6 per cent—of 40.8 million employed in 2016 work in the services sector.[10] This, together with the finding that despite growth in the manufacturing sector employment growth there remains stagnant at about 8 per cent, seems to support the strategy of trying to focus on growing high-productivity services rather than the traditional focus on the manufacturing sector in order to generate quality employment.

The agricultural sector, on the other hand, suffered a decline in farm output of 1.4 per cent in 2016 due to very dry conditions from El Niño and wet conditions from typhoons.[11] Farm output worsened from 2015 and declined in all quarters of 2016 except the third quarter.

Why is the decline in farm outputs significant? Most of the poor are in rural areas. More importantly, according to de Dios and Dinglasan, 44 per cent of those employed in the agricultural sector are poor.[12] Of 33.9 million employed Filipinos—26.9 per cent are in the agricultural sector[13]—a number that has not changed much since 2010.

Another important feature of the unemployment problem is that 78 per cent of the jobless comprise young workers between 15 and 34 years of age. In fact, half of unemployed youth are 24 years old and younger, with more than one in three (34 per cent) having attended college, and one in five (20.5 per cent) a college graduate.[14]

Despite relatively low unemployment rates, underemployment remains high at 18 per cent—as a low unemployment rate does not necessarily capture a high underemployment rate.

De Dios and Dinglasan explain that using open unemployment to measure the welfare effects or inclusiveness of growth is incorrect.[15] They also point out that given the large informal employment sector in the Philippines, with an absence of unemployment insurance, open unemployment is primarily a middle-class phenomenon—the unemployed are not predominantly poor, and the poor are not predominantly unemployed. Using data from the Labor Force Survey and Family Income and Expenditure Survey, de Dios and Dinglasan also show that in 2009, there was 17 per cent poverty among the unemployed, while among those employed poverty was higher at 22.8 per cent.[16] Of those employed, the incidence of poverty was also higher at 35.8 per cent among the underemployed compared to 19.4 per cent among the fully employed. Furthermore, the majority of poor people in the Philippines are not unemployed but rather among the employed. Of 13 million people officially classified as poor in 2009, less than 4 per cent were unemployed. Most of the poor in 2009 were employed—42 per cent even fully employed—while 21 per cent were underemployed.[17] De Dios and Dinglasan therefore conclude that unemployment is a middle-class phenomenon. Unemployment was lowest among the poorest fifth of the population at only 5.1 per cent then rose steeply to between 7 and 9 per cent among the middle classes.[18]

The data on unemployment emphasize the fact that government programmes and policies need to be focused on the right issue to become truly inclusive. Clearly, policies to simply reduce unemployment rates would miss the point. There is a need to raise productivity and incomes of people who are employed. The 10-point socioeconomic agenda is on the right path by emphasizing the importance of investment in human capital—including education and health—and in trying to raise agricultural productivity—as most of the poor live in rural areas. Public and private investment in agriculture and agro-processing linking farmers to markets and higher value-added global supply chains will not only increase incomes but also pave the way for structural transformation to higher productivity service sector employment.

Perhaps the new paradigm of economic development will shift away from the necessary role of manufacturing sector growth in the Philippine's development. We have already seen that, despite growth in the manufacturing sector, the share of employment in manufacturing remained stagnant at about 8 per cent of total employment. There is also global evidence that more automation and labour-saving production techniques are already a reality in manufacturing. As service-related industries already account for almost half of all employment, the challenge is to enable more people to get jobs in high-productivity services like finance, business outsourcing, accounting, and other professional services—to not only raise incomes and growth, but to make growth more inclusive. To grow the services sector and solve the problem of low-productivity employment, there needs to be investment in infrastructure—roads, energy, water—human capital, faster and reliable internet services, communications facilities and other service-related industries.

GOVERNMENT SPENDING AND INFLATION

The Duterte administration has a very ambitious and justifiable programme of spending on infrastructure, given the lack of adequate infrastructure in the country. The amount of government spending on infrastructure rose by over two-fifths to PhP426.3 billion in the January–November 2016 period, according to data from the Department of Budget and Management. The end-November infrastructure spending accounted for 80 per cent of the revised full year 2016 programme.[19] According to the government, annual investment equivalent to 7 per cent of GDP needs to be undertaken, from the programmed 5.3 per cent of GDP for infrastructure amounting to PhP850 billion in 2017—in order for the country to attain high-income status in one generation.[20] Half of this amount is to be raised through an improvement in tax collection and efficiency while the other half is to come from tax policy reform.

There is, however, a real danger that fiscal gains—including the Philippine's return to investment grade status, and the ample fiscal space created by the previous administration—will be reversed if tax reforms remain in limbo.

Recently, Phase I of the tax reform law was passed by Congress and took effect on 1 January 2018. Unfortunately, the upward adjustment of taxes on petroleum came at a bad time, when world oil prices are even higher than they were in 2016. Dubai oil prices had been under US$50 per barrel before December 2016. However, Dubai's oil price exceeded US$50 per barrel in the first week of December 2016 as members of the Organization of Petroleum Exporting Countries (OPEC) agreed to reduce production. Prices of domestic petroleum products followed suit. Had the increase in oil excise taxes been applied earlier, the government would have generated more revenue. Instead, not only did the government earn less revenue due to the higher price of oil products, it is more difficult to increase the excise oil tax when prices of petroleum products are already high due to reduction in oil supply production. In any case, increases in transport and food prices followed the increase in the excise taxes on petroleum products, which impact the poor disproportionately.

The tax reform bill is designed to both generate necessary revenue to fund infrastructure and social expenditure and to make the tax system more progressive and fairer. Aggressive spending on infrastructure has not yet taken off in earnest. Two years since the start of the Duterte administration, Secretary of Budget and Management Diokno has proposed shifting to a cash-based budget to hasten spending, but many in Congress oppose this proposal. Serious structural bottlenecks in the spending ability of the government remain, e.g., there are not enough contractors and engineers to undertake government infrastructure projects. There are also nationality limits as to who can undertake infrastructure projects. The bureaucracy has a limited ability to plan and implement projects—the Department of Transportation a prime example. As in the past, nothing has yet happened. The Commission on Audit has evidently also become stricter in its audits, making government agencies more cautious in spending and thus also prolonging project implementation, and procurement laws, in general, do not lend themselves to quick spending.

Meanwhile, the government's budget position swung to a deficit of PhP19.1 billion in November 2016, reversing the surplus of PhP6 billion in November 2015.[21] The weakening of the peso (PhP) against the US dollar raises the value of the government's outstanding debt—at a record high of PhP6.105 trillion at the end of the first eleven months of 2016. Foreign debt rose 0.7 per cent month-on-month to PhP2.166 trillion. The depreciation of the peso vis-à-vis the US dollar by PhP1.26 in November from October 2016 led to an increase in the growth in external obligations of PhP55.99 billion.[22] The further depreciation of the peso to the US dollar recently has increased the value of external obligations.

For the full-year 2016, headline inflation stood at 1.8 per cent, slightly below the 2–4 per cent target of the BSP. However, inflation was expected to rise sharply in 2017 and average 3.3 per cent, which the BSP stated was manageable.[23] According to NEDA, inflation in January 2017 rose slightly to 2.7 per cent from 2.6 per cent in the previous month due to upward price movements in non-food items. Higher price adjustments in the heavily weighted housing sector, water, electricity, gas and other fuels pushed up overall inflation. The Deputy Governor of the BSP sees uncertainty in global economic prospects as posing the key risk to inflation.

SOURCES OF FUNDS: TAXES, FOREIGN DIRECT INVESTMENT, EXPORTS, REMITTANCES

Taxes

While the Bureau of Internal Revenue (BIR) collections grew by 9.55 per cent year-on-year in 2016 to PhP1.54 trillion—surpassing the PhP1.44 trillion in 2015—the adjusted goal of PhP1.62 trillion for 2016 was still missed.[24] Even this target of PhP1.62 trillion for 2016 was a reduction from the original 2016 target by the previous administration of PhP2.026 trillion—because the Duterte administration saw this target as unattainable due to below-target performance in the final six months of the Aquino administration.

Phase 1 of Duterte's tax reform proposal contains a proposed reduction in top personal income tax rates to correct income tax creep. Phase 1 also includes a shift to a simplified gross taxation system, a reduction in estate and donor taxes, an expansion in the Value-added Tax (VAT) base, and increases in the automobile and petroleum products excise taxes. The projected loss in revenue from decreases in personal income and estate and donor taxes in the first year of implementation alone is PhP139.6 billion in 2018, to be offset by revenue gains from the VAT of PhP92.5 billion, the automobile excise tax of PhP31.4 billion, and the excise tax on petroleum products of PhP120.9 billion. The Department of Finance estimates a net revenue gain of PhP162.5 billion in the first year of implementation.[25] These additional revenues are meant to partially benefit about 10 million poor and vulnerable households, 6 million of the poorest of the poor plus current 4M 4P Program recipients, who would receive unconditional cash grants. The NEDA Director General also stated that the non-approval of the tax reform package by 2017 would make the 2018 budget extremely difficult to fund because the revenue side would be uncertain and the government would not know what assumptions to apply.[26]

Foreign Direct Investment

Bangko Sentral ng Pilipinas data for foreign direct investment (FDI) inflows show that such inflows peaked to a seven-month high in November 2016 at US$756 million—exceeding the 2016 target of US$6.7 billion. Net FDI inflows at the end of November 2016 amounted to US$6.97 billion, growing by 25.4 per cent year-on-year and higher than the US$5.56 billion in the same period in 2015. Most FDI was in sectors such as the arts, entertainment, recreation, finance and insurance, professional, scientific and technical activities, real estate, wholesale and retail trade. In short, the majority of FDI went into the services sector, not manufacturing. Reliance on the manufacturing sector to grow the economy and provide high-productivity employment is once again not borne out by sectoral destinations of FDI.

While these numbers seem to suggest impressive growth in FDI inflows, it bears emphasizing that in general, the Philippines is starting from a low base and lags behind its ASEAN neighbours in attracting FDI. Among the original five ASEAN countries and including Vietnam, countries generally saw large increases in net FDI starting in 2012, according to United Nations Conference on Trade and Development (UNCTAD) data. The Philippines' net FDI at US$2 billion in 2012 was practically the same as US$1.9 billion in 2011. In contrast—between 2011 and 2012—Vietnam's net FDI rose from US$7.5 billion to US$8.4 billion and Thailand's from US$1.2 billion to US$9.2 billion. In 2016, Vietnam's FDI inflow hit US$15.8 billion, up 9 per cent from the preceding year. The Philippines FDI inflows pale in comparison.

The annual net FDI of the Philippines from 1990 to 2009 was US$1.4 billion. During the period 1970–89, net FDI only averaged US$200 million, suggesting political instability deters FDI. During the period 1990–2009, net FDI of the Philippines averaged a much higher US$1.4 billion. Net FDI almost reached US$3 billion in 2006 and 2007, declining sharply to US$1.54 billion in 2008 during the start of the Global Financial Crisis. In 2009 there was an increase to US$1.95 billion.

Recent political events seem to raise the uncertainty and hence, the risks, faced by potential investors. There is a seeming intolerance by the Duterte administration for any kind of opposition. Examples of how the administration deals with opposition are: the jailing of arch critic Senator Leila de Lima; the attempt to discredit Vice President Robredo; the emergence of former Police Superintendent Arturo Lascanas who testified in the Senate about the existence of the Davao death squads and the president's apparent role; and the firing of several officials for alleged corruption—including cabinet members—charges made by Senator Trillanes relating to the president's alleged multimillion peso accounts in a local bank. Other examples include: the back-and-forth pronouncements of the president about temporarily setting aside the International Court of Justice ruling on the islands in the West Philippine Sea in favour of the Philippines—then his pronouncement ordering the military to occupy these islands and his intention to plant the Philippine flag on one of them. The breakdown of the ceasefire with the Communist Party of the Philippines (CPP) and the New People's Army (NPA) amidst killings of soldiers and policemen by the NPA, with the capitulation of the president to a group of urban poor who occupied housing units intended for policemen and military also demonstrate the rule of law is under threat.

President Duterte has more frequently lambasted the media and the Church, and several apparently government-sponsored (or at least, led by appointed officials) rallies meant to show support for the president were held at the Luneta. The president's health is also a matter of speculation, despite pronouncements he is generally in good health. Meanwhile, daily traffic jams, and trains breaking down daily, plus the delicate balancing act between meeting the demands of the Left to release more political prisoners and distribute land—while aligning the country more closely with China, on the one hand, and keeping the military happy on the other—continue. Whether the seeming descent into anarchy will make the president declare martial law, something he has also mentioned in speeches, gives rise to uncertainty.

There is also greater uncertainty because of shifting positions while new initiatives such as the passage of the different phases of the tax reform bill have yet to happen. With greater spending and no apparent additional revenue sources, there is a risk that macroeconomic performance will deteriorate. This, in turn, will have a negative effect on FDI, which is closely linked to trade. The European Union (EU) threatened to cancel the Generalized System of Preferences Plus (GSP+) privileges for the Philippines due to extrajudicial killings and human rights abuses under the Duterte administration.

Exports

The Philippines posted seventeen successive months of declining exports before posting a 5.5 per cent year-on-year increase in September 2016, based on data from the Philippines Statistics Authority. This positive export growth moderated to 3.7 per cent in October 2016, however, these gains were not enough to improve the performance of merchandise exports for the year relative to the previous year's performance. This was the second year of weak export performance given the 5.1 per cent decline in the growth of merchandise exports in 2015. Abrenica opines the recent modest recovery in export growth may not represent a reversal of the downward trend given the bearish forecast for global trade in 2017.[27] While the current account is still in surplus, it is quite thin at less than 1 per cent of GDP.

The "pivot to China" appears to have been happening even prior to President Duterte's declaration. China is an important export market of the Philippines. The volume of Philippine exports to China increased ninefold and its share in total exports—10.9 per cent in 2015 based on UN Comtrade data—doubled from 2001 to 2016. In contrast, the share of the US market declined from 22 per cent to 15 per cent, even as the volume of Philippine exports to the US was relatively steady at about US$9 billion annually.[28]

The US-China economic and military relationship has important consequences on the world, including the Philippines. China is an important pillar in regional and global production networks. What happens to China's economy—as a result of trade relations with the US—impacts not only on China but on all countries. China is moving towards more domestically oriented sources of growth, weaning its dependence on exports. How successful China will be in this rebalancing act and how sustainable this will be over the medium-run is unclear. If there is a trade war with the US, countries in the region, including the Philippines, will be adversely affected.

In 2000, the EU share of Philippine exports amounted to 17 per cent. Despite this relatively small EU share of Philippines exports, the value of exports going to the EU amounted to US$7.2 billion in 2015. The EU is openly sensitive to human rights violations, so there is a risk that market access in the EU and the GSP+ granted to Philippine exports in the EU that are not subject to tariffs—could be removed.

OFW Remittances

There was a rapid increase of 5.2 per cent growth in remittances amounting to US$24.34 billion from January to November 2016 relative to the same period in 2015. The US$2.22 billion amount of cash remittances in November 2016 represented an 18.5 per cent increase over US$1.87 billion recorded in November 2015[29]—the fastest growth in remittances since July 2008. The main sources of remittances were Japan, Qatar, Saudi Arabia, the United Arab Emirates (UAE) and the United States.

However, not all these remittance data reflect an optimistic outlook. The World Bank report "Trends in Remittances, 2016: A New Normal of Slow Growth", warns that the Philippines was "likely to see the slowest remittance expansion in the past decade, to 2.2 per cent, reflecting a decline in overseas worker deployments".[30] The forecast in growth in remittances of the World Bank is lower than the BSP's projection of 4 per cent. The 2016 World Bank report cites cheap oil prices as being partly to blame.

External Risks

Apart from internal risks, there is greater uncertainty in the global economy given the election of President Trump—whose policy stance is unclear, yet whose pronouncements indicate a more insular and protectionist United States—which would reduce world trade. Business process outsourcing companies (BPOs) and overseas Filipino workers (OFWs) are both sensitive to external risks. Seventy per cent of BPOs in the Philippines are US-owned. The BPO industry generated US$22 billion in revenue last 2017 and employs about a million people. Anti-US rhetoric may affect US FDI to the Philippines, including to BPOs. The US administration's announcement of a border adjustment tax could adversely impact the BPO industry and other US FDI as expenses from operations abroad will no longer be deductible by US firms. Unequal treatment of exports and imports may not comply with the World Trade Organization (WTO) rules and it is possible that the border adjustment tax will be challenged by the EU, for example. FDI is affected by uncertainty.

The US-China relationship, as noted, is very important to the Philippines and the world. Any trade war between these two nations, or among an allied bloc will reduce trade and welfare globally.

Equally, Brexit and the shift towards more inward-looking policies could shrink global trade and the deployment of workers overseas if other countries follow the United Kingdom.

MARKET PERCEPTIONS AND RATINGS

Bond investors have become increasingly nervous given political events and statements from President Duterte and the weakening of the peso against the US dollar by about 16 per cent in the last six months of 2016. The peso continues to be one of the worst performing currencies in the region vis-à-vis the US dollar.

Bond investors were seeking protection from defaults through so-called covenants—in which borrowers are tied down with conditions ranging from credit ratings to debt servicing ratios. In 2016, three out of five Philippine debt issues came with such covenants—a significant increase from 2015 and double the average of the preceding seven years.[31] This is an indication of a fear of deteriorating credit profiles, in large part due to high leverage ratios and shrinking profit margins of non-financial corporations. Lenders could suffer from reduced access to US dollar financing in the wake of political uncertainties and risks brought about by government spending without commensurate ways to finance such spending.

The Fed's impending interest rate hikes could adversely affect balance sheets of domestic firms and banks, especially those with US dollar-denominated debt and floating interest rate debts. Reactions could cause a liquidity shortage in domestic credit markets and put even greater pressure on the peso—further depreciating its value.

Business and investor sentiment will worsen from reduced domestic financing coupled with incomplete or non-implementation of the tax reform plan and the socioeconomic agenda and political problems—which could result in a self-fulfilling downward spiral of the economy. The Philippines' ranking in Transparency International's annual Corruption Perceptions Index of the public sector in 168 countries already slipped from 95th in 2015 to 101st in 2016.[32]

According to the World Justice Project Rule of Law Index, the Philippines was the "biggest decliner" among countries in East Asia and the Pacific—ranked 70th of 113 countries in 2016.[33] According to Chief Justice Sereno, the Philippine's ranking had worsened from 60th of 99 countries surveyed in 2014 and 51st of 102 countries surveyed in 2015—when improvements in the rule of law resulted in part from judicial reform initiatives. Chief Justice Sereno attributed the worsening score to the "brazen" killings of the government's war on drugs and as being indicative of a "serious erosion of trust in the criminal justice system, the civil justice system, and in regulatory agencies, whether singly or combined".[34]

SUMMARY

The Duterte administration inherited a robustly growing economy and unveiled an ambitious 10-point socioeconomic plan aimed at raising growth, reducing poverty, and making growth more inclusive to put the Philippines in the upper-middle income category by 2022. The plan aims to reduce the incidence of poverty from 21.6 per cent to 14 per cent, and lift about 6 million Filipinos out of poverty.

Among the challenges facing policymakers in making growth more inclusive is being able to make correct inferences from economic data. While manufacturing sector growth has risen impressively more recently, the share employment in the manufacturing sector remains stagnant at a little over 8 per cent. Meanwhile, the services sector employs more than half of all employed persons. The usual stages of development and indicators of structural transformation may need to be revised to put more emphasis on the role of high-productivity services as a provider of quality employment. Low unemployment rates may not be an accurate indicator of inclusive growth when underemployment is high—44 per cent of the employed in agriculture are poor, the unemployed are not predominantly poor and the poor are not predominantly unemployed. Unemployment is a largely middle-class phenomenon. The Philippines also has a very high rate of youth unemployment. The policy imperative is to raise the productivity and incomes of people already employed rather than focusing on further lowering the open unemployment rate. The emphases in the 10-point socioeconomic plan on investment in human capital, education and health, and in physical capital to raise productivity are in the right direction.

Annual investment equivalent to 7 per cent of GDP needs to be undertaken—from the programmed 5.3 per cent of GDP for infrastructure amounting to PhP850 billion in 2017—in order for the Philippines to attain high-income status in a generation. Half of this amount is to be raised through an improvement in tax collection and efficiency while the other half is to come from tax policy reform.

There is a real danger that the fiscal gains—including the Philippines returning to investment grade status, and the ample fiscal space created by the previous administration—will be reversed if tax reforms remain in limbo. The president needs to use some political capital to get his allies in Congress to pass the tax reform package *in toto* as soon as possible to pay for increased government spending on infrastructure and socioeconomic programmes. The tax reform package also needs to be passed as the government's budget deficit is rising and external liabilities are rising as the peso continues to depreciate against the US dollar. With tightening finance conditions in the world, the US federal government is looking to raise interest rates in the United States. Rising inflation rate in the Philippines and continuing depreciation of the peso vis-à-vis the US dollar will temper expansionary monetary policy domestically, covenant attached to bonds issued by Philippines corporations, and create greater uncertainty in the global economy—all of which may make financing conditions in the future more difficult.

With export growth still weak and the current account surplus under 1 per cent of GDP, FDI increased but remains low relative to FDI inflows to the Philippine's regional neighbours—and may be sensitive to domestic political events. Remittances increased in the first eleven months of 2016 but are projected to grow slower in the future—with threats of greater protectionism in the world under Trump, after Brexit in the United Kingdom, and with China's inward-sourced growth strategy—resulting in future prognostications being more guarded. An ambitious reform programme is indeed more difficult to undertake given the challenges posed by an uncertain global environment as well as populism—in the Philippines and abroad.

Notes

1. Ben O. De Vera, "PH Economy Expands a Robust 6.6 Percent in the Fourth Quarter", *Philippine Daily Inquirer*, 27 January 2017, p. A12.
2. Ibid.
3. Ibid.
4. "UN hails Du30's RH Order", *Philippine Daily Inquirer*, 14 January 2017, p. A2.
5. De Vera, "PH Economy Expands".
6. Ibid.
7. Cielito F. Habito, "Wanted: More Jobs for the Young", *Philippine Daily Inquirer*, 17 January 2017, p. A.11.
8. Ibid.
9. Ben O. De Vera, "Jobless Rate Down", *Philippine Daily Inquirer*, 23 December 2016, p. B1.
10. Ibid.
11. Rommel W. Domingo, "Farm Output Declined 1.4% in 2016", *Philippine Daily Inquirer*, 21 January 2017, p. B1.
12. Emmanuel de Dios and Katrina Dinglasan, "Just How Good is Unemployment as a Measure of Welfare? A Note", *Philippine Review of Economics* LII, no. 2 (2015): 234–45.
13. De Vera, "Jobless Rate Down".
14. Habito, "Wanted: More Jobs for the Young".
15. De Dios and Dinglasan, "Just How Good is Unemployment as a Measure of Welfare?".
16. Ibid., pp. 236–37.
17. Ibid., pp. 241–42.
18. Ibid.
19. Ben O. De Vera, "Infra Spending Picks Up at End-November", *Philippine Daily Inquirer*, 23 January 2017, p. B6.
20. Doris Dumlao Abadilla, "Investors Bet on a Golden Age of Infrastructure", *Philippine Daily Inquirer*, 27 January 2017, pp. B3-1.
21. Ben O. De Vera, "Govt Posts P19.1B Budget Gap", *Philippine Daily Inquirer*, 29 December 2016, p. B4.
22. Ibid.
23. Iris Gonzales, "Inflation to Remain-Manageable-BSP", *Philippine Star*, 21 January 2017.
24. "BIR Collections Rose 9.55% to P1.54T in 2016", *Philippine Daily Inquirer*, 10 January 2017, p. B1.
25. "Urgent Tax Reform", Editorial, *Philippine Daily Inquirer*, 6 February 2017.
26. Ben O. De Vera, "Tax Reform Program Pushed", *Philippine Daily Inquirer*, 22 December 2016, p. B4.

27. Ma. Joy A. Abrenica, "Notes on Recent Performance of Philippine Merchandise Exports", unpublished, 11 January 2017.
28. Ibid.
29. "OFW Remittances Up 5.2% to $24.34B in First 11 Months of 2016", *Philippine Daily Inquirer*, 17 January 2017, p. B1.
30. Ben O. De Vera, "Growth in OFW Remittances in 2016 Seen Slowest in 10 Years", *Philippine Daily Inquirer*, 8 October 2016, p. B1.
31. Andy Mukherjee, "Philippine Bond Jitter Bode Ill", *Bloomberg*, 6 December 2016.
32. Damien Stroka, "Transparency International: Rise in Populism Risks Worsening Corruption; Philippines Ranks 101 of 176", *Agence France-Presse/Interaksyon.com*, 25 January 2017.
33. Tricia Aquino, "Sereno Laments 'Brazen' Killings as OH Becomes 'Biggest Decliner' in Region's rule of Law Index", *Interaksyon.com*, 27 January 2017.
34. Ibid.

5

The Philippine Economy: Renewed Dynamism, Old Challenges

Christopher Cabuay and Hal Hill

INTRODUCTION

The transition from the second Aquino administration to the Duterte administration is a critical period in Philippine economic history. For most of the current decade, the Philippines has been one of the most dynamic economies in the world, growing at a rate not far short of the Asian giants, China and India, and a good deal faster than its traditional neighbouring comparator, Thailand. The Philippines appears to have discarded its "sick man of Asia" epithet. The record is all the more notable for having occurred in the aftermath of the global financial crisis, and during an era characterized by slow global growth and considerable financial volatility.

However, earlier periods of economic dynamism have not been sustained. The Philippines has a history of boom and bust economic cycles, in which periods of economic growth are followed by a crisis, or at least a major growth slowdown. The question is, will this time be different? The current growth acceleration broadly coincides with the 2010–16

Aquino administration. Yet, in spite of the current political controversies, the economic dynamism continued into the first eighteen months of the Duterte administration.

It is premature to pass judgement on the Duterte administration's economic record. This chapter therefore provides an analytical narrative of the drivers and outcomes of the Philippine's recent economic performance. Some of the key development challenges will be explored, including the importance of maintaining macroeconomic stability—and, by extension, crisis avoidance—and constructing a more inclusive growth path.

Section 2 provides an economic survey, including growth, structural change and macroeconomic management. Section 3 then investigates some key development issues and challenges—including the business process outsourcing (BPO) success story, overseas employment, regional (subnational) dynamics, living standards, and institutional development. Section 4 sums up.

Where relevant, we compare and contrast the recent Philippine economic record with its middle-income neighbours—Indonesia, Thailand and Vietnam. Historically, Thailand was the most frequently used comparator. Around 1960 Philippine per capita income was about double that of Thailand. By the mid-1990s, the relativities had been reversed owing to Thailand's faster growth and the Philippines' "lost decade" of the 1980s. In this twenty-first century, the Philippines has begun to catch up. Comparison with Indonesia is relevant due to similar economic and political crises of both countries—albeit twelve years apart—and their subsequent political and institutional paths. The two also share geographic similarities, although Indonesia has a richer natural resource base. Vietnam was historically much poorer than the Philippines, but since its Doi Moi reforms of the 1980s, has been converging towards its higher income neighbours.

THE ECONOMY: A COMPARATIVE OVERVIEW

Growth and Structural Change

The Philippine economy has been growing strongly in recent years. In fact, during the twenty-first century its growth rate has been similar to Indonesia and Thailand. The Philippines maintained positive growth during the global financial crisis, and in recent years has been growing at a similar rate to that of the high-growth Asian economies—China, India and Vietnam. The Philippines has now recorded the longest period of continuously positive economic growth, over a period of seventy-two quarters[1]—a remarkable achievement that reflects both the major macroeconomic reforms during the 1990s and the essential political compacts that operated during the democratic era. The 2016 elections and change of government had little perceptible impact on this economic dynamism, with growth of 6.7 per cent in 2017. The sectoral sources of growth have been reasonably broad-based, including manufacturing, trade, real estate and business services. The latter two are closely connected to international remittances and the booming BPO sector—examined in more detail in section 3.[2]

Figure 5.1 shows the Philippine growth record compared to its three ASEAN neighbours over the period 2000–16. Although drivers of growth vary across the four countries, as broadly open economies there are similarities in the cyclical growth paths—albeit with country-specific factors at work—including political disturbances in the Philippines in 2001, and the commodity boom in Indonesia over the decade 2004–14. Only Thailand was sharply affected by the global financial crisis—reflecting its higher export dependence—especially in the contracting global electronics and tourism industries in 2009. Importantly for all the economies in the region, especially Indonesia, China maintained high economic growth over the years 2008–10.

Figures 5.2, 5.3 and 5.4 show greater variability in sectoral growth rates across the Philippines and neighbours. Agriculture typically grew more slowly than other sectors (see Figure 5.2). Consistent with the process of economic development, the agricultural share of the economy contracts over time. Agricultural growth is also affected by climatic conditions and natural disasters, as illustrated in the Philippines by two particularly severe typhoons that hit the country in 2016. Agriculture's share in Philippine GDP in 2016 was 9.7 per cent, a figure broadly comparable to its neighbours—Indonesia (13.9 per cent), Thailand (8.7 per cent) and Vietnam (18.9 per cent). One important distinction is that, unlike the other three, the Philippines is not a significant agricultural exporter, reflecting its relative natural resource endowments and restricted opportunities for expansion in its "frontier" agricultural region of Mindanao.[3]

The Philippine industrial record has been extensively documented.[4] The Philippines was the first Southeast Asian country to embark on comprehensive import substitution. In the late 1940s, the newly independent

FIGURE 5.1
Economic Growth, the Philippines and Neighbours, 2000–16

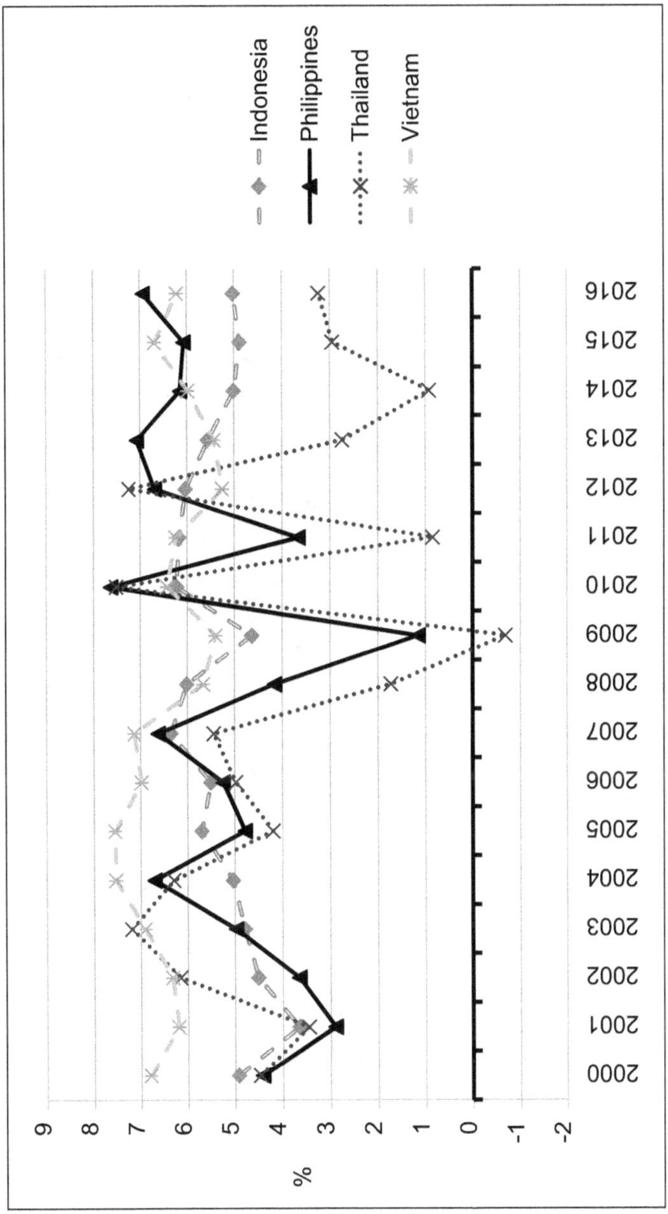

Source: World Bank, World Development Indicators.

The Philippine Economy

FIGURE 5.2
Agricultural Growth, the Philippines and Neighbours, 2000–16

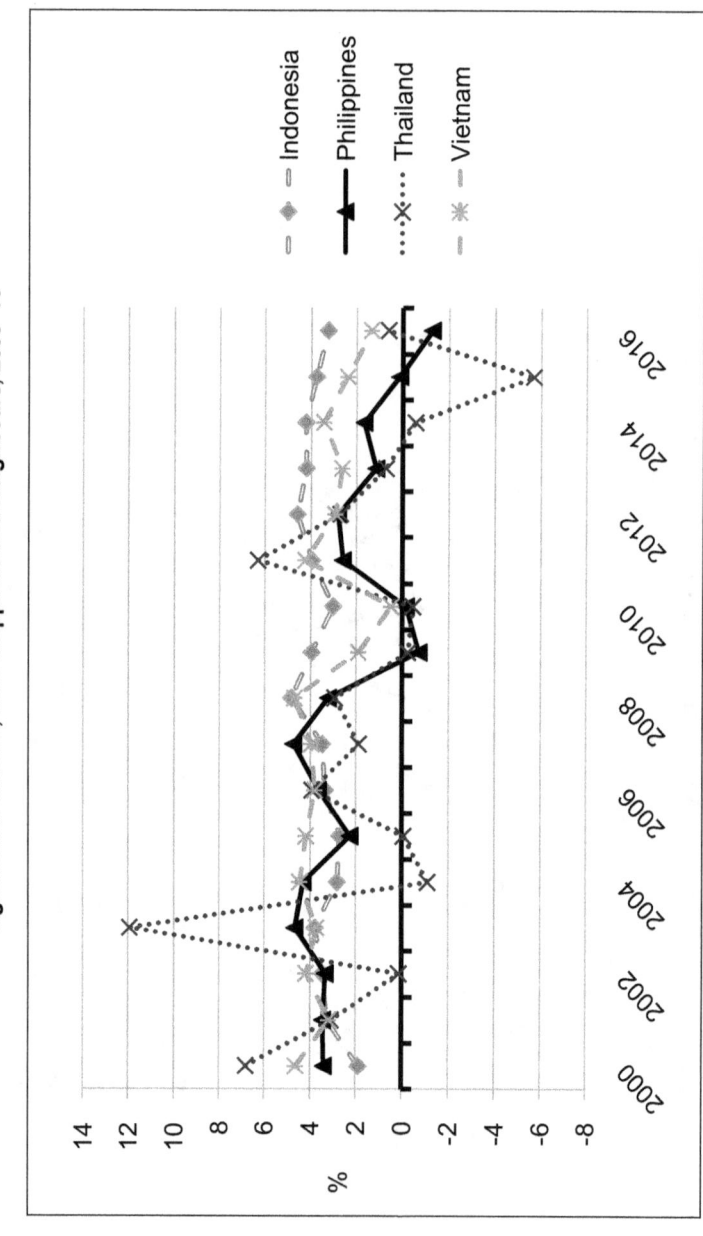

Source: World Bank, World Development Indicators.

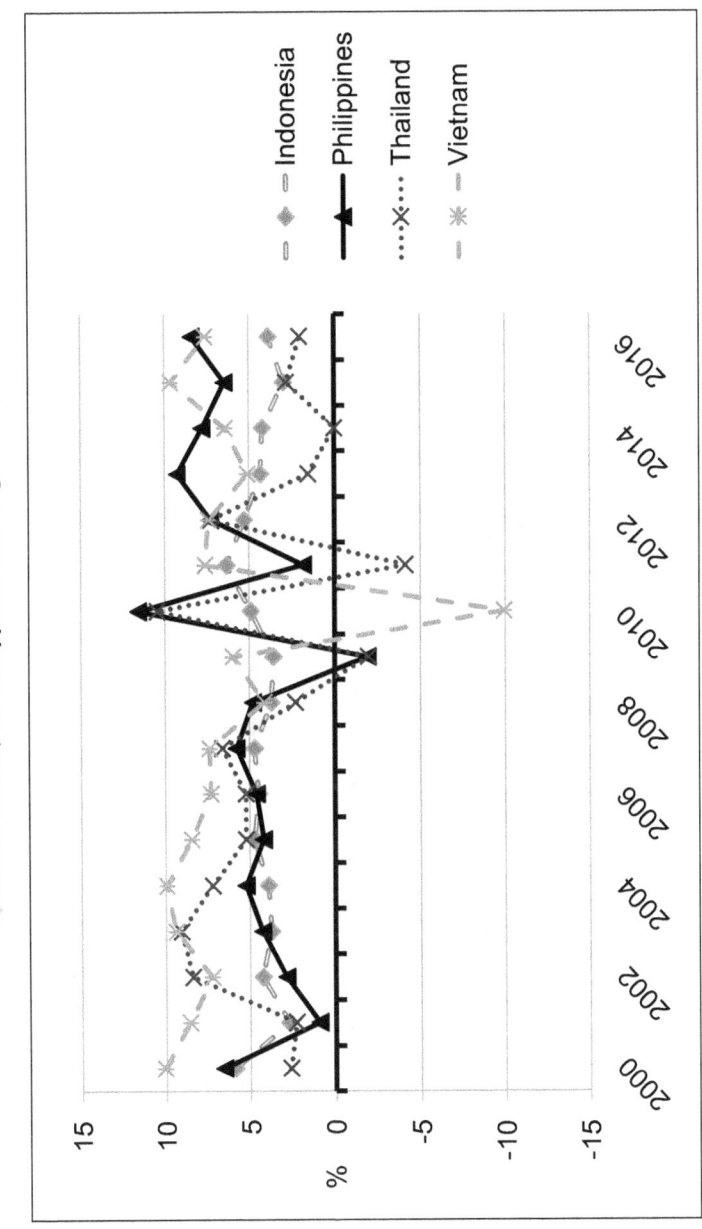

FIGURE 5.3
Industrial Growth, the Philippines and Neighbours, 2000–16

Source: World Bank, World Development Indicators.

The Philippine Economy 151

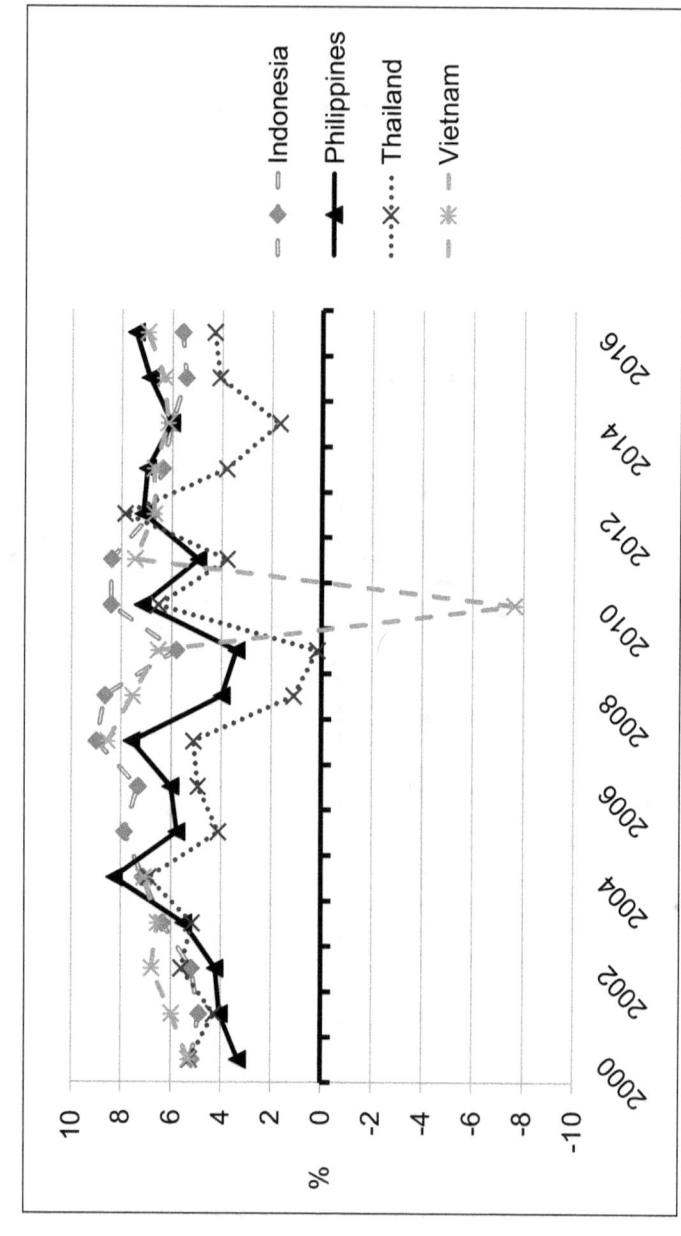

FIGURE 5.4
Services Growth, the Philippines and Neighbours, 2000–16

Source: World Bank, World Development Indicators.

administration introduced a series of temporary import restrictions in response to a balance of payments crisis. These import restrictions became embedded in the country's political economy structures, proving extremely difficult to remove. Power and Sicat's seminal study stated:

> The adoption of a strategy of encouraging manufacturing behind protection was more or less inadvertent ... and what began as an emergency tactic in balance of payments policy became the principal instrument for promoting industrialization over the decade of the 1950s.[5]

When reforms eventually commenced in the late 1970s, it proved extremely difficult to overturn these high levels of protection. The deep economic crisis of the 1980s then overwhelmed reforms, which both delayed their implementation and resulted in the country almost missing out on major industrial relocations from Japan and the Newly Industrializing Economies (NIE) to Southeast Asia. The Philippines only began to effectively adopt an export-oriented strategy—already successfully implemented by its neighbours—in the 1990s.

The Philippine industrial record has been mixed since the 1990s (Figure 5.3). One perspective on the Philippine's record is its export performance in the world market for three labour-intensive manufactures—electronics, garments and footwear—which have been the backbone of East Asia's successful export-oriented industrialization.[6] Electronics now account for over half of intra-ASEAN and intra-East Asian trade. Electronics are typically referred to as "fragmentation trade", reflecting the fact that much of the trade is in parts and components are manufactured for assembly in the final destination market—most commonly China.[7] The 1990s reforms paid dividends for the Philippines, as the country's global share of the fragmentation trade at the turn of the century was a respectable 3.2 per cent—higher than Thailand and well above its lower middle-income neighbours. By 2015, however, this had halved, and was overtaken by Thailand and Vietnam, but not Indonesia. A similar pattern was evident in garments, where, over the same period the Philippine share fell from 1.4 to 0.4 per cent, below all the major ASEAN economies—including Cambodia with 1.4 per cent. In footwear the Philippine share was minuscule, at less than 0.1 per cent, with the comparable figures for Indonesia and Vietnam at 3.7 per cent and 10.1 per cent respectively.

These three areas of manufacturing are just one aspect of Philippine industrialization—albeit a crucial aspect. These labour-intensive industries have had transformative labour market and effects on poverty in neighbouring economies and are a factor in understanding the country's relative slow record in poverty reduction, which we discuss below. It is also indicative of the unfinished reform agenda in the Philippines, including its relatively restrictive foreign investment regime, tightly regulated labour market, and lagging internationally oriented logistics.

As is well documented, the services sector has been the most dynamic in the Philippines and is the largest sector, generating about 59 per cent of GDP and 55 per cent of employment. The Philippine GDP share is higher than Malaysia and Thailand, even though these two countries have much higher per capita incomes—and therefore would be expected to have a higher service share. The story is mixed, featuring a dynamic modern sector, much of it BPOs (see section 3) alongside low productivity, "last-resort" employment activities. For this reason, the implied relative labour productivity, which is similar to the economy-wide average, conceals a lot of intra-sector variability. Figure 5.4 shows services growth has been subject to less volatility, reflecting the absence of seasonality and other factors that cause growth fluctuations in agriculture and industry. In recent years, international remittances—which typically drive a lot of service industry—have remained buoyant, and largely unaffected by global economic volatility.[8]

Macroeconomic Management

A defining feature of the Philippine economy since the 1980s economic crisis has been greatly improved macroeconomic management, particularly monetary policy and the exchange rate. This reflects the far-sighted decision to re-establish the central bank, now the Bangko Sentral ng Pilipinas (BSP), as an independent, professional entity with clearly defined policy objectives. As Figure 5.5 shows, the Philippines has now become a moderately low inflation economy. It has achieved this record in spite of periodic political turbulence, for example, during the Macapagal Arroyo administration, occasional Congressional fiscal logjams, and international financial shocks. In this respect, its record now closely resembles that of traditionally low inflation Thailand, more than it does that of Indonesia and Vietnam, with their histories of hyperinflation and which occasionally still struggle to contain inflation.

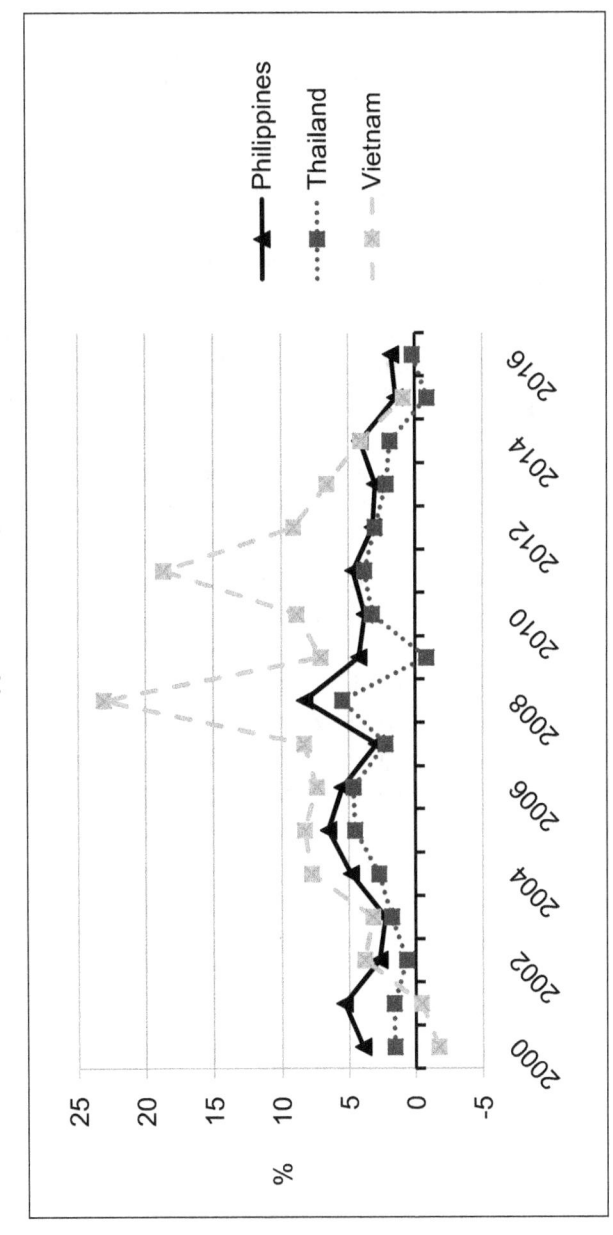

FIGURE 5.5
Inflation, the Philippines and Neighbours, 2000–17

Source: World Bank, World Development Indicators.

The floating rate regime has been managed well by the BSP. The BSP "depoliticized" the exchange rate, and also played a role as a shock absorber, enabling the Philippine peso to adjust to changing domestic and international circumstances. Figure 5.6 shows the Philippine currency has tended to depreciate in periods of domestic political and economic uncertainty—as in the early mid-2000s, when events triggered capital flight—and to appreciate during periods of stronger economic growth. Note that in Figure 5.6 an upward movement represents a currency depreciation. The rates are normalized at 100 for the base period of 2000. Movements in terms of trade have not had a major impact on the Philippine exchange rate—reflecting the broader range of factors influencing the country's international transactions than was historically the case. The relatively stable rate during the global financial crisis, 2008–9, is also noticeable compared to Indonesia, for example, indicating both the country's economic resilience over this period and the buoyant international remittances.

Exchange rates and the stock market are two of the most closely observed early indicators of a country's economic and political circumstances. With an open international capital account, which the Philippines has, capital flows are highly sensitive to changed circumstances. Other data series, notably the national accounts, move more slowly since they also incorporate the effects of investment decisions taken several quarters earlier. As we have seen above, the country's economic momentum has changed little in the transition from the Aquino to the Duterte administration. What do these short-term indicators—the exchange rate (Figure 5.6) and the stock market (Figure 5.7)—tell us about the response of international capital markets to the Duterte administration? Here too, we need comparative data, since for small open economies like those in Southeast Asia, international capital flows and general sentiments towards emerging market economies may be more important than domestic factors. Figure 5.7 therefore also includes stock market data for Indonesia and Thailand. Vietnam does not yet have a fully functional stock market, and its exchange rate is more heavily managed.

The Philippine peso (PhP) has weakened since the election of President Duterte, but it is important not to draw conclusions at this stage. Neither the president's more inflammatory speeches directed at the European Union (EU) and the United States nor the Marawi conflict appear to have affected investor sentiment in any significant way.

FIGURE 5.6
Exchange Rates, the Philippines and Neighbours, 2000–17

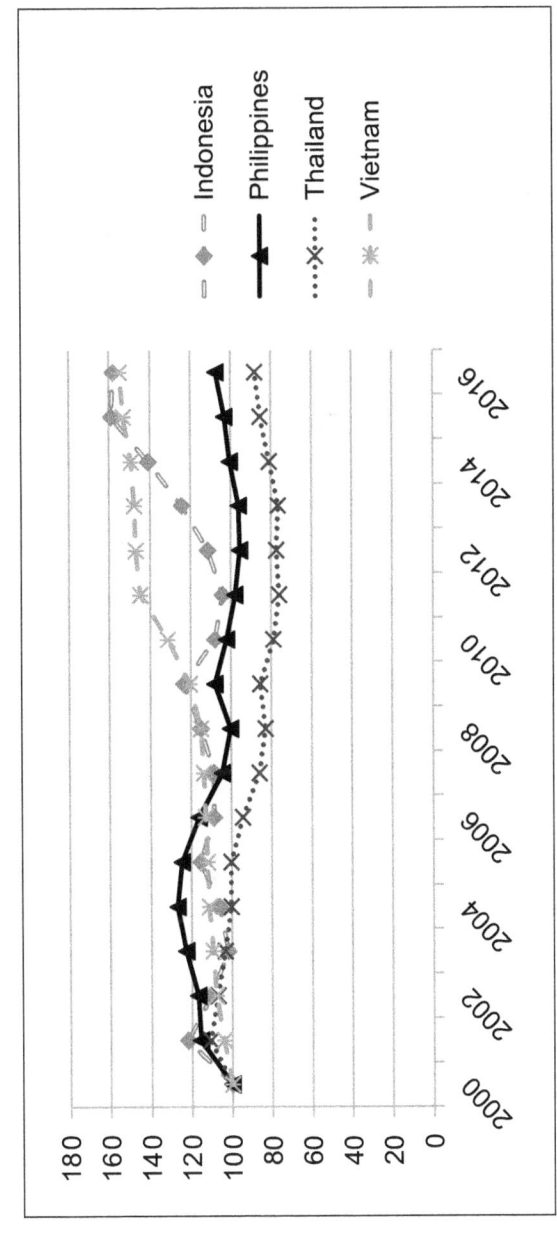

Note: LCU per US dollar, year 2000 exchange rate = 100 used as an index.
Source: World Bank, World Development Indicators.

FIGURE 5.7
Stock Market Indices, the Philippines and Neighbours, 2013–17

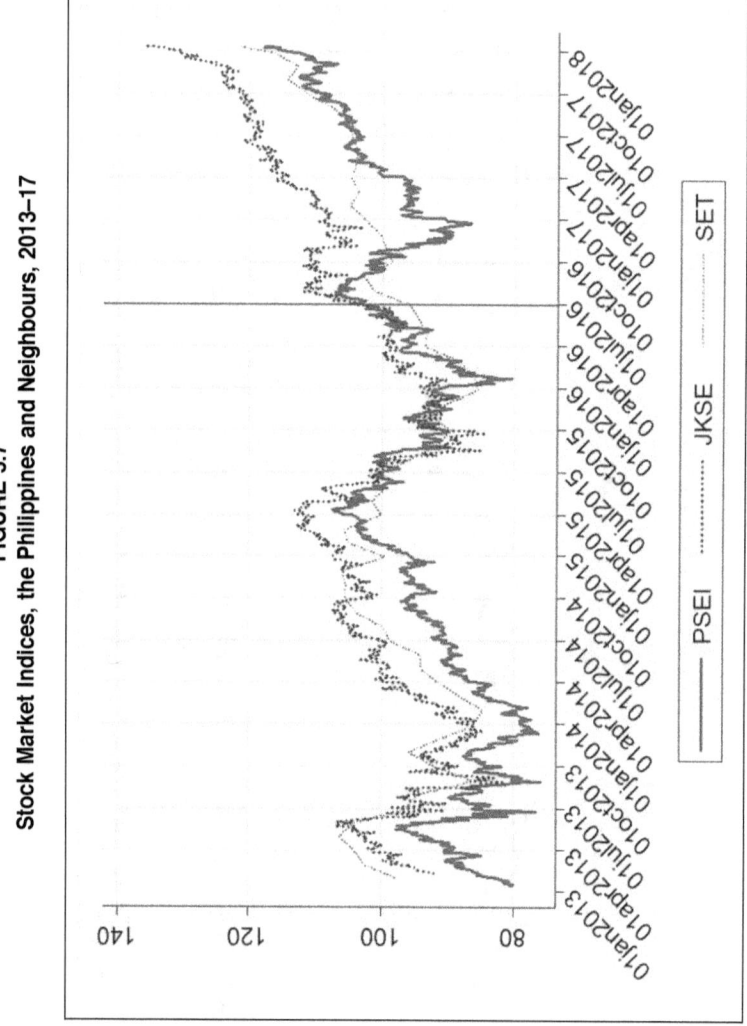

Note: Series for Stock Exchange of Thailand (SET) uses only a monthly index due to data limitation. The indices of June 2016 were set to 100 to make indices comparable, otherwise, the PSEI would be around 7,000's, JKSE at 5,000's, and SET at 1,400's.
Source: Yahoo Finance Stock Exchange Indices.

There is no inherent virtue in having a "strong" currency, as the exchange rate simply reflects supply and demand factors for the country's currency. The exchange rate therefore adjusts, for example, to lower or higher exports and imports, and sentiments in capital markets. The weakening peso also provides a competitive boost, increases domestic purchasing of remittances, and is consistent with the economy now running a current account deficit—which reflects large capital inflows to support the government's aggressive infrastructure programme.[9]

There was a significant decline in the Philippine stock market in the first six months of the Duterte administration. By the end of 2017, however, the stock market had recovered, with the Philippine Stock Exchange Index (PSEI) reaching a record high, breaking through the 8,000 ceiling. The stock markets of Indonesia and Thailand moved in a similar direction, outperforming the Philippines, highlighting the importance of both domestic and international factors in these outcomes (Figure 5.7).

The Philippines, like most of its neighbours, has run a current account surplus for most of the period since the Asian financial crisis, 1997–98 (Figure 5.8). This is contrary to the traditional pattern of formerly high-growth developing economies needing to draw on foreign savings to finance their development. Perversely, these poor countries are lending their savings to the rest of the world, and such a pattern reflects their saving-investment imbalance. With slower growth, and more restrictive foreign investment regimes in some cases, these poorer countries are less attractive investment destinations, while domestic savings—except for the Philippines—remain quite strong. A current account surplus implies that net external liabilities are declining. In the case of the Philippines, with its history of high external indebtedness, the risk of debt crisis is lessened. A modest current account deficit, now emerging, is not detrimental to the extent that it reflects stronger foreign investor interest. The key issues are that imported capital flows are directed to productive investments and not dominated by short-term, speculative flows that may suddenly exit the country. These are the two markers by which to evaluate the transition from surplus to deficit on the current account.

The improved monetary policy has only been partially accompanied by better fiscal outcomes. Put simply, successive Philippine administrations have been unable to raise the requisite revenue to supply the goods and services that the community expects. Government revenue has been about 15 per cent of GDP for most of this century—now somewhat higher

FIGURE 5.8
Current Account Balances, the Philippines and Neighbours, 2000–16

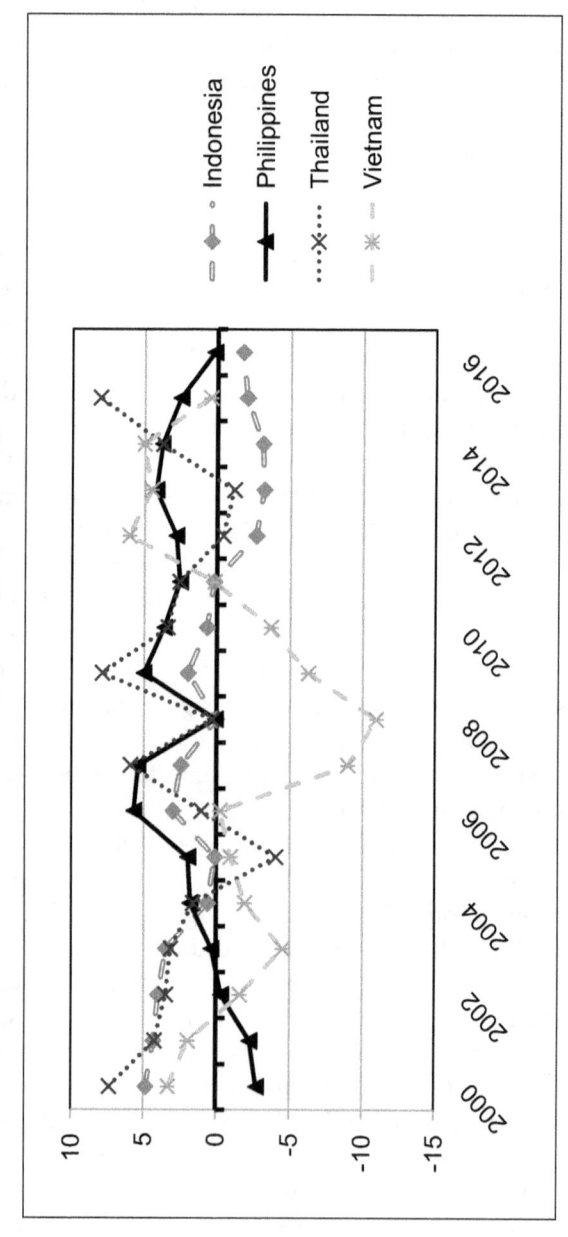

Note: Current account balances as a percentage of GDP.
Source: World Bank, World Development Indicators.

than Indonesia but well below more advanced neighbours, and Vietnam (Figure 5.9). The problem was particularly serious during periods of the Macapagal Arroyo administration, when congressional blocks simply resulted in a re-enactment of the previous year's budget, resulting in significant real expenditure cuts.

Government revenue increased modestly during the Aquino administration. The Duterte administration has signalled its intention to intensify the tax effort through its Tax Reform for Acceleration and Inclusion (TRAIN) initiative—an ambitious and welcome initiative, aimed at widening the tax base, simplifying tax structures, and improving tax progressivity. TRAIN will provide a much-needed boost to infrastructure spending, as well as securing the future of the social policy initiatives. Negotiating the package through Congress was predictably complex, with politicians favouring concessional measures in the package but baulking at the compensating tax increases. Eventually a major reform was enacted with Republic Act No. 10963, passed into law on 27 December 2017. This constitutes phase one of the tax reforms, generating an expected PhP90 billion of additional annual revenue, not far short of the initial target of PhP130 billion. Further tax reform measures are scheduled in the future.[10]

KEY DEVELOPMENT ISSUES AND CHALLENGES

With strong economic momentum seemingly firmly established in the Philippines, we now briefly examine some of the drivers of economic growth, and some of the key policy challenges required to maintain this growth and ensure that benefits are widely distributed. We look at five topics in particular: the BPO success story; international remittances; regional (subnational) development; living standards; and institutional development.

The BPO Success Story

BPOs have quickly emerged as a Philippine success story this century, and the country now ranks as second only to India among developing countries. From a very small base at the turn of the century, the sector now employs over 1 million Filipinos in relatively well-paid jobs. It contributes over 8 per cent of GDP and its revenue of over US$16 billion are over half that of international remittances. Figure 5.11 compares the

FIGURE 5.9
Government Revenue, the Philippines and Neighbours, 2000–16

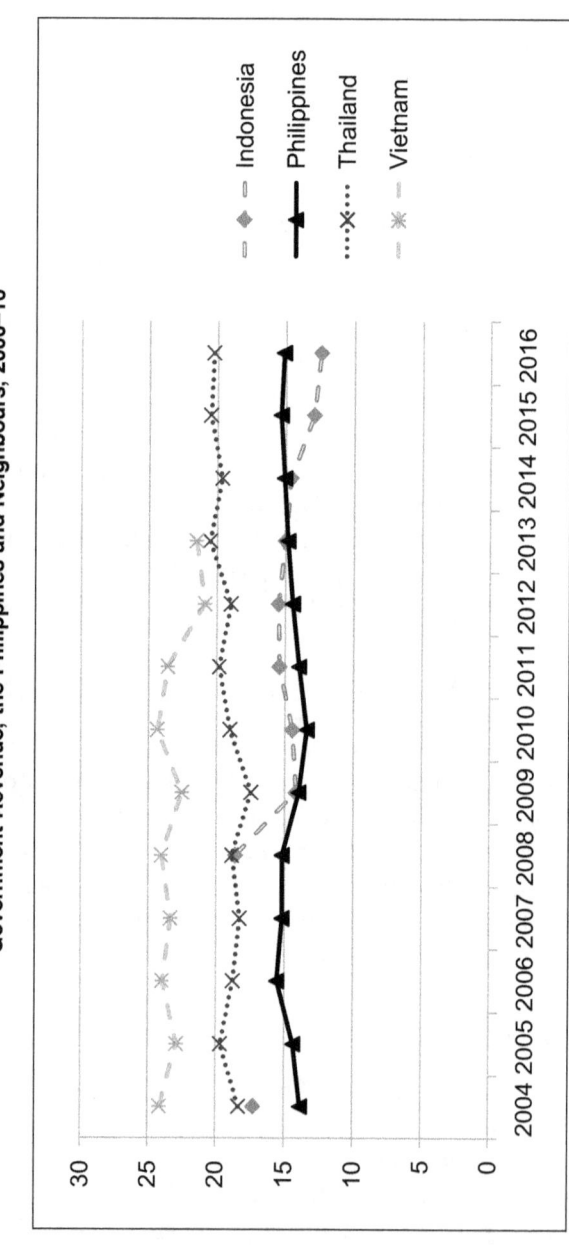

Note: Government revenue as a percentage of GDP.
Source: World Bank, World Development Indicators.

FIGURE 5.10
Fiscal Balances, the Philippines and Neighbours, 2000–16

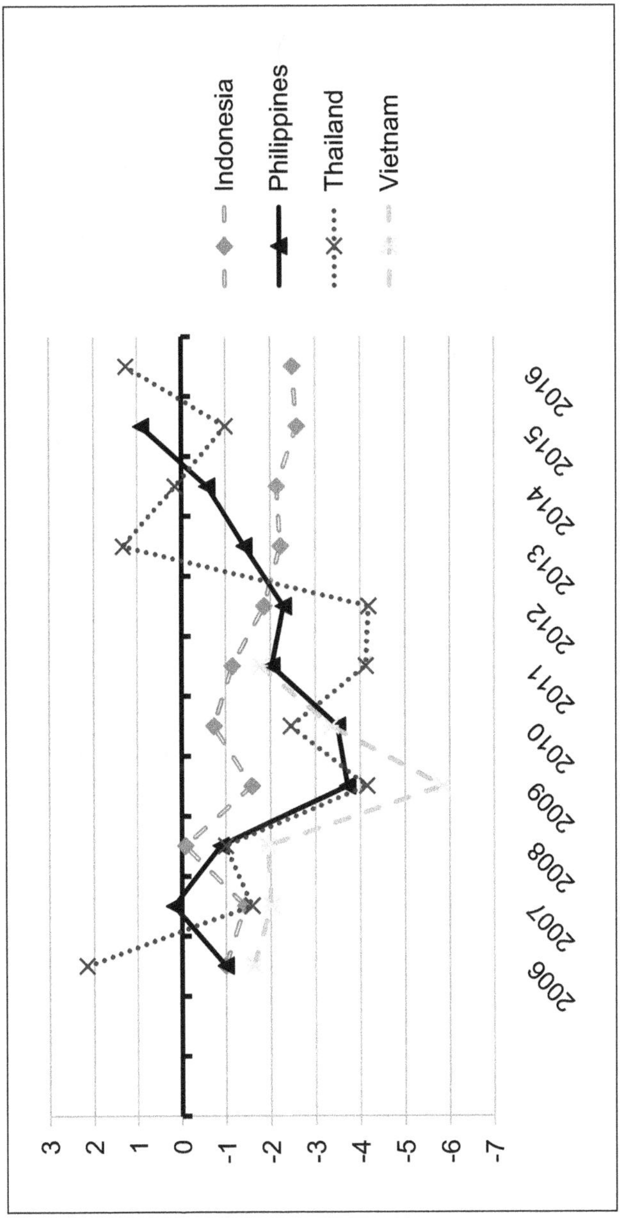

Note: Fiscal balances as a percentage of GDP.
Source: ASEAN Statistical Yearbook 2016.

FIGURE 5.11
Remittances and BPO Revenues, 2000–17

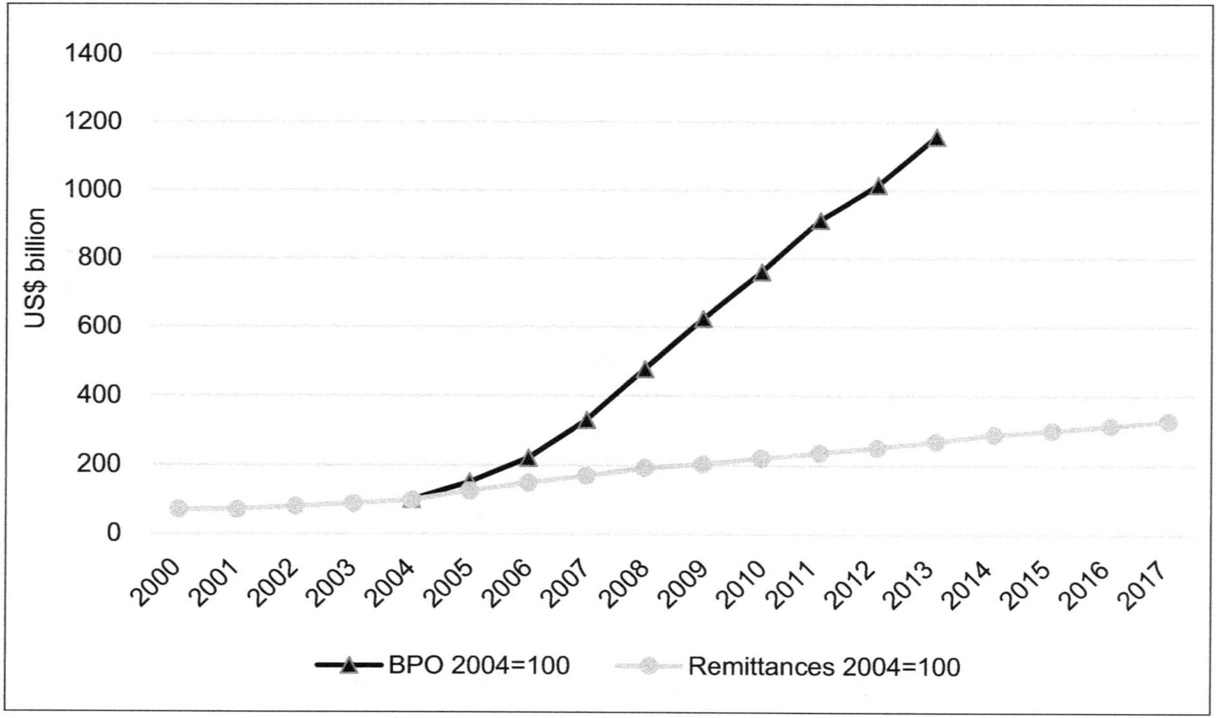

Note: Index where revenue in 2004 = 100.
Source: Bangko Sentral ng Pilipinas, 2013 Survey of IT-BPO Services.

trajectory of BPO revenues and remittances since 2000, basing each series at their 2004 levels. While remittances have remained buoyant over this period—more than tripling in value—the growth of BPO revenues from a much smaller base has been spectacular, increasing some twelvefold through to 2013.

BPOs are essentially internationally traded services that constitute a range of outsourced and offshore business services. Contrary to popular perceptions, they are much more than "call centres". BPOs comprise: voice operations; customer service and technical support; back-office knowledge processing related to finance accounting and human resource administration; data transcription, particularly for the health sector; animation for advertising and other creative industries; game development; software development; and engineering development. Over time, as the industry's reputation and skills have developed, the range and complexity of tasks performed within BPOs have expanded rapidly.

There is a continuing debate about the origins and prospects of BPOs. Two fortuitous factors clearly drove the success. Firstly, the technological revolution in telecommunications since the 1990s enabled these cross-border services to flourish. Secondly, the Philippine proficiency in English language and its cultural and commercial connections to the United States—the major market and foreign investor—gave the country a head start. Fortunately, there had also been a major telecommunications liberalization in the Philippines during the 1990s with the advent of cellular telephony. At the margin, the Philippine investment environment improved as these changes swept across the globe. The country's fiscal concessions, administered through the Philippine Export Zone Authority (PEZA), also attracted some investments—although there is continuing debate about the cost/benefit calculus of these incentives, and whether they are simply second-best measures compensating for the complexities of the country's regulatory regime (see below).

The BPO industry is increasingly competitive globally, as other countries attempt to emulate the success of India and the Philippines. To remain competitive, Philippine telecoms need to be more efficient and competitive.[11] Intellectual property rights need to be strengthened to guard against cybercrime. A more effective system of Information and Communications Technology (ICT) education also needs to be instituted.[12]

Contrasting fortunes of the Philippines in the provision of internationally traded manufactures (through global production networks) and internationally traded services (through BPOs) shed light on the country's commercial environment. Both traded manufactured goods and BPOs involve semi-skilled and unskilled activities. Why does the Philippines perform strongly in BPOs but not manufacturing? The answer appears to be twofold. Firstly, manufactured goods have to be shipped through ports and airports, requiring high-quality international logistics systems—an area where the Philippines lags (see below). BPO outputs obviously do not face this constraint. Secondly, the Philippines has relatively high minimum wages compared to per capita income. Manufacturing firms hire in the segment of the labour market where wage regulations push up labour costs. By contrast, BPOs recruit white-collar college graduates whose remuneration packages are well above the regulated minimum. This illustration demonstrates the importance of "getting the policy right", and how the absence of reform has cost the country dearly in terms of creating employment.

Overseas Employment

The Philippines has long been a labour exporter, dating back to the American colonial period, growing rapidly from the 1970s. As the developing world's fourth largest recipient of international remittances, the Philippines is sometimes characterized as a "remittance economy".

In 2013 the Commission on Filipinos Overseas (CFO) estimated that were some 10.2 million Filipinos overseas, slightly more than 10 per cent of the then population.[13] Of these, about 48 per cent were permanent migrants, 41 per cent temporary migrants, and the rest "irregular". Permanent migrants tended to locate in countries open to such migration flows, with the United States, Canada and Australia as major destinations. Temporary workers went mainly to the Middle East and East Asian countries such as Malaysia that have large migrant worker communities. Presumably many of the "irregulars" were the very large workforce employed as seafarers and on cruise ships where Filipinos constitute the largest single nationality. In 2017 remittances were estimated to be about US$25.3 billion, equivalent to almost 10 per cent of GDP. Most overseas workers were historically engaged in construction, domestic duties and other unskilled occupations. Over time, the range of skills has diversified, with large numbers now in health care, information technology (IT), business services and the entertainment industry.

Drivers of migration include a range of push and pull factors. The Philippines has a large stock of relatively well-trained, English-speaking workers. During periods of indifferent economic performance, there were large incentives to seek employment abroad. Demographic factors are also involved, with a youthful population readily finding employment in rapidly ageing societies. Once these global employment channels became well established, information costs fell rapidly, further facilitating the outflows.

Costs and benefits of overseas employment have been well documented.[14] International remittances are an important means of supplementing and diversifying the sources of household income. Balisacan showed that estimates including remittances lower poverty per capita by several percentage points,[15] and slightly increase inequality—since remittances tend to flow to higher income households. Remittances have been remarkably stable—more so than any other international capital flow—thus providing an economic buffer during periods of international financial volatility. There have of course been costs of overseas employment, including the breakdown of family and societal structures, and risks of mistreatment abroad. There is an ongoing debate about whether migration results in "brain drain" or "brain circulation". In the case of permanent outflows, there will clearly be some loss of skills—although migrants locating in high-skill countries may have enhanced capacity to maintain their contributions to Philippine society. The opportunities for skill acquisition are limited for migrants in temporary unskilled employment. However, the experience may broaden their horizons and aspirations.

There is little the Philippines government can do to regulate these migrant flows in a world of globalized labour markets. If the objective is to reduce the outflows, the only effective strategy is a stronger economy with beneficial employment opportunities at home. As already noted, there is some evidence that this is occurring, particularly through the dynamic BPO sector. The government has a clear role to play in providing education and protection for Filipinos going abroad—especially to some of the more dangerous Middle East locations. There is also a case for developing a more flexible and responsive capital market that broadens investment opportunities for these remittances, beyond the traditional focus of real estate.

Regional (Subnational) Dynamics

Geography is a defining feature of the Philippines. It is the world's second largest archipelagic state and features great diversity in its economy, society and ecology. Governments therefore need to accord a high priority to regional development, especially since large disparities are generally both the cause and consequence of local discontent and conflict. Although the Philippines has not been threatened with territorial disintegration to the extent of neighbouring Indonesia, it is no coincidence that the areas of greatest armed conflict and insurrection are those with the greatest socio-economic deprivation.

The major 1991 decentralization measures transformed the regional economic and political landscape which, while retaining the nation's unitary political structure, devolved much administrative and financial authority to the cities and provinces. Much of these resource flows are automatic and formula-driven through the Internal Revenue Allotment (IRA), further increasing a region's autonomy. The system is now effectively functional, even if—as in Indonesia—there has been no noticeable improvement in local service delivery directly attributable to decentralization measures. President Duterte has recently signalled an interest in adopting a federal political and economic structure. While the ideas and motivations for this proposed reform remain unclear, with a general concern that it may be directed towards further consolidating his political power, it is indicative of the ongoing importance of the general issue of regional development.[16]

Table 5.1 illustrates the Philippine's regional economic diversity. It shows per capita Gross Regional Product (GRP) for the major administrative regions relative to the national figure.[17] Several features of the country's economic geography are immediately apparent. Firstly, Manila dominates the national economy, with a per capita income almost three times the national average, and well over double the next richest region—Calabarzon. Much of Calabarzon is an extension of the capital city. The capital and its immediate surrounds generate about 37 per cent of the country's GDP, depending precisely on where de facto boundaries are drawn. Seen in this light, Manila is one of the world's major primate cities in terms of national economic and political power. Among the other regions, it is no coincidence that the country's second and third cities— Cebu and Davao respectively—are the keys to the regions' prosperity

TABLE 5.1
Philippine Regional GDP, at constant 2000 prices in PhP

		2010	2016ᵖ
	Philippines (PhP billion)	61,570	78,712
	National Capital Region	278.5	295.8
Luzon	Cordillera Administrative Region	120.4	95.6
	Ilocos Region	61.4	62.8
	Cagayan Valley	50.1	49.7
	Central Luzon	81.5	87.2
	CALABARZON	129.4	120.5
	MIMAROPA	60.1	50.6
	Bicol Region	34.1	34.0
Visayas	Western Visayas	51.9	52.7
	Central Visayas	81.2	88.2
	Eastern Visayas	59.6	47.3
Mindanao	Zamboanga Peninsula	55.6	54.8
	Northern Mindanao	79.5	81.1
	Davao Region	78.8	83.6
	SOCCSKSARGEN	59.6	57.8
	Caraga	43.0	45.4
	Autonomous Region of Muslim Mindanao	23.7	17.0

Note: For values at regional level, index generated using national level = 100 as reference.
Source: Philippine Statistical Yearbook, 2016.

and dynamism. Per capita income is at least 80 per cent of the national average in these regions.

At the other end of the spectrum are the very poor regions. Here the counterpart to Manila's relative affluence is the Autonomous Region of Muslim Mindanao (ARMM). In 2016 the ARMM per capita income was only 17 per cent of the national figure, and just 6 per cent of that of Manila. This estimate predates the Marawi siege of 2017, and thus the current figure would be even lower. To put the ARMM figure in some perspective, its income is about half that of the poorest region in Luzon, Bicol, and about one-third of the poorest region in the Visayas, Eastern Visayas, comprising Samar and Leyte.

Manila's economic pre-eminence is long established, reflecting the concentration of political power, financial and human capital, and global connections. The other relatively prosperous regions surrounding Manila—in addition to Cebu, Davao and Northern Mindanao—have been established for decades. Bicol and Eastern Visayas have always had deeply entrenched poverty. Regional inequality has therefore remained high but fairly stable over time—consistent with Manasan and Chatterjee's estimates for the period 1975–2000.[18] The main exception to these estimates is the conflict-affected areas of Mindanao—mainly in the southwest and through the Sulu archipelago—that have slipped further behind the rest of the country. Interregional migration patterns are also evidence of this slippage, with historic patterns of in-migration to much of Mindanao reversed in recent years.

The regional policy reform agenda has been clearly articulated, but is yet to translate into major change. The division of responsibilities between central and local governments is reasonably clear in principle. However, the national government's responsibility to enforce a clear set of minimum governance standards has wavered—most notably in the case of health—which has been decentralized to local governments. Interjurisdictional coordination issues also remain complex, particularly in areas such as provision of infrastructure. Deficiencies in infrastructure have also retarded development in poor regions, which have been unable to exploit their potential in agriculture and tourism. In conflict areas such as Marawi, the overwhelming national priority is, of course, to establish a durable peace and quickly rebuild the economy.

Living Standards

The Philippines has struggled to overcome deep-seated problems of inequality and poverty. Historically, poverty in the Philippines has declined more slowly than most of its neighbours, owing to slower growth and the fact that poverty has been less "growth-responsive"—for a given growth rate, poverty fell less in the Philippines than neighbours.[19] With rapid growth now apparently established, the challenge is to both maintain that growth and ensure it is more inclusive.

Figure 5.12 illustrates both aspects of the poverty story—the country's relatively high poverty compared to its neighbours, and the relatively slow decline in poverty incidence. In the mid-1980s, the incidence of poverty in the Philippines was well below that of Indonesia and Vietnam, and not much above Thailand. By around 2015, absolute poverty in Thailand had been almost eliminated, Vietnam actually had a lower incidence of poverty, and Indonesia and the Philippines had similar rates of poverty. To facilitate inter-country comparisons, these data employ the standard World Bank

FIGURE 5.12
Poverty Incidence, the Philippines and Neighbours, 1985–2016

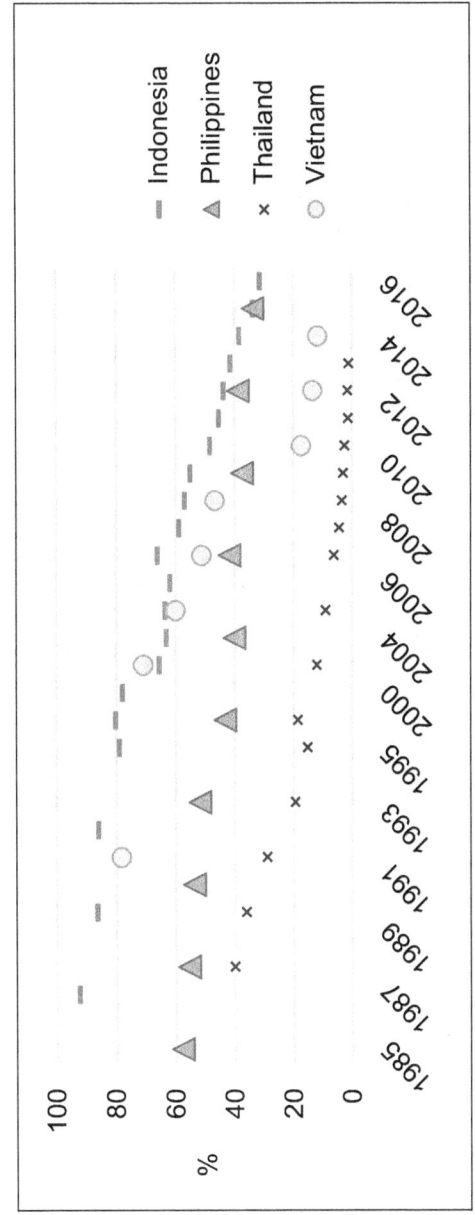

Note: Based on World Bank World Development Indicators' povery headcount ratio at $3.20/day (2011 PPP).
Source: World Bank, World Development Indicators.

international poverty line of US$3.20 per day expressed in purchasing power parity (PPP) terms. Each country defines a national poverty line considered directly relevant to its circumstances. Although these poverty lines generally show a similar trend to international estimates, levels of poverty are not directly comparable.

The relative unresponsiveness of poverty to growth in the Philippines reflects the country's high levels of interpersonal, interhousehold and interregional inequality. The Philippines and Malaysia historically had the highest inequality in Southeast Asia, reflecting colonial histories of agrarian inequality. However, over time the neighbours have "caught up"—dating back to the 1970s in Thailand, and more recently in Indonesia and Vietnam. This convergence is revealed in Table 5.2, showing the ratio of top-to-bottom income shares. The data suggest that the Philippines is now in accordance with ASEAN "norms". However, the usual caveats need to be attached to this conclusion. Income data are less accurately measured than expenditure data. For this reason, poverty statistics, which are expenditure-based, are more accurate than income-based inequality data. Income at both ends of the spectrum is typically understated, resulting in underestimates of inequality. Moreover, imputed income in remote and subsistence economies is extremely difficult to measure.[20]

International literature emphasizes the importance of three key policy interventions that assist in making poverty more responsive to growth—

TABLE 5.2
Top and Bottom Income Shares, the Philippines and Neighbours

	Earliest Ref. Year*	Income Share of Top 20%	Income Share of Bottom 40%	Ratio of Top 20% to Bottom 40%	Latest Ref. Year*	Share of Top 20%	Share of Bottom 40%	Ratio of Top 20% to Bottom 40%
Indonesia	—	—	—	—	2013	47.4	27.9	1.70
Malaysia	2004	51.4	26.3	1.95	2009	51.4	26.4	1.94
Philippines	2000	49.8	26.7	1.87	2015	47.3	28	1.69
Thailand	2000	49.7	27.1	1.83	2013	46.3	28.5	1.62
Vietnam	2002	45.4	28.6	1.59	2014	43	29.3	1.47

Note: * reference years based on data availability in the period 2000–17.
Source: World Bank, World Development Indicators.

efficient and flexible labour markets, broad-based and inclusive education systems, and targeted social welfare policies. It is important to note that these interventions need to be undertaken in a manner that does not disrupt growth momentum.[21]

The first and key policy intervention is the labour market. As noted, the Philippine economy has been unable to generate enough "good jobs", thus forcing many Filipinos to seek employment abroad. While globalized labour markets are a reality, and a positive option for many Filipinos, an anaemic labour market hurts the poor, who typically have nothing to sell but their labour, and for whom mobility options are limited.

The Philippines has historically struggled with high levels of unemployment and underemployment, a feature shared with Indonesia, but not with the labour-scarce economies of Thailand and Malaysia—now major labour importers (Figure 5.13). The less regulated Vietnamese labour market also has low unemployment. Unemployment was high for much of the Macapagal Arroyo administration, but has fallen over the past decade thanks to stronger growth and overseas employment opportunities.[22] The composition of the unemployed in the Philippines also illustrates the nature of the country's labour market. A relatively high proportion (21 per cent) of college graduates are unemployed—suggesting a mismatch between needs of the labour market and education suppliers, which may also indicate extended job searching periods by graduates exploring options at home and abroad.

The second policy intervention, an inclusive and high-quality education system, is essential for lifting people out of poverty—a traditional strength of the Philippines, but one where historic advantage is eroding over time as other countries catch up. Most Southeast Asian countries have achieved close to universal primary school enrolments and literacy (Table 5.3). Rates have been rising rapidly at the secondary level, and the Philippines is no longer an outlier. Education "survival" rates are also high, rising slightly in most cases. However, in this respect the Philippines appears to be lagging behind its neighbours, which is cause for concern. These survival rates correlate with socioeconomic status and region, and therefore tend to reinforce rather than ameliorate inequality.[23] Although the Philippines performs strongly in the quality of its education sector, much of the public and private systems produce graduates of indifferent quality. The Philippines is not a regular participant in various international testing exercises, such as the Trends in International Mathematics and Science

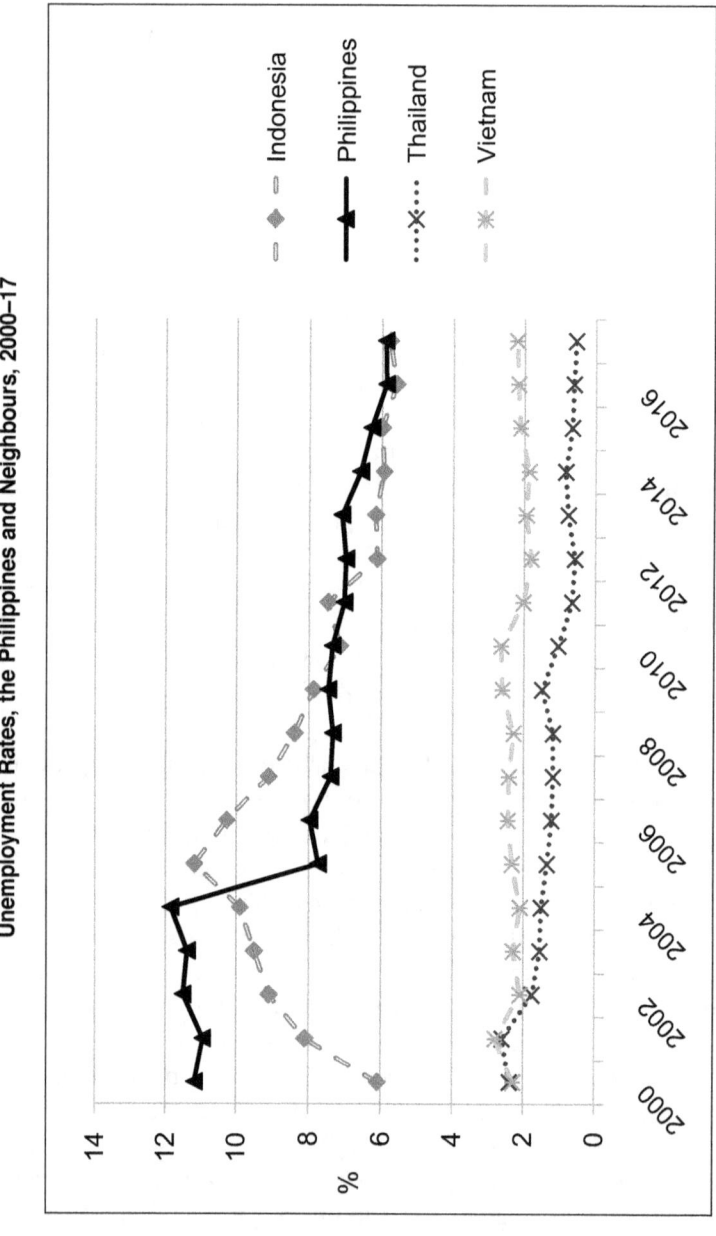

FIGURE 5.13
Unemployment Rates, the Philippines and Neighbours, 2000–17

Source: World Bank World Development Indicators.

TABLE 5.3
Education Enrolment and Survival Rates, the Philippines and Neighbours (%)

Panel A: Primary Enrolment Rate						
Country	2000	2005	2008	2011	2013	2015
Indonesia	—	88.8	92.9	93.3	90.2	89.7
Malaysia	97.8	100.0	97.2	96.6	98.8	98.1
Philippines	—	88.6	88.7	—	96	—
Thailand	—	—	95.1	—	—	90.8
Vietnam	97.2	90.2	96.9	98.0	98	—

Panel B: Secondary Enrolment Rate						
Country	2000	2005	2008	2011	2013	2015
Indonesia	—	53.4	64.1	73.0	75.2	75.5
Malaysia	66.0	68.4	65.2	65.6	67.5	68.5
Philippines	—	58.8	61.1	—	67.4	—
Thailand	—	—	77.2	81.8	—	82.6
Vietnam	—	—	—	—	—	—

Panel C: Primary Survival Rate					
Country	2000	2005	2008	2011	2013
Indonesia	—	—	87.9	89.0	81.9
Malaysia	—	98.9	—	—	94.2
Philippines	—	70.4	75.8	—	—
Thailand	93.6	—	—	—	—
Vietnam	85.7	92.1	—	97.5	89.6

Panel D: Lower Secondary Survival Rate					
Country	2000	2005	2008	2011	2013
Indonesia	—	97.4	92.8	94.6	—
Malaysia	84.7	77.6	91.5	90.8	90.3
Philippines	—	84.0	86.2	—	—
Thailand	—	—	—	—	—
Vietnam	78.2	—	—	82.7	89.4

Source: UNESCO Institute of Statistics.

Study (TIMSS) and Program for International Student Assessment (PISA), and when it has participated it ranks poorly. A major priority area for the Philippine government is to better fund the public system to ensure better performance on quality and equity indicators.

The third element of the "growth with equity" strategy is targeted conditional cash grants. These grants were initiated during the Macapagal Arroyo administration, and are known as the *Pantawid Pamilyang Pilipino Program* (the 4Ps)—modelled on the Latin American *Opportunidades* and similar programmes. To be eligible, families are identified as "poor" from regular Family Income and Expenditure Surveys (FIES) data. Eligible families must have children aged between 0 and 18 years—or expecting a child—and willing to meet the conditions of the programme. These conditions include that the children remain in school, and have regular check-ups—including up-to-date immunization cards, regular deworming—and pre-natal and post-natal care in the case of pregnancies. Monthly grants range from PhP500 to PhP1,400—equivalent to about US$9.8 to US$27.3. A proxy mean test based on the 2006 FIES and Labor Force Survey was used to achieve targets.

There is a large body of literature describing and evaluating this important and innovative programme.[24] Nothing like this had been attempted in the Philippines, especially the targeting aspects. The Philippine administrative structure—including the implementing agency, the Department of Social Welfare and Development (DSWD)—has not been attuned to implement this type of transfer payment. The scheme's viability depends on a healthy national budget, which, while much improved, is still not assured. The programme also requires a degree of financial and IT sophistication not yet developed in rural and remote regions. Local democratic accountability is also crucial to check on the operation of the programme—it is common knowledge that local elites exert strong political power in some regions.[25]

Despite these constraints, evaluations to date are cautiously optimistic. School enrolments and attendance have been positive, as has health care access. There are inevitably "type I" and "type II" errors—recipients who should not be receiving payments and those who are entitled to payments but are not receiving them.[26] There are also frequent reports of outright corruption, but it is difficult to obtain accurate information on the national incidence rate. This is clearly one of the most important policy initiatives in recent Philippine history—as a direct poverty alleviation strategy and also a test case of the government's ability to effectively construct a modern social welfare net.

Institutions and the "Supply Side"

Philippine institutional development and quality of governance are well documented—a story of continuity and change.[27] The obvious and major achievement has been the restoration of democracy since 1986, and implementation of five reasonably credible national elections since then—including mostly peaceful transfers of power from one administration to the next.[28] Alongside the challenge to maintain a democracy has been the difficulty of translating this democratic achievement into quality governance.

We now briefly review this record, in a comparative regional context. Institutions may be regarded as providing "rules of the game" or certain organizational structures, both formal and informal. When effective, institutional structures reduce transaction costs and uncertainty, internalize externalities, and provide secure property rights. Equity objectives can also be achieved, as—in their absence—outcomes are more likely to be determined by access to wealth and political power—unequally distributed in the Philippines. It is important to emphasize that—even though data bases and conceptual sophistication have improved greatly—measurement of institutions and their quality is imperfect and subjective. The following discussion should therefore be treated as indicative, not conclusive.

We select three of the most widely used indicators available for which comparative time series data exist. The first is the World Bank's "ease of doing business" (EODB) indicator—that attempts to measure regulatory aspects of the business environment, from business start-ups to labour regulations and the legal system. The Philippine regulatory complexity is illustrated in Figure 5.14. Across countries, rankings of these indicators typically correlate with countries' levels of development. The Philippines now ranks below not only Thailand but also Indonesia and Vietnam. However, the position of the Philippines has been improving since around 2010, coinciding broadly with the start of the Aquino administration. Perhaps the surprising aspect is that neither democracy nor decentralization have had an appreciable impact on regulatory quality in the Philippines. Deeper reform is needed—bureaucratic reform and an overhaul of licensing procedures.[29]

Another widely used comparative series is the World Bank's Logistics Performance Index (LPI). This data series attempts to evaluate the cost and quality of logistics—broadly defined to include hard and soft infrastructure

FIGURE 5.14
Ease of Doing Business, the Philippines and Neighbours, 2004–17

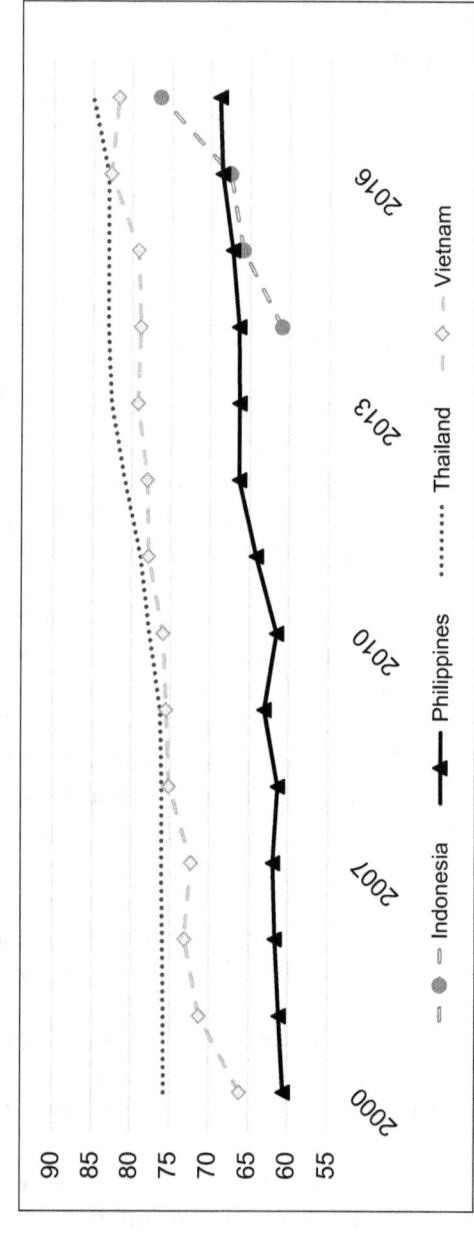

Note: Figures represent Distance to Frontier (DTF) for Starting a Business. Lower scores connote higher distances.
Source: World Bank, Doing Business.

and domestic and international transactions. The inclusive LPI methodology is important. For example, countries may have efficient ports and airports but complex customs and immigration procedures, and the converse may apply. Country rankings are also broadly consistent with their per capita incomes. Thailand is well ahead of the lower middle-income group (Figure 5.15). In most years the Philippines ranks last among the four countries. Customs inefficiency, border management, trade and transport infrastructure and the quality of logistics services all contribute to the Philippine's lower ranking in 2018.

Costs of poor logistics affect the whole economy. Poor farmers pay more to market their crops, city-dwellers suffer long commutes in inadequate urban amenities, and, as previously discussed, major employment opportunities have been lost through the country's low participation in global production networks. There are better prospects ahead—both the Aquino and the Duterte administrations have prioritized infrastructure—Duterte through the "build, build, build" programme. As LPI data remind us, however, better infrastructure requires both money and reform. Reform includes streamlined procedures at borders—especially reform of the corruption-prone Bureau of Customs—simplified (but equitable) land acquisition procedures, and much more.[30]

A third dimension concerns corruption of public office, and rent-seeking. These estimates are survey-based and therefore highly subjective. The data do not distinguish between grand and petty corruption—arguably the former is more corrosive. The data are, however, plausible, suggesting the Philippines has a similar ranking to its lower middle-income neighbours (Figure 5.16). There are variations over time, including an improvement in some of the Aquino years, but no clear overall trend emerges. Data reported in Figure 5.16 are from the Transparency International (TI) Corruption Perceptions Index (CPI). The World Bank's Worldwide Governance Indicators have similar results. Klitgaard's formula that "corruption equals monopoly plus discretion minus accountability" remains a useful framework for understanding the persistence of corruption in the Philippines, notwithstanding its vibrant democracy and a vigorous press.[31] Much of the persistence of corruption can be explained by poorly paid civil servants who implement a complex licensing and regulatory regime, with limited practical oversight and penalties for malfeasance, aided by a permissive political system. These elements also shed light on the dimensions of the reform agenda going forward.

FIGURE 5.15
Logistics Performance Index, the Philippines and Neighbours, 2007–16

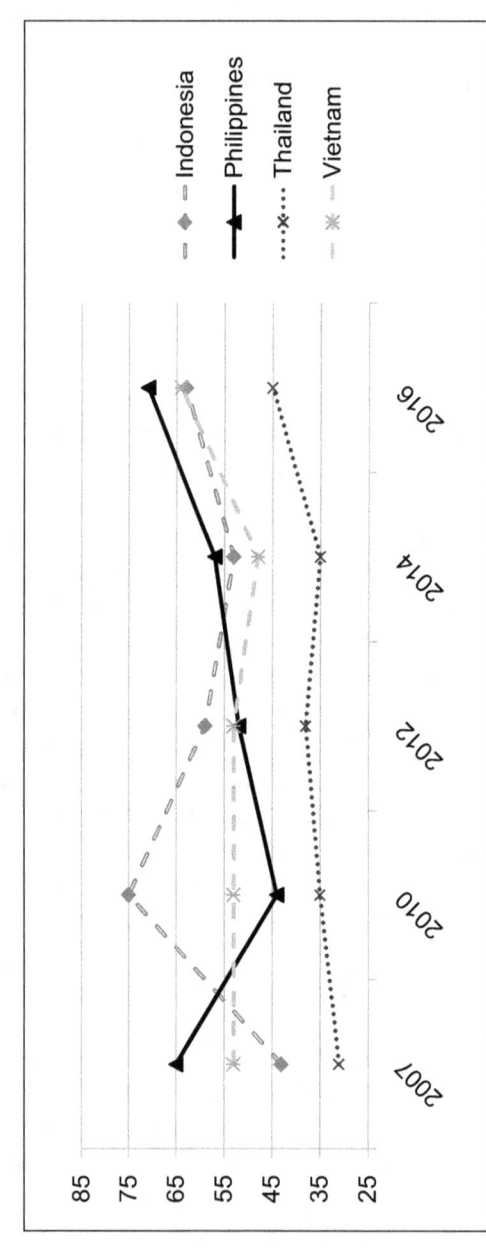

Note: Figures represent ranking out of 160 countries.
Source: World Bank, Logistics Performance Index.

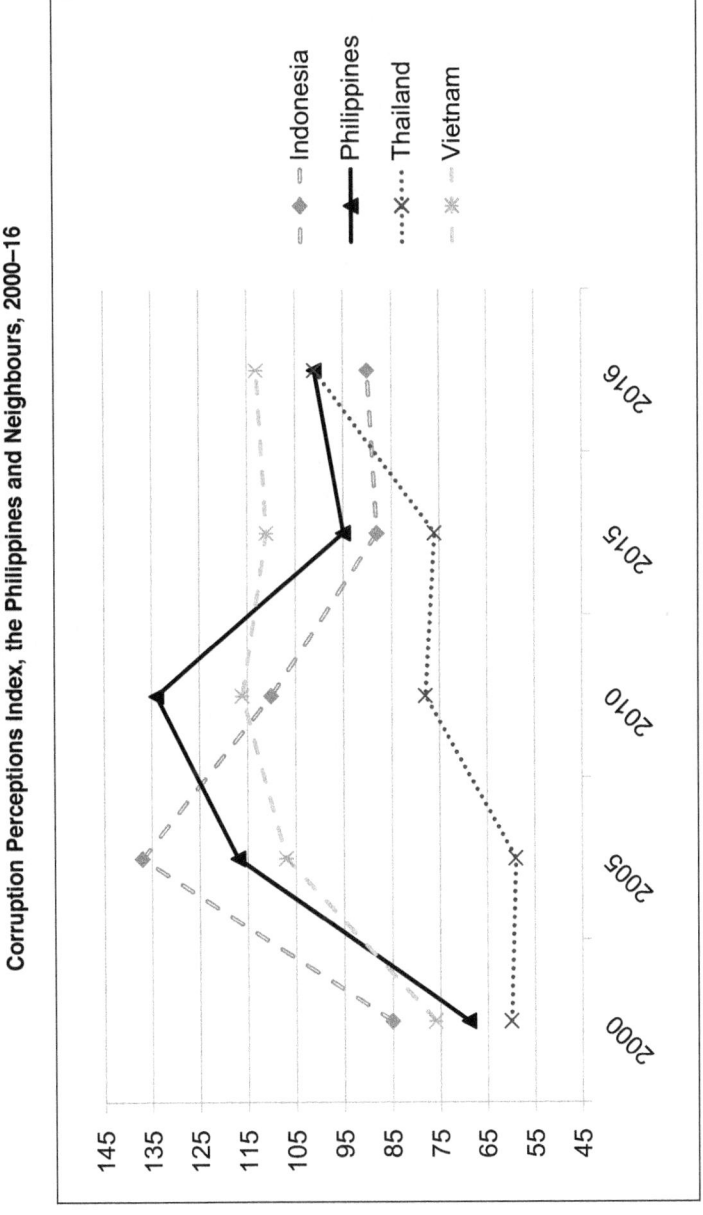

FIGURE 5.16
Corruption Perceptions Index, the Philippines and Neighbours, 2000–16

Note: Figures represent ranking out of 173 countries.
Source: Transparency International, Corruption Perceptions Index.

SUMMING UP

The Philippine economy is in a historically unprecedented period of consistently strong growth for almost a decade. Cast for a long time as the "sick man of Asia", the country now enjoys the unusual moniker of being one of Asia's—and therefore the world's—most dynamic economies. On current projections, the Philippines will graduate to the ranks of the upper middle-income economies in less than a decade. Importantly, this dynamism, which originated in the 1990s economic reforms, has now straddled three successive administrations—in a country historically known for boom and bust growth and policy reversals across single-term presidencies.

Barring unforeseen political developments, there are good prospects that this growth will be maintained in the coming years. The macroeconomic policy framework looks reasonably secure. Growth may be narrowly based, depending heavily as it does on BPOs and remittances, but there are encouraging signs that the economic base is broadening. There can also be no doubt that the growth potential is even higher. Factors that have been holding the Philippines back in the past include the following four.

1. The international economy is now strengthening, and appears more stable.
2. If—and it may be a very big if—peace can be secured in the troubled regions of Mindanao, it would unleash increased economic activity in agriculture, tourism and other sectors.
3. Increased infrastructure investment would remove a major bottleneck on growth, and improve quality of life for long-suffering users of these services.
4. More inclusive growth through improved social safety nets would not only improve societal cohesion but also raise the social productivity of millions of Filipinos who have thus far missed out on the general improvements in living standards.

All manner of negative scenarios can, of course, be constructed. One only needs recourse to Philippine history for examples. The Duterte presidency remains quite popular according to major opinion surveys, but his polarizing governance style—particularly his controversial war on drugs—could at some future stage create deep societal schisms.

Peace in Marawi has been secured for now, but it is precarious, costs of reconstruction are large, and there are fertile grounds for the penetration of Islamic terrorist groups and ensuing conflict. The still narrow economic base means if there were major disruptions to the country's two main export earnings—BPOs and remittances—the country would be hit hard. As noted, the government's fiscal position is secure for now. Navigating major fiscal reforms through Congress, however—especially those that involve significant increases in much-needed government revenue—could encounter difficulties if Duterte's popularity begins to wane or he experiences health problems. In these scenarios, major expenditure increases could be unfunded, aggravating the fiscal deficit. There is also the question of international relations and regional security. The economy has been largely unaffected by the president's attacks on the EU and the United States so far, while the administration has pragmatically recognized China's pre-eminence in the South China Sea. Risks still abound for the Philippines—a country dependent on foreign investment and goodwill.

Notes

This paper was written in early 2018. Owing to the space constraint, this paper aims to provide a broad overview of recent economic developments in the Philippines. See R. Clarete, E.S. Esguerra and H. Hill, eds., *The Philippine Economy: No Longer the East Asian Exception?* (Singapore: ISEAS – Yusof Ishak Institute, 2018) for a more detailed examination of some of the issues we highlight.

1. Note of course that this record refers to GDP growth, not growth in GDP per capita. In low-growth years, such as 2009, GDP per capita fell slightly.
2. Unless otherwise indicated, when we cite Philippine statistics they are sourced from the Philippine Statistical Authority (PSA), including its website (http://psa.gov.ph) and various press releases and other communications.
3. Note here that agriculture's employment share in the Philippines is about three times that of its output share. In other words, agricultural labour productivity is about one-third that of the economywide average, a figure that is indicative of the sector's low earnings and deep-seated poverty.
4. Gerardo P. Sicat, *Cesar Virata: Life and Times through Four Decades of Philippine Economic History* (Quezon City: University of the Philippines Press, 2014).
5. John H. Power and Gerardo P. Sicat, *The Philippines: Industrialization and Trade Policies* (Oxford: Oxford University Press, 1971), p. 33.
6. The statistics in this paragraph draw on Hal Hill and Deasy Pane, "Indonesia and the Global Economy: Missed Opportunities?", in *Indonesia in the New*

World: Globalization, Nationalism and Sovereignty, edited by Muhamad Chatib Basri, Mari Pangestu, and Arianto Patunru (Singapore: ISEAS – Yusof Ishak Institute, 2018). Our thanks to Deasy Pane for computing these numbers.
7. Prema-Chandra Athukorala, "Global Production Sharing and Trade Patterns in East Asia", in *Oxford Handbook of the Economics of the Pacific*, edited by Inderjit Kaur and Nirvikar Singh (New York: Oxford University Press, 2014), pp. 333–61.
8. Of note in Figure 5.4 is the sharp decline in Thai services growth in 2009–10, presumably reflecting the global fall in tourism during the global financial crisis. This sector has great (but largely unrealized) potential in the Philippines.
9. The issues are clearly set out in Raul Fabella, "Who's Afraid of a Weak Peso?", *Business World*, 25 September 2017, http://bworldonline.com/whos-afraid-weak-peso/.
10. See Cesar E.A. Virata, "Economic wins and lives lost during Duterte's first year", *East Asia Forum*, 8 February 2018, http://www.eastasiaforum.org/2018/02/08/economic-wins-and-lives-lost-during-dutertes-first-year/.
11. A third provider has now been licensed in addition to the current duopoly, although the liberalization was implemented in a non-transparent manner.
12. For a set of policy recommendations see Tereso S. Tullao, Jr., Rhory Fernandez, Chris Cabuay, and Denise Serrano, "IT-BPO Industry Profile, Prospects, Challenges and Issues for Growth and Employment", *AKI Policy Brief* IV, no. 2 (2012).
13. More up-to-date statistics from the CFO are expected shortly, pending revisions to its methodology for estimating the number of Filipinos living abroad.
14. Tereso Tullao and Chris Cabuay, "International Migration and Remittances: A Review of the Economic Impacts, Issues, and Challenges from the Sending Country's Perspective", in *Entrepreneurship and Trade*, edited by Paulynne Castillo (Manila: De La Salle University Publishing House, 2012).
15. Arsenio Balisacan, "Poverty and Inequality", in *The Philippine Economy: Development, Policies, and Challenges*, edited by Arsenio Balisacan and Hal Hill (New York: Oxford University Press, 2003), pp. 311–41.
16. See Chapter 4 for further discussion of these issues. For a general review of regional development in the Philippines through to the early 2000s, and in comparative East Asian context, see the papers in Arsenio N. Balisacan and Hal Hill, *The Dynamics of Regional Development: The Philippines in East Asia* (Cheltenham: Edward Elgar Publishing and ADB Institute, 2007).
17. Note that these regions are administrative units not major units of governance. The funds transferred through the Local Government Act flowed to the cities and provinces below these units. Note also that, owing to frequent changes in administrative boundaries, the data presented here refer only to the more recent period of the current boundaries.

18. Rosario Manasan and Shiladitya Chatterjee, "Regional Development", in *The Philippine Economy*, edited by Balisacan and Hill, pp. 342–80.
19. Arsenio Balisacan, "The Growth-Poverty Nexus: Multidimensional Poverty in the Philippines", in *Sustainable Economic Development: Resources, Environment and Institutions*, edited by Arsenio Balisacan, Ujjayant Chakravorty, and Majah-Leah V. Ravago (Amsterdam: Elsevier, 2014), pp. 445–68.
20. For a discussion of these issues in the Southeast Asian context, see Peter Warr, "Poverty Reduction and the Composition of Growth in the Mekong Economies", in *Sustainable Economic Development*, edited by Balisacan, Chakravorty, and Ravago, pp. 469–82.
21. For example, it is important to ensure that education and social expenditures are maintained in the context of overall fiscal discipline. Programmes which endanger macroeconomic stability and therefore result in a fiscal and economic crisis, actually hurt the poor. This seems to be the case currently in the much-discussed Brazilian social programmes.
22. Note that there is a series break in 2004–5 owing to definitional changes and so the data can be compared only within the two subperiods.
23. W. Villamil, "Education and Training", in *The Philippine Economy*, edited by Clarete, Esguerra, and Hill, pp. 151–89.
24. See, for example, Luisa Fernandez and Rosechin Olfindo, "Overview of the Philippines Condition Cash Transfer Program: the Pantawid Pamilyang Pilipino Program", Social Protection and Labor Policy and Technical Notes 62879 (Manila: World Bank, 2011); Celia Reyes, Aubrey Tabuga, Christian Mina, and Ronina Asis, "Promoting Inclusive Growth through the 4P's", Research Paper Series 2015-01 (Makati: Philippine Institute for Development Studies, 2015); Aniceto Orbeta Jr. and Vicente Paqueo, "Pantawid Pamilya Pilipino Program: Boon or Bane?", Discussion Paper Series No. 2016-56 (Makati: Philippine Institute for Development Studies, 2016); and Melba Tutor, "The Impact of the Philippines' Conditional Cash Transfer Program on Consumption", *The Philippine Review of Economics* 51, no. 1 (2014): 117–61. Much of this research has been undertaken by the country's pre-eminent policy think-tank, the Philippine Institute for Development Studies, which enhances the credibility of the findings.
25. Emmanuel De Dios, "Local Politics and Local Economy", in *The Dynamics of Regional Development*, edited by Balisacan and Hill.
26. According to early estimates reported by Fernandez and Olfindo in *Overview of the Philippines Condition Cash Transfer Program* about 72 per cent of the recipients come from the poorest 20 per cent of the population, suggesting a creditable targeting outcome.
27. R.U. Mendoza and R. Olfindo, "Governance and Institutions", in *The Philippine Economy*, edited by Clarete, Esguerra, and Hill, pp. 375–417.

28. The major exceptions are of course the extra-parliamentary removal of President Estrada in 2001, and the contested ("Hello Garci") election of 2004.
29. The future of the EODB series may be in doubt in the wake of the high-profile resignation in early 2018 of the World Bank's chief economist which was reportedly triggered in part by his dissatisfaction with the methodology and politicization of the data.
30. For a comprehensive analysis of the country's logistics system and reform priorities, see Gilberto Llanto, "Philippine Infrastructure and Connectivity: Challenges and Reforms", *Asian Economic Policy Review* 11, no. 2 (2016): 243–61.
31. See Robert Klitgaard, "International Cooperation Against Corruption", *Finance and Development* 35, no. 1 (March 1998): 4.

6

Competition Law and Policy in the Philippines:
A Role in Sustained and Inclusive Economic Growth

Rachel Burgess

INTRODUCTION

The Philippines has experienced one of Southeast Asia's fastest growth rates.[1] Between 2010 and 2015, the Philippines experienced an average GDP growth rate of more than 6 per cent, its highest since the 1970s.[2] The GDP growth in 2017 was 6.69 per cent, more than Indonesia, Malaysia and Thailand, and only marginally behind China and Vietnam.[3] The hope is that the Philippines can sustain this growth rate for the foreseeable future in a way that is inclusive.

The introduction of competition law and policy into the Philippines is believed to be a necessary step towards achieving sustained and inclusive growth. In September 2016, the Chairman of the then newly established Philippines Competition Commission (PCC), Arsenio Balisacan, called the Competition Act a "game-changer for the economy" and "one of the key components of the overall strategy to make economic growth more enduring and more inclusive".[4]

Whether competition law does in fact contribute to enduring and inclusive growth will depend on a number of outcomes being achieved. The law must be applied in a way that benefits the nation's poor as this is the only way it will achieve inclusive growth. The key to this will be levelling the playing fields so entrepreneurs and micro, small and medium-sized enterprises (MSMEs) can prosper on a national and international scale. The country is dominated by oligarchs and oligopolies, which prevent—or, at the very least, deter—new entrants. The Filipino business and wider communities must understand and accept the benefits of competition law and policy to enable a "culture of compliance". This will, in turn, lead to sustained growth as Filipino businesses are able to operate in a truly globally competitive way and enable the Philippines to continue to attract foreign direct investment (FDI). Existing government policies which—perhaps inadvertently—impede competition need to be addressed. The actual and perceived success of the regulator, the PCC—in enforcing competition law provisions—will underpin all these outcomes.

OVERVIEW OF PHILIPPINES' COMPETITION LAW AND POLICY

Having been introduced into Congress more than twenty-five years before, the Philippine Competition Act (the Act) was finally passed on 21 July 2015. Although the law came into force on 8 August 2015, the two-year transitional period (section 53) gave businesses time to review and revise agreements and practices to avoid sanctions. The merger regime has been operative since 2016.

Competition Law in the Philippines

Prior to introduction of the Act, thirty separate laws of the Philippines contained provisions dealing with competition issues, including the Philippines constitution.[5] Most of these laws are still in operation, although that may change following completion of the National Competition Review (see below).

Relevant provisions of the Philippines Constitution[6] are worth noting. Article XII, section 1 provides:

> The goals of the national economy are a more equitable distribution of opportunities, income, and wealth; a sustained increase in the amount of goods and services produced by the nation for the benefit of the people; and an expanding productivity as the key to raising the quality of life for all, especially the underprivileged.
>
> The State shall promote industrialization and full employment based on sound agricultural development and agrarian reform, through industries that make full and efficient use of human and natural resources, and which are *competitive in both domestic and foreign markets. However, the State shall protect Filipino enterprises against unfair foreign competition and trade practices.*
>
> In the pursuit of these goals, all sectors of the economy and all regions of the country shall be given optimum opportunity to develop. Private enterprises, including corporations, cooperatives, and similar collective organizations, shall be encouraged to broaden the base of their ownership. [emphasis added]

Section 19, Article XII provides: "The State shall regulate or prohibit monopolies when the public interest so requires. No combinations in restraint of trade or unfair competition shall be allowed".

There is already some jurisprudence in the Philippines on competition law. For example, in the case of Francisco S. Tatad v. Secretary of Department of Energy and Secretary of Department of Finance[7] (1997), the Supreme Court stated:

> the fundamental principle espoused by Section 19, Article XII of the Constitution is competition for it alone can release the creative forces of the market. But the competition that can unleash these creative forces is competition that is fighting yet is fair. Ideally, this kind of competition requires the presence of not one, not just a few but several players. A market controlled by one player [monopoly] or dominated by a handful of players [oligopoly] is hardly the market where honest-to-goodness competition will prevail. Monopolistic or oligopolistic markets deserve our careful scrutiny and laws which barricade the entry points of new players in the market should be viewed with suspicion.

Monopolies and oligopolies are prevalent in the Philippines, so these words of the Supreme Court have significance for the PCC, discussed below.

Competition law provisions also exist in other Filipino legislation, such as: the Price Act 1992 (which, *inter alia*, prohibits cartels in relation to "basic necessity" or "prime commodity" goods); the Downstream Oil Industry Deregulation Act 1998 (which prohibits cartels and predatory pricing in relation to oil); and the Corporation Code of the Philippines 1980 (which regulates mergers and acquisitions).

Thus, the introduction of the Philippine Competition Act brings a more comprehensive competition law into operation in the Philippines with key prohibitions located in one piece of legislation that applies across all sectors. The Act can therefore be regarded as more traditional, as it regulates the three key pillars of competition regulation—anticompetitive agreements, abuse of dominance and anticompetitive mergers and acquisitions. The Act establishes the PCC as an independent, quasi-judicial body (section 5) and gives the PCC significant powers to investigate potential breaches of the law, including the ability to undertake inspections of an entity's business premises (section 12(g)). The Office for Competition in the Philippines Department of Justice is responsible for criminal investigations and prosecutions under the Act (section 13).

The Act draws on a range of concepts from established competition law jurisdictions. For example, definitions of "dominant position" and "relevant market" are drawn from European case law, while concepts such as "contract, arrangement or understanding" and "substantial lessening of competition" are terms used in Australia's competition legislation. The available jurisprudence may assist the PCC and Filipino courts in interpreting the law. The Act imposes civil and criminal sanctions for serious breaches of competition law—cartels—and provides for a leniency regime under which reductions in fines may be available for parties who provide information to the PCC about the existence of a cartel. In key respects, competition law in the Philippines is now consistent with many competition laws around the world.

The Philippines also has sector regulators—including the Energy Regulatory Commission (ERC), National Telecommunications Commission and the Philippine Port Authority—with powers to address competition issues. The United Nations Conference on Trade and Development (UNCTAD) reported the ERC was the most active in competition oversight.[8] One of the key tasks for the PCC is to establish arrangements under which it can work with these regulators to ensure an effective and efficient enforcement of competition law provisions.

Statements of Competition Policy in the Act

The Act sets out a number of policy statements that will guide the PCC in exercising its mandate. Section 2 sets out the main declaration of policy. The State is said to recognize "that past measures undertaken to liberalize key sectors in the economy need to be reinforced by measures that safeguard competitive conditions". Section 2 goes on to oblige the State to "enhance economic efficiency and promote free and fair competition in trade, industry and all commercial activities". The requirement to penalize anticompetitive agreements, abuse of dominant position and anticompetitive mergers and acquisitions is stated to be with the "objective of protecting consumer welfare and advancing domestic and international trade and economic development".

The PCC states that it:

institutes a regulatory environment for market competition to:

1. *Protect consumer welfare* by giving consumers access to a wider choice over goods and services at lower prices, and;

2. *Promote competitive businesses* and encourage market players to be more efficient and innovative. Competition also benefits small and medium businesses.

In its capacity as a regulatory body, the PCC helps protect markets from anti-competitive behaviour of firms, and works with other government agencies to promote a culture of competition.

A level playing field improves the growth prospects of local firms, and could also result in a more active market participation of foreign players. In the process, competition expands economic opportunities in the country and improves overall welfare.[9]

There are a number of other provisions of the Act relevant to policy considerations. Section 26(d) of the Act imposes an obligation on the PCC to balance the need to ensure competition is not prevented or substantially restricted with the "risk that ... development of priority areas or industries in the general interest of the country may be deterred by overzealous or undue intervention". Section 28 of the Act allows for forbearance if the PCC determines "enforcement is not necessary to the attainment of the policy objectives" of the Act. It is not yet clear what approach the PCC will take to forbearance but it is recommended this section be applied sparingly.

The importance of key consumer markets is also recognized in the Act. Under section 41 of the Act violation of the law that involves "basic necessities", defined to include products such as rice, sugar, coffee, fresh eggs, fresh vegetables, fresh and processed milk, and "prime commodities", defined to include products such as fresh fruits, school supplies, cement, batteries and light bulbs, are subject to triple fines.[10] Section 41 creates an additional deterrent to those active in markets that would have the greatest impact on the nation's poor and recognizes the important role that competition law and policy can play in the reduction of poverty.

Competition Law and Policy as a Tool for Economic Development in the Philippines

The introduction of competition law and policy in the Philippines is intended to contribute to the wider goal of "rapid and sustainable economic growth and development".[11] A study on the relationship between competition law and policy and economic development is beyond the scope of this chapter. However, it is worth noting a few interesting points identified in the considerable literature on this topic.

Singh[12] discusses studies undertaken to try to identify the nature of the relationship between competition and economic development. Singh notes the relationship is "controversial, both in economic theory and in relation to empirical evidence" and concludes that "a suitable combination of cooperation and competition is more likely to enhance societal welfare than competition alone". Cooperation refers to the need to balance competitive markets with the ability to attract investment. If a market becomes too competitive—leading to price wars and other aggressive behaviour—ongoing foreign investment, which is needed to increase productivity, may be deterred. In these cases, government intervention may be necessary to prevent overcapacity, thereby ensuring profits for the private sector.

This concept is important for the Philippines. The intention to increase foreign direct investment (FDI) is critical for the Philippines' sustainable economic growth. The PCC needs to carefully balance the desire to increase competitiveness in relevant markets with the need to continue to attract foreign investment. Sections 26(g) and 28 of the Act give the PCC some scope to achieve this balance.

To achieve sustainable and inclusive growth and development, UNCTAD argues that competition policy needs to be part of a wider mix of trade, economic, social and environmental policies.[13] It makes a number of recommendations to help achieve this. Firstly, UNCTAD recommends inclusive engagement with stakeholders—governments, businesses, consumers, academia and civil society. The importance of advocacy for a new competition authority cannot be overstated (discussed below).

Secondly, the competition regulator should identify priority sectors relevant to the economy and poor people—such as agriculture. In the Philippines, the Act requires the establishment of a National Competition Policy (section 2(a)). The National Economic Development Authority (NEDA) are undertaking a National Competition Review to inform the development of the Philippines National Competition Policy. The National Competition Review, together with other government agencies, has identified five priority sectors for competition analysis and enforcement in the medium term—agriculture, manufacturing, power/electricity, telecommunications and transportation/logistics.[14]

Thirdly, UNCTAD recommends each country consider the necessity for exemptions for certain sectors, such as farmers' cooperatives—the United States and the European Union (EU) have exemptions in the agricultural sector. As noted above, agriculture has an important role to play in the Philippines economy, particularly in relation to the nation's poor. The PCC may wish to consider whether exemptions are needed in this area (discussed below).

To act as a tool for economic development in the Philippines, competition law and policy will need to "level the playing field", as recognized in Chapter 16 of the Philippine Development Plan 2017–2022.[15] There are many challenges that will need to be overcome in the Philippines to achieve this, including market issues arising from the country's oligarchs and monopolies/oligopolies, opening markets up to the high number of entrepreneurs and MSMEs, and changing entrenched business practices and government policies that may deter competition. These are discussed below.

(a) Oligopolies

The problem of power resting with an elite few in the Philippines is well recognized, with seven corporate groups dominating the Philippine economy—San Miguel Corp, Ayala Corp, First Pacific, SM Investments Corp, JG Summit, DM Consunji and Aboitiz.[16] In fact, a 2016 article in the *Manila Times* classified the Philippines as an oligarchipelago.[17] This may change if President Duterte is able to "destroy the oligarchs that are embedded in government".[18]

It is likely that the country's oligopolistic markets will be high on the list of priority sectors for the new competition authority, especially given their significant impact on development and consumer welfare. (It is pleasing to see power/electricity and telecommunications already on the list of priorities.) Oligopolistic market conditions are conducive to anticompetitive behaviour and, as the Philippine Supreme Court has already identified in the Tatad case, do not facilitate "honest-to-goodness" competition.

The telecommunications industry has already made its way to the forefront of PCC's attention. In May 2016, the two main telecommunications firms in the Philippines, PLDT and Globe, announced they were each buying a 50 per cent interest in San Miguel's telecom business—the only other rival in the market. In their Preliminary Statement of Concerns, the PCC's Mergers & Acquisitions Office (MAO) concluded:

> The joint acquisition of SMC's telecommunications businesses is likely to further entrench the dominant position of PLDT and Globe, in markets where outcomes have not traditionally served consumers well. The MAO therefore currently believes that the Transaction is likely to substantially prevent, restrict or lessen competition within the relevant market(s) in the Philippines.[19]

However, PLDT was successful in obtaining an order from the Court of Appeals restraining the PCC from investigating the acquisition on the basis that it was "deemed" approved because it was completed prior to the commencement of the Act's Implementing Rules and Regulations. The PCC subsequently filed a petition at the Supreme Court, asserting its authority under the law to review the acquisition under the merger rules. The PCC petition illustrates its commitment to tackling the oligopolies, in the interests of consumers: "How [the Court of Appeal] ended up according paramount importance to protecting dominant industry players from these alleged [business] losses and inconveniences over the State's duty of ensuring the consumer welfare of millions of Filipinos remains a mystery."[20]

The PCC Chairman Arsenio M. Balisacan stated that the PCC petition "also sends a message to consumers and businesses. The country's first-ever competition authority will not back down or be intimidated by companies who have grown accustomed to unregulated business practices that hamper competition and ultimately hurt the consumers."[21]

At the time of writing, the matter remains unresolved.

(b) Entrepreneurs and Micro, Small and Medium-Sized Enterprises

Entrepreneurship and small business are key to breaking the cycle of poverty in many developing countries. Many poor people do not work in regular jobs—undertaking entrepreneur-style activities to make money on a day-to-day basis. Drexl notes competition policy has a key role to play as it can help to ensure individuals and small businesses have access to level playing fields and competition authorities can regulate anticompetitive conduct of larger businesses.[22] The need to level the playing field in areas that impact MSMEs may therefore be high on the PCC priority list. Sectors such as agriculture and fisheries—key to the Filipino poor—may warrant particular attention.

According to the Philippines Development Plan 2011–2016 (2016 PDP), agriculture and fisheries contributed approximately 18.4 per cent to GDP from 2004 to 2010 and employed more than 11.8 million people. If the entire agricultural value chain is considered, the contribution to GDP would have been 35 per cent and the industry would have employed more than half of the entire Filipino workforce.[23] More than 96 per cent of enterprises involved in the agricultural industry are small and medium enterprises (SMEs).[24]

The 2016 PDP highlights a number of challenges faced in the sector that may be able to be addressed by an effective competition law. Costs of inputs such as fertilizers and pesticides are reported to account for 20–30 per cent of production cost, and the cost of livestock and poultry feeds represent a staggering 70 per cent. Between 2007 and 2008, the cost of fertilizer alone increased 135 per cent. The competition authority may seek to understand the reasons for such a steep rise. Similarly, inefficiencies in the agricultural supply chain—for example, distribution costs reported as being 20–30 per cent higher than in developed countries[25]—are also likely to improve if competition increases. It is encouraging to see that the Philippines Development Plan 2017–2022 (2022 PDP) commits to reviewing market competition in key inputs to production such as fertilizer and seeds.[26]

(c) Business Practices and the Role of Trade Associations

Recognizing the important role that trade associations can play in business environments, section 48 of the Act confirms the competition law does not "prohibit the existence and operation of trade associations organized to promote quality standards and safety issues". However, it is made clear that the associations should not be used as a vehicle for anticompetitive behaviour.

The PCC needs to educate businesses in the Philippines on the dos and don'ts of competition law as part of its advocacy programme. The PCC advocacy should include advice on potential risks for businesses if business owners discuss commercially sensitive matters in the context of otherwise legitimate discussions at trade association meetings. MSMEs in other ASEAN countries have infringed competition laws in the early years of competition law enforcement—often through their trade associations. In Malaysia, for example, six of the first seven cases involved a breach of the competition law by SMEs that had reached agreement through their trade associations. Similar issues arose in Singapore.[27]

(d) Government Policies

The PCC will need to start educating other government departments about competition law, in particular how government policies may be leading, intentionally or unintentionally, to anticompetitive practices. In developing countries like the Philippines, government intervention into markets can be significant, particularly in relation to price controls. One example is the need to tackle the issue of price intervention by the National Food Authority (NFA). The 2016 PDP notes that the NFA's attempt to stabilize rice prices—with the objectives of securing farmer's profits whilst maintaining affordability—led to a number of downsides including an increase in volatility of domestic prices and discouraging the private sector from investing in distribution and storage facilities.[28] This type of intervention obviously distorts a truly competitive market.

Based on a 2017 press release, the PCC is acutely aware of the need to allow market forces to drive prices, rather than a regulator:

> For the longest time, the [Department of Trade and Industry (DTI)] through the National Price Coordinating Council has been setting prices that guide both consumers and suppliers. But now that we have the Philippine Competition Act, we support DTI in its efforts to promote industry efficiency and consumer welfare by allowing market forces to dictate the prices of goods instead of issuing Suggested Retail Prices or (SRPs), Chairman Arsenio M. Balisacan said.[29]

In 2017, the PCC commenced a project to identify a strategy plan to promote market competition in the rice industry, an industry that is critical to the nation's poor. It is not clear whether this project has been completed. More recently, in a policy note published by the Philippine Institute for Development Studies in October 2018 on the future of the National Food Authority, the key role of the PCC was recognized: "the Philippine Competition Commission must consistently enforce fair competition in the rice market".[30]

The PCC will need to continue to work closely with the government to determine if, how, and when, pre-existing government policies and interventions should be removed.

OBSTACLES TO COMPETITION LAW AND POLICY FOR INCLUSIVE AND SUSTAINED GROWTH

To successfully implement the Act, the PCC will need to overcome a number of challenges—which will require time and patience from the Philippine government, businesses and the public.

(a) Challenges in the Law

The law is complex, and many concepts in competition law will be new to the Filipino government, businesses, legal and academic communities. For this reason, one of the most crucial tasks for the PCC is its advocacy role.

An active advocacy programme will help create a competition culture within the Philippines, where the general public and businesses accept a competitive market as the norm. As in many ASEAN countries, the introduction of competition law in the Philippines represents a significant change in the way of doing business. In Malaysia, for example, businesses were accustomed to meeting to discuss prices, and the idea that this could not be done any longer came as a considerable shock to businesses.[31] Education of the general public and businesses is therefore critical for the successful implementation of competition law in the Philippines.

The PCC will also need to ensure other government departments and sector regulators understand the new law—particularly in relation to the potential impact of government policies and procurement.

Assisting the judiciary to understand competition law is also significant in the Philippines as a decision of the PCC can be appealed to the Court of Appeals. If the PCC's decisions are supported by the government and judiciary, the PCC will become a well-respected competition regulator. The civil system in the Philippines may pose particular challenges—compared with a common law system where the judiciary is accustomed to interpreting laws to "fill in" gaps—which is critical in competition law.[32]

The PCC will also need to prioritize capacity building. Competition law and policy is a complex area, requiring expertise not only in law but also in economics and investigations. Building skills needed to implement and enforce the Act—in a manner that earns the respect of the Philippines' business community and general public as well as other competition regulators—will take time.

In addition to capacity building within the PCC, there will be a need to coordinate with other government departments and regulators, particularly those that have competition powers, to ensure that an agreed manner of working is established. A consistent, clear approach to enforcing competition laws will be crucial to earning the respect of the business and other stakeholder communities. Towards this end, the PCC has already agreed several Memoranda of Agreement with key government departments (Securities and Exchange Commission, the Bangko Sentral ng Pilipinas, the Department of Justice – Office for Competition, the Philippine Statistics Authority, the Public Private Partnership Center and the Commission on Audit and Office of the Ombudsman (specifically relating to public procurement and bidding)) but initiatives such as joint training and capacity building are still to be pursued.

(b) Challenges Faced as a Regulatory Body

The independence of the PCC is critical to effective implementation of the Philippines' competition law. The risk of "regulatory capture" must be acknowledged alongside inherent corruption issues in the Philippines.

"Regulatory capture" involves the idea that a certain group is able to exercise influence over a regulator to ensure the regulator serves the group's own interests. Baxter describes "regulatory capture" where "one interest group among many in a field contesting for recognition of their disparate interests has seized control of the umpires, such that the game is no longer taking place on a level playing field".[33] In the context of competition law, Mariniello, Neven and Padilla highlight risks associated with competition policies with multiple objectives:

> The multiplicity of objectives for competition policy, and in particular the adoption of non-competition goals, opens the door to discretionary decisions, political intervention and more generally the capture of enforcement decisions by particular interests.[34]

The declaration of policy contained in the Act arguably includes non-competition objectives—such as advancing international trade and economic development—with broader underlying policies of sustained and inclusive growth and the reduction of poverty. The result of this broader purpose may be to expose the PCC to a greater risk of regulatory capture.

A challenge already faced by the PCC is the complexity of legal and economic issues associated with competition law and policy. Ultimately, competition authorities have a substantial amount of discretion—both in choosing which issues to investigate and, often, also deciding whether to find an infringement and the appropriate level of a penalty—although jurisdictions like Australia and the United States are dependent on the courts to determine both liability and the penalty. This discretion exposes competition regulators to the threat of regulatory capture.[35]

Ergas finds the link between corruption and regulatory capture "far from reassuring" and that countries with weak governance and high levels of corruption have adopted competition policy in recent years. In Ergas' view, this combination of poor governance, weak human resources and the complexity of competition policy could mean less developed countries end up with worse outcomes than if there were no competition laws in place.[36]

To avoid the risks of regulatory capture, the PCC will need to ensure it remains independent, impartial and accountable. This balance may be delicate for the PCC in its early years, as it struggles to gain recognition and apply a complex law to complex markets. Although, the PCC has been established as an independent, quasi-judicial body, it is attached to the Office of the President and its Chairperson and four Commissioners are also appointed by the President. Such appointments may result in questions regarding whether the PCC can truly be independent. There are protections built into sections 6 and 7 of the law: the appointees must have distinguished service in the fields of law, economics, finance, commerce or engineering; they must not have been candidates for preceding elections; and, perhaps most importantly, they have security of tenure—seven years on a staggered basis, such that for the first set of appointments, the Chairman and two Commissioners serve for seven years, while the other two Commissioners serve for five years.

All final decisions, orders and rulings of the PCC are required to be published on the PCC's website for transparency. The PCC has already made a large number of documents publicly available, including merger decisions and the Preliminary Statement of Concerns in relation to the PLDT/Globe acquisition. This open and transparent approach is to be applauded.

Unfortunately, problems of corruption persist in the Philippines. According to the Transparency International Corruption Perception Index 2017,[37] the Philippines continues to be perceived to have high levels of corruption, with a ranking of 111 (out of 180) and a score of 34/100—where 0 indicates highly corrupt and 100 indicates completely clear of corruption. The 2017 result is a slight improvement on a score of 35 for 2016 and 2015 and a score of 38 for 2014.

In a 2018 Asian survey, perception of corruption in the Philippines returned a score of 6.85 out of 10, with 10 the worst score. However, the results do show a steady improvement in the perception of corruption since a peak at 9.35 in 2012 (8.28 (2013), 7.85 (2014), 7.43 (2015), 7.05 (2016), and 7.00 (2017)).[38] Although it is difficult to determine the precise reasons for the change in perception, the 2016 report (no longer publicly available) considered the improvement to reflect the strong leadership under Aquino III. The continued improvement may be due to Duterte's pledge that his fight against corruption "will be relentless and sustained".[39]

(c) Government Policy Responses

The PCC will need to work with the government to address bid rigging issues. The oligopolistic nature of many Filipino markets means they are particularly susceptible to "bid rigging" and other cartel behaviours. The World Bank *Philippines—Country Procurement Assessment Report* (2008) reported "a perception that collusion or rigging of bids is common, particularly for big ticket contracts" with only about three participants in each tender process. This number increased to five in 2010.[40]

Bid rigging is recognized as one of the most harmful anticompetitive practices. Fines imposed on entities that engage in bid rigging are high and, in some jurisdictions, those who participate can be subjected to individual fines and imprisonment. In developing countries, bid rigging takes on even greater significance. Anticompetitive practices such as bid rigging have a disproportionate impact on the poor—who are most reliant on government services. If the government is overpaying as a result of bid rigging, the ability of the government to provide key services is reduced.[41]

In other ASEAN member states, uncovering bid rigging has been a priority, in recognition of the harmful effect these agreements have on markets. In Singapore, a number of the early decisions of the Competition and Consumer Commission of Singapore (CCCS) were in relation to bid rigging. Malaysia issued a publication entitled *Help Us Detect Bid Rigging*[42] quite early in its operation and ran a series of workshops on bid rigging, aimed at government officials.

CONCLUSION

Aldaba's 2012 discussion paper for the Philippine Institute for Development Studies reported "weak competition is one of the fundamental factors that explain limited growth, productivity, [and] employment in the economy".[43] The Asian Development Bank stated that "appropriate enforcement of competition law both enhances the attractiveness of an economy as a location for foreign investment and is important for maximizing the benefits that flow from such investment".[44] Against the backdrop of such statements, those responsible for enforcing the new competition law have a high burden placed on them.

The PCC recognizes the enormity of the task ahead. Not only does the PCC have to build a successful competition regulator with highly skilled staff, it needs to undertake a broad advocacy programme on the benefits of competition law and policy to educate Filipino businesses, the public and stakeholders. The landscape is challenging as many Filipino markets are run by oligopolies, the country is geographically widespread—raising particular issues for competitive markets, and corruption is still pervasive.

The manner in which the PCC chooses to apply the law will have a significant bearing on its economic impact. Wider policy issues may need to be considered to maximize the potential benefit of competition law and policy on the Philippines economy. The PCC is likely to come under criticism—from business, the public and possibly even its own government—and must withstand that criticism and apply the competition law in a fair and transparent manner in order to succeed in building a well-respected, well-recognized competition authority.

The mood in the Philippines remains upbeat with a president making decisive, if unconventional, changes to address old problems. Economic growth is strong and forecasts are positive. The PCC is progressing at an impressive pace, with numerous publications, communications and public events taking place. The stage is set for competition law and policy to make a valuable contribution to sustainable and inclusive growth for the benefit of all Filipinos.

Notes

1. Antoinette Raquiza, "Changing Configuration of Philippine Capitalism", *Philippine Political Science Journal* 35, no. 2 (2014): 225–50.
2. Philippines Congress, Philippines Congressional Record, 16th Congress, Third Regular Session, House of Representatives, 27 July 2015 (Quezon City: Philippine Congress, 2015), p. 2.
3. World Bank data on Gross Domestic Product, https://data.worldbank.org/indicator/NY.GDP.MKTP.KD.ZG?locations=PH-CN-MY-TH-VN (accessed 23 October 2018).
4. Arsenio Balisacan, "Conference Keynote Address" (presented at the Australian National University Philippine Update Conference 2016 on "Sustaining the Momentum for Change beyond 2016", Canberra, 2 September 2016).
5. For a full list of the laws including competition provisions, see UNCTAD, 2014. "Voluntary Peer Review of Competition Law and Policy: Philippines Full Report" (New York and Geneva: UNCTAD, 2014).
6. Available at https://www.officialgazette.gov.ph/constitutions/1987-constitution/ (accessed 15 October 2018).

7. G.R. No. 124360, 5 November 1997.
8. Ibid., n. 5.
9. PCC, "PCC Mission", https://phcc.gov.ph/about-us/phcc-mission/ (accessed 15 October 2018).
10. See section 3, Republic Act No. 7581, The Price Act of 1992 for definitions of "basic necessities" and "prime commodities".
11. National Economic Development Authority, "Philippine Development Plan 2011–2016" (Pasig City: NEDA, 2011).
12. Ajit Singh, "Competition and Competition Policy in Emerging Markets: International and Development Dimensions", G-24 Discussion Paper Series (New York and Geneva: UNCTAD, 2002), p. 8.
13. UNCTAD Secretariat, "The Role of Competition Policy in Promoting Sustainable and Inclusive Growth", TD/RBP/CONF.8/6, 27 April 2015, https://unctad.org/meetings/en/SessionalDocuments/tdrbpconf8d6_en.pdf (accessed 23 October 2018).
14. Arsenio Balisacan, "Prioritization of Competition Actions: The Case of the Philippine Competition Commission", Meeting of High-Level Representatives of Asia-Pacific Competition Authorities, OECD Conference Centre, Paris, 6 December 2017.
15. NEDA, "Philippines Development Plan 2017–2022" (Pasig City: NEDA, 2017); PCC, "PCC Mission", n. 9.
16. Mark Williams and Ruby Ann S. Jalit, "The Philippines", in *The Political Economy of Competition Law in Asia*, edited by Mark Williams (Cheltenham: Edward Elgar, 2013).
17. Yen Makabenta, "Has the Philippines Become an Oligarchipelago?", *Manila Times*, 6 August 2016, http://www.manilatimes.net/has-the-philippines-become-an-oligarchipelago/278206/ (accessed 1 December 2016). For an interesting discussion on the manner in which the Filipino business elite are growing their businesses, including a reliance on joint ventures with foreign companies providing resources and technical expertise, see Raquiza, "Changing Configuration of Philippine Capitalism", n. 1.
18. Speech to election volunteers by President Rodrigo Duterte quoted in Keren Blankfeld, "Duterte's War on Oligarchs", *Forbes*, http://www.forbes.com/sites/kerenblankfeld/2016/08/24/philippines-50-richest-2016-president-rodrigo-duterte-wages-war-on-oligarchs/#3f5b5efb371d (accessed 2 December 2016).
19. The PCC Preliminary Statement of Concerns is no longer publicly available.
20. PCC, "PCC asks SC to lift CA injunction blocking review of P69.1-B telco deal", press release 2017-012, 19 April 2017, http://phcc.gov.ph/pcc-asks-sc-lift-ca-injunction-blocking-review-p69-1-b-telco-deal/ (accessed 31 May 2017).
21. Ibid.
22. Josef Drexl, "Economic Integration and Competition Law in Developing

Countries", in *Competition Policy and Regional Integration in Developing Countries*, edited by Josef Drexl et al. (Cheltenham: Edward Elgar, 2012).
23. NEDA, Philippines Development Plan 2011–2016 (Pasig City: NEDA, 2011).
24. Rafaelita Aldaba, "Small and Medium Enterprises' (SMEs) Access to Finance: Philippines", Philippine Institute for Development Studies Discussion Paper Series No. 2012-05 (Makati City: Philippine Institute for Development Studies, 2012).
25. NEDA, Philippines Development Plan 2011–2016 (Pasig City: NEDA, 2011).
26. NEDA, "Philippines Development Plan 2017–2022" (Pasig City: NEDA, 2017), p. 252.
27. Rachel Burgess, "Trade Associations: Competition Law Advocates or Offenders?", in *Competition Law, Regulation & SMEs in the Asia-Pacific: Understanding the Small Business Perspective*, edited by Michael T. Schaper and Cassey Lee (Singapore: ISEAS – Yusof Ishak Institute, 2016).
28. NEDA, Philippines Development Plan 2011–2016 (Pasig City: NEDA, 2011).
29. PCC, "Let Market Forces Dictate Prices, Not SRPs", Press Release 2017-010, 5 April 2017, https://phcc.gov.ph/press-releases/pcc-let-market-forces-dictate-prices-not-srps/ (accessed 23 October 2018).
30. Philippine Institute for Development Studies, "Options for Reform of the National Food Authority", Policy Note 2018-09, p. 6, https://pidswebs.pids.gov.ph/CDN/PUBLICATIONS/pidspn1809.pdf (accessed 24 October 2018).
31. Shila Dorai Raj and Rachel Burgess, "SMEs and Malaysia's New Competition Law: Experiences to Date", in *Competition Law, Regulation & SMEs in the Asia-Pacific*, edited by Michael T. Schaper and Cassey Lee (Singapore: ISEAS – Yusof Ishak Institute, 2016).
32. Henry Ergas, "Should Developed Countries Require Developing Countries to Adopt Competition Laws? Lessons from the Economic Literature", *European Competition Journal* 5, no. 2 (2009): 347–66.
33. Lawrence G. Baxter, "Understanding Regulatory Capture: An Academic Perspective from the United States", in *The Making of Good Financial Regulation: Towards a Policy Response to Regulatory Capture*, edited by Stefano Pagliari (Surrey: International Centre for Financial Regulation, 2012), pp. 31–39.
34. Mario Mariniello, Damien Neven and Jorge Padilla, "Antitrust, Regulatory Capture and Economic Integration", *Bruegel Policy Contribution* (2015): 2–13.
35. Ergas, "Should Developed Countries Require Developing Countries to Adopt Competition Laws?", n. 32.
36. Id.
37. https://www.transparency.org/news/feature/corruption_perceptions_index_2017#table (accessed 24 October 2018).
38. Political and Economic Risk Consultancy (PERC), *Asian Intelligence Report*

No. 992, 28 March 2018, http://www.asiarisk.com/subscribe/exsum1.pdf (accessed 23 October 2018).
39. President Rodrigo Duterte, "State of the Nation Address", Quezon City, 25 July 2016, http://newsinfo.inquirer.net/799060/full-text-president-rodrigo-duterte-first-sona-state-nation-address-2016 (accessed 21 October 2016).
40. World Bank, *Philippines: Country Procurement Assessment Report* (Washington, D.C.: World Bank, 2008), http://documents.worldbank.org/curated/en/598131468107676796/Philippines-Country-procurement-assessment-report.
41. Nick Godfrey, *Why Is Competition Important for Growth and Poverty Reduction?* (London: Department for International Development, 2008), p. 4.
42. MyCC, http://www.mycc.gov.my/sites/default/files/handbook/MYCC_Handbook_HelpUsDetectBidRigging.pdf (accessed 15 October 2018).
43. Rafaelita Aldaba, "Small and Medium Enterprises' (SMEs) Access to Finance: Philippines", Philippine Institute for Development Studies Discussion Paper Series No. 2012-05 (Makati City: Philippine Institute for Development Studies, 2012).
44. Asian Development Bank, *Asian Development Outlook 2005* (Metro Manila: Asian Development Bank, 2005).

PART III

Peace Process in Mindanao

7

Prospects for Lasting Peace in Mindanao:
Peacemaking and Peacebuilding under the Aquino and Duterte Administrations

Matthew Stephens

INTRODUCTION

The Philippines has an impressive record of securing political settlements with non-state armed groups. However, its record for implementing them is disappointing. This is not unusual. Many peace agreements have been signed around the world in the last fifty years and as many as half of them fail.[1] But the Philippines' inability to move from peacemaking to peacebuilding has left parts of the country stuck in an uncomfortable equilibrium of low-level conflict and poverty.

There are few signs so far that the government of President Duterte has the capacity to build a just and lasting peace that addresses the root causes of the conflict in Mindanao of historical injustice, insecurity, weak governance and lack of economic opportunity. The emergence of violent extremism linked to the so-called Islamic State (IS)—epitomized by the May 2017 attack on Marawi City—demonstrates how violence can evolve in disturbing new directions when these issues are left to fester.

There is still time to turn things around. The Bangsamoro Organic Law (BOL) was finally passed by Congress in July 2018, delivering the core of the 2014 Comprehensive Agreement on the Bangsamoro (CAB). Pursuant to the BOL, a new autonomous political entity will be established in 2019 to replace the existing Autonomous Region in Muslim Mindanao (ARMM). This provides the peace process an anchor and some welcome impetus. A number of the major armed groups have expressed support for the BOL, increasing the prospects of stability in the immediate term. However, delivering on the promise of the BOL to deal once and for all with the "Bangsamoro problem" requires decisive and sustained action to strengthen institutions, counter the threat of violent extremism and tackle entrenched poverty in conflict-affected Mindanao. Failure to do so would see the situation continue to drift into highly dangerous territory for security in the Philippines and Southeast Asia as a whole.

Drawing on nearly ten years of direct participation in most aspects of the peace process in Mindanao, this chapter reviews achievements of the administration of Benigno Aquino III, highlighting successes on peacemaking and critiquing a peacebuilding approach that never moved sufficiently beyond confidence-building measures. I describe the first two years of the Duterte administration's approach to peace and development, noting some bold steps, and identifying major gaps on peacebuilding that leave the process precariously placed. The chapter concludes with some suggestions on how to address these gaps to achieve the elusive shift from making to building peace.

KEY CONCEPTS

The key concepts used in this chapter will be briefly defined in this section. I use the UN definition of peacemaking: "Peacemaking generally includes measures to address conflicts in progress and usually involves diplomatic action to bring hostile parties to a negotiated agreement."[2] For the purposes of this chapter, peacemaking refers to the political process of negotiating peace between the government and various armed groups.

Peacebuilding is a process of addressing the social and political sources of conflict. According to the Alliance for Peacebuilding, it *"addresses root causes of violence and fosters reconciliation* to prevent the return of instability and violence" [emphasis added].[3] Braithwaite et al. take a human security approach, conceiving peacebuilding as "the craft of supporting institutions, including non-state institutions, in a process of growing to provide human security".[4] Braithwaite et al.'s approach clarifies that peacebuilding is not synonymous with building a modern state, though may include elements of it. Peacebuilding must also work with non-state institutions and with the realities of shadow governments.

Building peace requires an understanding of the structural causes of conflict and the factors that strengthen community security, upon which peacebuilding strategies can be built. As Braithwaite has also stated, "pick problems and fix them; pick strengths and expand them".[5] Fisher looked at peacebuilding as a precursor to peacemaking—also recognizing it can proceed in parallel depending on the context—"only peacebuilding will address the relationship qualities and basic needs that are at the heart of the conflict".[6]

Peacebuilding activities must be tailored to the specific context and can include humanitarian and development assistance to meet basic needs, transitional justice, disarming combatants and strengthening state and non-state institutions.

This chapter is influenced by the framework from the 2011 World Development Report (WDR) *Conflict, Security and Development*.[7] The key message from the 2011 WDR is that breaking cycles of violence requires legitimate institutions to provide citizen security, justice and jobs. The WDR concludes that in the best of circumstances, coming out of conflict can take twenty to thirty years to build legitimate institutions with technical capacity and accountability. Recognizing no government is given twenty to thirty years to deliver improved security, justice and jobs—inclusive coalitions for reform must be built—and governments need to generate quick wins to build confidence and buy time for long-term institutional reform. The emphasis on institutions, security, justice and jobs resonates in Mindanao and is used as the main framework for conceptualizing peacebuilding in this chapter.

THE STRAIGHT PATH TO PEACE? ASSESSING THE ACHIEVEMENTS OF THE AQUINO ADMINISTRATION

From the outset of his presidency, Benigno Aquino III positioned peace in Mindanao as an issue that would define his legacy. The Mindanao peace process was included in the "Social Contract with the Filipino People" that defined the parameters of the Aquino administration and was highlighted in the President's first State of the Nation Address in 2010: "Our foundation for growth is peace. We will continue to be shackled by poverty if the crossfire persists." On the political front, much was achieved in his six-year term from 2010 to 2016. The highlight was undoubtedly signing of the Framework Agreement on the Bangsamoro (FAB) with the Moro Islamic Liberation Front (MILF) in October 2012, followed by the more detailed Comprehensive Agreement on the Bangsamoro (CAB) in March 2014. Much less was achieved on the peacebuilding agenda, although a solid foundation was established.

Two-Track Strategy

The Aquino administration hit the ground running after assuming office in July 2010. Under the leadership of Secretary Teresita Quintos-Deles, the Office of the Presidential Adviser on the Peace Process (OPAPP) articulated a two-track strategy for peace and development—the political track and complementary development track.[8]

The political track covered the peacemaking agenda and aimed to conclude agreements with the MILF and the Communist Party of the Philippines/New People's Army/National Democratic Front (CNN). The government also undertook to ensure "closure" of previously signed agreements with the Moro National Liberation Front (MNLF) and communist splinter groups such as the Cordillera People's Liberation Army (CPLA) and the *Rebolusyonaryong Partidong Manggagawang Pilipinas*/Revolutionary Proletarian Army/Alex Boncayao Brigade (RPM-P/RPA/ABB).

The second track was called the "development track" but actually encompassed a broad peacebuilding agenda to address "the causes of armed conflict and other issues that affect the peace process". This complementary track was defined in the Mid-Term Update of the Philippine Development Plan to include: building community resilience against armed violence; strengthening institutions; and mainstreaming conflict-sensitive, peacebuilding and gender-sensitive lens in governance.[9] The main strategy to implement this track was the PAMANA (*Payapa at Masaganang Pamayanan*) programme, which extended government development assistance to conflict-affected areas across the country.[10]

The definition in the Philippine Development Plan mid-term update reflected the influence of the 2011 World Development Report on the thinking of key OPAPP officials, including Secretary Deles.[11]

Securing political settlements and addressing the socioeconomic and institutional drivers of conflict in a six-year term was ambitious, however, much was achieved during the 2010–16 period, as described below.

Key Achievements: Political Track

Signing the FAB and CAB was Aquino's crowning achievement. Ending seventeen years of negotiations, these agreements set out a framework for enhanced autonomy for the Bangsamoro, acknowledging deficiencies in the existing ARMM. The agreements also addressed issues such as transitional justice, decommissioning of combatants and the transformation of the MILF camps into peaceful and productive communities.

The parties involved established a series of joint or independent institutions to implement the CAB, including:

- an Independent Commission on Policing;
- the Bangsamoro Transition Commission—to draft the Bangsamoro Basic Law to create the Bangsamoro entity;
- the Joint Normalization Committee to oversee the security transition;
- the Transitional Justice and Reconciliation Commission (TJRC)—on historical injustice; and
- the Coordination Team for the Transition—to prepare for the administrative transition from ARMM to the Bangsamoro entity.

Among these different bodies, the report of the TJRC—issued in March 2016—was perhaps the most significant achievement.[12] Although the report garnered little public attention, it represents a powerful acknowledgement by the state of the historical injustices perpetrated against the Bangsamoro people.

Together, the CAB and the institutional architecture it spawned tied the MILF leadership to peaceful resolution of the so-called "Bangsamoro problem". Figure 7.1 shows how few vertical conflict incidents there were between the MILF and the government during the 2011–16 period. Most incidents recorded are horizontal in nature—involving clashes between MILF commanders or between the MILF and other armed groups—such

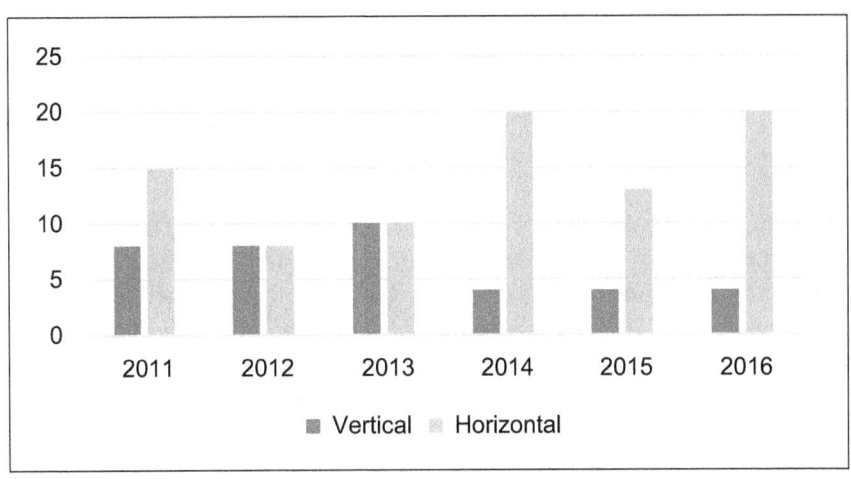

FIGURE 7.1
MILF Vertical and Horizontal Conflict Incidents, 2011–16

Source: Bangsamoro Conflict Monitoring System.

as the breakaway Bangsamoro Islamic Freedom Fighters.[13] The MILF has also begun the formal transition from armed group to political movement through the formation of the United Bangsamoro Justice Party (UBJP)—launched in December 2014.

Despite the MILF retaining the capacity to return to armed conflict, in reality it has evolved from adversary to security partner of the government. The MILF's commitment to peace was tested following the non-passage of the Bangsamoro Basic Law during the term of President Aquino. The absence of the type of violence seen after the collapse of the 2008 Memorandum of Agreement on Ancestral Domain (MOA-AD) speaks to the extent to which the MILF leadership is now vested philosophically and institutionally in the peace process.

Two other factors explain the relative security. First is the continued effectiveness of the joint government-MILF security and ceasefire mechanisms.[14] Second is the role of the international community. The involvement of state and non-state parties in bodies such as the International Contact Group and the Third Party Monitoring Team has provided helpful technical and moral support to the MILF and government. More importantly, the international recognition and legitimacy this provides the

MILF was hard-earned and the MILF are loath to give it up by a return to war.

Beyond the direct political gains of the peace process with the MILF, solid progress was made promoting convergence between the MILF and some parts of the MNLF. Leaders of the MNLF had been spurious about the MILF peace process, insisting on full implementation of the 1996 Final Peace Agreement and asking how the government could provide "two sets of keys to the same car without telling the other driver".[15] Facilitation through the Organization of Islamic Cooperation and mechanisms such as the Bangsamoro Coordination Forum (BCF) laid the foundation for the more inclusive agreement pursued by the Duterte administration.

The January 2015 Mamasapano incident landed a killer blow to the prospects of the Bangsamoro Basic Law (BBL) in Congress, but many of the political gains remained in place, giving the Duterte government a base on which to build.

Key Achievements: Complementary Track—Development and Institution-Building

On the complementary track, the government sought to address underlying drivers of conflict by expanding economic opportunity and strengthening local institutions. Two major programmes were launched for economic development. In 2010 the government conceived the PAMANA programme for "peace-building and development in areas affected by and vulnerable to conflict".[16] PAMANA comprises three pillars: (1) Building Foundations for Peace, (2) Establishing Resilient Communities, and (3) Promoting Sub-Regional Economic Development.

It has mostly targeted areas influenced by the NPA and communist splinter groups and MNLF territory. The programme had less traction with the MILF, which dismissed it as counterinsurgency. From 2012 to 2016 the total budget for PAMANA was PhP34 billion (US$733 million).

The bulk of funding under pillar two went into small-scale community development investments—such as farming equipment, day care centres, post-harvest facilities and water systems—through the Departments of Social Welfare and Development, Agriculture and Agrarian Reform. Much of this investment was spread in small grants of PhP300,000 (approximately USD$7,000) equally among *barangays* in conflict-affected municipalities identified by the Armed Forces of the Philippines. Pillar 3 investments are larger—such as farm-to-market roads—and implemented through central government agencies including the Department of Interior and Local Government.

The second plank of the development track was Sajahatra Bangsamoro. The first joint Government of the Philippines (GPH)-MILF development initiative, Sajahatra commenced with much fanfare in early 2013, when President Aquino travelled for the first time to the MILF heartland in Maguindanao province for the ceremonial launch. Pitched explicitly as a confidence-building measure, Sajahatra provided assistance in MILF communities for health, education and livelihood. A counterpart MILF-appointed Project Management Team (PMT) worked hand-in-hand with government agencies such as the Department of Education, the Commission on Higher Education, the Technical Education and Skills Development Authority, and the Departments of Social Welfare and Development, Health and Agriculture. The MILF PMT opened up security access on the ground, identified beneficiaries and monitored implementation. Assistance included free health insurance, cash-for-work, university study grants, technical vocational training fellowships and agricultural inputs and equipment for

FIGURE 7.2
Annual Budget for PAMANA (in PhP billion)

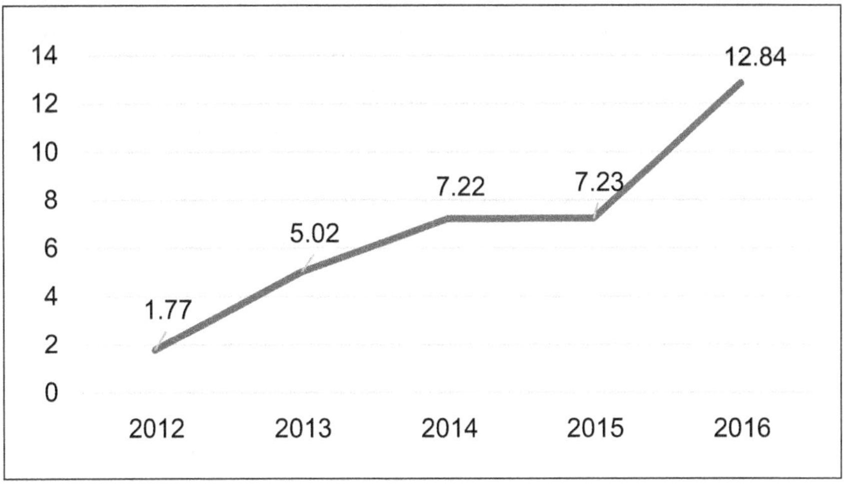

Source: OPAPP.

farmers. Over the period 2013–15, Sajahatra benefited over 50,000 people across conflict-affected areas of Mindanao.[17]

The other main element of the complementary track was an effort to strengthen institutions. The primary target was the ARMM regional government. In 2011 the national government suspended elections in an ARMM region still reeling from the aftermath of the 2009 Maguindanao massacre.[18] The suspension synchronized voting in the region with the national election schedule. The main reason for this move was to professionalize and clean up ARMM, which President Aquino had described as a "failed experiment".[19] Mujiv Hataman was appointed as an interim Regional Governor, with a remit for reform. As governance improved, the ARMM annual budget was massively increased during the 2011–16 period from PhP11 to PhP28 billion.[20]

Measuring success or otherwise of the government's initiatives on the complementary track is difficult. PAMANA had no baseline or rigorous evaluation, leaving the government uncertain as to whether almost US$750 million in spending had achieved any peacebuilding aims.[21] However, with or without these data it is evident the government's approach was never going to be sufficient to "address the causes and impacts of all internal armed conflicts and other issues affecting the peace process".[22] PAMANA, Sajahatra and the increased expenditure in ARMM delivered important benefits to needy communities. I have seen these programmes in hundreds of rural villages across conflict-affected Mindanao—from Surigao in the northeast to Tawi-Tawi in the southwest. It is clear the programmes were appreciated by communities and played a confidence-building role by meeting some basic needs and expanding the presence of the state into previously neglected areas.[23]

Despite these successes, the government's approach to development lacked a strategy beyond confidence-building—a critical precondition for peacebuilding—but as the 2011 WDR states, "is not an end in itself. Progress will not be sustained unless underlying problems are addressed to prevent a recurrence of violence."[24]

This is where the Aquino government's approach fell short. Many members of various armed groups in Mindanao fight for ideological reasons, but a large number are also driven by poverty and unemployment or underemployment.[25] PAMANA was designed to address this problem by generating jobs and economic opportunity to "build community resilience against armed violence", yet PAMANA was not suited to this purpose. Global evidence and from the Philippines show that community development programmes like PAMANA's pillar two are effective at providing services to poor communities and can build social cohesion and trust in the government. Together with larger investments under pillar 3 they had the potential to link remote communities to market opportunities. Operating mostly in isolation, evidence suggests, however, that such programmes do not generate employment at the scale required to offer a serious alternative to joining an armed group—nor can they be expected to reduce violence.[26]

In the case of PAMANA, grants were initially made available to villages identified as conflict-affected. In response to complaints from neighbouring local chief executives whose villages missed out on funding, OPAPP changed the system so all villages in a conflict-affected municipality would receive a PAMANA grant. This was done in the name of equity and to extend state presence into as many areas as possible. The expansion of sites without additional budget meant many communities received a per capita level of funding that an evaluation of the Philippine government's own national community development programme had shown was insufficient to generate meaningful economic impacts.[27]

Under Sajahatra Bangsamoro, assistance actually directed towards jobs and income-generation—such as technical vocational skills training—was often misdirected. The MILF allowed beneficiaries to select training courses not necessarily suited to the local market. The government acquiesced for relationship-building purposes.[28] Consequently, in a number of villages, I met young men who had received fellowships in computer maintenance who then returned to villages with neither electricity nor computers. Vocational training was not complemented by the job referral and counselling systems or start-up capital generally needed to translate skills into employment. Agricultural support for farmers often comprised whatever the Department of Agriculture had available and was not always related to needs identified in the target villages.[29]

The suite of assistance on offer did not generate jobs required to underpin stability and support more inclusive growth. In fairness to the government, the MILF has long opposed large-scale development initiatives, asserting that the development track must never move ahead of the political. But assistance could have been provided to match real needs of farmers in what is an agrarian economy. Larger-scale and longer-term cash-for-work and other active market labour programmes to stabilize conflict-affected areas could have been pursued. Incentives provided to attract private sector investment for more sustained employment creation were minimal.

While the government was able to mobilize more funding for conflict-affected areas during the Aquino administration, much more was needed. To catch up to the current national Gross Domestic Product (GDP) per capita, ARMM would require regional GDP growth per annum of 21.4 per cent for ten years.[30]

The previous analysis is not intended as a criticism of OPAPP, which was able to oversee an expansion of development programmes in conflict-affected areas. OPAPP's focus on confidence-building was consistent with its mandate. To truly address the socioeconomic drivers of conflict in Mindanao requires a concentrated and dedicated long-term, whole-of-government effort and a level of resources that the Aquino administration was unable to muster.

Limited Investment in Institutions

The WDR framework highlights the importance of legitimate institutions to break cycles of violence. Recognizing this, the mid-term update of the Philippine Development Plan expanded the emphasis of "complementary track" from development through PAMANA to institutions in conflict-affected areas.[31] Yet, with government capacity already stretched by the challenges of the political track, PAMANA and Sajahatra, less was achieved on the institutional agenda.

Some progress was made in terms of reform in ARMM. The regional government passed the central government's Good Governance Conditions for the first time in history.[32] The number of ARMM Local Government Units (LGUs) who received the Department of the Interior and Local Government's Good Financial Housekeeping award for meeting audit and transparency standards increased from 15 per cent in 2014 to 63 per cent in 2016—against a national average of 93 per cent. Six of the 123 LGUs in ARMM—4.8 per cent—received the more robust Seal of Good Local Governance in 2016—up from zero two years earlier—with a national average of 18.8 per cent.[33] Major improvements were achieved in internal management systems, with the Office of the Regional Governor and the ARMM Technical Education and Skills Development Authority receiving ISO certification for Quality Management.[34] Some service delivery improvements were also recorded. For instance, road construction expanded from 40 kilometres in 2012 to 505 kilometres in 2015. According to the 2013 Functional Literacy, Education and Mass Media Survey (FLEMMS), basic literacy increased to 86.1 per cent in 2013 from 81.5 per cent in 2008. Private sector investment in the region also reached record levels, albeit from a low base (see Figure 7.3). The 2016 decline was expected as an election year, but still surpassed the target of PhP900 million.

These achievements helped to restore credibility to the ARMM regional government. However, socioeconomic impacts remain variable. In 2015 the Gross Regional Domestic Product actually declined by 0.4 per cent after years of positive growth, rebounding by 0.3 per cent in 2016. The 2015 data also indicated that poverty had barely declined in the region, despite increased expenditure and apparent governance improvements (see Figure 7.4). Turning ARMM around is clearly a long-term challenge.

While spending billions of pesos on community development with the aim of building resilience against conflict—the government overlooked two crucial institutional reform agendas that would have genuinely built such resilience—the performance of local government units and the institutions of justice.

FIGURE 7.3
Private Sector Investments in ARMM, 2012–16 (in PhP million)

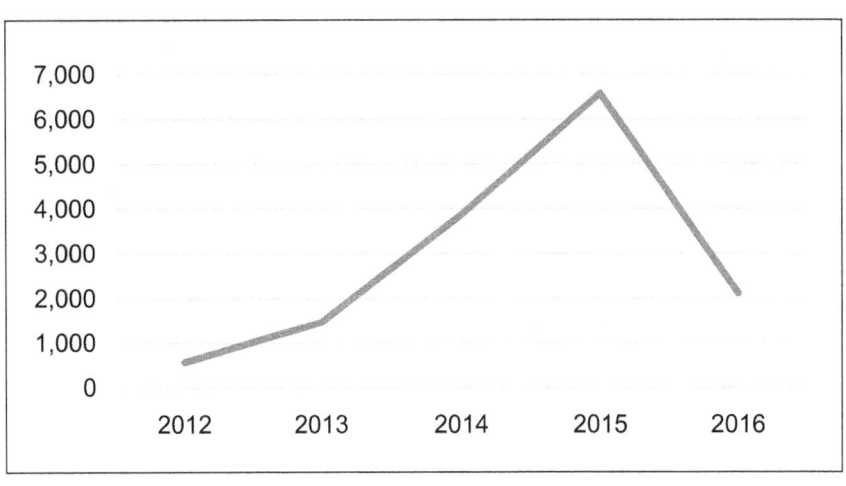

Source: ARMM Regional Board of Investments 2016, Accomplishment Report.

FIGURE 7.4
Poverty Incidence among Population in ARMM, 2006–15

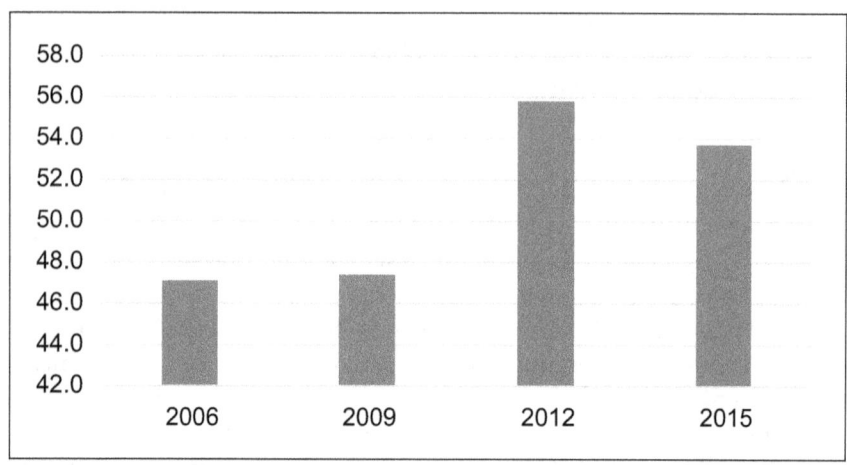

Source: Philippine Statistics Authority 2015, Official Poverty Statistics.

Local Governance: Security and Development Challenge

Weak local governance is widely acknowledged as one of the key drivers of poverty and insecurity in Mindanao.[35] Although there are exceptions, local government performance in ARMM is characterized by a lack of accountability, absenteeism and poor service delivery. In Mindanao and, particularly in ARMM, many local officials maintain private armies or use local Philippine National Police (PNP) units as de facto private armies.[36] According to the PNP, there are eighty-five private armed groups in the Philippines—80 per cent of which are in ARMM and Central Mindanao.[37]

Often led by powerful families who control both politics and the economy, LGUs have proven resistant to measures to extract accountability for performance. The 1991 Local Government Code established an intergovernmental fiscal framework providing LGUs with an automatic appropriation regardless of performance. Elections have generally proven ineffective as a means of holding local officials accountable.[38]

Of total government resources available in ARMM, only 2.2 per cent is own-sourced revenue—indicating low technical capacity and little formal sector economic activity to tax.[39] This low percentage also reflects the reality that much of the ARMM economy is informal or illicit and that politicians who control the local economy have little interest in taxing themselves, their family members or their financiers.[40]

The inability of local governments in conflict-affected areas to deliver services or maintain security is a major challenge to peacebuilding, which requires among other things, meeting basic human needs. Senior officials in the Aquino administration were cognizant of this problem—with many expressing concerns that clans and "traditional politicians" would hijack the proposed Bangsamoro political entity. Rather than promoting peace and development, the CAB would then simply serve to entrench the power of existing elites who benefit from the status quo of poverty, insecurity and impunity.

Despite recognizing this risk, the government did not launch serious reform of the LGUs. There are three main reasons for this. Firstly, the national legal framework limits options for reform. As already noted, the Local Government Code guarantees an automatic appropriation from the national government to all LGUs, regardless of performance. The "autonomous" ARMM government has no hierarchical relationship over the region's constituent LGUs, which receive the bulk of their funds from Manila—and few levers to drive LGUs to improve service delivery or security. Since its passage in 1991, the Local Government Code has proven effectively untouchable as Congress wishes to maintain LGU dependence on Manila for political reasons.[41]

Secondly, it is practically very difficult to improve the performance of local governments in much of ARMM. Dynastic political structures abound across the Philippines, particularly in Mindanao. The Herfindahl index measures concentration of political power and was formulated based on the proportion of mayoral terms between 1988 and 2013 held by one political family in a particular municipality. The index ranges from zero to one—the higher the value, the greater concentration of political power. A score of one could mean a single family controlled all nine mayoral terms in the period in question. The average political Herfindahl index at the municipal level in Mindanao is 0.51, higher than Luzon at 0.45 and the Visayas at 0.46.[42] In Mindanao, the three ARMM island provinces of Basilan, Sulu and Tawi-Tawi have the highest index at 0.58. While there are some progressive dynasties, there is a strong correlation between limited political competition and poverty.[43] The clans and political dynasties have a very strong hold on power, limiting both competition and incentives to reform.

The third, and most crucial, reason is political. Establishing the Bangsamoro entity requires two steps. Congress has completed the first of these by passing the BOL. The BOL now needs to be ratified by the population through a plebiscite in affected areas. Voting patterns are to a large degree determined by local chief executives across the Philippines—particularly in ARMM where feudalism and dynastic politics remain strong.[44] Thus, securing public support for a plebiscite to establish the Bangsamoro requires the support of ARMM's existing local political elites. As already mentioned, many of these figures maintain private armies with the capacity to generate insecurity. Any moves to limit their power by removing existing privileges or strengthening regional control over local governments would, therefore, constitute political suicide for the Bangsamoro project. The government and MILF felt they had no choice but to shelve plans to reform local governance in return for the political support of the clans for the BOL.

The government also invested limited resources in strengthening the justice sector or addressing historical injustice, a key driver of violent conflict in Mindanao.[45] Land administration and management agencies are weak in Mindanao.[46] At the same time, a number of effective dispute resolution mechanisms operate in different parts of Mindanao, resolving *rido* (clan feuds) and grievances over land and natural resources.[47] The government and MILF formed a Transitional Justice and Reconciliation Commission (TJRC) to study historical injustice, including over land dispossession. Up to 2018, the TJRC report launched in March 2016 has not received a response from the GPH and MILF panels.

The government spent PhP34 billion (US$733 million) on PAMANA. Allocating as little as 10 per cent of that budget to strengthen local dispute resolution mechanisms, build the capacity of land administration and management agencies, and begin to address social and economic impacts of unjust land dispossession would arguably have been more effective in "building community resilience against armed conflict". No serious investment of resources was made, however, to enhance the performance of the justice sector or land-related agencies during Aquino's term.

SUMMARY: AQUINO ADMINISTRATION

The Aquino administration made solid gains on peacemaking. The political track was undermined, however, by insufficient attention to constituency-building that saw the BBL fail in Congress.

Increased development spending delivered valuable benefits to communities for peacebuilding. The development strategy did not, however, reach beyond confidence-building and was of insufficient scale to address the economic drivers of conflict.

In terms of institutional development, the ARMM reforms demonstrated the Bangsamoro people are more than capable of exercising self-governance. However, other key institutions—particularly local governments and the justice sector—remain inadequate for long-term peacebuilding. Incentive structures for these institutions have not changed and business as usual prevails.

In security terms, the Aquino administration was not able to address the "causes of armed conflict and other issues that affect the peace process". Data from International Alert's Bangsamoro Conflict Monitoring System demonstrate that—despite very few incidents involving the MILF or MNLF—overall levels of violence increased in the proposed Bangsamoro territory between 2011 and 2016.

Private armed groups (PAGs) remain prevalent in Mindanao. The government and MILF established a task force to disband the PAGs but it was never convened.[48] Senior government officials told me they expected the MILF to "take care of" PAGs once in government. Senior

FIGURE 7.5
Violent Conflict Incidents and Deaths in the Proposed Bangsamoro Territory, 2011–16

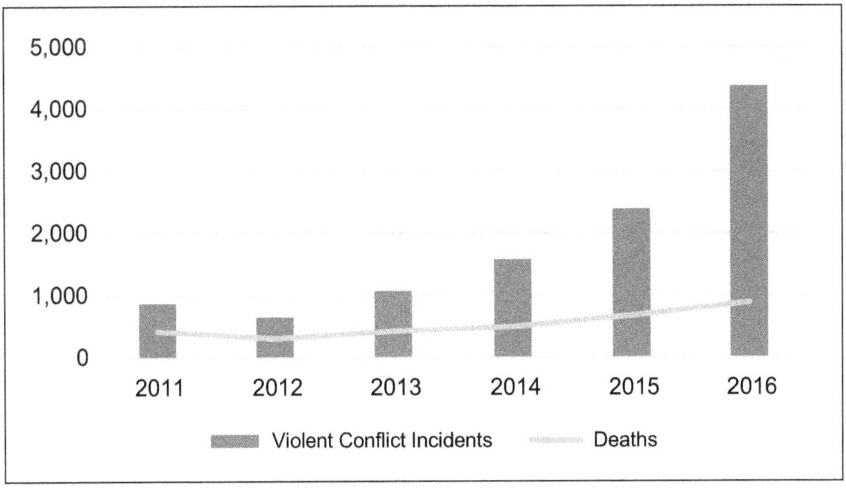

Source: Bangsamoro Conflict Monitoring System.

MILF representatives said they expected government to come up with a plan.[49]

The Aquino administration handed over the peacebuilding challenges of addressing injustice, jobs, security and strengthening institutions to the new government in July 2016. The next section examines how the Duterte administration has tackled those challenges over the first two years.

A MINDANAOAN IN MALACANANG: THE DUTERTE OPPORTUNITY

The election of Rodrigo Duterte was met with a sense of optimism by most proponents of the peace process. Here was a Mindanaoan, who understood the issues, personally knew the key players, came with a track record of negotiation with communist insurgents in Davao City and even claimed Moro blood. Duterte carried a mandate for change and appeared to be an atypical politician who could confront difficult issues, seemingly unburdened by the shackles of vested interests.

The early signs were promising. In July 2016, OPAPP launched a new road map for peace and development that included several bold features distinguishing it from its predecessor. Firstly, the road map insisted on convergence between the two Moro fronts. Secondly, constitutional change was put on the table as a viable option. Thirdly, it offered the prospect of federalism to make genuine autonomy for the Bangsamoro more politically feasible. Lastly, talks with communist insurgents were resurrected.

The road map elicited a positive response from civil society, leaders of the MILF and the international community. Inclusivity and Moro convergence had the potential to forge a more robust peace that could unify ethnic groups and clans across the mainland-island divide. Federalism could provide useful political cover for the Bangsamoro process. Over several decades Congress had proven wary of "rewarding" a rebellious minority with special autonomy—which would become more politically palatable if the entire country were to benefit under a federal system.

Mindanaoans were appointed to many key positions in government, including OPAPP Secretary, Jesus Dureza. Dureza rapidly shifted the narrative from negotiating to implementing peace. Peace panels were changed from "negotiating" to "implementing" panels. The Malaysian facilitator and International Contact Group were retained but sidelined—no longer seen as central players in the implementation phase. There were calls for rapid action, as Secretary Dureza himself said in August 2016, "these ... steps are in line with President Duterte's avowed commitment to quicken the pace of the peace process to bring about an early and much-needed end to conflict."[50]

The major achievement in the intervening period has been the passage of the BOL in July 2018. Despite this milestone achievement, the initial optimism has largely turned to concern. Talks with the CNN have collapsed. Moro convergence has been partially successful, but MNLF founder Nur Misuari remains outside the process. The government is ill-equipped to address violent extremism, even after the shock of the 2017 occupation of Marawi City by a coalition of groups affiliated with the so-called Islamic State (IS).[51] Like the preceding government, Duterte's administration has also left the challenging peacebuilding agenda largely untouched.

Despite the limited progress, Duterte's ongoing high public popularity means he retains the political capital to ensure full government attention to addressing the root causes of conflict.[52] As Professor Tony La Viña of Ateneo University stated in mid-2017, "the present political climate presents a most opportune time to stop the bloodshed and create peace."[53] There are a number of obstacles before the parties can move beyond the peacemaking stage and on to deeper progress on peacebuilding. The next section examines these challenges.

CHALLENGES TO PEACEMAKING

Rebuild Momentum

Despite the early talk of speeding up, progress has been slow. The President took four and a half months to reconstitute the Bangsamoro Transition Commission to draft the new BBL[54] and another three months to appoint its members. Over the subsequent several months the BTC was not provided with a budget, forcing it to rely on credit from friendly hotels for meetings and consultations and personal contributions from Commissioners to cover travel costs. As noted, there has still been no response to the report of the Transitional Justice and Reconciliation Commission. Four and a half years since the CAB was signed there is still no clear plan for the transition of MILF combatants to civilians or to address Mindanao's broader security challenges.

There are many reasons for the slow progress, but the most important has been a political strategy that vacillated between pursuing the BBL/BOL or federalism. Duterte's public statements on the issue varied, stating before he ran for the presidency that the BBL should be a back-up option if federalism was not supported by the public.[55] As president, Duterte's public position was that the BBL should be passed before federalism, serving as a template for the rest of the country.[56] Mixed messages on the president's real strategy were conveyed to different stakeholders over the first two years of the administration, causing confusion and frustration.

Whatever the reasoning, the government allowed the Bangsamoro peace process to drift. Many in government felt this was a low-risk approach, as they no longer considered the MILF to be an existential threat to the state. While this may well be true in relation to the senior MILF leadership—which is so deeply ensconced in the peace process that it has few options but to stay the course—it is not the case with all MILF combatants or some of its military commanders, who are at risk of being driven by frustration to other armed groups or indeed to split completely.[57]

Evidently the government did not foresee that IS-affiliated groups would develop the capacity to launch large-scale attacks as the Bangsamoro peace process drifted. However, the siege in Marawi City was the peak event in what had been an emerging pattern of activity by IS-affiliated groups—including the temporary capture of territory in Butig town, Lanao del Sur in June and November 2016, the September 2016 bombing in Davao City and the April 2017 attempt to kidnap foreign tourists in Bohol.

The extremist threat would have existed with or without the BBL, but the failure to move more quickly on the Bangsamoro process fomented frustration, particularly among Bangsamoro youth. Amina Rasul, head of the Philippine Center for Islam and Democracy, warned in February 2017, "government inaction on the passage of the Bangsamoro Basic Law is adding fuel to the fire. This we cannot afford as the reach of violent extremism has expanded globally."[58] These warnings were seemingly unheeded. With the "success" of Marawi as a selling point, violent extremist groups are still recruiting, and foreign fighters continue to arrive in Mindanao.[59] Lack of progress also affected credibility of the MILF leadership, who saw their legitimacy as the vanguard of Moro aspirations for autonomy dissipating.

Understanding and Addressing the Extremist Threat

The scale of the attack on Marawi City surprised even the most well-informed analysts. It was a game changer for violent conflict in the Philippines that escalates the risk to other cities in Mindanao and beyond, including Manila.

Almost a year and a half after Marawi, the government is currently drafting a National Action Plan to counter violent extremism. The plan needs to be based on a better understanding of the nature of the threat by mapping out the origin, composition, funding sources, local and international support networks and recruitment approaches of the different groups. Such information should in turn inform the formulation—as has been done in Indonesia—of a comprehensive strategy that goes beyond the current narrow and ineffective security approach.[60] The strategy should include enhanced security and intelligence approaches, coupled with community-based programmes that work with religious leaders in prisons, schools and universities. Enhanced cooperation with Indonesia, Malaysia and Singapore will be necessary given regional linkages.[61]

Bringing youth more effectively into the peace process would help policymakers to better understand the nature and appeal of the extremist threat. The Duterte government prioritized an inclusive peace process. The 2011 WDR states that coalitions for peace need to be "inclusive enough". So, not all stakeholders need be brought on board, but rather only those with the influence to make or break the process.

The government identified the MILF, MNLF, Indigenous Peoples, the ARMM, traditional Muslim leaders (Sultans) and religious leaders as key parties. More "inclusive" has, therefore, mostly meant more groups of old men sitting around the table. Bangsamoro youth have not been given a serious voice in the process.

As the Moro fronts have committed to the compromises inherent in negotiating peace, they have inevitably become—and become seen as—moderate. Consequently, the more radical political space they once occupied is now open. Youth leaders and intellectuals in the Bangsamoro raised concerns about the radicalization of Bangsamoro youth before the Marawi attack, led by the youthful Maute Group. Substantive engagement should be pursued with male and female youth leaders to bring them into the peace process.

CHALLENGES TO PEACEBUILDING

The deeper problems of peacebuilding must be addressed to complement passage of the BOL. The government has defined its peacebuilding approach in a draft Strategic Framework for Peace and Development.[62] The UN states that peacebuilding strategies "should comprise a carefully prioritized, sequenced, and relatively narrow set of activities".[63] The Strategic Framework is too broad to provide useful guidance on priorities and sequencing.[64]

The remainder of this section sets out some suggested actions to provide prioritization. These actions are required for the government to address the root causes of the conflict—historical injustice, insecurity, weak governance, and lack of economic opportunity.

Historical Injustice

In his first State of the Nation Address in July 2016, President Duterte acknowledged, "there's a historical injustice committed against the Moro people. We have to correct it."[65] The report of the Transitional Justice and Reconciliation Commission documents a history of discrimination, human rights violations and unjust dispossession of land. Launched in March 2016, the report includes over ninety recommendations, to which the parties are yet to respond. This omission undermined confidence in the government's sincerity and should be addressed as a matter of priority.

Security

Of the 14,873 incidents of violent conflict recorded in ARMM by International Alert's Bangsamoro Conflict Monitoring System between 2011 and 2017, only 124 involved the MILF and 26 the MNLF.[66] This does not mean that the MILF and MNLF are no longer a threat to security. A splintered MILF would actually be the greatest risk to security in the region. Rather, the data demonstrates that, in a region with multiple private armed groups and as many as 800,000 loose firearms, translating the CAB and BOL into improved security will require a broad-based strategy beyond retiring the threat from the Moro fronts.[67]

The normalization programme under the Bangsamoro peace process includes police reform, redeployment of military personnel and decommissioning of MILF troops and weapons. The GPH-MILF Joint Normalization Committee has met regularly since its establishment but is yet to issue clear plans or come up with a workable operational model. There is also deep unhappiness in the MILF about how 145 combatants ceremonially decommissioned in June 2015 were handled by the government—raising concerns about how the larger estimated number of 30,000 to 40,000 will be managed. The Philippine government has a poor track record of demobilizing combatants dating back to the 1980s and remains far from ready to deal with the MILF caseload. The government needs to work with the international community to prepare a detailed plan. The BOL is also not fully consistent with the Annex on Normalization to the CAB, which provides the roadmap for the normalization process. The GPH and MILF will need to revise and update the Annex to align it with the provisions of the BOL.

A credible security strategy would need to build on normalization with four additional features. Firstly, decommissioning assistance for MILF combatants should be expanded to include other groups and individuals with conflict carrying capacities to neutralize the security risk they pose. This would need to include the MNLF, private armed groups and government militia.[68] Secondly, targeted trials should be launched to reduce the number of small arms and light weapons in circulation in Mindanao through initiatives such as gun amnesties and buy-back schemes. Third, local dispute resolution mechanisms should be strengthened. In different parts of Mindanao, initiatives involving traditional and religious leaders, the government, the security sector and civil society have proven effective in resolving local resource conflicts.[69] More can be done to assist existing mechanisms and create new bodies. Finally, major investments will be needed to strengthen land administration and management, including dealing with the history of unjust dispossession of land. The TJRC report recommends actions to strengthen land governance and to deal with the past through restitution and reparations. Implementing these recommendations will be difficult and costly but should be considered a top priority to improve security and the environment for business.

Local Governance

Local governance challenges in conflict-affected Mindanao are well understood and freely acknowledged in the ARMM's 2017–2022 Regional

Development Plan.[70] No amount of training and technical capacity-building can fix this problem. Incentive structures must be adjusted to promote better service delivery and accountability to meet the basic needs of the Bangsamoro people.

The Bangsamoro peace process offers the opportunity to recraft the local governance framework. According to Article VI, section 10 of the Bangsamoro Organic Law (Republic Act 11054),

> The authority of the Bangsamoro government to regulate the affairs of its constituent local government units shall be guaranteed in accordance with this Organic Law and a Bangsamoro local government code to be enacted by the Parliament. The privileges already enjoyed by local government units under Republic Act No. 7160, otherwise known as the Local Government Code of 1991 as amended, and other existing laws shall not be diminished.

The BOL seems to bestow authority on the proposed Bangsamoro parliament to exercise more authority over the LGUs and dilute their dependence on Manila. Given the new Bangsamoro government will be reliant on the mayors and governors to guarantee stability, however, it is unlikely it would have the political capital to aggressively assert regional control. The central government will need to step in and provide incentives to local chief executives to accept a more powerful regional government that can exact accountability and drive better performance from the LGUs.

Creating Economic Opportunity: Transforming the Mindanao Economy and Generating Jobs

The government should agree on a comprehensive, conflict-sensitive strategy to transform the economy of Mindanao—focusing on job creation and education. The vision should be for Mindanao—and conflict-affected Mindanao in particular—to catch up to the rest of the country within twenty years.

For a long time, there has been no clear lead in government on strategic planning for economic development in Mindanao's conflict-affected areas. Under the Duterte administration, OPAPP and the Mindanao Development Authority (MinDA) share this role through joint stewardship of the Strategic

Framework for Mindanao Peace and Development. They are trying to secure an Executive Order to oblige key government line agencies to support the Framework. These agencies include Departments of Agriculture, Public Works and Highways, Social Welfare and Development and Transport and Communications. Mobilizing national government agencies—traditionally wary of heavily investing in the country's most difficult region—will require the direct intervention of the President.

The development approach should prioritize massive job creation as a stabilization measure, starting with a Mindanao-wide youth employment programme to reach out to the most vulnerable and neglected areas. In addition, incentives will be needed for private sector investment and support extended to smallholder farmers, complemented by a major push on education—including literacy—and skills. Alternative service delivery means through local and international non-governmental organizations should be explored as an interim measure in areas where the government is not capable.[71]

The strategy will need to look at the Mindanao economy as a whole, not just the conflict-affected areas. Large parts of Mindanao—including cities such as General Santos, Davao, Iligan and Cagayan de Oro—are growing rapidly. Sustaining growth in these locations can generate jobs to absorb labour from conflict-affected regions.[72]

The investments in development and institutions required to stabilize and catch up will take twenty to thirty years of dedicated financial and technical assistance. Whether the Duterte government has the capacity or willingness to head down that path is unclear. The slow pace of reconstruction in Marawi would suggest it has neither,[73] but without it, the inclusive growth required to underpin stability and address the economic drivers of conflict in Mindanao will remain an aspiration.

CONCLUSION

The administration of President Aquino made strong progress on the peacemaking agenda, highlighted by the conclusion of agreements with the largest insurgent group, the Moro Islamic Liberation Front.

Less progress was made on long-term peacebuilding. Addressing structural causes of protracted social conflict is time-consuming and difficult. Philippine governments have rarely been able to apply sufficient dedicated financial and technical resources to challenges requiring long-term, concerted attention.

The election of Rodrigo Duterte promised change—in line with his image as a "man of action". Senior Duterte government officials distinguished themselves from the civil society workers and peace advocates who worked in the Aquino administration as wheelers and dealers who would shift the process from negotiation to implementation.

So far, the record has not lived up to those expectations. Hamstrung by a confused political strategy, a narrow focus on security-based approaches to combating violent extremism and little attention to peacebuilding challenges, limited progress has been made overall. In the meantime, the ground has shifted as the IS threat has emerged as a major risk to national and regional security.

Despite difficulties, the opportunity to turn the situation around remains. The passage of the Bangsamoro Organic Law is an important achievement that has addressed a core historical grievance, restored the credibility of the political process and reduced space for recruitment by extremist groups.

Autonomy is not, however, the panacea to Mindanao's ills. An MILF-led autonomous government will comprise people with limited experience in governing. Key appointments will inevitably have to place a premium on political accommodation over technical capacity. This relatively weak government will continue to face the root causes of conflict.

A long-term commitment is required to build institutions that can gradually improve security and transform the economy. This will be a massive test of the will and capacity of the Philippine state to finally deal with the Mindanao question.

The root causes of conflict cannot be settled during the term of the current government, but without serious action along that path, conflict-affected Mindanao will, at best, remain trapped in poverty and low-level violence. At worst, the national and regional security implications are too serious to allow for continued inaction in what is a rapidly evolving context. How Duterte tackles these peacebuilding challenges may well determine his legacy as president.

Notes

The views expressed in this article are those of the author rather than the institutions to which he is, or has been, affiliated.
1. Nigel Roberts, "Mindanao: the Political Psychology of Peace", *Philippine Daily Inquirer*, 30 March 2014, http://opinion.inquirer.net/73092/mindanao-the-political-psychology-of-peace (accessed 30 August 2016).

2. United Nations Peacekeeping, http://www.un.org/en/peacekeeping/operations/peace.shtml (accessed 23 July 2017).
3. Alliance for Peacebuilding, http://www.allianceforpeacebuilding.org/what-is-peacebuilding/ (accessed 23 July 2017).
4. John Braithwaite, Sinclair Dinnen, Matthew Allen, Valerie Braithwaite, and Hilary Charlesworth, *Pillars and Shadows: Statebuilding as Peacebuilding in Solomon Islands* (Canberra: ANU Press, 2010), p. 1.
5. John Braithwaite, *Regulatory Capitalism: How It Works, Ideas for Making It Better* (Cheltenham: Edward Elgar, 2008), pp. 115–26.
6. Ronald J. Fisher, "The Potential for Peacebuilding: Forging a Bridge from Peacekeeping to Peacemaking", *Peace & Change* 18, no. 3 (1993): 259.
7. World Bank, *World Development Report 2011: Conflict, Security and Development* (Washington, D.C.: World Bank Group, 2011).
8. See Chapter 9 of National Economic and Development Authority (henceforth NEDA), *Philippine Development Plan 2011–2016* (Pasig City: NEDA, 2011).
9. See Chapter 8 on "Peace and Security" of NEDA, *Philippine Development Plan 2011–2016 Midterm Update* (Pasig City: NEDA, 2013).
10. For more information on PAMANA, see http://www.pamana.net/.
11. See above note 7. OPAPP senior officials adopted elements of the WDR 2011 framework following a presentation from co-Director Nigel Roberts in early 2012. Roberts returned to the Philippines several times at the request of OPAPP to present on the framework to various stakeholders, including OPAPP staff.
12. Transitional Justice and Reconciliation Commission, "Report of the Transitional Justice and Reconciliation Commission", 2016, www.tjrc.ph.
13. Former OPAPP Secretary Quintos-Deles claimed that no encounters occurred between the MILF and the government between 2012 and March 2016 except for the January 2015 Mamasapano incident (see "Closing Remarks of Sec. Teresita Quintos-Deles on the Commemoration of the 2nd Anniversary of the Signing of the CAB" at http://www.opapp.gov.ph/resources/closing-remarks-sec-teresita-quintos-deles-commemoration-2nd-anniversary-signing-cab (accessed 27 August 2016). But this is not consistent with International Alert's Bangsamoro Conflict Monitoring System data—available at www.conflictalert.info.
14. These include the Joint Coordination Committee for the Cessation of Hostilities and the Ad Hoc Joint Action Group. An International Monitoring Team also oversees the ceasefire.
15. Author's interview with senior adviser to then Cotabato City Mayor and MNLF (Sema) Secretary-General, Muslimin Sema, Cotabato City, August 2009.
16. Office of the Presidential Adviser on the Peace Process, "PAMANA Progress Report 2015", http://pamana.net/resources/pamana-status-reports, 2016 (accessed 27 August 2016).
17. See Mindanao Trust Fund 2015, "GPH-MILF Sajahatra Bangsamoro Program Implementation Lessons Learned Documentation", unpublished document.

Prospects for Lasting Peace in Mindanao 233

18. On 23 November 2009, fifty-eight people were killed in an election-related massacre in Ampatuan, Maguindanao province. No convictions have yet been recorded, but the principal suspects include then ARMM Regional Governor, Zaldy Ampatuan, his brother, Andal Ampatuan Jr. and their father, the late Andal Ampatuan Sr. who was then Maguindanao Governor.
19. Benigno S. Aquino III, "Speech of President Aquino on the Framework Agreement with the MILF, October 7, 2012", http://www.officialgazette.gov.ph/2012/10/07/speech-of-president-aquino-the-framework-agreement-with-the-milf-october-7-2012-full-english/ (accessed 21 July 2017).
20. Additional funds of around PhP8 billion were also provided to ARMM through the Transitional Investment Support Program, a product of the Disbursement Acceleration Program, which was later declared unconstitutional by the Supreme Court.
21. The government undertook a qualitative evaluation of PAMANA, but the results have not been widely shared.
22. NEDA, *Philippine Development Plan 2011–2016 Midterm Update*, p. 187.
23. In the interests of transparency, the author notes that the World Bank supported the MILF's Sajahatra Bangsamoro Project Management Team under the Mindanao Trust Fund (www.mtf.ph), provided some technical assistance for the initial design of PAMANA in 2010 and has been a partner of ARMM on various initiatives.
24. World Bank, *World Development Report 2011* (Synopsis), http://web.worldbank.org/archive/website01306/web/pdf/english_wdr%202011_synopsis%20no%20embargo.pdf (accessed 27 August 2016).
25. A survey from five countries in the 2011 WDR showed that unemployment/idleness was the main reason respondents joined armed groups—see above, note 7 at p. 9. A recent study from Colombia also showed a mix of ideological and economic reasons for taking up arms—see Paola Pena, Joaquin Urrego and Juan M. Villa, "Civil Conflict and Conditional Cash Transfers: Effects on Demobilization", *Universidad Aefit Working Paper on Economics & Finance* No. 15-10 (Medellín: Universidad EAFIT, 2015). In the Institute of Bangsamoro Studies and Centre for Humanitarian Dialogue, *Armed Violence in Mindanao: Militia and Private Armies* (Geneva: Centre for Humanitarian Dialogue, 2011), p. 40, a sample of government militia members identified poverty/lack of employment opportunities as the main motive for joining. We cannot extrapolate that members of private armed groups or non-state armed groups are equally driven by poverty, but it is very likely that many are. Poverty and joblessness are acknowledged even by the MILF as an important cause of conflict.
26. On the impact of community development programmes on conflict, see Susan Wong, *What Have Been the Impacts of World Bank Community Development Programs?* (Washington, D.C.: World Bank, 2012), p. 32. See also Patrick Barron, "CDD in Post-Conflict and Conflict-Affected Areas: Experiences from

East Asia", World Development Report 2011 Background Paper (Washington, D.C.: World Bank, 2010), http://siteresources.worldbank.org/EXTWDR2011/Resources/6406082-1283882418764/WDR_Background_Paper_Barron.pdf (accessed 21 July 2017).
27. World Bank, *Philippines: The KALAHI-CIDSS Impact Evaluation—A Revised Synthesis Report* (Manila: World Bank Group, 2013).
28. Confirmed in a number of discussions with senior OPAPP officials working on Sajahatra Bangsamoro.
29. Findings from multiple site visits to Sajahatra Bangsamoro locations from 2013 to 2015, including as documented in World Bank Aide Memoire #10, Mindanao Trust Fund-Reconstruction & Development Program, 22–26 September 2014.
30. Moro Islamic Liberation Front, *Bangsamoro Development Plan* (Cotabato City: Bangsamoro Development Agency, 2015), p. 23.
31. The WDR argues that all countries face internal and external stresses. Legitimate institutions—those with technical capacity and accountability—can withstand such stresses and prevent them from turning into violence.
32. See official website of the Autonomous Region in Muslim Mindanao, "ARMM Passes Good Governance Tests", http://www.armm.gov.ph/armm-passes-good-governance-tests/ (accessed 28 August 2016).
33. Details on the Department of Interior and Local Government, Reports and Resources, http://www.dilg.gov.ph/reports-and-resources/seal-of-good-local-governance/12/ (accessed 1 August 2017).
34. On TESDA-ARMM, see official website of the Bureau of Public Information "TESDA-ARMM receives ISO certification", http://www.armm-info.com/2014/10/tesda-armm-receives-iso-certification.html. For the Office of the Regional Governor, see official website of the Autonomous Region in Muslim Mindanao, "The ISO Certification of ORG-ARMM", https://armm.gov.ph/iso-certification/ (both accessed 21 July 2017).
35. See Mindanao Development Authority, *Mindanao 2020: Peace and Development Framework Plan 2011–2030* (Davao City: MinDA, 2011), p. 149; and Human Development Network, *Philippines Human Development Report: Peace, Human Security and Development in the Philippines* (Manila: Human Development Network, 2005), p. 47. The government's 2017 draft "Mindanao Strategic Framework for Peace and Development" also recognizes that "the conflicts have persisted due in large part to a deep sense of injustice stemming from poor or failed governance over many decades" at p. 6.
36. See Institute of Bangsamoro Studies and Centre for Humanitarian Dialogue, *Armed Violence in Mindanao* (Geneva: Centre for Humanitarian Dialogue, 2011).
37. Germelina Lacorte and Judy Quiros, "PNP: Most of Private Armed Groups

Found in ARMM, Central Mindanao", *Philippine Daily Inquirer*, 1 April 2016, http://newsinfo.inquirer.net/777325/pnp-most-of-private-armed-groups-found-in-armm-central-mindanao (accessed 29 August 2016).
38. See Romulo A. Virola, Severa B. de Costo, Noel S. Nepomuceno, Kristine S. Agtarap, Ma. Ivy T. Querubin, and Mai Lin Villaruel, "Governance Statistics: Did Performance Matter in the 2007 Elections?" (paper presented at the 10th National Convention on Statistics, Manila, 1–2 October 2007).
39. World Bank and Department of Foreign Affairs and Trade Australia, *Making Education Spending Count for the Children of the Autonomous Region in Muslim Mindanao: Public Expenditure and Institutional Review for ARMM Basic Education* (Washington, D.C.: World Bank Group, 2015), p. 20.
40. For more on the illicit and illegal economy, see Francisco Lara, Jr. and Steven Schoofs, eds., *Out of the Shadows: Violent Conflict and the Real Economy of Mindanao* (Manila: International Alert, 2013).
41. While there is a forest of analysis identifying local governance deficiencies across the country, there have been no major revisions to the Local Government Code since 1991, as the Code creates a loyalty to and dependence on Manila that has served national-level powerbrokers well. So long as local chief executives deliver the vote, Congress and the President will ensure the Internal Revenue Allotment is delivered. For an analysis of this dynamic, see Nathan G. Quimpo, "Mindanao, Southern Philippines: The Pitfalls of Working for Peace in a Time of Political Decay", in *Autonomy and Ethnic Conflict in South and South East Asia*, edited by Rajat Ganguly (London: Routledge, 2012).
42. This analysis comes from World Bank (2017) "Conflict-Affected Mindanao", unpublished background paper for World Bank, *Mindanao Jobs Report: A Strategy for Mindanao Rural Development* (Washington, D.C.: World Bank Group, 2017).
43. Ronald Mendoza, Edsel Beja Jr., Victor Vedina, and D. Yap, "Political Dynasties and Poverty: Measurement and Evidence of Linkages in the Philippines", *Oxford Development Studies* 44, no. 2 (2016): 189–201.
44. See Julio Teehankee, "Electoral Politics in the Philippines", in *Electoral Politics in Southeast and East Asia*, edited by Gabriele Bruns, Aurel Croissant, and Marei John (Singapore: Friedrich Ebert Stiftung, 2002); and Brand Lab, "The Mindanao-Sulu Power Game: An Ethnography of Emergent Players", unpublished report submitted to the US Naval War College, Department of Navy and Department of Defence, 2011.
45. The government did complete a cadastral survey of political boundaries across the country, but this did not extend to individual land plots. The results in ARMM have not been released for fear of generating insecurity.
46. See, for instance, World Bank and International Organization for Migration, *Land: Territory, Domain and Identity* (Washington, D.C: World Bank Group, 2017).
47. See, for instance, Nell Bolton and Myla Leguro, *Local Solutions to Land Conflict*

in Mindanao (Manila: Catholic Relief Services, 2015), https://www.crs.org/sites/default/files/tools-research/local-solutions-to-land-conflict-in-mindanao.pdf (accessed 1 August 2017).

48. Office of the President Memorandum Circular No. 83 entitled "Creating the National Task Force for the Disbandment of the Private Armed Groups (NTF-DPAGs) in the Areas of the Proposed Bangsamoro and the Adjacent Regions IX to XII", issued 8 September 2015. The circular lapsed once Aquino's term ended and no further action has been taken since.
49. Discussions with senior members of the government and MILF peace panels, Davao City, September 2015.
50. "Statement of Philippine Peace Adviser Jesus Dureza after end of two-day talks on the Bangsamoro in Kuala Lumpur, Malaysia", http://www.opapp.gov.ph/milf/news/statement-philippine-peace-adviser-jesus-dureza-after-end-two-day-talks-bangsamoro-kuala (accessed 30 August 2016).
51. For more on this issue, see Institute for Policy Analysis of Conflict (henceforth IPAC), "Pro-ISIS Groups in Mindanao and their Links to Indonesia and Malaysia", IPAC Report No. 33 (Jakarta: IPAC, 2016); and IPAC, "Marawi, the East Asia Wilayah and Indonesia", IPAC Report No. 38 (Jakarta: IPAC, 2017).
52. The September 2018 Pulse Asia national survey showed the president enjoyed a 75 per cent approval rating and 72 per cent trust rating: see Pulse Asia, "September 2018 Nationwide Survey on the Performance and Trust Ratings of the Top Philippine Government Officials and Key Government Institutions", http://www.pulseasia.ph/september-2018-nationwide-survey-on-the-performance-and-trust-ratings-of-the-top-philippine-government-officials-and-the-performance-ratings-of-key-government-institutions/ (accessed 14 October 2018).
53. Antonio G. La Viña, "BBL 2014 vs. BBL 2017: An Initial Analysis", *MindaNews*, 19 July 2017, http://www.mindanews.com/mindaviews/2017/07/rivermans-vista-bbl-2014-vs-bbl-2017-an-initial-analysis/ (accessed 22 July 2017).
54. Executive Order 8 of 7 November 2016.
55. In 2014—"Duterte favors federalism over BBL", *Politiko*, http://politics.com.ph/duterte-favors-federalism-over-bbl/ (accessed 22 July 2017); Pia Ranada, "Duterte: If Filipinos don't want federalism, I will support BBL", *Rappler*, 8 July 2016, http://www.rappler.com/nation/139086-duterte-filipinos-federalism-support-bbl (accessed 22 July 2017).
56. See Ryan Rasauro and Nico Alconaba, "There will be a Bangsamoro Country", *Philippine Daily Inquirer*, 18 July 2017, http://newsinfo.inquirer.net/914677/there-shall-be-a-bangsamoro-country (accessed 22 July 2017).
57. Keep in mind that the leaders of a number of other armed groups in Mindanao come from the ranks of the MILF, including the Bangsamoro Islamic Freedom Fighters and Ansar Khalifa Philippines (AKP).

58. "Peace and Federalism", *Business World*, 6 February 2017, http://politics.com.ph/duterte-favors-federalism-over-bbl/ (accessed 23 July 2017).
59. Interview, member of the Third Party Monitoring Team, October 2018. Also see International Crisis Group, "Philippines: Addressing Islamist Militancy after the Battle for Marawi", 17 July 2018, and *Philippine Daily Inquirer*, 2 October 2018, "Islamic State fighters return to Mindanao", https://newsinfo.inquirer.net/1038080/islamic-state-fighters-return-to-mindanao (accessed 14 October 2018).
60. Indonesia has established a dedicated national body, the National Anti-Terrorism Agency. For more, see IPAC, "Countering Violent Extremism in Indonesia: Need for a Rethink", IPAC Report No. 11 (Jakarta: IPAC, 2014).
61. A meeting on counter-terrorism cooperation between the Philippines, Indonesia, Brunei, Malaysia, Australia and New Zealand was held in Manado, Indonesia on 29 July 2017: Tom Allard, "Southeast Asian States Vow Cooperation on 'Growing' Militant Threat", *Reuters*, 29 July 2017, https://ca.reuters.com/article/topNews/idCAKBN1AE0EL-OCATP (accessed 1 August 2017). This is a good start but, as noted in IPAC, "Pro-ISIS Groups in Mindanao", trust deficits on counter-terrorism between Indonesian, Malaysian and Philippine authorities will need to be addressed for this cooperation to be effective.
62. "The Philippine Government Strategic Framework for Mindanao Peace and Development", provided by OPAPP.
63. See United Nations Peacebuilding Fund, "What is Peacebuilding?", http://www.unpbf.org/application-guidelines/what-is-peacebuilding/ (accessed 23 July 2017).
64. Under the overall goal of "A peaceful, cohesive, secure and inclusively developed Mindanao where communities are resilient and free from violence and deprivation of dignity, rights, injustice, access to basic services and economic opportunities", the Framework has five interlinked strategic outcomes: (1) Resilient Communities Built; (2) Effective Governance Promoted; (3) Inclusive Economic Growth and Jobs Ensured; (4) Security Environment Stabilized; and (5) Consensus for Peace Strengthened. The June 2017 draft includes close to fifty indicators of success, so will require simplification and prioritization.
65. "Full Text: President Duterte's 1st State of the Nation Address", *Rappler*, 26 July 2016, http://www.rappler.com/nation/140860-rodrigo-duterte-speech-sona-2016-philippines-full-text (accessed 23 July 2017).
66. International Alert, *Conflict Alert 2018: War and Identity* (Manila: International Alert, 2018).
67. The number of light weapons cited is an estimate. Small Arms Survey estimated there were 4.2 million loose firearms in the Philippines in 2002. Quitoriano cites AFP data from 2010 that suggests 19 per cent of them were in Mindanao in

Eddie Quitoriano, "Shadow Economy or Shadow State? The Illicit Gun Trade in Conflict-Affected Mindanao", in *Out of the Shadows*, edited by Lara and Schoofs.

68. The Police militia are the Civilian Volunteer Organizations or CVOs and the Armed Forces of the Philippines para-militaries are the Citizen Armed Force Geographical Unit or CAFGUs.
69. See, for instance, World Bank and International Organization for Migration, *Land: Territory, Domain and Identity*, p. 66.
70. See Chapter 5 of Autonomous Region in Muslim Mindanao, *ARMM Regional Development Plan 2017–2022*, http://rpdo.armm.gov.ph/rpdo/index.php/rdp-2017-2022 (accessed 1 August 2017).
71. This is the approach adopted in countries in transition such as Afghanistan and Timor Leste. In ARMM already, the Bangladeshi NGO BRAC is running alternative schools: BRAC, "Education", http://www.brac.net/brac-philippines/item/789-education (accessed 1 August 2017).
72. For more on economic development strategies for Mindanao and conflict-affected Mindanao, see World Bank, *Mindanao Jobs Report: A Strategy for Mindanao Regional Development*.
73. On the reconstruction in Marawi, see Carmela Fonbuena, "Marawi One Year after the Battle: A Ghost Town Still Haunted by Threat of ISIS", 22 May 2018, https://www.theguardian.com/global/2018/may/22/marawi-one-year-siege-philippines-ghost-town-still-haunted-threat-isis (accessed 14 October 2018); and CNN Philippines, "Rebuilding of Marawi ground zero to start on 'liberation' anniversary", 12 October 2018, http://cnnphilippines.com/news/2018/10/12/Rebuilding-of-Marawi-ground-zero-to-start-on-liberation-anniversary.html (accessed 14 October 2018).

8

Prospects for the Normalization Process in the Southern Philippines:
An Architecture of Uncertainty?

Georgi Engelbrecht

INTRODUCTION

On 16 June 2015, more than a year after the signing of the Comprehensive Agreement on the Bangsamoro (CAB), with seventeen years of ceasefire and several decades of on-and-off peace talks, the Moro Islamic Liberation Front (MILF) dared to take a historic step and decommissioned 145 combatants and 75 firearms. This step in the peace process was not only a clear commitment to a political solution by the government to the "Bangsamoro question" but also part of the elaborate pattern of agreements reached between both sides in the last years. To achieve normalization—a return to a peaceful and stable life for communities—is the ultimate goal of the peace agreement.

But Mindanao's woes and worries cannot be isolated from the conflict between the Government of the Philippines (GPH) and the MILF—although many issues are strongly intertwined with this major conflict trajectory. The situation on the ground is often very complicated and different layers of armed violence, armed groups and governance systems will challenge the implementation period of the peace process. Apart from journalistic pieces and a limited number of essays, little has been written about this normalization period initiated after the CAB—or scholarly reviews or assessments of demobilization and disarmament published. The lack of published material is not surprising, considering the initiated formal process of normalization is only recent.

This chapter will look back at the foundations of normalization—in particular security aspects—as well as examine future prospects and trajectories. This is part of the broader scholarship on the Mindanao conflict and also an initial study on demobilization of combatants in a post-conflict situation. Existing literature on Disarmament, Demobilization and Reintegration (DDR) and Mindanao, official documents and peace agreements between GPH and MILF, media articles, press statements and fieldwork—community immersion, interviews, participant observation—undertaken in the southern Philippines between 2012 and 2015, are discussed. The first section outlines the history of conflicts in the southern Philippines, including some notions on the particularities and characteristics of these conflicts. DDR is discussed before the third section outlines the Moro National Liberation Front (MNLF) following the 1996 Final Peace Agreement (FPA)–DDR efforts with other groups in the Philippines. The fourth section looks at the Framework Agreement on the Bangsamoro (FAB), the CAB and the Normalization Annex—with an assessment of the implementation of these agreements so far. The conclusion places the normalization architecture into the context of the current security situation in Mindanao and identifies factors on which the improvement of human security—the aim of normalization—would depend.

THE DYNAMICS OF THE MINDANAO CONFLICT AND THE ROAD TO PEACE

The armed conflict in the southern Philippines between the government and a number of separatist groups for over forty years—with a historical discourse of discrimination and injustices—is one of the longest-running in the world and one of the most difficult to resolve.[1] This identity-based conflict revolves around the integration and accommodation of a Muslim minority in the predominantly Christian nation state on the southern island of Mindanao and the Sulu Archipelago. An important additional perspective to the conflict dynamics is the violent mode of decision making "over the particular terms and conditions by which large sections of the Muslim population wish to integrate within this state and cannot be understood as a conflict solely in opposition to the state".[2] Violence is therefore understood to be a continuation of conflict resolution.

Islam predated Christianity in the Philippines for centuries and one of the strongest manifestations of a precolonial state existed as different Sultanates in the southern Philippines.[3] The arrival of Spanish and American powers resulted in conquest and domination over the indigenous polities—yet a number of Muslim rulers resisted and avoided permanent subjugation—laying the foundation for strong narratives of self-determination and independence. In the beginning of the twentieth century, the US administration started to promote the settlement of Christians in Mindanao and change existing laws in favour of the settlers.[4] The newly formed independent Philippine state continued this practice. An influx of Christian farmers from Luzon and Visayas permanently changed the demographic balance so that in the 1960s Moros were already reduced to a minority. Grievances about the loss of land led to first communal clashes between Muslims and Christians and the formation of armed militias on both sides.

Land and property were often the initial root causes of these localized encounters. Religion, ideology and the rhetoric of self-determination against oppressive regimes fuelled a more militant Moro nationalism.[5] The Martial Law Regime of Ferdinand Marcos—introduced in 1972—caused an even stronger escalation of hostilities between resistance groups led by the MNLF, and the Armed Forces of the Philippines (AFP). Mindanao, Sulu and Palawan were de facto in a state of civil war. Even though a peace agreement was concluded in 1976 and full-scale civil war in Mindanao stopped, on-and-off clashes continued as the MNLF insisted that this accord was not implemented properly.[6] In addition, in 1977 a faction of fighters led by the Islamic scholar Salamat Hashim split from Misuari's MNLF and vowed to continue the struggle for an independent Islamic state in Mindanao. The newly born MILF soon became the strongest armed group in Central Mindanao and established de facto governance structures in hundreds of villages. Both MNLF and MILF simultaneously yet separately conducted guerrilla warfare against government troops throughout the 1970s and

1980s. However, some resistance fighters were co-opted by the government and took on important roles within regional governments in Mindanao.⁷ This divide-and-rule strategy and degrees of elite accommodation have been strong features in Mindanao until present day.

The end of the Marcos regime in 1986 led to negotiations with the MNLF and the creation of the Autonomous Region of Muslim Mindanao (ARMM) in 1989 and inauguration of ARMM in 1990—through the legislative action of an Organic Act. Whilst MNLF rebels were actively talking to the government, MILF continued to engage in protracted jungle warfare. The FPA between the government and MNLF was signed in 1996, but the enhanced ARMM under Nur Misuari and other MNLF rebels-turned-leaders did not succeed in resolving the root causes of the Moro conflict or addressing governance flaws. Many commanders were co-opted by the state and integrated into the Philippine security forces. The MNLF organization continued to split and exists now as a loose umbrella coalition of commanders across the Bangsamoro area—nominally in two factions—many having joined the political game in the country based on patronage and clan relations and a monopoly of violence.

The MILF continued its struggle for independence, although a ceasefire was agreed with the government in 1997. Talks between the GPH and MILF continued with periods of peace being regularly interrupted by skirmishes and larger hostilities. The government launched major all-out-war campaigns in 2000 and 2003 which significantly diminished the MILF's military capability—without achieving complete victory. MILF combatants retreated to their hinterlands, whilst other groups such as the Abu Sayyaf—a hybrid crime-terror offshoot of the MNLF in the Sulu Archipelago—and disgruntled MNLF members launched periodic attacks against the Philippine state. These grievances were also one the reasons for the birth of the Abu Sayyaf Group.⁸ The latest episode was the Zamboanga Siege in September 2013 when a commander of the Misuari-MNLF-faction launched an attack on Zamboanga City, resulting in three weeks urban warfare, 200 dead and over 150,000 displaced persons.

The security situation improved with the deployment of the International Monitoring Team (IMT) in 2004 to monitor the ceasefire between the GPH and MILF—with Malaysia as a third-party facilitator. After a few years, negotiations resulted in the Memorandum of Agreement on Ancestral Domain (MOA-AD)—a proposed settlement. However, the Supreme Court deemed the agreement as unconstitutional and subsequent clashes broke out leading to dozens killed and hundreds of thousands of internally displaced persons. It took years before another initiative on both sides led to a better climate for negotiations and "initial decision points on principles" were agreed by both sides in early 2012.[9] A breakthrough came with the FAB—a road map for the successful war-to-peace transition—followed two years later by the CAB. The only major political setback related to the peace process was the non-passage of the Bangsamoro Basic Law (BBL)—a law stipulating details on autonomous governance in Bangsamoro and creating a new political entity as proposed and laid out in the FAB, its annexes and the CAB. The new administration intended to continue the peace process with another "enabling law", building on the legacy of the BBL and avoiding its constitutional shortcomings. Duterte assured the MILF he will honour all agreements signed between the GPH and MILF.

TRAJECTORIES OF VIOLENCE AND CONFLICT IN MUSLIM MINDANAO

Whilst the peace process made overall significant progress and the level of violence has decreased, everyday violence in the southern Philippines continues.[10] Recent recognition of different manifestations of violence in literature and practice is the "heterogeneous and ambiguous" character of violence in Mindanao being shaped by competition and struggles over the local political economy.[11] Certain areas of Maguindanao and Lanao are trapped in a state of fragility where the boundary between war and peace is heavily blurred.[12] Conflicts often occur over political appointments, power and resources such as land—as clan feuds or firefights involving MILF/MNLF commanders, political warlords and local strongmen. This "horizontal violence" has been acknowledged by various studies to fuel insecurity in Mindanao.[13] Many armed conflicts between 2012 and 2015 which led to intervention of humanitarian actors and monitoring bodies were motivated by fierce competition over power in its diverse forms—at localized levels, fuelled by local grievances and (mis)perceptions.[14]

The Bangsamoro areas are also affected by activities of other armed groups, the most prominent being the Bangsamoro Islamic Freedom Fighters (BIFF)—a MILF-splinter which repeatedly staged attacks on military facilities in North Cotabato and Maguindanao, and was repeatedly targeted in military operations.[15] With seemingly never-ending activities of the Abu Sayyaf in Basilan/Sulu and the jihadist-influenced Maute group in Lanao del Sur–armed groups in Mindanao continue to inflict insecurity on localized pockets of violence—or "ungoverned spaces" of power vacuums benefiting entrepreneurs of violence.[16] A major trend in 2016 was the number of law enforcement operations by the military against lawless groups—which could be interpreted as an effort of the state to regain ungovernable spaces and "unilaterally" normalize them.[17] Three ceasefire violations between the GPH and MILF in 2016 were indirect results of these operations—and triggered misencounters.

Continuous conflict in these areas during a constantly slow rate of peace implementation and the transitional character of actors still assessing the costs and benefits of peace might result in an "insecurity trap"—which needs to be bridged in order to avoid a larger fallout.[18] The localized character of violence comes back to former notions of localized space—both in peace and war.[19] Root causes of violence across the *barangays* of Mindanao—including the vertical conflict between government and Moro fronts—are often very similar. Addressing human security in the Bangsamoro is the ultimate goal of both the GPH and MILF as the strongest of all Moro armed groups—but cannot be limited to those two actors.

DEALING WITH NON-STATE ARMED ACTORS AFTER WAR: DISARMAMENT, DEMOBILIZATION AND REINTEGRATION

The GPH and MILF peace panels were looking at lessons learned from other countries vis-à-vis war-to-peace transitions, and both sides agreed the Philippine context requires something special and tailor-made.[20] The legacy of a protracted armed conflict and several other forms of political violence left Mindanao and the Sulu Archipelago in a state where entrepreneurs of violence and combatants are heavily armed and ubiquitously present. The peace process with the MILF so far focused only on decommissioning the Bangsamoro Islamic Armed Forces (BIAF), but as already discussed, other non-state armed groups also contribute to the insecurity.

The standard model of dealing with combatants of armed groups in a transition context refers to processes usually called DDR—disarmament, demobilization and reintegration—which have been implemented for almost three decades by a variety of international and national actors. More than sixty DDR processes had been initiated since the early 1990s[21] with various DDR programmes throughout the world differing in objectives, size and duration. The majority of initiatives were completed in Africa and there is also significant experience in Asia, Latin America and Europe.

"Disarmament" refers to the collection of weapons and ammunition belonging to combatants and documentation of the process. Reducing amounts of firearms of armed groups circulating in the post-conflict area usually results in a lower supply of weapons. Registering and categorizing guns belonging to non-state armed actors are usually the first steps before destruction or putting these firearms "beyond use". "Demobilization" is the formal and controlled discharge of combatants from military units. In practice, fighters are often gathered in one or several locations—so-called cantonments or demobilization sites—then registered at assembly areas and officially discharged.[22] The harder and more challenging aspect of DDR is long-term transition to civilian life. All measures which aim to help former combatants adjust fully to civilian life are commonly understood as "Reintegration". Packages include education and training, material assistance, a cash-lump sum, and credit loans, for example. Reintegration has to essentially address needs of ex-combatants—to reduce the appeal and incentives of a return to war or criminal activity. DDR therefore has an overall objective to attain a basic level of security conducive for long-term development. Reintegration is usually the most critical stage of DDR—as studies show failed implementation may lead to "spoilers" and breakaway groups of the mainstream rebel faction—or a reversal in perceptions of peace.[23] As peace can be won at the grassroots level, reintegration is a long-term tool to close the insecurity trap prevalent in many post-conflict contexts.

Behind the details and design of every DDR programme, implementation lays the fundamental question about a programme's ultimate objective. The first generation of DDR programmes from the 1980s to the 1990s emphasized a military-centric approach to disarmament and looked at transition from a national security perspective. In the 1990s–2000s, this slightly narrow understanding of DDR was expanded towards a broader, human security dominated interpretation. The reintegration phase was particularly emphasized as a significant step in the process to ensure the sustainability of gains following disarmament and demobilization— described as "second-generation" DDR.[24] Most DDR initiatives are now embedded in recovery and rehabilitation programmes which make up a variety of transition instruments—to facilitate return to civilian life for combatants and improve human security in conflict-affected areas.[25] These initiatives also address hybrid conflicts involving militias, paramilitaries and political armed groups—therefore could find space in the conflict areas of Mindanao. Disarmament, demobilization and reintegration are interrelated and interdependent, and—although initially understood as sequential—are now accepted with a more concurrent approach. This current thinking aligns with the paradigm shift of DDR—from a surgical and technical intervention towards stabilizing and reconfiguring the state.[26]

Muggah suggests DDR processes should neither be delayed nor designed in a hurry following a peace agreement.[27] Studies indicate, on average, a year should pass before the process starts. Ideally, peace agreements and subsequent guidelines or communiqués should include details such as organizational framework, funding, timing, scope, stages, sequencing, ownership, supervision and reintegration packages—not forgetting broader principles such as expectation management, sustainability of the programme and overall coherence of the process.[28] In the long run, state security forces also need to adapt to changing security environments in post-conflict situations. DDR cannot work without adequate steps to restructure armed forces—in turn affected by dismantling of non-state armed groups. DDR is therefore not a panacea or "magic bullet"[29] and should always be viewed as one variable in a wider equation of re-configuring security.

THE PHILIPPINES: LESSONS LEARNED

A major part of DDR research focuses pragmatically on design and implementation of programmes, aiming to make relevant recommendations to policymakers. Lessons learned from the process and insights into the efficacy of DDR as a response to a particular conflict are equally important. The Philippine government has undergone some of the DDR process with the MNLF and some of the communist groups. The results have been mixed and were a factor to be considered in the task of normalizing the Bangsamoro.

One such case is the Cordillera People's Liberation Army (CPLA). The group is a splinter group of the Maoist New People's Army fighting in the Cordilleras region of Luzon for self-determination of the indigenous population. A ceasefire has been in effect since 1986, but the peace deal implemented was murky, and factionalized bickering within the CPLA challenged implementation. The government gave attention to only one faction of the CPLA, excluding at least three, and despite many inclusive elements in the accord—final disposition of forces, economic reintegration, community development and symbolic gestures—the original objective of autonomy was not included. Areas where the peace agreement did not reach are prone to political violence. Selective project implementation and budgetary constraints were other drawbacks of the process. Integration of ex-CPLA into security forces was relatively successful, but many CPLA members rejoined an armed group through taking part in paramilitary outfits such as Civilian Armed Forces Geographical Units (CAFGUs)— around 800 personnel. There is little chance for re-escalation of violence in Cordilleras, but in the end only limited demobilization was achieved.[30] The 700-man strong Revolutionary Proletarian Army–Alex Boncayo Brigade (RPA-ABB) in Negros Occidental is another example of an NPA splinter, with mixed demobilization efforts. Members are said to be hired as local goons and exploited by political elites without sustaining gains of reintegration.[31]

The main purpose of the FPA with the MNLF was to have a political, cultural and economic compromise between the GPH and the MNLF— leaving aside aspects of disarmament and demobilization.[32] Dealing with the rebels meant their integration into the government. In September 1996, the FPA foresaw three major regulations on the military integration of MNLF members estimated to be between 17,000 and 18,000 in number—some literature cites up to 50,000 MNLF including community mass support.[33] 1,500 MNLF members were to be integrated into the Philippine National Police and 5,750 MNLF members into the Philippine Army—with special socioeconomic and educational programmes to be conducted for the rest. Packages for MNLF members would contain all types of support to address grievances and socioeconomic needs such as technical and livelihood training. The FPA did not therefore attempt a general demobilization or disarmament of the MNLF, rather aiming to provide a comprehensive safety net for combatants who could not be integrated into government forces for political and financial reasons.[34]

Some researchers and practitioners agree that the implementation of these integration provisions had mixed results.[35] Around 1,600 MNLF joined the police and 5,160 joined the AFP. Although the integration was lauded by MNLF leaders, their combatants were often perceived as "friendly forces" by the military. Many MILF commanders had apprehensions of these MNLF strongmen, which in turn led to several local conflicts.[36] Though the integration was lauded by MNLF leaders, their combatants were often perceived as "friendly forces" by the military. Many MILF commanders have their apprehensions of these MNLF strongmen, which in turn has led to several local conflicts. The vast number of MNLF combatants remained on the ground—armed, self-ascribed as "active" members and potentially susceptible to political persuasion or autonomous behaviour as entrepreneurs of violence. The majority of violent incidents in Mindanao involving MNLF commanders or elements stem from this paradox of an armed group being party to a peace accord, with factions or members periodically taking up arms and regrouping if there is a need or order.[37] The limited disarmament of the MNLF ultimately had little impact on the security situation in the ARMM.[38]

The integration of the MNLF did not lower the number of firearms or reduce the violent potential of remnants of the armed group.[39] In the years following the FPA, for example, several programmes were undertaken by international and national agencies—as well as non-government organizations (NGOs)—with the number of beneficiaries in the thousands.[40] Firearms still remain in circulation and are considered illegal, although no seizure operations are implemented if the group is not engaged in lawless activity. Some MNLF members drifted back to armed struggle in the MILF or joined the more radical Abu Sayyaf group,[41] others are openly active in local governments as mayors or officials—while still commanding smaller armed units. Moreover, research findings suggest that the number of clan feuds (*ridos*) has increased despite the 1996 FPA.[42] MNLF personalities are involved in clan feuds with individual MILF commanders over land or political positions—as seen in several cases September/October 2016 in the municipalities of Matalam and Kabacan, Cotabato Province.

THE PROMISE OF NORMALIZATION

1. Normalization Structure

1.1 Framework Agreement on the Bangsamoro

The FAB expanded on several aspects for the first time to be incorporated into future agreements.

Firstly, "normalization" is defined as a state whereby:

> Communities can return to conditions where they can achieve their desired quality of life, which includes the pursuit of sustainable livelihoods and political participation within a peaceful deliberative society. The aim of normalization is to ensure human security in the Bangsamoro. Normalization helps build a society that is committed to basic human rights, whereby individuals are free from fear of violence or crime and where long-held traditions and values continue to be honoured.[43]

The term "normalization" is noteworthy—as opposed to DDR—which still has a bitter aftertaste for armed groups in Mindanao who understand DDR to mean a form of counterinsurgency equated with surrender. The distinction is not academic only. During field visits and activities, the author has observed the affinity communities and MILF have been developing towards "normalization"—showing that the term has been chosen well. The common narrative is that normalization does not equal "surrender". Normalization carries a connotation of inclusivity, as it does not only refer to the mechanically formal act of decommissioning, but also the broad improvement of human security as in the definition. Officially, MILF distanced itself from "DDR" as early as 2006 as it was deemed a rather strong term.

Secondly, "police" is defined as a professional body free from partisan political control which shall be civilian in character—efficient and effective in law enforcement, fair and impartial, and accountable for its actions. Recommendations on policing are to be given by an independent commission. Ultimately, law enforcement functions shall be transferred from the military to the Bangsamoro police force.

Thirdly, the MILF shall undertake a graduated programme for decommissioning of its forces so all weapons are "put beyond use"—an expression modelled after the Good Friday Agreement in Northern Ireland.[44] Coordination between government and MILF forces shall be coordinated by a Joint Normalization Committee (JNC) through which MILF will also assist in maintaining peace and order in the area of Bangsamoro until decommissioning will be completed. The parties also agree on development efforts for rehabilitation, reconstruction and development of the Bangsamoro, and institute programmes to address the needs of MILF combatants and communities, internally displaced persons (IDPs), and poverty-stricken and conflict-affected communities.

Finally, GPH and MILF commit to work in partnership for the reduction and control of firearms in the area and the disbandment of private armies and other armed groups.

1.2 Annex on Normalization

The Annex on Normalization (the Annex) was signed on 25 January 2014 and affirms and specifies certain features laid out in the FAB.[45] Divided into ten sections, the Annex identifies the following to be handled in the implementation of the peace agreement:

1. policing;
2. transitional components of normalization and the creation of steering bodies;
3. decommissioning of MILF-combatants;
4. redeployment of the armed forces;
5. UXOs (unexploded ordnances) and landmines;
6. disbandment of private armed groups;
7. socioeconomic development programmes.
8. transitional justice and reconciliation;
9. resource mobilization; and
10. confidence-building measures.

The interplay of these elements aims to make a successful normalization process possible.

The relevant sections of the Annex for the decommissioning process are: steering of the normalization process is with the Joint Normalization Committee (Section B1); security aspects shall be handled by the so-called Joint Peace and Security Committee (JPSC)—which is to liaise with the government and MILF military leadership—and develop guidelines on the implementation of the security provisions of FAB and the Annex (Section B2). Most importantly, the JPSC will also guide integrated Joint Peace and Security Teams (JPST) consisting of AFP, Bangsamoro Islamic Armed Forces (BIAF) and Philippine National Police (PNP) members. These localized teams have the mandate to track and document private armies and other armed groups, support the maintenance of the ceasefire between GPH and MILF and potentially support grassroots conflict resolution (Section B3).

With respect to actual demobilization, the MILF affirms the commitment to gradually put their weapons beyond use. The process will be steered by an International Decommissioning Body (IDB) tasked to:

(a) conduct an inventory, verification and validation of BIAF members, arms and weapons;
(b) develop and implement a schedule of decommissioning of BIAF forces;
(c) plan, design and implement techniques and technologies for weapons collection or retrieval, transport, and storage and putting weapons beyond use in accordance with the agreement of the parties; and
(d) report on the progress of its work and submit its terminal report to the GPH and MILF peace panels.

Needs assessments for combatants shall also be undertaken, maximizing the outcome of the future reintegration. The decommissioning is supposed to occur "parallel and commensurate" to the CAB implementation—essentially a safety pin for the MILF based on a quid pro quo principle. The Annex also mentions the objective of managing and reducing small arms and light weapons (SALW) as an integral part of decommissioning—without specific details.[46]

Related to decommissioning of the MILF are necessary steps to avoid a security imbalance or vacuum in the Bangsamoro areas which could arise from removal of a vast force of combatants. The Annex identifies the AFP and Private Armed Groups (PAGs) as two sectors in need of a harmonized and calibrated approach. With respect to the military, AFP units and troops shall be redeployed from or within the Bangsamoro after a joint security assessment and inventory. Installations necessary for national defence and security shall be maintained. Likewise, PAGs in the Bangsamoro shall be disbanded upon the identification of said groups with help of a clear assessment and planning.

Reintegration of MILF combatants should also be addressed by community-based socioeconomic programmes that shall foster social cohesion and preserve the unity of communities whilst addressing the needs of demobilized BIAF, internally displaced persons, women-auxiliary forces and marginalized communities. Needs assessments shall guarantee harmonized interventions. Moreover, the six recognized camps of the MILF are to be transformed into "peaceful and productive communities.

1.3 Comprehensive Agreement on the Bangsamoro

The CAB did not stipulate new rules. In respect to normalization the CAB only mentioned both parties commit to the process of full implementation towards "the gradual normalization of previously conflict-affected areas".[47] Normalization is closer to second-generation DDR initiatives—while all types of DDR focus on security first, the process in the Bangsamoro aims to emphasize governance.[48] The CAB serves as a reference anchor and document of commitment to previously outlined agreements, uniting several aspects of war-to-peace transitions. The CAB also recognizes that decommissioning is necessary, yet insufficient as the only means for normalization in Mindanao.[49] The decommissioning has the following original timeline:

Phase 1: Signing of Normalization Annex until complete validation of MILF forces by IDB (completed).
Phase 2: Completion of validation until passage of BBL (30 per cent to be decommissioned).
Phase 3: Passage of BBL until the creation of the Bangsamoro Police (35 per cent to be decommissioned).
Phase 4: From the operationalization of the police until the exit agreement (35 per cent to be decommissioned).

2. Implementation

2.1 The JNC was launched in May 2014 and also created the JPSC—initial work was focused on meetings and planning processes. A joint security assessment has been started, and is still in the initial, basic phase. JNC's coordination is dependent on instructions and ideas of both sides and the mechanism has not yet grown into an organic and autonomous unit—carried mostly by respective counterparts. In 2016, the JNC was relatively out of the loop vis-à-vis major security developments in conflict-affected areas—law enforcement by government, anti-drugs operations, *rido*-resolution interventions. However, they gained momentum in the subsequent years, even though nominally still under the Peace Implementing Panels.

2.2 The Independent Commission on Policing (ICP) produced a report on a Bangsamoro police force whose recommendations were submitted to the Peace Panels. Major recommendations of the study were incorporated in the Draft BBL submitted to Congress in 2014. Trainings and workshops on community policing since then have been organized by Canada, the UK and various NGOs. Yet, according to President Duterte's statements, he does not seem to agree with a separate Bangsamoro police force.[50] The set-up of the police in the future Bangsamoro will thus be mostly aligned with the national structure.

2.3 Ceremonial decommissioning of 145 MILF combatants and the turnover of 75 weapons—51 high-powered firearms and 24 crew-served weapons—was successfully organized and completed on 16 June 2015. The firearms are stored at the secure arms storage area in Camp Abubakar, the current headquarters of the 37th Infantry Battalion of the Philippine Army. JPST personnel and IDB are guarding the inner perimeter whilst AFP and BIAF provide outer security. All ex-combatants were registered and officially decommissioned from the BIAF, each combatant receiving a grant of PhP25,000 and one health insurance card.[51] Later, 141 ex-combatants underwent a needs assessment in order to determine the most suitable socioeconomic package for them. Its implementation did not occur without hiccups in terms of pace and content of the delivery, but at a lessons learnt assessment has been undertaken in 2018.[52]

2.4 The IDB needed some time to be properly established—after its constitution and the signing of its Terms of Reference—around January 2015. IDB's main achievement so far was the symbolic decommissioning of the first BIAF batch (see below). IDB continues to prepare for the second batch through the creation of an inventory of BIAF members and weapons and needs assessment with other agencies. This inventory activity was on hold due to the non-passage of the BBL in 2015–17. However, the IDB has conducted some studies on various aspects of decommissioning—canton sites, scheduling, lessons learned from the first batch—and the sequencing programme is clear. The challenge lies in the tie-in of the three remaining steps to the political benchmarks. Fortunately, with the passage of the Bangsamoro Organic Law (BOL) in July preparations for the second batch have started and a list of verification sites and the final decommissioning zones are being discussed. A complete database of combatants remains in development, so that the second batch could be most likely decommissioned only at the end of 2019.

2.5   1,380 members of JPSTs have been organized and trained in three batches so far—50 per cent BIAF, 50 per cent AFP-PNP. The first batch is securing the decommissioned firearms of the first decommissioned MILF. The JPST will be deployed in sensitive hot spot areas to maintain peace and also fulfil additional security tasks. In July 2016, the trainings were put on hold but gained momentum after two years with the passage of BOL; as of the time of the writing, a curriculum and training schedule for further batches of JPSTs is in the making.

2.6   The camp-to-community transformation is ongoing. Task forces for each of the six recognized MILF camps are meeting to plan the process ahead, with the Bangsamoro Development Agency (BDA) taking the lead in planning for the socioeconomic development in these camps towards productive communities. However, only one camp has been profiled so far. Delineation efforts are ongoing and temporary agreements for the purpose of project development achieved. In early 2016, the Department of Agriculture—in spirit with the normalization process—provided agricultural assistance and equipment to the camps. Assessment is ongoing—but expected to be properly taking off after the BOL is approved in the plebiscite in January 2019.

2.7   The challenge of private armed groups remains difficult to tackle. PAGs and followers of local strongmen are often involved in armed violence.[53] The Aquino administration created a "National Task Force for the Disbandment of Private Armed Groups in the areas of the proposed Bangsamoro and the adjacent regions IX to XII" in September 2015—only one meeting occurred by December 2015 and the momentum for the very challenging aspect of private armies was later lost.[54] The issue on PAGs remains among the greatest challenges in the normalization process.

2.8   AFP redeployment remains, as expected, unhurried. Apart from repositioning of the 603rd Infantry Brigade from Camp Abubakar—though it was replaced by the smaller unit 37th Infantry Battalion—no major shifts have occurred. Additional troops from the Visayas arrived in sensitive spots of Maguindanao province, Lanao and Sulu in 2015 and 2016.[55] Mindanao remains a highly militarized zone—with approximately 40 per cent of countrywide military deployment with the army at the forefront of countering security challenges and even taking over law enforcement functions.[56]

3. Future Assessment

When the term of President Aquino ended and Rodrigo Duterte took over in July 2016 the prospects for further implementation were only partially clear. The second batch of BIAF could not be decommissioned, as it was linked to the passage of the BBL or—as it was renamed—the enabling law. The IDB is optimistic it can proceed with further decommissioning after the passage of this legislation. While talks on working group level continued until the last weeks of the Aquino administration—and preparations by the new peace panels ("implementing teams") were undertaken—no major policy decisions have been made.[57] However, a boost of the preparations was achieved in July 2018 with the final passage of the—now slightly differently titled—Organic Law.

The Duterte government expressed its commitment to fully implement the CAB, although—as and implementation mechanism—the BBL will be replaced by another, more inclusive law. No existing mechanisms were abrogated by President Duterte, yet a shift from "normalization" to "CAB implementation" is noticeable—which goes hand-and-in-hand with the inclusive Bangsamoro Transition Commission (BTC) and a relative stagnation of normalization activities. The year 2016 started with a surge of law enforcement operations on the ground, and ended with the flare-up of several clan feuds in Maguindanao and Lanao during November. Involvement of several MILF commanders indicated the need to transform violent social capital of non-state armed groups towards positive action— enabling the potential for peace rather than creating incentives for armed conflict. The same pattern continued until the end of 2018 and although the implementation of the CAB is moving, it did not yet fully accelerate. The process is dependent on a number of variables and the coming year of 2019 might be considered a possible game-changer with the imminent formation of the Bangsamoro government.

CONCLUSION: AN ARCHITECTURE OF UNCERTAINTY?

The normalization process is scheduled to move on and socioeconomic aspects expected to continue as planned. The security aspect remains a point of discussion, and complications—such as the status/role of MNLF within the new inclusive peace process and new benchmarks for the MILF's decommissioning—will require hard bargaining. As Muggah writes, the "management of the ostensibly political issues associated with reconciliation, peace building and the meaningful reform of judicial, government and economic structures" will make normalization a success—or a misstep.[58] CAB's advantage over the FPA may be a wider understanding of the Bangsamoro problem as a holistic and interdependent issue. The integrative outlook of security provisions of the CAB is directed at a plethora of armed groups and aims to avoid local security dilemmas. Kalyvas rightly points out that armed conflict is about real issues on the local level that are being addressed through violence.[59] Decommissioning is a beginning—not the end—of ensuring adequate human security on the local level and a wider process of transformation in Mindanao.

At the time of writing, the peace process was being continued by the Duterte administration, but some details remain unclear. Normalization will continue, and the fine architecture build-up by the CAB likely to continue only on the socioeconomic level. Decommissioning might need reconfiguring within the CAB normalization framework—in a holistic context where MNLF has been re-elevated to prominent status.[60] Moreover, the security environment is highly fluid, and might affect the decommissioning flow. It certainly will not be as easy as one AFP officer said: "The decommissioning can be just realigned to federalism, right?". Moreover, whilst the arena for normalization has been prepared with the passage of BOL in July 2018, the law needs to be further approved in a plebiscite—an enterprise taking up much time and effort in late 2018. After the law is approved by the public, the focus will shift to transition and governance. A scenario might emerge that the steps to be taken to ensure qualitative normalization will pale in comparison to the immediate gains of the MILF ascending to political position. Thus, to achieve genuine human security in the Bangsamoro and minimize potential fallout from uncertain and inconsistent steps, the following factors need to be considered:

(1) Policy coherence: An adjustment of the decommissioning process to the new peace process roadmap presented by Duterte and its subsequent implementation is needed to avoid security dilemmas and support implementation of the peace agreement through appropriate initiatives at ground level. AFP redeployment

and disarmament of PAGs are examples of such measures to approach this "interlocking landscape" of conflicts.[61] In addition, complementarity of the political and socioeconomic tracks should be ensured to avoid misperceptions. Preparatory work for the normalization stage should be continued despite the absence of the enabling law.

(2) Community-centric approach: As most of the BIAF—and other armed groups in Mindanao—are located in their communities, an appropriate approach is to take this combatant/civilian dichotomy into consideration, as the combatants are "embedded rebels" who do not need to return to their place of origin.[62] Full completion of the socioeconomic packages to the first batch of demobilized BIAF should also be achieved. In addition to socioeconomic packages, other forms of communitarian peacebuilding need to be crafted within the context of the Bangsamoro.

(3) Local normalization: Good analysis and assessment is at the beginning of every successful initiative. Intertwined horizontal and vertical conflicts in the Bangsamoro areas are rooted in local issues—pulled by the macronarrative of the struggle for self-determination and violent conflict resolution—and need a local response. LGUs could help their constituents to alleviate security dilemmas and curb the need to carry firearms or be active in an armed group. Other bodies from MILF or the JPSTs can take over more responsibilities in dealing with horizontal conflicts such as clan feuds—contributing to conflict resolution. It is essential the demand for arms and continuous availability of weapons in Mindanao is decreased. The privatization of violence within the broader normalization framework is also vital. The GPH and MILF cannot ignore guns owned by civilians, political elites and syndicates.[63]

The outcome of any future programme in the Bangsamoro will ultimately depend on the lens various parties use to look at human security situation in the area. Political will, and commitment, of both GPH and MILF to implement the ambitious goals stipulated in the agreements are essential to how successfully they could manage the various challenges on the ground. In the case of the MNLF, disarmament was not the government's top agenda item as it prioritized a peace settlement above all means. Smaller

FIGURE 8.1
MILF Decommissioning in Context

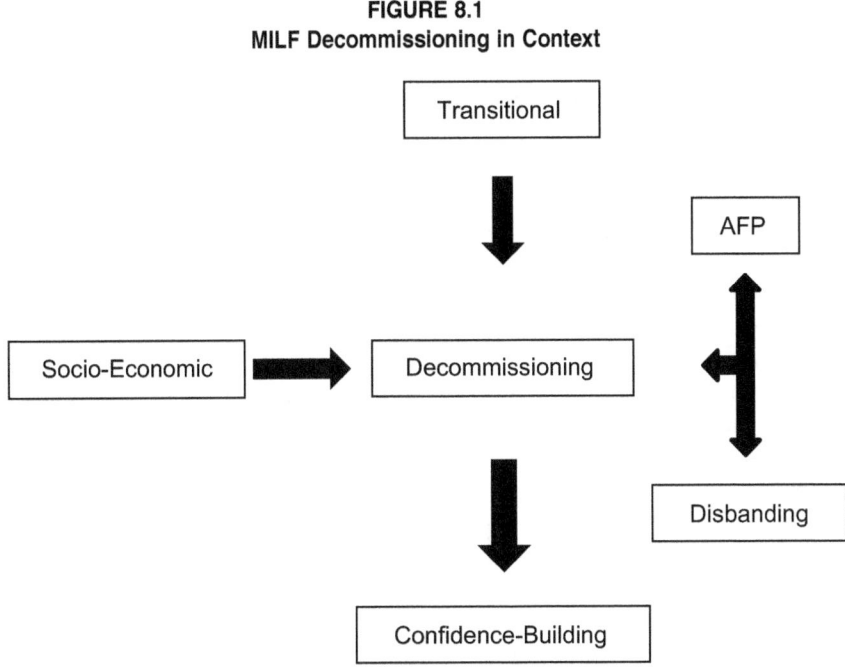

insurgent groups in the Philippines were only partially decommissioned, as were violence potential of these groups carried over to new settings. Signing diverse peace agreements and roadmaps may not be adequate to achieve sustainable peace without considering the microfoundations of the conflict. It is also important that communities in Mindanao support and embrace normalization efforts.

Notes

The views expressed in this article are those of the author rather than the institutions to which he is, or has been, affiliated.

1. Francisco Lara Jr. and Phil Champain, *Inclusive Peace in Muslim Mindanao: Revisiting the Dynamics of Conflict and Exclusion* (London: International Alert, 2009).
2. Jeroen Adam, Boris Vebrugge, and Dorien Vanden Boer, "Peacemaking and State-Society Interactions in Conflict-Torn Mindanao, Philippines", Justice and Security Research Programme Paper (Ghent University, 2014), p. 2.

3. Cesar Majul, *The Contemporary Muslim Movement in the Philippines* (Berkeley: Mizan Press, 1985); Thomas McKenna, *Muslim Rulers and Rebels: Everyday Politics and Armed Separatism in the Southern Philippines* (Berkeley: University of California Press, 1998); Patricio Abinales, *Making Mindanao: Cotabato and Davao in the Formation of the Philippine Nation-State* (Quezon City: Ateneo De Manila University Press, 2000).
4. Majul, *The Contemporary Muslim Movement*; Abinales, *Making Mindanao*.
5. Majul, *The Contemporary Muslim Movement*.
6. Salah Jubair, *Bangsamoro, A Nation Under Endless Tyranny* (Kuala Lumpur: IQ Marin, 1999).
7. Ibid.; McKenna, *Muslim Rulers and Rebels*.
8. Human Rights Watch, "Philippines: Mistreatment, Hostage-Taking in Zamboanga", https://www.hrw.org/news/2013/09/19/philippines-mistreatment-hostage-taking-zamboanga (accessed 27 September 2018).
9. GPH-MILF Decision Points on Principles, 2012.
10. Francisco Lara Jr. and Steven Schoofs, eds., *Out of the Shadows: Violent Conflict and the Real Economy of Mindanao* (London: International Alert, 2013).
11. Adam, Vebrugge, and Vanden Boer, "Peacemaking and State-Society Interactions in Conflict-Torn Mindanao, Philippines".
12. Maguindanao province in the ARMM is one of the most militarized provinces in the Philippines with at least 5,000 MILF-BIAF. It is also home to one military infantry division, two brigades, four battalions and a number of paramilitary-force-multiplier support units to the AFP.
13. Wilfredo Magno Torres III, ed., *Rido: Clan Feuding and Conflict Management in Mindanao* (Makati City: Asia Foundation, 2007); Francisco Lara Jr., *Insurgents, Clans and States: Political Legitimacy and Resurgent Conflict in Muslim Mindanao, Philippines* (Manila: Ateneo de Manila University Press, 2014).
14. Fermin Adriano and Thomas Parks, *The Contested Corners of Asia: The Case of Mindanao, Philippines* (San Francisco: The Asia Foundation, 2013).
15. One civil society activist has described the group as "the latest vanguard of the Bangsamoro struggle". Interview with the author in Cotabato City, 2013.
16. ICG, 2016.
17. This goes back to arguments presented among others by Giorgio Agamben and his theory of the *state of exception*.
18. Macartan Humphreys and Jeremy Weinstein, "Demobilization and Re-integration", *Journal of Conflict Resolution* 51, no. 4 (2007): 531–67.
19. Rosalie Hall, "From Rebels to Soldiers: An Analysis of the Philippine and East Timorese Policy Integrating Former Moro National Liberation Front and Falintil Combatants into the Armed Forces", Toronto Meeting Paper (American Political Science Association, 2009).

20. Kristian Herbolzheimer, "Normalization after a Peace Agreement", Conciliation Resources Discussion Paper (London: Conciliation Resources, 2012).
21. Robert Muggah, "Innovations in Disarmament, Demobilization and Reintegration Policy and Research: Reflections on the Last Decade", Norwegian Institute of International Affairs Working Paper 774 (Oslo: Norwegian Institute of International Affairs, 2010); International Crisis Group, "The Philippines: Dismantling Rebel Groups", Asia Report No. 248 (Brussels: International Crisis Group, 19 June 2013).
22. http://unddr.org/what-is-ddr/introduction_1.aspx (accessed 27 September 2018).
23. Michael Brzoska, "Embedding DDR Programmes in Security Sector Reconstruction", in *Security Governance in Post-Conflict Peacebuilding*, edited by Alan Bryden and Heiner Hänggi (Geneva: Geneva Centre for Democratic Control of Armed Forces, 2006); Robert Muggah, "No Magic Bullet: A Critical Perspective on Disarmament, Demobilization and Reintegration (DDR) and Weapons Reduction in Post-conflict Contexts", *The Round Table* 94, no. 379 (2005): 239–52; Dave McRae, "Reintegration and Localised Conflict: Security Impacts beyond Influencing Spoilers", *Conflict, Security and Development* 10 (2010): 403–30.
24. Nat Coletta and Robert Muggah, "Context Matters: Interim Stabilization and Second Generation Approaches to Security Promotion", *Conflict, Security & Development* 9, no. 4 (2009): 425–53; Muggah, "Innovations in Disarmament"; Jairo Munive and Finn Stepputat, "Rethinking Disarmament, Demobilization and Reintegration Programs", *Stability: International Journal of Security & Development* 4(1), part 48 (2015): 1–13.
25. Willemijn Verkoren, Rens Willems, Jesper Kleingeld, and Hans Rouw, "From DDR to Security Promotion: Connecting National Programs to Community Initiatives", *International Journal of Peace Studies* 15, no. 2 (2010): 1–32.
26. Muggah, "Innovations in Disarmament"; World Bank, *World Development Report 2011: Conflict, Security and Development* (Washington, D.C.: World Bank, 2011).
27. Robert Muggah, ed., *"Security and Post-Conflict Reconstruction. Dealing with Fighters in the Aftermath of War"* (New York: Routledge, 2010); Muggah, "Innovations in Disarmament".
28. Alpaslan Özerdem, "Disarmament, Demobilization and Reintegration of former combatants in Afghanistan: Lessons Learned from a Cross-Cultural Perspective", *Third World Quarterly* 23, no. 5 (2002): 961–75.
29. Muggah, "No Magic Bullet".
30. Albert Caramés Boada, "Past, Present and Future in Mindanao: Analysis of the MNLF and MILF Peace and Reintegration Processes", Peacebuilding Papers 07(Barcelona: Escola de Cultura de Pau, 2009).

31. Soliman Santos Jr. and Paz Santos, ed., *Primed and Purposeful: Armed Groups and Human Security Efforts in The Philippines* (Geneva: South-South Network for Non-State Armed Group Engagement and the Small Arms Survey, 2010).
32. Merliza Makinano and Alfredo Lubang, *Disarmament, Demobilization and Reintegration: The Mindanao Experience* (Ottawa: International Security Bureau, Department of Foreign Affairs and International Trade, 2001); Friedrich Plank, "Not Enough Pieces of the Cake? The Moro National Liberation Front (MNLF) in the Mindanao Final Agreement", *Asian Security* 11, no. 2 (2015): 154–77.
33. Makinano and Lubang, *Disarmament, Demobilization and Reintegration*; Hall, "From Rebels to Soldiers"; Santos Jr. and Santos, *Primed and Purposeful*.
34. Hall, "From Rebels to Soldiers"; Santos Jr. and Santos, *Primed and Purposeful*.
35. Santos Jr. and Santos, *Primed and Purposeful*.
36. Interview with a local CSO activist, July 2016.
37. Santos Jr. and Santos, *Primed and Purposeful*; Boada, "Past, Present and Future in Mindanao".
38. Santos Jr. and Santos, *Primed and Purposeful*.
39. Hall, "From Rebels to Soldiers".
40. Among others: Livelihood Assistance Program (ELAP) providing 2,000 MNLF members with skills on growing corn (Plank, "Not Enough Pieces of the Cake?"). The Growth with Equity in Mindanao (GEM) focused on around 3,800 MNLF combatants and taught seaweed farming. Both initiatives were funded by USAID which has overall provided a training/development programme for 21,000 MNLF ex-combatants (Boada, "Past, Present and Future in Mindanao). USAID and UN agencies have launched integration programmes for more than 50,000 MNLF members including the community-base support.
41. Santos Jr. and Santos, *Primed and Purposeful*; Plank, "Not Enough Pieces of the Cake?".
42. Lara Jr. and Champain, *Inclusive Peace in Muslim Mindanao*.
43. Framework Agreement on the Bangsamoro, 2012.
44. The expression "put beyond use" was modelled after Good Friday Agreement in Northern Ireland. See also http://news.bbc.co.uk/2/hi/uk_news/northern_ireland/4607913.stm (accessed 27 September 2018).
45. The Annex on Normalization, https://peacemaker.un.org/sites/peacemaker.un.org/files/PH_140125_AnnexNormalization.pdf (accessed 27 September 2018).
46. SALW in Mindanao is one of the bigger challenges and only a few initiatives have been undertaken so far. Firearms reduction needs a very holistic approach. Some experts even point out that firearms' registration in Mindanao has increased. Arms continue to flow and proliferate and are a major impediment to sustainable peace. On this, see: International Crisis Group, "The Philippines: Dismantling Rebel Groups"; Santos Jr. and Santos, *Primed and Purposeful*.

Getting rid of high-powered firearms won't necessarily result in a reduction of violence.
47. Comprehensive Agreement on the Bangsamoro, 2014, p. 4, para. 4.
48. Benedicto Bacani, ed., "Normalization in the CAB and Proposed BBL: Trajectories and Convergence", Institute for Autonomy and Governance Policy (IAG) Report (Cotabato City: IAG, 2015).
49. Zachary Karazsia, "Evaluating the 'Success' of Disarmament, Demobilization, and Reintegration Programs: The Case of Congo-Brazaville", *Journal of Interdisciplinary Conflict Science* 1, no. 2 (2015).
50. Pia Ranada, "Duterte on BBL: No Separate Bangsamoro Police, Military", *Rappler.com*, https://www.rappler.com/nation/203782-duterte-condition-bangsamoro-basic-law-no-separate-police-military (accessed 27 September 2018).
51. Third Party Monitoring Team. "Second Public Report, January 2014 to January 2015", 13 February 2015. "Third Public Report, January 2015 to February 2016", 26 February 2016.
52. Interview with an MILF Technical Expert, 17 August 2018.
53. Lara Jr. and Champain, *Inclusive Peace in Muslim Mindanao*.
54. Late 2016, the military launched an operation against the armed group of a mayor in Maguindanao province. However, it was more due to necessary action than a principled decision. Most of the PAGs in Mindanao remain active and untouched. Across the Philippines, 76 PAGs have been monitored by the police, mostly in ARMM. On this, see: ICG, 2016.
55. In Maguindanao, the 34th Infantry Battalion from Samar arrived after the months-long all-out-offensive of government forces against BIFF and the 19th Infantry Battalion replaced the 45th Infantry Battalion which supported the offensives in Sulu against the Abu Sayyaf Group. In Lanao, a battalion aims to secure the sensitive area where the Maute group is highly active. Sulu and Basilan experienced a "surge" since Duterte pronounced war on the Abu Sayyaf—albeit with mixed results.
56. Boada, "Past, Present and Future in Mindanao".
57. Interview with one technical working group member of the MILF, June 2016.
58. Muggah, "No Magic Bullet". p. 10.
59. Stathis Kalyvas, "The Ontology of Political Violence: Action and Identity in Civil Wars", *Perspectives on Politics* 1, no. 3 (2003): 475–94.
60. Interview with the author, May 2016.
61. World Bank, World Development Report 2011.
62. Veronique Dudouet, Hans Giessmann, and Katrin Planta, "From Combatants to Peacebuilders. A Case for Inclusive, Participatory and Holistic Security Transitions", Policy Report (Berlin: Berghof Foundation, 2012).
63. Eddie Quitoriano, "Firearm Law can Subvert the Bangsamoro Disarmament Process", *Action for Economic Reforms*, 4 October 2015, http://aer.ph/firearm-law-can-subvert-the-bangsamoro-disarmament-process/.

PART IV

International Environment

9

The Philippines and the South China Sea/ West Philippine Sea Conflict:
Challenges and Prospects for Peace, Diplomacy, and External Defence Capability

Noel M. Morada

INTRODUCTION

This chapter examines the Philippines' government policy towards the South China Sea (SCS) dispute since 1995 in the context of bilateral relations with China as well as membership in the Association of Southeast Asian Nations (ASEAN). Specifically, it looks at how the country has managed its maritime dispute with China since the Mischief Reef incident in 1995 and the implications of the international court's ruling in July 2016 for its bilateral ties with China and ASEAN regional diplomacy, as well as its external defence posture. Using a neoclassical realist perspective,[1]

I argue that—despite the favourable ruling of the international court—the Philippines under the new administration of President Duterte still faces a number of challenges in managing its maritime conflict with China. These challenges include: difficulties in renormalization of relations with Beijing; the push for a regional Code of Conduct (COC) between China and the ASEAN in the SCS; and the dismal state of the Philippines' external defence capability. This author also contends that, under new leadership, the Philippines should seriously consider embarking on developing self-reliance or self-help capability as part of its internal balancing strategy, which should have been the country's core defence strategy since 1992, to effectively protect its interests in the West Philippine Sea.

Self-help is fundamentally a principle of action in an anarchical system of states where each state actor is responsible for their own survival or security.[2] Realists do not consider it prudent for states to rely on other states or institutions to ensure their security.[3] While powerful states can pursue military or defence build-up when they feel threatened by other states, this may not be adequate for smaller states especially if they face a more powerful hegemonic state. To compensate, small states may resort to balance of power strategies by aligning with a more powerful state or forming alliances with other states to counter a perceived hegemony.[4] From a neorealist perspective, states can pursue balance of power internally, by mobilizing internal resources to build economic and defence capability, and externally, by forming alliances or bandwagoning with other states. According to Waltz,[5] power is a means to ensure a state's security and the concern of states is ultimately to maximize security.[6]

Neoclassical realists argue that external vulnerabilities generate incentives for states to emulate security practices of other states or counter such practices through innovation.[7] In this context, Taliaferro argues that state power—defined as the degree to which states can coercively extract or contractually mobilize societal resources—serves as an intervening variable between external vulnerabilities and the adaptive strategies of states to promote their survival.[8] For neoclassical realists, "politicians, military leaders, and bureaucrats make foreign policy choices based on their perceptions and calculations of relative power and other state's intentions" and "in the short and medium terms, different states' foreign policies may not be objectively 'efficient' or predictable based on an objective assessment of relative power".[9] More importantly, neoclassical realists recognize that "the identities and scope of those central-decision-making actors depends on the specific characteristics of a country's political system" and executive decision-makers "may be influenced in their thinking by cumulative actions" of diverse actors and "by the process of bargaining with them".[10] Accordingly, the state's national interest and conduct of foreign policy are defined by leaders, based not only on their assessment of relative power and other states' intentions, but also on domestic constraints.[11]

Literature over the last ten years on the SCS dispute focused on ASEAN engaging China in the process of promoting and negotiating a code of conduct following the signing of the Declaration on the Code of Conduct of Parties in the South China Sea in 2012.[12] Some works also examined strategies adopted by ASEAN states in the context of external balancing vis-à-vis China—including hedging and bandwagoning—in response to China's rise as an economic and military power in the region.[13] Some scholars and opinion makers have assumed that the Philippines' mutual defence treaty with the United States serves as a security guarantee against China's growing assertiveness in the SCS even though commitment from Washington to defend its weak ally remains vague in its commitment in defending its weak ally amidst growing tensions in the area.[14] Notwithstanding the Obama administration's "pivot in Asia" and the signing of the Enhanced Defence Cooperation Agreement (EDCA) with the Philippines in 2014, the United States was not able to prevent China from effectively taking control over Scarborough Shoal in 2012 and subsequent reclamation projects in some reefs in the SCS prior to and after the international court's decision in July 2016 declaring the "nine-dash line" as illegal under the 1982 United Nations Convention on the Law of the Sea (UNCLOS). This raises serious questions about the reliability of the United States as an ally and security guarantor for the Philippines. From a neoclassical realist perspective, it also raises important questions about how the Philippines as a weak state has been undertaking internal balancing amidst some growing scepticism at home about the effectiveness of its external balancing strategies vis-à-vis China. The Philippines under Duterte should pay more serious attention to developing self-reliance or self-help capabilities to assert claims in the SCS and protect its exclusive economic zones (EEZs) that overlap with China's nine-dash line—declared illegal under UNCLOS.

The next section of this chapter provides an overview of the Philippines' stance and foreign policy behaviour on the SCS conflict vis-à-vis China and how the Philippines responded to China's growing assertiveness and maritime claims in the region.

OVERVIEW

Conflicting claims in the SCS have been a major security concern for the Philippines and ASEAN—especially after the end of the Cold War and withdrawal of US military facilities from the Philippines in 1992. The Manila Declaration adopted by ASEAN-5 in 1992 clearly expresses the concerns and hopes of member states at the time for "concerned parties"— including China and Vietnam—to "exercise restraint with the view to creating a positive climate for the eventual resolution of all disputes".[15] Consensus among ASEAN members on the Manila Declaration was not difficult to achieve at the time given that Cambodia, Laos, Myanmar, and Vietnam— the CLMV countries—were not yet part of the group. ASEAN was also trying to navigate an uncertain post-Cold War regional security environment during this period following the closing down of American military bases in the Philippines—which some in the region saw as creating a "power vacuum".[16] ASEAN was forced under this uncertain environment to consider creating a post-Cold War security framework to promote regional peace and stability by engaging through dialogue and "norm-building" both traditional Western dialogue partners and non-traditional partners like China, Russia and North Korea. ASEAN was also preparing at the time to engage Vietnam and other Southeast Asian countries with a view towards inviting them to become members of the regional organization. From a strategic perspective, expanding the membership of ASEAN to include the CLMV countries was aimed at ensuring the region would no longer be divided due to the influence of external powers. Against this backdrop the ASEAN Regional Forum (ARF) was born in 1994, which served as an important post-ministerial conference of ASEAN to engage external actors beyond the region. Among other security concerns, the SCS issue continued to be on ASEAN's agenda even after the CLMV countries joined the group and in the ARF after China joined the dialogue forum.

China's takeover of Mischief Reef in 1995—which is claimed by the Philippines—upset the government in Manila and other ASEAN members as this takeover took place at a time when ASEAN was trying to engage China as part of the bloc's confidence-building efforts to promote regional peace and stability. Prior to this takeover of Mischief Reef, China seized Subi Reef in 1988—which is within the Philippines' continental shelf—and built a radar structure and military facilities.[17] The Philippines strongly denounced the occupation of Mischief Reef, invoked the Manila Declaration, and called on China to abide by the Manila Declaration's principles in an effort to avoid further destabilizing the region. China did not abandon its occupation of Mischief Reef and instead tried to persuade the Philippines to resolve the issue through bilateral negotiations. Realizing its limited options in dealing with Beijing on this issue, Manila started to embark on a military modernization programme aimed at beefing up its external defence capability.[18] The Philippines used ASEAN and the ARF as the main vehicles for exerting diplomatic pressure on China to abandon its occupation of Mischief Reef. This did not sit well with Beijing as it did not want the SCS issue to be included in any international multilateral forums like the ARF. One of the reasons for Beijing's initial reluctance in joining the ARF was the risk of being dominated by Western powers like some ASEAN claimant states that could "regionalize" the SCS dispute. The Philippines remained adamant in including the SCS dispute in the agenda of ASEAN and the ARF. Manila wanted to rally international public opinion against China over the SCS issue, running counter to Beijing's efforts to limit the SCS dispute within a framework of bilateral relations between China and the claimant states.[19]

Notwithstanding the Philippines' efforts in internationalizing the SCS dispute, the Philippines also kept the door open to bilateral talks with China in the search for a "win-win" solution to the conflict. During the Ramos and Arroyo administrations, Manila specifically expressed willingness to negotiate with Beijing—and later in a tripartite agreement that included Vietnam—for joint scientific explorations in the SCS even as the parties agreed to put aside sovereignty claims in the area. In 2004, the Philippines signed a memorandum of understanding (MOU) on joint marine seismic undertaking in the SCS with China and Vietnam. After the MOU lapsed in 2008 it was not renewed following public criticisms at home that it compromised the Philippine's sovereignty. China's willingness to sign an agreement with other claimant states for joint explorations in the SCS is part of its strategy to convince other states that parties in the dispute could put aside sovereignty claims. This may be considered part of Beijing's "charm offensive" in the region—trying to convince ASEAN about China's "peaceful rise" and desire to play the role of a "responsible stakeholder" so to speak—in order to promote regional peace and stability.

Following the Mischief Reef incident in 1995, tensions in the SCS increased more after China adopted a domestic law in 1998 on China's exclusive economic zone and continental shelf—including a provision asserting "historic rights" in the area. These developments forced ASEAN to start pushing for a legally binding Code of Conduct (COC) in the SCS. China and other ASEAN claimant states are expected to comply with a COC. In 2002, the ASEAN Declaration on the Conduct of Parties in the SCS was adopted in the summit of leaders in Phnom Penh—also signed by then Chinese Special Envoy Wang Yi—now China's Foreign Minister. The Declaration called on claimant and other states to stop undertaking activities "that would complicate or escalate disputes and affect peace and stability including, among others, refraining from action of inhabiting on the presently uninhabited islands, reefs, shoals, cays, and other features". The Declaration also reaffirmed the commitment of parties to the purposes and principles of the Charter of the UN, the 1982 Convention of the Law of the Sea, the Treaty of Amity and Cooperation in Southeast Asia, and the Five Principles of Peaceful Coexistence. The Declaration also reaffirmed "respect and commitment to the freedom of navigation in and overflight above the South China Sea as provided by the universally recognized principles of international law, including the 1982 UN Convention of the Law of the Sea".[20]

Meanwhile, in May 2009, China filed a map in the UN with the so-called "nine-dash line" in an effort to assert its territorial claim in the SCS. This move was aimed to challenge a prior submission made by Vietnam and Malaysia earlier the same month that extended their continental shelves in the SCS. The Philippines filed a protest three months later on 4 August 2009 against claims made by Vietnam and Malaysia but not against China's "nine-dash line" over the Spratly islands—which happened two years later on 5 April 2011, a month prior to the scheduled visit of President BS Aquino to Beijing.[21]

Prelude to 2012

China's assertiveness in the SCS increased following former Secretary of State Hillary Clinton's declaration in July 2010 during the ASEAN post-ministerial ARF meeting in Hanoi—that freedom of navigation in the SCS is in the "national interest" of the United States. As expected, the statement angered many leaders in Beijing and also spurred debates within China on whether to elevate Chinese sovereignty claims in the SCS as "core interest" as for Taiwan and Tibet.[22] In an essay written for *Foreign Policy* magazine in October 2011, Hilary Clinton expounded on President Obama's US "pivot" in Asia, which reiterated freedom of navigation in the SCS is in the national interest of the US. Secretary Clinton said:

> maintaining peace and security across the Asia-Pacific is increasingly crucial to global progress, whether through defending freedom of navigation in the South China Sea, countering the proliferation efforts of North Korea, or ensuring transparency in the military activities of the region's key players.[23]

Secretary Clinton's words also underscored the importance of America's defence alliances in the region and the value of supporting ASEAN's efforts to find a peaceful resolution to competing claims in the SCS. Some government and military officials in Beijing, however, viewed the United States' "pivot" in Asia as part of Washington's grand strategy of containing China's rise—possibly linked to the SCS dispute.[24] Chinese officials have indirectly rejected US concerns about freedom of navigation in the SCS even—and also expressed suspicions that freedom of navigation is an excuse to increase American presence in the region.[25]

Since 2011, China has become more aggressive in the SCS. In February 2011, a Chinese frigate reportedly fired at Philippine fishing boats in the area of Qurino Reef (Jackson Atoll) after these boats were asked to leave the area. In March 2011, the Philippines military presence was bolstered in its western maritime border following an encounter with two Chinese boats that threatened to ram a survey ship conducting seismic testing in the area. In May 2011, China built military garrisons and outposts in six reefs within the Kalayaan Island Group claimed by the Philippines. In July, Beijing protested against Manila's invitation for exploration bids in Areas 3 and 4 in the Reed Bank and called on the Philippines to "refrain from any action that infringes on China's sovereignty and sovereign rights" in the area. Later, in October 2011, a Philippine naval ship rammed into a Chinese fishing vessel in the Reed Bank, which resulted in a prompt apology from Manila to the Chinese embassy for the incident—which it called an accident.[26] The Department of Foreign Affairs significantly began using the term "West Philippine Sea" in 2011, to refer to the area of the SCS within its 200-mile EEZ.[27]

2012 Stand-off in Scarborough Shoal

The Scarborough (Panatag) Shoal became the centre of the Philippine-China maritime dispute throughout 2012. The stand-off in the area began on 8 April after Chinese fishing vessels ventured into the shoal and were spotted by a Philippine navy plane. Two days later, the Philippine Navy deployed a newly acquired and refurbished ship *BRP Gregorio Del Pilar* to the area. This prompted China to send surveillance ships to Scarborough Shoal to warn the Philippine Navy to leave the area—which led to the stand-off. The Philippine navy's ship pulled out of the area the next day as China sent a third ship into the disputed shoal. In May 2012, both the Philippine and Chinese governments imposed a ban on fishing in the Scarborough Shoal area. China then blocked Philippine ships and fishing vessels from the lagoon of the Scarborough Shoal in July—by setting up barriers at the entry point. After three months of impasse over the Scarborough Shoal, China informed the Philippines in November 2012 that its coast guard vessels will stay permanently in the area.[28] China also announced the creation of Sansha in 2012—to "formally garrison" the SCS.[29] The Philippines named the western side of the archipelago as West Philippine Sea under Administrative Order No. 29 in September 2012. In November, the Philippines also protested against China's decision to print the image of the "nine-dash line" on e-passports, showing China's claim over the entire SCS.[30]

The stand-off in Scarborough Shoal between the Philippines and China also had an impact on ASEAN's position on the issue. During the ASEAN foreign ministers' meeting in Phnom Penh in July 2012, the Philippines insisted on a statement on the SCS at the conclusion of the meeting—including the situation in the Scarborough Shoal. However, Cambodia—as chair of ASEAN at the time—refused to accommodate the request of the Philippines largely in deference to the wishes of China, Cambodia's major source of aid and investments. Despite the support of other ASEAN members for the Philippines, the Cambodian government remained adamant in its position. Ultimately, the ASEAN foreign ministers failed to issue a communiqué or Chairman's statement for the first time in forty-five years since the regional organization was established in 1967.[31]

Indonesia's Foreign Minister Marty Natalegawa attempted to save the situation by undertaking shuttle diplomacy between Manila, Hanoi, and Phnom Penh for two days after the ASEAN ministerial meeting. Natalegawa was attempting to ensure a joint statement could still be issued in lieu of an ASEAN communiqué— instead he could only deliver a short statement titled "Six Point Principles on the South China Sea" read out by Cambodian Foreign Minister Hor Namhong on 20 July 2012. The statement:

> Reaffirmed the commitment of ASEAN member states to:
> 1. the full implementation of the Declaration on the Conduct of Parties in the South China Sea (2002);
> 2. the Guidelines for the Implementation of the Declaration on the Conduct of Parties in the South China Sea (2011);
> 3. the early conclusion of a Regional Code of Conduct in the South China Sea;
> 4. the full respect of the universally recognized principles of International Law, including the 1982 United Nations Convention on the Law of the Sea (UNCLOS);
> 5. the continued exercise of self-restraint and non-use of force by all parties; and
> 6. the peaceful resolution of disputes, in accordance with universally recognized principles of International Law, including the 1982 United Nations Convention on the Law of the Sea.[32]

In the aftermath of events in 2012, the Philippines decided to file an arbitration case against China before the UN Permanent Court of Arbitration (PCA) in January 2013 to settle their maritime dispute. As expected, China refused to participate in the arbitration case and claimed that Manila's case was legally infirmed and "carried unacceptable allegations against Beijing".[33] Chinese ships continued to harass Philippine navy ships and fishing vessels between 2014 and 2015, specifically in areas claimed by the Philippines—Scarborough Shoal, Mabini Reef, and Panganiban Reef. In April 2014, the Philippines signed the EDCA with the United States, which allowed for enhanced rotational presence of US military forces and supplies to be stationed in military bases in the country within a period of ten years. In July 2014, the PCA began hearing the Philippines' oral arguments on whether the PCA has jurisdiction over the case filed against China. The PCA ruled in October 2015 that it had jurisdiction over the case despite claims by China to contrary. Meanwhile, China began to take bolder actions in the SCS by constructing airstrips in 2014 and undertaking reclamation projects in 2015 in some reefs claimed by the Philippines—for example, Mabini (Johnson) Reef, Panganiban (Mischief) Reef, and Kagitingan (Fiery Cross) Reef.

On 12 July 2016, the PCA ruled in favour of the Philippines. As expected, China refused to recognize the decision of the international tribunal that effectively rejected its "nine-dash line" claim in the SCS. President Xi Jinping asserted the court's ruling would not affect China's "territorial sovereignty and maritime rights" in the SCS and also insisted that the country is still committed to resolving disputes with its neighbours.[34]

CHALLENGES

Even prior to the international court's decision, the new administration of President Rodrigo R. Duterte was clear that it would not use the court's favourable verdict to taunt China. Foreign Secretary Perfecto Yasay called for restraint and sobriety even as he hailed the PCA's decision.[35] On 27 July 2016, President Duterte convened a meeting of the National Security Council—attended by four past presidents—to discuss the PCA's decision.[36] Duterte then appointed former President Fidel V. Ramos as special envoy to explore steps in opening bilateral talks with China on the SCS. On 13 August 2016, Ramos travelled to Hong Kong to meet with the former envoy of China to Manila, Ambassador Fu Ying, and Professor Wu Shicun, President of China's National Institute for South China Sea Studies. Potential areas of cooperation that could build mutual trust and confidence between the Philippines and China were discussed.[37] Although China welcomed Ramos to come to Beijing as special envoy, he opted to return to Manila to discuss the next steps with President Duterte.

What then are the major challenges ahead following the PCA's decision for the Philippines and ASEAN?

RENORMALIZING BILATERAL RELATIONS WITH CHINA

A major challenge for the administration of President Duterte is how to renormalize ties with Beijing even as the Philippines asserts its sovereignty in the West Philippine Sea—anchored on the recent decision of the international court. China has stated bilateral talks cannot proceed if the Philippines insists on China complying with the decision of the court.

Foreign Minister Wang Yi reportedly expressed willingness to talk about the ruling in an "unofficial engagement" with his Filipino counterpart during the Asia-Europe meeting in Mongolia in July 2016.[38] A perception within China is that nationalist sentiments in the Philippines must calm down following the court's ruling—and that the new government must find a balance in dealing with opposition, public opinion, and external pressures from the United States and Japan.[39]

Access to the area of the Scarborough Shoal for Filipino fishermen is a good starting point to resume bilateral talks between the two countries. This issue was covered in informal talks agreed upon by former President Ramos in his meeting with Chinese diplomats in Hong Kong in August 2016—specifically with regard to managing tension and promoting fishing cooperation in the area.[40] President Duterte himself has already appealed twice to the Chinese ambassador in Manila to allow Filipino fishermen access to Scarborough Shoal area out of humanitarian consideration.[41]

However, the Philippines must also be realistic in its expectations about how far bilateral talks with China can proceed in an attempt to renormalize their relations, especially concerning other sensitive issues related to the SCS dispute. For example, the exploitation of marine resources as well as the protection of maritime environment within the EEZ of the Philippines could be contentious issues with China given the ongoing reclamation projects that China has already undertaken in the SCS. China's exploration, reclamation, and military build-up in the disputed SCS do not appear to be winding down any time soon. The Philippine government should therefore seriously consider its options in managing and responding to a range of scenarios that could arise from China's continuing intransigence and aggressive behaviour in dealing with the Philippines and other claimant, and non-claimant, states in the region. On the issue of SCS since 1995, the new leadership in Manila should begin a candid assessment of important lessons learned in dealing with China and gaps in capabilities that must be given priority in the near- and medium-term. This assessment should include an honest examination of the government's weaknesses, particularly in diplomacy and building external defence capability. Convening a meeting of the National Security Council (NSC) at the start of President Duterte's term is a step in the right direction. Subsequent meetings of the NSC should give priority to developing a national consensus on how to move forward in searching for a pragmatic and realistic approach in dealing with the SCS dispute with China.

ASEAN AND THE CODE OF CONDUCT IN THE SCS

Since the takeover of Mischief Reef by China in 1995, the Philippines has relied primarily on ASEAN's framework to engage with the rising power in the north—specifically in managing the conflict in the SCS. The Philippines supported efforts by ASEAN in developing instruments that could eventually lead to the adoption of a regional code of conduct for concerned parties in the SCS dispute. This approach is anchored on the belief that norm-building—the mantra of ASEAN since 1967—is key to managing regional conflicts. The ARF, created in 1994, is also anchored on the belief of norm-building—with the aim of exporting norms in the larger context of East Asia and beyond. The centrality of ASEAN in managing regional security is at the core of the ARF, which members assumed would be respected by external powers including China.

ASEAN has been convinced for some time there is value in socializing China to its norms so this rising power could eventually be persuaded to act responsibly by adhering to joint declarations and agreements it signed with the group—respecting relevant international laws and conventions mutually recognized and committed to. The Declaration of Conduct of Parties in the South China Sea (DOC) signed by ASEAN and China in 2002 was hailed at the time as an important milestone in ASEAN-China relations. DOC purportedly demonstrated—at least on paper—an indication that Beijing was willing in the medium term to negotiate a binding Code of Conduct (COC) with other claimant states in the region. Since China's filing in the UN of a map containing the "nine-dash line" in 2009 and the subsequent developments that took place in the region over the last five years—ASEAN's efforts in negotiating a legally binding COC with China have been eclipsed. The Philippines' filing of a case in the PCA in 2013 against China made the COC negotiations even more difficult.

How then would the court's ruling in favour of the Philippines impact on the COC negotiations?

At best, one could be cautiously optimistic. A COC can be viewed as a "face-saving" alternative for Beijing to the PAC's ruling, which was rejected by China. Given that Beijing has been supporting the idea of a COC with ASEAN, it is possible Beijing will show some flexibility and accommodate some interests of ASEAN claimant and non-claimant (for example, Indonesia) states—such as access to fishing boats. China and ASEAN may, however, have some difficulties in negotiating a COC that deals with issues such as oil exploration, exploitation of marine resources, and even protection of maritime environment. The Philippines and Vietnam are likely to take a hard-line stance against including these issues in the COC. As well, Cambodia's close ties with China could again be a factor in developing a consensus within ASEAN on what are the negotiable and non-negotiable elements that must be included in the COC.

The Philippines should continue to support the collective efforts of ASEAN in pushing for a COC with China in the SCS. The Philippines must also have realistic expectations about what such an agreement can do to protect Philippine interests in the West Philippine Sea—and learn important lessons about the way other ASEAN members responded to the international court's ruling. The Philippines may have difficulty using the international court's ruling as basis for a COC following controversy in the 2016 ASEAN Foreign Ministers' Meeting in Laos on what to include in the final statement related to the SCS dispute. More importantly, the Philippines should realize by now that ASEAN's centrality has been undermined since 2012—particularly on the issue of SCS—partly due to China's strong influence on some members. Another factor that constrains the group from developing consensus on the SCS is internal political dynamics in some ASEAN states. Even presumed natural leaders within the group are reluctant to push for that much-needed consensus.

External Defence Capability

What is the use of a favourable decision by the international court if the Philippines, alone, cannot enforce that decision within its own EEZ? This is the fundamental question that should have been in the minds of Philippine leaders since 1995. While the Ramos administration attempted to beef up the country's external defence capability following the Mischief Reef incident, succeeding administrations did not seriously follow through on his initiative for a number of reasons. Firstly, in the aftermath of 9/11, managing internal security threats remained a priority in resource allocation of the state for the defence establishment. Counterterrorism was high on the agenda of bilateral relations with the United States—particularly during the administration of President Arroyo—which had close ties with the Bush administration. Although these close relations continued under the administration of President Benigno Aquino—culminating in the signing of the EDCA in 2014—the SCS dispute with China became a significant addition to the *raison d'être* for enhancing security ties between the two countries.

Some questions still remain in the minds of many Filipinos on whether the United States is committed to defending the Philippines in the face of China's growing aggressive behaviour in the SCS. Will the United States continue with "strategic vagueness" on this question? Who benefits more from EDCA and to what extent will the existing Mutual Defence Treaty be useful in deterring China's encroachment into the West Philippine Sea? To what extent is US military assistance to the Philippines—including refurbished World War II ships—a reflection of US commitment to defend an ally? What is the "redline" for both allies in dealing with China's aggressive behaviour in the West Philippine Sea?

The administration of President Duterte should take a long hard look at these difficult questions from a strategic perspective, and seriously examine the Philippines' journey in dealing with internal and external security threats. Duterte's strong commitment in "waging" peace at home by ending communist and Muslim rebellions, as well as in containing corruption, criminality, and poverty—should enable his government to focus more on external security—hopefully sooner than later. The dismal state of the country's external defence capability vis-à-vis China and other claimant states in the SCS should compel the Duterte government to embark on developing self-reliance or self-help, which should have been at the core of the Philippines defence strategy since 1992. The Philippines should take serious steps to mobilize and allocate more resources to build a more modern coast guard to protect its EEZs and improve naval defence capabilities to assert legitimate claims in the SCS. The Philippines also needs to diversify sources or suppliers of coast guard and defence technologies and develop appropriate defence weaponry through research and development. The country cannot continue with second-hand or refurbished naval ships from traditional allies even if these may serve some useful—albeit more symbolic—purpose in the short term. The Philippine government should also take advantage of opportunities to develop the country's shipbuilding capability through technology transfer from South Korea, for example, which already has a shipbuilding facility in Subic—a former US naval base.

Filipino leaders have been self-effacing in acknowledging the country's weak external defence capability—without coherent and consistent efforts to address the root causes. Security alliances and multilateral diplomacy should only complement—not substitute—self-reliance or self-help when it comes to dealing with external threats and managing the country's security environment. The sooner Filipino leaders realize the Philippines is alone—and cannot always count on its allies or neighbours—the better the country will be in the long term. At the same time, the Philippines should also learn from its neighbours—in particular, Vietnam and Indonesia—on how to assert rights under international law, based on a strong sense of political will and ways to enforce the law. Vietnam, for example, consistently protested against Chinese oil explorations in its EEZs and in the Paracels that forced China to withdraw an oil rig in 2016.[42] Vietnam also imported more defence weapons than South Korea and Singapore between 2011 and 2015 amidst rising tensions in the SCS in an effort to build its naval and air force capability.[43] Hanoi signed several agreements in 2016 with India to improve its defence capability—for a strategic partnership and defence cooperation with New Delhi including a contract for the sale of Indian fast patrol boats.[44] Vietnam also received its fifth submarine from Russia in 2016[45] and it was reported that Hanoi was "eyeing" some refurbished maritime surveillance planes from South Korea.[46] Indonesia also asserted claims over its EEZs around the Natuna islands—which overlaps with China's "nine-dash line"—and enforced claims in its maritime EEZs amidst some encroachment by Chinese coast guard and fishing vessels in the area.[47] Jakarta plans to set up a new base in the Natuna islands following several clashes with Chinese coast guard and fishing boats in early 2016.[48] In a strong signal to China, President Joko Widodo held a cabinet meeting in June 2016 aboard a ship on the Natuna islands as part of asserting the country's sovereignty over the EEZs in the area.[49]

CONCLUSION

This chapter examined Philippines policy towards the SCS dispute since 1995 in the context of bilateral relations with China and membership in ASEAN—using a neoclassical realist framework. The foregoing discussion is clear that—despite the favourable ruling of the international court in July 2016 on the case filed against China—under the new administration of President Duterte, the Philippines still faces a number of challenges in managing its maritime conflict with China. Challenges include the renormalization of relations with Beijing, the push for a regional Code of

Conduct between China and ASEAN in the SCS, and the dismal state of the Philippines external defence capability. This author argues that, under the new leadership, the Philippines should seriously consider embarking on developing its self-reliance or self-help capability—which should have been its core defence strategy since 1992—in order to protect interests in the West Philippine Sea. Security alliances and multilateral diplomacy should complement—and not be a substitute for—this core strategy. Improving the Philippine's external defence capability ultimately depends on how successful President Duterte's administration is in waging peace at home by putting an end to internal rebellion and containing corruption and crime, and improving poverty. A weak state like the Philippines needs to mobilize resources to pursue sustained economic development that would contribute to improving external defence capabilities. The Philippines would then be able to lessen current dependence on external balancing in what appears to be a constrained bilateral security alliance with the United States and uncertain hedging with ASEAN vis-à-vis China in the South China Sea.

Notes

1. Neoclassical realism was coined by Gideon Rose in his 1998 *World Politics* review article, in which he pointed out that this framework, in contrast to both classical realist and neorealist (or structural realist) perspectives, "explicitly incorporates both external and internal variables, updating and systematizing certain insights drawn from classical realist thought. Its adherents argue that the scope and ambition of a country's foreign policy is driven first and foremost by its place in the international system and specifically by its relative material power capabilities. This is why they are realist. They argue further, however, that the impact of such power capabilities on foreign policy is indirect and complex, because systemic pressures must be translated through intervening variables at the unit level. This is why they are neoclassical." [As quoted from Nicholas Kitchen, "Systemic Pressures and Domestic Ideas: A Neoclassical Realist Model of Grand Strategy Formation", *Review of International Studies* 36, no. 1 (2010): 117.
2. See Tim Dunne and Brian C. Smith, "Realism", *The Globalisation of World Politics* (3rd ed.), edited by John Baylis and Steve Smith (Oxford: Oxford University Press, 2005), p. 164.
3. Ibid.
4. Ibid.

5. Kenneth N. Waltz, "Structural Realism after the Cold War", *International Security* 25, no. 1 (2000): 5–41.
6. Ibid.
7. See Jeffrey W. Taliaferro, "State Building for Future Wars: Neoclassical Realism and the Resource-Extractive State", *Security Studies* 15, no. 3 (July–September 2006): 464–95.
8. Ibid., pp. 485–86.
9. Ibid., p. 485.
10. Nicholas Kitchen, "Systemic Pressures and Domestic Ideas: A Neoclassical Realist Model of Grand Strategy Formation", *British International Studies Association* 36, issue 1 (2010): 117–43.
11. Ibid.
12. See, for example, Carlyle Thayer, "ASEAN, China and the Code of Conduct in the South China Sea", *SAIS Review* 33, no. 2 (2013): 75–84; Hong Zhao, "The South China Sea Dispute and China-Asean Relations", *Asian Affairs* 44, no. 1 (2013): 27–43; Alice Ba, "ASEAN's Stakes: The South China Sea's Challenge to Autonomy and Agency", *Asia Policy*, no. 21 (January 2016): 47–53.
13. See, for example, Ann Marie Murphy, "Beyond Balancing and Bandwagoning: Thailand's Response to China's Rise", *Asian Security* 6, no. 1 (2010): 1–27; Cheng-Chwee Kuik, "How Do Weaker States Hedge? Unpacking ASEAN States' Alignment Behaviour towards China", *Journal of Contemporary China* 25, no. 100 (2016): 500–14 ; Kaewkamol Pitakdumrongkit, "Coordinating the South China Sea Issue: Thailand's Roles in the Code of Conduct Development", *International Relations of the Asia Pacific* 15 (2015): 403–1; Ristian Supriyanto, "Out of Its Comfort Zone: Indonesia and the South China Sea", *Asia Policy*, no. 21 (January 2016): 21–28; Evan Laksamana, "The Domestic Politics of Indonesia's Approach to the Tribunal Ruling and the South China Sea", *Contemporary Southeast Asia: A Journal of International and Strategic Affairs* 38, no. 3 (2016): 382–88; Carlyle A. Thayer, "Chinese Assertiveness in the South China Sea and Southeast Asian Responses", *Journal of Current Southeast Asian Affairs* 30, no. 2 (2011): 77–104; and Phuong Nguyen, "Deciphering the Shift in America's South China Sea Policy", *Contemporary Southeast Asia: A Journal of International and Strategic Affairs* 38, no. 3 (2016): 389–421.
14. See, for example, Renato Cruz De Castro, "The Risk of Applying Realpolitik in Resolving the South China Sea Dispute: Implications on Regional Security", *Pacific Focus* 27, no. 2 (August 2012): 262–89; Richard Javad Heydarian, "Why the New US-Philippine Defense Pact Could Be a Double-Edged Sword", *The Diplomat Online*, 27 January 2016, http://thediplomat.com/2016/01/why-the-new-us-philippine-defense-pact-could-be-a-double-edged-sword/ (accessed 17 April 2017); Richard Javad Heydarian, "Opinion: Scarborough Shoal: Will America Help Us?", *ABS-CBN News Online*, 27 March 2017,

http://news.abs-cbn.com/opinions/03/27/17/opinion-scarborough-shoal-will-america-help-us (accessed 17 April 2017); and Richard Javad Heydarian, "Will America Go to War for the Philippines?", *The National Interest online*, 27 January 2016, http://nationalinterest.org/feature/will-america-go-war-the-philippines-15031?page=show (accessed 17 April 2017).

15. https://cil.nus.edu.sg/wp-content/uploads/2017/07/1992-ASEAN-Declaration-on-the-South-China-Sea.pdf.
16. See, for example, Denny Roy, "Assessing the Asia Pacific 'Power Vacuum' ", *Survival* 37, no. 3 (1995): 45–60; Ralf Emmers, *Cooperative Security and the Balance of Power in ASEAN and the ARF* (London and New York: Routledge, 2003); and Noel M. Morada, "The ASEAN Regional Forum: Origins and Evolution", in *Cooperative Security in the Asia-Pacific: The ASEAN Regional Forum*, edited by Jurgen Haacke and Noel M. Morada (London: Routledge, 2010), pp. 13–35.
17. "Timeline: The Philippines-China Maritime Dispute", *Rappler.com*, 12 July 2016, http://www.rappler.com/world/regions/asia-pacific/139392-timeline-west-philippine-sea-dispute (accessed 29 August 2016).
18. See Noel M. Morada and Christopher Collier, "The Philippines: State Versus Society?", in *Asian Security Practice: Material and Ideational Influences*, edited by Muthiah Alagappa (Stanford: Stanford University Press 1998), p. 573.
19. Ibid., pp. 573–75.
20. "ASEAN Declaration on the Conduct of Parties in the South China Sea", 2002, http://asean.org/?static_post=declaration-on-the-conduct-of-parties-in-the-south-china-sea-2 (accessed 29 August 2016).
21. Tessa Jamandre, "PH protests China's '9-dash line' claim over the Spratlys", *Yahoo! Southeast Asia*, 13 April 2011, https://sg.news.yahoo.com/blogs/the-inbox/ph-protests-china-9-dash-line-claim-over-20110413-064347-870.html (accessed 29 August 2016).
22. Edward Wong, "China Hedges Over Whether South China Sea Is a 'Core Interest' Worth War", *New York Times Online*, 30 March 2011, http://www.nytimes.com/2011/03/31/world/asia/31beijing.html (accessed 27 August 2016).
23. Hillary Clinton, "America's Pacific Century", *Foreign Policy*, 11 October 2011, http://foreignpolicy.com/2011/10/11/americas-pacific-century/ (accessed 27 August 2016).
24. Michael D. Swaine, "Chinese Leadership and Elite Responses to the U.S. Pacific Pivot", *China Leadership Monitor*, no. 38 (2012), p. 10, http://www.hoover.org/sites/default/files/uploads/documents/CLM38MS.pdf (accessed 27 August 2016).
25. Ibid.
26. *Rappler.com*, "Timeline: The Philippines-China Maritime Dispute".
27. Ibid.

28. Ibid.
29. Reuters, "China to Formally Garrison Disputed South China Sea", *Reuters.com*, 22 July 2012, http://www.reuters.com/article/us-china-sea-idUSBRE86L08B20120722 (accessed 29 August 2016).
30. *Rappler.com*, "Timeline: The Philippines-China Maritime Dispute".
31. See Ernest Z. Bower, "China Reveals Its Hand on ASEAN in Phnom Penh", *CSIS*, 20 July 2012, https://www.csis.org/analysis/china-reveals-its-hand-asean-phnom-penh (accessed 29 August 2016).
32. ASEAN Foreign Ministers, "ASEAN's Six-Point Principles on the South China Sea", Phnom Penh, Cambodia, 20 July 2012, http://www.asean.org/wp-content/uploads/images/AFMs%20Statement%20on%206%20Principles%20on%20SCS.pdf (accessed 29 August 2016).
33. *Rappler.com*, "Timeline: The Philippines-China Maritime Dispute".
34. Tom Phillips, Oliver Holmes, and Own Bowcott, "Beijing Rejects Tribunal's Ruling in South China Sea Case", *The Guardian Online*, 13 July 2016, https://www.theguardian.com/world/2016/jul/12/philippines-wins-south-china-sea-case-against-china (accessed 29 August 2016).
35. Joel Guinto, "Philippines Hails Arbitration Win, Calls for Restraint", *ABS CBN News*, 12 July 2012, http://news.abs-cbn.com/news/07/12/16/philippines-hails-arbitration-win-calls-for-restraint (accessed 29 August 2016).
36. Yas D. Ocampo and Roy C. Mabasa, "FVR wants Security Council Meeting before China Mission", *Manila Bulletin Online*, 25 July 2016, http://www.mb.com.ph/fvr-wants-security-council-meeting-before-china-mission/ (accessed 29 August 2016).
37. "Former President and Special Envoy Fidel V. Ramos Meets with Chinese Diplomats in Hong Kong", *Eaglenews.ph*, 13 August 2016, http://www.eaglenews.ph/former-president-and-special-envoy-fidel-v-ramos-meets-chinese-diplomats-in-hongkong/ (accessed 29 August 2016).
38. Li Xiaokun and Wang Qingyun, "China Offers Philippines Chance to Discuss Ruling, Spokesman Says", *China Daily*, 20 July 2016, http://www.chinadaily.com.cn/china/2016-07/20/content_26155904.htm (accessed 30 August 2016).
39. Ibid.
40. *Eaglenews.ph*, "Fidel V. Ramos Meets with Chinese Diplomats". The seven areas identified in the informal discussions include (1) encouraging marine preservation; (2) avoiding tension and promoting fishing cooperation; (3) anti-drug and anti-smuggling cooperation; (4) anti-crime and anti-corruption cooperation; (5) improving tourism opportunities; (6) encouraging trade and investment facilitation; and (7) encouraging track II (think-tank) exchanges on relevant issues of mutual concern and interest.
41. Margaux Torres, "Duterte Pleads with China for Filipino Fishermen", *Kami*.

com.ph, 30 August 2016, https://kami.com.ph/46275-disturbing-footage-shows-woman-trampling-wreaths-laid-tribute-first-world-war-soldiers.html (accessed 30 August 2016).

42. Katie Hunt, "South China Sea: Vietnam Says China Moved Oil Rig into Contested Water", *CNN Online*, 21 January 2016, http://edition.cnn.com/2016/01/20/asia/vietnam-china-south-china-sea-oil-rig/index.html (accessed 17 April 2017).
43. Trefor Moss, "Vietnam Adds Military Muscle as South China Sea Tension Escalate", *Wall Street Journal Online*, 21 February 2016, https://www.wsj.com/articles/vietnam-adds-military-muscle-as-south-china-sea-tensions-escalate-1456095603 (accessed 18 April 2017).
44. Gordon Chang, "India and Vietnam Unite against China", *World Affairs Journal Online*, 7 September 2016, http://www.worldaffairsjournal.org/blog/gordon-g-chang/india-and-vietnam-unite-against-china (accessed 17 April 2017).
45. Prashanth Parameswaran, "Vietnam Gets Fifth Submarine from Russia," *The Diplomat Online*, 10 February 2016, http://thediplomat.com/2016/02/vietnam-gets-fifth-submarine-from-russia/ (accessed 17 April 2017).
46. Reuters, "Vietnam, S. Korea Eye Lockheed Planes Amid China Buildup", *ABS-CBN News Online*, 6 June 2016, http://news.abs-cbn.com/global-filipino/world/06/06/16/vietnam-s-korea-eye-lockheed-planes-amid-chinese-buildup (accessed 17 April 2017).
47. Ristian Atriandi Supriyanto, "Breaking the Silence: Indonesia vs China in the Natuna Islands", *The Diplomat Online*, 23 March 2016, http://thediplomat.com/2016/03/breaking-the-silence-indonesia-vs-china-in-the-natuna-islands/ (accessed 17 April 2017).
48. Prashanth Parameswaran, "Indonesia Plays Up New South China Sea 'Base' After China Spat", *The Diplomat Online*, 28 March 2016, http://thediplomat.com/2016/03/indonesia-plays-up-new-south-china-sea-base-after-china-spat/ (accessed 17 April 2017).
49. "Indonesia Sends a Strong Signal Asserting Sovereignty over Southern South China Sea", *BigNewsNetwork.com*, 24 June 2016, http://www.bignewsnetwork.com/news/245243991/indonesia-sends-a-strong-signal-asserting-sovereignty-over-southern-south-china-sea (accessed 17 April 2017).

10

Fall from Grace, Descent from Power?
Civil Society after Philippine Democracy's Lost Decade

Aries A. Arugay

INTRODUCTION

Since the 1986 *Epifanio de los Santos Avenue* (EDSA) People Power Uprising that toppled the dictatorship of Ferdinand Marcos, civil society mobilization has occupied an increasingly prominent role in contemporary Philippine politics. The restoration of democratic rule aided in the proliferation of social forces and non-governmental organizations (NGOs) that now form one of the most robust and politically active civil societies in Asia.[1] Throughout their existence, Filipino civil society organizations (CSOs) have wielded considerable mobilization and coalitional power in pressing demands for good governance, advocating policy reforms, and even challenging the legitimacy of elected governments. With an affinity with democracy, civil society is considered appropriate and effective for channelling popular discontent against corrupt and abusive governments.[2] Different civil society groups have been at the forefront of the Philippines' struggle for good governance, social justice, and sustainable development.

There is consensus among some scholars and policymakers that a strong civil society is one of the most effective bulwarks against threats to democracy.[3] The celebrity status of civil society members makes them the heroes of ongoing stories of democracy-building around the world.[4] As Asia's oldest democracy, the Philippines confirms—to a large extent—the inexorable relationship between steady progress towards democratization of regimes and the density and health of civil society.[5]

Not all actions by Philippine civil society in the post-Marcos era adhered to constitutional rules and promoted democratic consolidation. During the Philippines' tumultuous period from 2001 to 2010, civil society and rival factions mobilized and collaborated with elites and other political actors—engendering an atmosphere of heightened and polarized conflict.[6] This prolonged democratic crisis started with the opposition against populist president Joseph Estrada resulting in his extraconstitutional removal in 2001. Known as the country's "lost decade of democracy", social forces claiming to be civil society were front and centre in a contentious and vicious political cycle that included the removal of a democratically elected president—and subsequent military coup plots, impeachment crises, and violent repression of protests during the tenure of Estrada's successor, Gloria Macapagal Arroyo (2001–10).[7]

In this chapter, I discuss the political issues confronted by CSOs in the Philippines since the country's "lost decade of democracy". Particular attention is given to the ways the crisis of legitimacy faced by the Estrada and Arroyo administrations further fragmented civil society—decreasing their ability to challenge state power, and their standing to embody popular interests—thereby weakening their position to influence public policy. Despite the reputation of civil society as the bulwark of Philippine democracy, the weakened state of various societal actors manifested in their inability to exercise influence during the Aquino II administration. Examples of this are the pork-barrel scandal, the Reproductive Health Law debate, and the 2013 mid-term elections. A hostile split within civil society was apparent with the Catholic Church and other conservative social groups at odds with more liberal and progressive NGOs in the campaign for the adoption of the Reproductive Health Law. At the height of the pork-barrel scandal, civil society groups—particularly left-leaning organizations allied with the Aquino presidency—refused to mobilize against the government, leaving other factions of the Philippine left and middle-class NGOs to lead the demonstration. The 2013 elections also divided civil society as more moderate and middle-class groups endorsed the administration candidates—while the opposition received significant backing from urban poor movements and radical left groups.

Because of partisan involvement in elite conflicts and hostile divisions, civil society groups were unable to overcome their differences and create a united front against the successful populist challenge of Rodrigo Duterte in the 2016 elections. I discuss the preliminary relationship between the Duterte administration and civil society groups, concluding with the prospects of civil society action and resistance against the current erosion of liberal democracy in the Philippines.

CIVIL SOCIETY AFTER DICTATORSHIP: BETWEEN DEMOCRATIZATION AND CRISIS

What is now known as Philippine civil society was born—to a large extent—out of the country's struggle against Marcos' constitutional authoritarian regime from 1972 to 1986. Civil society was significantly shaped by the "dangerous, heady experience of organizing oppressed people under martial law".[8] Despite these repressive conditions, societal organizations steadily flourished, extending their networks and incrementally building an infrastructure of political contention against the government.[9]

The ultimate power of civil society was demonstrated in a grand display of non-violent collective action—known as the 1986 People Power Uprising—which ended the Marcos regime and paved the way for Corazon Aquino to assume the presidency. The role of civil society in regime change became its crucible for an expanded political role after the Marcos dictatorship. The 1987 Constitution and subsequent legal instruments provided civil society access to important policy processes.

Through a more critical lens, social forces that mobilized—claiming to be civil society—would form the de facto configuration of civil society in the Philippines—comprising NGOs and people's organizations (POs). These collective manifestations of Filipino civil society would be integrated with the extant hegemonic power bloc composed of economic elites, transnational actors, and the Catholic Church. In other words, civil society in the country helped realize a certain democratic vision characterized by moderation, liberalism, and a tolerance to inequality and the oligarchy.[10]

Corazon Aquino's administration (1986–92) survived despite numerous military coup attempts, crippling economic crises, and policy gridlock. While her presidency accomplished the critical task of democratic transition, this overriding goal sacrificed the potential for deepening democracy. Aquino's government eventually lost its revolutionary promise as the Philippines returned to a *"cacique* democracy".[11] Her successor—Fidel Ramos—also prioritized political stability and economic progress above addressing democratic deficits in the Philippine political system.[12] The Philippines' restored yet unconsolidated democratic regime would face its most challenging test during the presidency of Joseph Estrada.

Estrada's Populist Challenge and Civil Society Resistance

In 1998, the country's democracy was subjected to a litmus test with the electoral triumph of populist leader Joseph Estrada. As a former movie star and city mayor, Estrada was known more for his questionable morals and lack of intellectual credentials than effective leadership. Estrada's focus on the needs of the poor masses was, however, unprecedented in contemporary Philippine politics. His quest for a more deeply inclusive democratic mould was significantly shaped by intellectuals and personalities—former participants in the country's communist movement[13]—which became the spark for a polarizing conflict that defined the country from 2001 to 2010.

Backed by the Filipino masses, Estrada the populist ruled by stretching the limits of executive power. By 2000, Estrada's alleged involvement in illicit activities such as illegal gambling and money laundering became the tipping point for civil society to mobilize ranks against his abuses of power.[14]

The stakes against Estrada became higher as pillars of Philippine democracy—such as the Catholic Church and Cory Aquino—coalesced. The demand from these moral leaders revived the dormant political opposition led by then Vice-President Gloria Macapagal Arroyo—who quickly resigned from Estrada's cabinet. Previously weak and fragmented minority parties found a reason to bond together, while some of Estrada's party stalwarts deserted his coalition. By October 2000 these movements had contributed to a highly charged political conflict between Estrada and his loyal mass supporters on one side—and Arroyo, middle-class civil society, Catholic groups, and progressive social movements on the other.[15]

Emotional outrage displayed on the streets of Manila and beyond was tempered by Estrada's impeachment trial—which unfortunately unravelled before the president's guilt could be proven. In 2001, Estrada was removed extraconstitutionally through people power with the help of two crucial institutions—the armed forces and the Supreme Court. Estrada's removal was also made possible because of the significant role played by middle-class NGOs and leftist social movements, who mobilized and helped political opposition against him.[16]

Polarized Civil Society and Contested Democracy under Arroyo

At the outset, people power in 2001 was celebrated at home but criticized abroad. Rather than resolving the political conflict, the country was subjected to further political instability with civil society at the centre of this contentious period.[17] Among violent instances was the massive protest of pro-Estrada supporters in May 2001. Despite this uprising being violently repressed by the military, it displayed the mobilization power of organizations that could be considered part of civil society sympathetic to an ousted leader.[18] Although Estrada was an ineffective leader, this popular backlash represented resentment and longing for another vision of democracy not espoused by the Philippines' political elites and allied civil society groups.[19]

Civil society groups encountered a dilemma when Arroyo—elected as president in 2004—became embroiled in an electoral fraud scandal. The en masse resignation of several cabinet officials resulted in a crisis of legitimacy for the Arroyo administration. This time, however, CSOs were unable to tap into reliable power in order to mobilize and create a semblance of a new conflict to collectively defend democracy. The extraconstitutional nature of Estrada's removal dissuaded some CSOs from embarking on a similar initiative against Arroyo.[20]

While unpopular, Arroyo's government was politically strategic in co-opting the country's institutions—military, legislature, Church, judiciary, and bureaucracy. Arroyo's influence also reached civil society where some leaders appointed by Arroyo chose to remain in her government.[21] The anti-Arroyo coalition spearheaded by what remained of the anti-Estrada alliance was best described as a hotchpotch of familiar and strange bedfellows. Fragmented political opposition was also weak—by failing to impeach Arroyo—despite appeals made by some leaders for military intervention. The last serious destabilization attempt against Arroyo in February 2006 was unsuccessful because civil society groups—such as the Black and White Movement—were not able to effectively recruit protest participants.[22]

AQUINO'S *DAANG MATUWID* AND REFORMIST CIVIL SOCIETY

Philippine politics stabilized after the 2010 presidential elections with the convincing victory of Benigno Simeon Aquino. As former president Corazon Aquino's first-born, Benigno's sudden rise to head of state was largely due to his political pedigree rather than his competence or sterling track record. Filipino voters had enough of the destabilizing conflict between the Estrada and Arroyo political coalitions that had held the nation hostage for almost a decade—entrusting the presidency to a scion of one of the country's most powerful political dynasties.[23]

President Benigno Aquino's campaign centred on reforms that sought political accountability from wrongdoings committed by the Arroyo administration. His government's anticorruption stance—summarized in the slogan *Daang Matuwid* or the Straight Path—captured the longing of a nation for morality-oriented leadership.[24] Apart from prosecuting wrongdoing, the president also appointed prominent personalities in the country's anticorruption institutions.

President Benigno Aquino appointed leaders of reform-oriented civil society groups to join his administration. In particular, he appointed leaders who belonged to the anti-Arroyo Black and White Movement—a predominantly liberal and middle-class coalition of civil society groups who mobilized against Arroyo. Benigno Aquino aligned with political parties with extensive linkages to social movements and democratic NGOs. One of them—a segment of the Philippine left, the Akbayan Party—proudly sought to instigate "new politics" by advocating reforms and participatory politics. The Akbayan Party was described as "a coalition of academics, ex-CPP cadres, social democrats, populists, trade unionists, and peasant leaders, and NGO/civil society activists".[25] Akbayan and its allies in civil society became, to a large extent, beneficiaries of the Aquino administration, dubbing it "remarkable in a political system where such positions traditionally fall to the President's own party or to supporters from other mainstream political parties within the coalition".[26] Apart from the traditional Liberal Party, this political bloc had a profound influence in determining Aquino's reform agenda.

Not everyone in Filipino civil society was invited to join Benigno Aquino's government. Other leftist formations such as political party Bayan Muna and its network of organizations deliberately chose to remain distant from Aquino. Porous boundaries between political parties, social movements, and NGOs—enabling CSOs to easily shift alliances—were also possible because of weak and clientelistic-based parties.[27] Even if Benigno Aquino's reform agenda largely overlapped with the progressive agenda of left-oriented civil society groups, not everyone was selected to assist in realizing his administration's goals.[28]

THE CHURCH'S FALL FROM GRACE: THE REPRODUCTIVE HEALTH DEBATE

Population control has been part of the government's agenda for decades. It was denounced however by the Catholic Church—a social institution that was one of the bastions of resistance against the dictatorship and a subsequent protector of post-martial law sociopolitical order.[29] Progressive social policy occupied an inferior position in post-Marcos administrations despite the support of some politicians. Civil society was similarly divided—with NGO networks such as the Philippine NGO Council on Population, Health, and Welfare clashing with the church on the issue.[30] The Catholic Church and conservative allies adamantly opposed the government's push for legislation on reproductive health or popular campaigns for artificial contraception use.[31] Other right-leaning presidents such as Arroyo only promoted natural family planning methods—guided either by principles or strategic appeasement of civil society groups who could mobilize against her government.

The second Aquino administration sought to finally put an end to the long-standing debate by advocating for an official policy on population control from a reproductive health orientation. This proposed legislation mandated the Philippine state to provide reproductive health services and family planning options to its citizens. Despite contradicting his mother's stance, Benigno Aquino's administration mobilized a multisectoral coalition that included key figures in the women's movement, progressive legislators, and non-Catholic religious groups.

The Catholic leadership—represented by the Catholic Bishops Conference of the Philippines—campaigned against the Reproductive Health (RH) Bill. To its surprise, Aquino declared his willingness to be excommunicated over the passage of the RH Bill. The president was labelled by one bishop as "anti-Christian" for this position.[32] Although Aquino's administration did not adopt a confrontational approach with the Church hierarchy, his position emboldened other like-minded civil society actors to face this powerful institution over reproductive health rights.

Acting on its stewardship role, the Church fought with Aquino over the RH Bill—however, the highly popular president had support from civil society health advocates. Rather than the classic clash between the Philippine state and a united civil society, it became a struggle between CSOs of different persuasions and visions for Filipino society.

The essentialist view of the confrontation had CSOs painted as reformists, against more conservative social forces who identified themselves as custodians of the moral order. Reproductive health advocates were also accused of being purveyors of vice and social permissiveness.[33] Both sides polarized—with the use of such labels from conservative and Catholic-based groups as "modern-day Herods" and "mass murderers" for RH advocates within the NGO community.[34] In retaliation, pro-RH CSOs such as women's groups called their opponents "extremists" and "Talibans". CSOs engaged in public discourse—framing each other negatively as either mindless harbingers of morally bankrupt foreign ideas—or as corrupt, backward, and oppressive unaccountable men professing to be on the side of piety.[35]

The Catholic Church was defending the untenable status quo from a position of weakness—given the decline in religiosity among Filipinos since 1986. Social Weather Stations (SWS) poll conducted in 2013 showed only 37 per cent of Catholics attended mass weekly, compared to 64 per cent in 1991. More salient, however, were various scandals faced by the Church—especially with regard to relations with the previous Arroyo administration. In June 2011, the Philippine Charity Sweepstakes Office cited a 2009 Commission on Audit report that several Catholic bishops received public funds to purchase sports utility vehicles.[36] The scandal weakened the anti-RH position since the bishops implicated in the report were part of the so-called "Malacañang diocese" who remained supportive of former president Arroyo.[37]

Weakened due to internal scandals and loss of faith among its flock, the Church's attempt to mobilize against the RH Law was also a failure because its largest gathering was only a few thousand people. While the Catholic Church's power to mobilize had prevented previous governments in adopting a population control policy, the Church could no longer muster sufficient popular outrage against a policy considered by the public as an idea whose time had finally come. With strong commitment from the Aquino government, the RH Law was signed by the end of 2012 and successfully hurdled all constitutional challenges two years later when the Supreme Court deemed it constitutional, albeit with some partial reservations.[38]

The passage of the RH Law symbolized increasing assertiveness of politicians against the tremendous influence of the Catholic Church on public policy matters. Previous governments were unable to institute policies that provided choices to poor families. The Catholic Church insisted on opposition based more on dogma and unwieldy assumptions about Filipino society than on grounded realities. This case did not simply signify the defeat of a formerly powerful member of civil society against the state as it was further proof of battles within Filipino civil society based on values and visions for society. The Catholic Church lost this particular battle because politicians benefitted from the support, expertise, and networks of other CSOs—specifically, progressive NGOs, academics, female academics, health advocates, and other religious groups.

SHADY NGOs AND THE PORK-BARREL SCANDAL

Philippine civil society has an established record of advocating for good governance, democratization, and community empowerment. Apart from holding government accountable and proposing progressive policies, civil society is also a crucial vehicle of service delivery to the public[39]—particularly relevant for marginalized sections of society or areas far from the reach of the government. CSOs are given participatory roles in decision-making and governance processes oriented towards a partnership between the state and civil society. The Philippines has rich narratives containing NGOs' noble and empowering pursuits towards a democracy more meaningful to ordinary citizens.[40]

Along the fringes of society, however, there are members of Filipino civil society who deviate from supposedly shared goals of democracy promotion and popular empowerment. The influx of foreign funding since the late 1980s provided a steady source of financial resources for NGOs. Democratizing functions mandated by law and credibility to participate in governance was previously exploited by "shady" political entities. For example, some politicians would rather co-opt CSOs or create their own CSO—thereby undermining the autonomy of existing CSOs. Academics labelled them as GONGOs (government-owned NGOs), GRINGOs (government-run or -initiated NGOs), FUNDANGOs (fund-driven NGOs), and even the humorous name Come N'GOs (fly-by-night NGOs).[41]

Civil Society as Scapegoats: The Pork-Barrel Scandal

The good reputation of NGOs as service providers became the impetus for what can be considered as the biggest scandal related to Filipino civil society. On 12 July 2013, the media exposed a multibillion peso scam dealing with the disbursement of "pork barrel" funds to legislators. A whistle-blower revealed at least three senators and eleven district representatives were involved in deals made by Janet Lim Napoles which had created some twenty dummy NGOs used to siphon state funds. In exchange for these funds, Napoles offered lawmakers about 40 to 60 per cent kickback from the defrauded money. The by-product of the collusion was billions of pesos of public monies channelled through beneficiary funds—mainly NGOs created by Napoles.[42] This kind of transactional rent-seeking behaviour by politicians using private entities as conduits of their patrimonial plunder has been previously studied.[43]

The pork-barrel scandal is historic and involved PhP6.156 billion of public money from just 2007–9 according to the government audit report—with Napoles receiving a disproportionate PhP2.1 billion despite owning only ten of the eighty-two NGOs identified by the report. Half of the amount given to Napoles came from three opposition senators who were subsequently indicted and suspended from office by the Ombudsman. Napoles, in this case, is an individual who brokered back-door deals away from the spotlight—that enabled her to amass a fortune out of taxpayers' money. Notable bogus NGOs involved were, for example, cooperatives and development NGOs such as the Masaganang Ani para sa Magsasaka Foundation Inc (MAMFI), Social Development Program for Farmers Development (SDPFFI), and Pangkabuhayan Foundation Inc (Pang-FI). The use of dummy corporations—usually run by her relatives—involved former and incumbent legislators as stakeholders in the NGOs.[44]

There were significant reputational costs of the pork-barrel scandal to President Aquino—to whom Napoles surrendered after the anomaly was exposed. There was a 15-point drop in his satisfaction ratings as an erstwhile popular president.[45] Not only was the integrity of Aquino's anticorruption posture a casualty of the scandal—members of his party were also involved. The institutionalized presence of CSOs in fiscal processes and service delivery made such plunder possible. The pork-barrel scandal was not only "the most serious political challenge that confronted the Aquino administration since it came to office", it also provoked broader public scepticism about the credibility of NGOs as the bulwark of Philippine democracy.[46]

On the supply side, the ability to create dummy NGOs was made possible because of the relatively lax regulatory framework provided by the government.[47] During the congressional investigative hearing on this scandal, it was revealed that NGOs submitted valid papers to the Securities and Exchange Commission—the regulatory agency tasked to accredit and monitor NGOs.[48] Non-state entities like Napoles were ultimately able to penetrate the fiscal system because of the institutionalized "umbilical cord" linking the state and CSOs and the lack of clear and extensive regulatory mechanisms for non-governmental entities. Apart from Napoles, it is still unknown whether other individuals or groups committed similar anomalous transactions using different kinds of public funds and dealings with other government agencies.

The Ombudsman ordered the preventive suspension of three sitting senators who belonged to the political opposition—separate to Napoles and other implicated individuals. There is also a money laundering case filed in a US court against Napoles and her family. The damage of fraudulent and corrupt practices of some NGOs involved in development work weighed heavily on the entire spectrum of Filipino civil society.[49] There is now an aversion to NGOs by government agencies afraid of being involved in plunder charges. The public mood also became distrustful of NGOs in the Philippines which affected even long-term advocates within civil society.

Civil Society as Mobilizers: The Million People March

The pork-barrel exposé caused popular outrage in Filipino civil society to an incumbent government that ironically acquired an electoral mandate because of its promise to curb corruption and enforce accountability. Despite recognizing the gravity of the scandal, President Aquino refused to abolish the pork-barrel system but promised to institute governance reforms. Pork-barrel funds are considered vital instruments left to the discretion of politicians in order to maintain loyalty to the chief executive—given the country's weak party system.[50] Aquino's stance further fuelled the anger of ordinary citizens as well as civil society groups not allied with the Aquino administration. Sparked by the emotional indignation of young Filipinos dubbed as "millennials", a planned mobilization dubbed the "Million People March" was held in Manila on 26 August 2013.[51]

Unlike mass mobilizations in the past, there was no clear civil society formation responsible for the planning and conduct of the Million People March. Most of the "usual suspects" labelled as street parliamentarians did not play leadership roles. There was also difficulty in maintaining the presence of protest participants in the absence of a central programme during the event. Apart from the call to wear "white", communication on the Million People March was transmitted through social media platforms such as Twitter and Facebook.[52] The Million People March superficially displayed the mobilization power of certain groups, but was a glaring indication of the continued fragmentation of civil society in the Philippines. The estimated number of participants ranged from 100,000 to 350,000 people attended—falling far short of the target of 1 million participants.[53]

The Million People March led by the middle class did not ultimately have a clear message of action towards the Aquino administration—neither calling for Aquino's resignation nor having coherent political demands. Class-led protest actions in the Philippines therefore require an infrastructure of contention often provided by civil society which draws from its own repertoires and mobilizing networks.[54] Multiple voices heard at the Million People March rally displayed the diversity of social forces comprising Philippine civil society—and also showed civil society less as a unified political agency fighting corruption and more as an arena of diverse groups contesting divergent political agendas.

THE 2016 ELECTIONS AND DUTERTE'S POPULIST CHALLENGE

Despite Aquino's anticorruption campaign convincing foreign audiences, there were significant weaknesses in his brand of leadership. Aquino's accountability drive was partisan—relentlessly punishing enemies while his allies remained untouched. The fruits of development from the growing economy were only advantageous for the top tier of the population with many ordinary Filipinos continuing to suffer from poverty.[55] *Daang matuwid* was inadequate to address problems like the country's inadequate infrastructure, insufficient social services, and widespread criminality. The outgoing president had, to a large extent, governed in safe mode, refusing to embark on building democratic institutions, promoting more transparency through a freedom of information law, and curbing political dynasties. Democratic quality was not, however, any better under Aquino, as the Philippines was only granted a "partly free" status—in terms of political rights and civil liberties throughout his tenure. The Aquino administration believed it satisfied the people so long as it blamed past administrations, selectively prosecuted politicians, and denied the existence of lingering issues.[56]

This political context surrounding the 2016 presidential elections spurred the serious populist challenge of Rodrigo Duterte. Duterte represented, to some extent, the antithesis of *cacique* politicians like Aquino. In the country's capital, Manila, Duterte appears brazen, tough talking, ineloquent, not well-born, foul-mouthed, and contemptuous of politics. During the 2016 electoral campaign, he severely criticized the Catholic Church, the United States, and oligarchic elites. Despite this, there was no concerted effort on the part of civil society to campaign against Duterte although Aquino warned that he constituted a serious threat to Philippine democracy.

Despite the challenges, Duterte had a convincing victory as the first president to hail from Mindanao—with an estimated 16.6 million of the 44 million votes cast in the election. While the liberal-democratic segment of Filipino civil society was unable to mobilize to prevent Duterte's victory—the surprise of the 2016 elections was the emergence of a citizen movement campaigning for Duterte. A cross-class coalition of conservative Filipinos, overseas labour migrants, the educated middle class, the urban poor, and informal workers, constituted a type of grassroots "army of true believers". This social force can be viewed as Filipinos discontented with mainstream civil society believing their interests are better represented by the populist leader.

The Marcos Burial Issue and Civil Society Immobilism

One of Duterte's first actions after assuming office was to fulfil a promise he made to the Marcos family. This was not a surprise as Duterte had already expressed during the electoral campaign his intention to give the late autocrat Ferdinand Marcos a state burial at the Cemetery of Heroes. This issue divided the nation, representing an unresolved issue on the legacy of dictatorship in Philippine democracy. The fact that Filipinos still voted for Duterte revealed the polarizing nature of this issue.

Many constituents were surprised at Duterte's swift move to push ahead with Marcos' burial. Duterte claimed there were no legal hurdles preventing him from bestowing military honours to Marcos as a war veteran and former head of state. The chief executive blamed Aquino's party for not passing a law prohibiting Marcos' burial in the Cemetery of Heroes. Duterte cracked down on dissenters—notably his own vice-president, Leni Robredo—after the latter attended mass protests during the actual day of Marcos' burial.[57]

Some civil society groups supported a case filed in the Supreme Court challenging the chief executive's decision—with the Court deciding after several months there were no constitutional violations in the burial of Marcos.[58] Multiple demonstrations—mostly by students from elite universities such as the University of the Philippines and Ateneo de Manila University—were subsequently mounted in Quezon City, Baguio City, Manila, Legazpi City, Los Banos, Cebu, Makati, Davao, and Cagayan de Oro.[59] A major mass action rally led by leftist social movements and called the National Day of Rage and Unity was held on 25 November 2016 at Luneta Park in Manila City. More moderate middle-class social groups held a rally at the People Power Monument. A similar demonstration was held on 30 November. Notably, there was no groundswell mobilization on the streets for either of these protests. The two civil society coalitions which organized the 25 November and

30 November rallies were reportedly "not working together despite their common anti-Marcos agenda".[60]

Lack of civil society unity on this issue has deep historical roots among those groups previously united—particularly ideological divides and internal bickering. In an unprecedented move, the Duterte presidency also sought to drive a wedge within Filipino civil society by extending an invitation to a faction of the Philippine left to join his cabinet with the promise of pursuing peace talks with the communist movement. During the campaign, Duterte stated he was a leftist, backing up this proclamation by appointing former members of the Communist Party of the Philippines (CPP).[61] Duterte's cabinet contained people endorsed by the CPP which invoked fear in the military establishment.[62] Duterte's strategic move also had an immobilizing effect as CSOs affiliated with the CPP-endorsed faction did not launch major protest actions against the government. The inability of the Duterte administration to defend their appointees against the Commission on Appointments ended the short-lived intimate relationship between the leftists and the president. Duterte was also furious when elements of the New People's Army attacked the countryside when martial law was declared in Mindanao after the siege of Marawi. At the time of writing, there are minor but inconsistent attempts to revive peace talks with communist insurgents while their front organizations in civil society are back on the streets protesting against the Duterte administration.

At some level, the immobilization of civil society was also evident in the inability to engage in political opposition against Duterte's bloody war on drugs. This highly popular war on drugs has resulted in the deaths of thousands of victims—mostly from low-income classes—with outrage and condemnation from the international community. To date, there has been no civil society-led large-scale coordinated effort to hold the perpetrators of this violence accountable. Despite sporadic protest actions against the Duterte administration, the war on drugs has not been the primary issue of mobilization. The Philippines has been flagged by international human rights NGOs such as Human Rights Watch for the spate of extrajudicial killings and, while foreign aid and other tools by the international community have been used to pressure the Philippine government, there has yet to be counterpart measures undertaken by Filipino civil society whose democratic credentials contain a steadfast commitment to human rights and the rule of law.

The war on drugs and Marcos burial issue did not generate pendular mobilizations, and protest issues did not escalate to street feuding akin to the protest cycle that took the country captive during the "lost decade" 2000–10. Mainstream civil society was obviously unable to tap into its reliable mobilization and coalition powers to prevent this action, which could be consistent with public opinion as a February 2016 poll revealed almost six out of ten respondents agreed to giving Marcos a hero's burial.[63]

The inability of previous governments to categorically deny space for the Marcos family to further influence Philippine politics also speaks to a failure of collective action against elements of authoritarianism in the Philippines. The political support received by members of the Marcos family when the late dictator's son almost became an elected vice-president is an example of the ambiguity that lends Duterte some legitimacy and allows him to transform the country into a delegative democracy where constraints to executive power are either downplayed or outrightly undermined.[64]

DUTERTE'S CIVIL SOCIETY: *KILUSANG PAGBABAGO*

The Philippines under Duterte is seen as a democracy under threat given his emphasis on security and order and his disdain for constraints on exercising his power. Duterte has also criticized pillars of the country's liberal-democratic order—such as the Catholic Church, the media, judiciary, and civil society. Apart from these negative remarks, Duterte's government is attempting to create its own civil society flank. Dubbed *Kilusang Pagbabago* or KP (Movement for Change), it is a national mass movement launched under the auspices of former priest-turned-rebel Cabinet Secretary Leoncio "Jun" Evasco Junior. Riding on the tide of Duterte's electoral victory— this government-created movement tries to harness the grassroots that believed in the president's call for change. Government plans for these KP civil society groups appear to be to help battle Duterte's war against drugs, crime, and corruption, assist in the provision of social services, and campaign for political projects such as the president's push for federalism. Parallels can be drawn between this and efforts of previous presidents such as Marcos and Estrada. *Kilusang Pagbabago*'s self-professed main goal is to provide civil society support to President Duterte as leverage against the backlash of old elites—and diminish their power by reforms of the Duterte administration.

Outside the machinery of Duterte's political party—the Partido Demokratiko Pilipino-Lakas ng Bayan (PDP-Laban)—KP is described as a "citizens partner of the Duterte administration". KP is envisioned to be closely integrated with line agencies and local governments, fulfilling three functions relative to the administration: as a watchdog; a platform to disseminate Duterte's agenda directly to people; and as a "defender of the republic during crisis and calamities"—especially against political destabilization from those negatively affected by the changes his government have instituted—such as drug cartels, politicians, judges, and oligarchs.[65]

Though still in its nascent stage of formation, KP bears an uncanny resemblance to organized civil society groups called Bolivarian Circles formed under President Hugo Chávez in Venezuela. These Venezuelan CSOs have a mixed record in promoting democracy. While they mobilized marginalized sectors and pursued community empowerment, they were vital in defending socialist policies of the late president and came to his aid during periods of crisis. It is highly doubtful that these organizations can be autonomous from the government.[66]

It is unclear whether KP CSOs will be taken seriously given that Duterte and other politicians have not fully endorsed the project at the time of writing. Whether or not the KP movement will be empowered will depend on the continued popularity of the incumbent administration as well as the presence of polarizing political conflict in the future. Unlike in Venezuela, it is unclear whether KP will be integrated to Duterte's political party with other civil society groups supportive of the president. The KP project contains contradictions on the autonomy of Filipino CSOs—a sacred operative principle that made civil society the bastion of democracy in the country. If members of civil society who claim to advance the country's democracy agenda will ultimately be co-opted by the state, can they still be considered a credible bulwark against threats to democracy?

CONCLUSION AND FUTURE PROSPECTS

This chapter discussed the role civil society played in Philippine politics after the polarizing and destabilizing period known as the country's lost decade for democracy (2001–10). Particular attention has been given to the stature and credibility of social forces who claim the mantle of civil society have been diminished as a combination of their own actions and deliberate moves by political entities seeking to lessen their power in the political arena. This chapter examined key events in the second Aquino administration (2010–16) and the early part of the Duterte presidency. Mainstream civil society's political influence was at its height during this lost decade and significantly diminished in the period 2010–16. Vital societal pillars—like the Catholic Church, social movements, NGOs, and other social formations—apparently no longer possess the political *gravitas* previously leveraged against the Philippine state in the pursuit of goals such as democratization, social justice, sustainable development, and popular empowerment. This chapter has discussed how the state fought with the Church and its allied social groups for the passage of the RH Law, the use of made-up CSOs in shady transactions such as the pork-barrel scam, and the inability of NGOs to mobilize the public in the streets all show that the country no longer has the strong and unified civil society that has astounded academics, policymakers, and others.

Discourse in this chapter has also revealed an important observation—that Filipino civil society is becoming less of a unified political actor with a single voice, representation, and set of interests. Rather, Filipino civil society must now be seen as an arena of competing social forces penetrated by powerful actors such as the state, capitalists, and external entities. The future of Philippine politics seems less about battles between the state and civil society, but rather a contest between groups within it together with the powerful blocs that bolster and sustain them. The Duterte administration is attempting to write a new constitution that could become a rallying point for disparate civil society groups—further polarizing the country—which might lead the Philippines into another debilitating cycle of pernicious polarization seen during the period of 2001–10.

The fate of civil society is inexorably linked with the fate of Philippine democracy. Assertions of component groups of civil society to have prominent roles in politics must be seen as struggles for deepening democracy—only true if civil society groups remain committed to democratic norms and principles. Civil society groups need to prevent being used by political elites in their squabbles, respect democratic institutions and processes, and have the conscious effort to be reflexive, allow diversity among their ranks, and build capacity for sustained action and engagement with the state. Such aims may be particularly difficult given the global retreat of democracy as well as Duterte's potent populist leadership. However, a strong civil society committed to a more grassroots, participatory and egalitarian vision could be the required protection against attacks on Philippine democracy.

Notes

The author would like to thank Justin Keith Baquisal for providing research assistance.
1. Mary Racelis, "New Visions and Strong Actions: Civil Society in the Philippines", in *Funding Virtue: Civil Society Aid and Democracy Promotion*, edited by Marina Ottaway and Thomas Carothers (Washington, D.C.: Carnegie Endowment for International Peace), pp. 159–87.
2. Muthiah Alagappa, "Civil Society and Political Change: An Analytical Framework", in *Civil Society and Political Change in Asia: Expanding and Contracting Democratic Space*, edited by Muthiah Alagappa (Stanford: Stanford University Press, 2004), pp. 25–57; Catalina Smulovitz, and Enrique Peruzzotti, "Societal Accountability in Latin America", *Journal of Democracy* 11, no. 4 (2000): 147–58.
3. Gordon White, "Civil Society, Democratization and Development: Clearing the Analytical Ground", in *Civil Society in Democratization*, edited by Peter Burnell and Peter Calvert (London: Frank Cass), pp. 6–21.
4. Nancy Bermeo, *Ordinary People in Extraordinary Times* (Princeton: Princeton University Press, 2003).
5. Gerard Clarke, *The Politics of NGOs in Southeast Asia: Participation and Protest in the Philippines* (London: Routledge, 1998).
6. Aries A. Arugay, "Saviors or Spoilers? Explaining 'Civil Society Coups' among Democratizing Regimes", *Thammasat Review* 16, no. 1 (2012): 167–87.
7. Aries A. Arugay and Dan Slater, "Polarization without Poles: Machiavellian Conflicts and the Philippines' Lost Decade of Democracy, 2000–2010", *Annals of the American Academy of Political and Social Science* 681, no. 1 (2019): 122–36.
8. Mary Racelis, "New Visions and Strong Actions: Civil Society in the Philippines", in *Funding Virtue: Civil Society Aid and Democracy Promotion*, edited by Marina Ottaway and Thomas Carothers (Washington, D.C.: Carnegie Endowment for International Peace), p. 172.
9. Ledivina V. Cariño, *Between the State and the Market: The Non-Profit Sector and Civil Society in the Philippines* (Quezon City: Centre for Leadership, Citizenship and Democracy, National College of Public Administration and Governance, University of the Philippines, 2002); Stephen Zunes, "The Origins of People Power in the Philippines", in *Nonviolent Social Movements: A Geographical Perspective*, edited by Stephen Zunes, Sarah Beth Asher, and Lester Kurts

(Oxford: Blackwell Publishers, Ltd., 1999), pp. 129–57; Mark R. Thompson, *The Anti-Marcos Struggle: Personalistic Rule and Democratic Transition in the Philippines* (New Haven: Yale University Press, 1995).
10. Eva-Lotta Hedman, *In the Name of Civil Society: From Free Election Movements to People Power in the Philippines* (Honolulu: University of Hawaii Press, 2006).
11. Benedict Anderson, "Cacique Democracy in the Philippines: Origins and Dreams", *New Left Review* 169, no. 3 (1998): 3–31.
12. Paul David Hutchcroft and Joel Rocamora, "Strong Demands and Weak Institutions: The Origins and Evolution of the Democratic Deficit in the Philippines", *Journal of East Asian Studies* 3, no. 2 (2003): 259–92.
13. Jennifer C. Franco, "The Philippines: Fractious Civil Society and Competing Visions of Democracy", in *Civil Society and Political Change in Asia: Expanding and Contracting Democratic Space*, edited by Muthiah Alagappa (Stanford: Stanford University Press, 2004), pp. 97–137.
14. Aries A. Arugay, "Mobilizing for Accountability: Contentious Politics in the Anti–Estrada Campaign", *Philippine Sociological Review* 52 (2004): 75–96.
15. Dan Slater and Aries A. Arugay, "Polarizing Figures: Executive Power and Institutional Conflict in Asian Democracies", *American Behavioral Scientist* 62, no. 1 (2018): 92–106.
16. Aries A. Arugay, "The Accountability Deficit in the Philippines: Implications and Prospects for Democratic Consolidation", *Philippine Political Science Journal* 26, no. 49 (2005): 63–88.
17. Paul D. Hutchcroft, "The Arroyo Imbroglio in the Philippines", *Journal of Democracy* 19, no. 1 (2008): 141–55.
18. Marco Garrido, "Civil and Uncivil Society Symbolic Boundaries and Civic Exclusion in Metro Manila", *Philippine Studies* 56, no. 4 (2008): 443–65.
19. Arugay and Slater, "Polarization without Poles".
20. Benjamin T. Tolosa, "Framing the Challenges of Political Empowerment and Engagement: Ideational Interventions for Democratization since 2005", in *Agenda for Hope: Democratizing Governance*, edited by Agustin Martin G. Rodriguez and Teresita Asuncion M. Lacandula (Quezon City: Ateneo de Manila University Press, 2009), pp. 49–75.
21. Ben Reid, "Crossovers Double-Crossed: NGOs, Semi-Clientelism, and Political Reform", in *The Routledge Handbook on the Contemporary Philippines*, edited by Mark R. Thompson and Eric Vincent C. Batalla (London: Routledge, 2018), pp. 386–95.
22. Aries A. Arugay, "The Military in Philippine Politics: Still Politicized and Increasingly Autonomous", in *The Political Resurgence of the Military in Southeast Asia: Conflict and Leadership*, edited by Marcus Mietzner (London: Routledge, 2011), pp. 85–106.

23. Mark R. Thompson, "Reformism vs. Populism in the Philippines", *Journal of Democracy* 21, no. 4 (2010): 154–68.
24. Wataru Kusaka, *Moral Politics in the Philippines: Inequality, Democracy and the Urban Poor* (Singapore: NUS Press, 2017).
25. Patricio Abinales, "The Philippines Under Aquino III, Year 2: A Ponderous Slog Continues", in *Southeast Asian Affairs 2013*, edited by Daljit Singh (Singapore: ISEAS – Yusof Ishak Institute, 2013), p. 231.
26. Aileen Baviera, "Aquino: Pushing the Envelope, Single-Mindedly", in *Southeast Asian Affairs 2012*, edited by Daljit Singh and Pushpa Thambipillai (Singapore: ISEAS – Yusof Ishak Institute, 2012), pp. 241–56.
27. Franco, "The Philippines: Fractious Civil Society".
28. Mark R. Thompson, "The Politics Philippine Presidents Make: Presidential-Style, Patronage-Based or Regime Relational?", *Critical Asian Studies* 46, no. 3 (2014): 433–60.
29. Robert L. Youngblood, *Marcos against the Church: Economic Development and Political Repression in the Philippines* (Ithaca: Cornell University Press, 1990).
30. Jennifer Sta. Ana, "The State and Church in the Debates over Reproductive Health and Population Control", *Pampubliko*, 2 February 2016, https://www.pampubliko.com/background-briefings/view/the-state-and-the-church-in-the-debates-over-reproductive-health-and-population-control.
31. Coeli M. Barry, "The Limits of Conservative Church Reformism in the Democratic Philippines", in *Religious Organisations and Democratisation: Case Studies from Contemporary Asia*, edited by Tun-jen Cheng and Deborah A. Brown (London: Routledge, 2005), pp. 167–89.
32. Baviera, "Aquino: Pushing the Envelope".
33. Coeli M. Barry, "Gender, Nation, and Filipino Catholicism Past and Present", in *The Routledge Handbook on the Contemporary Philippines*, edited by Mark R. Thompson and Eric Vincent C. Batalla (London: Routledge, 2018), pp. 330–40.
34. Nicole Curato and Jonathan Ong, "The RH Bill Debate and Responsible Participation", *ABS-CBN News*, 29 September 2012, http://news.abs-cbn.com/blogs/insights/09/28/12/rh-bill-debate-and-responsible-participation.
35. Kusaka, *Moral Politics in the Philippines*.
36. John Antiquerra, "The Media, the Bishops and the Missing Pajeros", Center for Media Freedom and Responsibility, 6 September 2011, http://cmfr-phil.org/media-education-3/the-media-the-bishops-and-the-missing-pajeros/.
37. Jocelyn Uy and Maricar Cinco, "Bishop Cruz Tells 'Pajero 7': Confess". *Philippine Daily Inquirer*, 29 June 2011, http://newsinfo.inquirer.net/19014/bishop-cruz-tells-%E2%80%98pajero-7%E2%80%99-confess.
38. Kristine Alave and T.J. Burgonio, "Massive Church Rally Set against RH bill",

Philippine Daily Inquirer, 3 August 2012, http://newsinfo.inquirer.net/241737/massive-church-rally-set-against-rh-bill.

39. Gerard Clarke, "NGOs in the Post-Marcos Era", in *The Routledge Handbook on the Contemporary Philippines*, Mark R. Thompson and Eric Vincent C. Batalla (London: Routledge, 2018), pp. 376–85.
40. Ma. Glenda S. Lopez and Marlon A. Wui, eds. *Philippine Democracy Agenda, Volume 2: State-Civil Society Relations in Policy-Making* (Quezon City: Third World Studies Center, 1998).
41. Karina Constantino-David, "From the Present Looking Back: A History of Philippine NGOs", in *Organizing for Democracy: NGOs, Civil Society, and the Philippine State*, edited by G. Sidney Silliman and Lela Garner Noble (Honolulu: University of Hawaii Press, 1998), pp. 26–48.
42. Nancy Carvajal, "NBI Probes P10-B scam", *Philippine Daily Inquirer*, 12 July 2013 http://newsinfo.inquirer.net/443297/nbi-probes-p10-b-scam0.
43. Paul David Hutchcroft, *Booty Capitalism: The Politics of Banking in the Philippines* (Ithaca: Cornell University Press, 1998).
44. Aries Rufo, "Bong, JPE, Jinggoy 'suki to Napoles NGOs", *Rappler.com*, 20 August 2013, https://www.rappler.com/newsbreak/36665-reville-enrile-estrada-suki-napoles-ngos.
45. John Sidel, "The Philippines in 2013: Disappointment, Disgrace, Disaster", *Asian Survey* 54, no. 1 (2014): 64–70.
46. Renato De Castro, "The Philippines in 2013: Popular President Confronts Daunting Challenges", in *Southeast Asian Affairs 2014*, edited by Daljit Singh (Singapore: ISEAS – Yusof Ishak Institute, 2014), p. 246.
47. Gerard Clarke, *Civil Society in the Philippines: Theoretical, Methodological, and Policy Debates* (Abingdon: Routledge, 2013).
48. Ayee Macaraig, "After 'Pork' Scam, COA to Issue New Rules for NGOs", *Rappler*, 17 March 2014, https://www.rappler.com/nation/53208-coa-new-guidelines-ngos-after-pdaf-scam.
49. Jorge V. Tigno, "The Philippines", in The *Routledge Handbook of Civil Society in Asia*, edited by Akihiro Ogawa (London: Routledge, 2017), pp. 110–28.
50. Yuko Kasuya, *Presidential Bandwagon: Parties and Party Systems in the Philippines* (Pasig City: Anvil Publishing, Inc, 2009).
51. Reynaldo Santos Jr. "Timeline: The Road to the Million People March", *Rappler.com*, 25 August 2013 https://www.rappler.com/nation/37271-timeline-road-to-million-people-march.
52. Gang Badoy, "Million People March Set at Luneta against Pork Barrel Scam", *Philippine Daily Inquirer*, 19 August 2013, http://newsinfo.inquirer.net/469217/million-people-march-set-at-luneta-against-pork-barrel-scam#ixzz5Cj5HeQ65.
53. Carmela Lapena, "Mascots and Music at the Million People March", *GMA*

News Online, 26 August 2013, http://www.gmanetwork.com/news/lifestyle/content/323659/mascots-and-music-at-the-million-people-march/story/.
54. Arugay, "Mobilizing for Accountability".
55. Bea Orante, "Despite High Economic Growth, PH Poverty on the Rise", *Rappler.com*, 24 September 2015, http://www.rappler.com/move-ph/106966-economic-growth-ph-poverty.
56. Aries A. Arugay, "The Philippines in 2016: The Electoral Earthquake and Its Aftershocks", in *Southeast Asia Affairs 2017*, edited by Daljit Singh and Malcolm Cook (Singapore: ISEAS – Yusof Ishak Institute, 2017), pp. 277–96.
57. Jorge V. Tigno, "The Philippines in 2017: Popularity Breeds Contempt", *Asian Survey* 58, no. 1 (2018): 142–48.
58. Ocampo et al. v. Enriquez, G.R. Nos. 225973, 225984, 226097, 226116, 226117, 226120, and 226294, 334012843082. For a full decision of the case, see http://news.abs-cbn.com/news/11/10/16/read-the-marcos-burial-cases-decision.
59. David Lozada and Raisa Serafica, "#ScrapPork Rallies Still a Go Despite Aquino's Reform Plans", *Rappler.com*, 25 August 2013, https://www.rappler.com/nation/37145-anti-pdaf-rallies-still-a-go.
60. Patty Pasion, "Protesters to Duterte, Marcoses: This Is What Democracy Looks Like", *Rappler.com*, 1 December 2016, https://www.rappler.com/nation/154118-duterte-marcos-burial-protest-rally-democracy.
61. Arugay, "The Philippines in 2016".
62. Carolina G. Hernandez, "The Philippines in 2016: The Year that Shook the World", *Asian Survey* 57, no. 1 (2017): 135–41.
63. Gerry Lirio, "Is Philippines Ready for a State Burial for Marcos?", *ABS-CBN News*, 14 March 2016, http://news.abs-cbn.com/halalan2016/focus/03/13/16/is-philippines-ready-for-a-state-burial-for-marcos.
64. Guillermo O'Donnell, "Delegative Democracy", *Journal of Democracy* 5, no. 1 (1994): 55–69.
65. Elias Baquero, "Kilusang Pagbabago Cebu Launched", *Sunstar*, 1 October 2016, http://www.sunstar.com.ph/article/101593/.
66. Kirk Andrew Hawkins and David R. Hansen, "Dependent Civil Society: The Círculos Bolivarianos in Venezuela", *Latin American Research Review* 41, no. 1 (2006): 102–32.

INDEX

Note: Page numbers followed by "n" refer to endnotes.

A
Abu Sayyaf, 242, 244
Abueva, Jose V., 66, 73, 83, 91n13
Administrative Discipline Unit, 115
Advocacy Commission (AdCom), 71
AFP. *See* Armed Forces of the Philippines (AFP)
agricultural support, 216
Akbayan Citizen's Action Party, 113
Akbayan Party, 290–91
Aldaba, Rafaelita, 200, 203n24
Amnesty International, 41
Annex on Normalization, 250–52
anti-charter change rally 1997, 65–66
anticorruption agencies, 105
anticorruption governance capacity
   Aquino, 112–16
   Arroyo, 106–12
   decentralized identification, 115
   Philippines, 105
   plans, 104, 109, 114
   political legitimacy, 111
   straight path to governance, 101, 116, 117
anticorruption machinery, 104–5, 115
anti-drug campaign, 51
anti-dynasty legislation, 13
Aquino, Benigno S., 106
Aquino, Corazon, 112, 113

Araneta, Salvador, 64
ARF. *See* ASEAN Regional Forum (ARF)
Armed Forces of the Philippines (AFP), 241, 251, 254
ARMM. *See* Autonomous Region in Muslim Mindanao (ARMM)
Arroyo, Gloria Macapagal, 2, 7, 9, 15, 16, 27, 42, 48, 57n27, 61n79, 63, 75, 175, 286, 288
   anti-charter change rally in 1997, 65–66
   anticorruption governance capacity, 106–12
   contested democracy, 289–90
   federalism project, 65–72
   good governance, 117
   interrogating federalism, 79
   lapse in judgement, 68
   Office of the Ombudsman, 110
   polarized civil society, 289–90
   political rhetoric, 107
ASEAN Regional Forum (ARF), 268–69, 276
Asian Development Bank, 200
Association of Southeast Asian Nations (ASEAN), 43
   CLMV countries, 268
   Declaration of Conduct, 276

Manila Declaration, 268
post-Cold War security, 268
Code of Conduct in the South
China Sea, 276–79
Austro-Hungarian Empire, 41
authoritarian regimes, 40
"autonomous" region, 24, 64, 71
Autonomous Region in Muslim
Mindanao (ARMM), 71, 168,
208, 215, 217, 219, 221, 242, 248,
259n12, 262n54
poverty incidence, 219
private sector investments in, 218

B
Balisacan, Arsenio, 166, 183n15, 186,
193, 196, 201n4
Bangko Sentral ng Pilipinas (BSP),
127, 135, 136, 139, 153, 155
Bangsamoro Basic Law (BBL), 8, 25,
29, 74, 85, 86, 88, 92n28, 213,
224–25, 243, 253, 255
Bangsamoro Coordination Forum
(BCF), 213
Bangsamoro Development Agency
(BDA), 254
Bangsamoro Islamic Armed Forces
(BIAF), 244, 250, 251, 253–55
Bangsamoro Islamic Freedom
Fighters (BIFF), 212, 243
Bangsamoro Organic Law (BOL), 74,
208, 221, 224, 228, 229, 253, 254
"Bangsamoro problem", 208, 211
Bangsamoro Transition Commission
(BTC), 86, 88, 211, 224, 255
barangays, 65, 71, 74, 244
basic literacy, 218
Batalla, Eric Vincent C., 49, 59n51
Bautista, Andres, 9, 10
Bayan Muna, 291
Beijing, 269, 273

Bertók, János, 102, 119n19
bid rigging, 200
Binay, Jejomar, 48
Bolivarian Circles, 301
bond investors, 140
bossism, 50, 82
brain drain, migration, 166
Braithwaite, John, 208
BRP Gregorio Del Pilar, 272
"build, build, build" programme, 26,
178
Bukovansky, Mlada, 111, 122n69
Bureau of Internal Revenue (BIR),
135
business practices, 195
business process outsourcing
companies (BPOs), 139
call centres, 164
remittances, revenues, 2000–17, 160,
163, 164
success story, 160, 163–65

C
CAB. *See* Comprehensive Agreement
on the Bangsamoro (CAB)
"*cacique* democracy", 6, 288, 297
CAFGUs. *See* Civilian Armed Forces
Geographical Units (CAFGUs)
call centres, 164
Cambodia, Laos, Myanmar, and
Vietnam (CLMV countries), 268
Camp Abubakar, 253, 254
camp-to-community transformation,
254
cantonments, 245
Carpio-Morales, Conchita, 9, 10, 27,
114
Catholic Bishops Conference of the
Philippines, 292
Catholic Church
"anti-Christian", 292

Index   311

civil society, 286
  fall from grace, 291–93
Catholic leadership, 292
Cebu, 80–81
Cebuano speakers, 50
Cemetery of Heroes, 298
Central European University (CEU),
    40
Centrist Democratic Party, 73
Centrist Democratic Party Institute
    (CDPI), 73
Chávez, Hugo, 301
China
  bilateral relations with SCS,
      274–75
  Code of Conduct, 276–77
  economic zone, 270
  export, 138
  Manila Declaration, 269
  Mischief Reef, 265, 268–70, 276
  National Institute for South China
      Sea Studies, 274
  "nine-dash line", 267, 270, 272, 274,
      276, 279
  Scarborough Shoal, 272–74
Citizens' Movement for a Federal
    Philippines (CMFP), 67–68, 70
Civilian Armed Forces Geographical
    Units (CAFGUs), 247
civil liberties, 39, 40
Civil Service Commission (CSC), 108,
    109
civil society
  after dictatorship, 287–90
  Aquino's reformist, 290–91
  church's fall from grace, 291–93
  contested democracy, 289–90
  country's "lost decade of
      democracy", 286
  Daang Matuwid and reformist,
      290–91

  between democratization and
      crisis, 287–90
  division in, 18
  Duterte's populist challenge,
      297–300
  2016 elections, 297–300
  Family Income Distribution, 17
  fragmentation of, 12–21
  Kilusang Pagbabago, 300–301
  Marcos burial issue, 298–300
  Million People March, 296–97
  non-violent collective action, 287
  PDP-Laban, 13
  political issues, 288
  pork-barrel scandal, 294–96
  post-Marcos era, 286
  president's ratings, 13–14
  reproductive health debate, 291–93
  resistance, 288–89
  role of, 287
  trust and satisfaction ratings, 18–21
civil society organizations (CSOs),
    285, 289
church's fall from grace, 291–93
Clinton, Hillary, 270–71, 282n23
code of conduct (COC), 266
  ASEAN *vs*. China, 266
  China, 276–77
  South China Sea, 270, 276–79
Cold War, 268
collective action problem, 100, 101,
    103
colonial rule, 62
Combating Corruption, 119n20,
    120n29, 121n48
Come N'GOs (fly-by-night NGOs),
    294
Commission on Audit (COA), 108,
    109, 114, 292
Commission on Filipinos Overseas
    (CFO), 165

Commission on Human Rights, 3, 15, 41
Communist Party of the Philippines (CPP), 137, 299
Communist Party of the Philippines–New People's Army (CPP-NPA), 15
community development, 218
community security, 209
Competition Act, 187
Competition and Consumer Commission of Singapore (CCCS), 200
competition law, 24, 187–89, 198, 201. *See also* Philippines Competition Commission (PCC)
competition law and policy, 186
　business practices, 195
　challenges in the law, 196–97
　economic development, 191–92
　entrepreneurs, 194–95
　government policies, 195–96, 200
　micro, small and medium-sized enterprises, 194–95
　oligopolies, 192–94
　regulatory capture, 198–99
　trade associations role, 195
complementary track, peacemaking, 210, 213–17
Comprehensive Agreement on the Bangsamoro (CAB), 79, 85, 88, 98n89, 208, 210, 211, 239, 243, 251, 252, 255, 256
ConCom. *See* Consultative Commission (ConCom)
conditional cash transfer (CCT), 45
Conditional Cash Transfer Program, 129
Constitution of the Philippines, 3, 6, 9, 13, 63, 65, 66, 68, 71, 79, 84, 87, 90n7, 92n22, 287

Article IX, 9, 10
Article XII, 188
opinion polls on amendment, 2014 and 2016, 76–77
constitutional change to 2001, 64–65
Constitutional Commissions, 9, 64, 66, 73, 83
constitutional provisions, 68–69
construction manufacturing, 130
Consultative Commission (ConCom), 68, 70, 71, 74, 79, 80, 89
Consultative Committee, 3, 52
Corbyn, Jeremy, 48
Cordillera People's Liberation Army (CPLA), 210, 246–47
Corona, Renato, 9, 47
Corporation Code of the Philippines 1980, 189
corrupt game, 100
corrupt politicians, 43
corruption
　codes of conduct, 102
　collective action problem, 100, 103
　developing countries, 102
　major public policy issue, 99
　normative framework, 102
　principal-agent problem, 100–103
　technical approaches, 100
corruption control
　critical capacities for, 102–5
　Klitgaard approach, 102
　Philippine, 101
　political capacity, 104
　principal agent model, 102
　strategies, 104, 109
Corruption Perceptions Index (CPI), 28, 43, 106, 141, 178, 179, 199
"Cory Constitution", 65
country's "lost decade of democracy", 286
coup d'états, 6, 107

crackdown on drug, 41, 42, 53
critical capacities
    anticorruption agencies, 105
    corruption control, 102–5
    political legitimacy, 111
"culture of compliance", 187
Curato, Nicole, 48

D
daang matuwid, 2, 7, 112, 115, 116, 290–91, 297
Dangerous Drugs Board (DDB), 55n15
Davao, 50, 128, 129, 137
David, Randy, 13, 49, 59n56, 64
de Dios, Emmanuel, 131, 132, 143n12
de Lima, Leila, 40, 61n79, 137
de los Santos, Kian, 53
deaths under investigation (DUI), 55n10
decentralized identification, 115
Declaration of Conduct of Parties in South China Sea (DOC), 276
demobilization, 245
democratic facade, 40
Department of Agriculture, 216
Department of Budget and Management, 133
Department of Finance, 80
Department of Interior and Local Government (DILG), 74
Department of Justice, 109
Department of Social Welfare and Development (DSWD), 175
Department of Trade and Industry (DTI), 196
developing countries
    bid rigging, 200
    business process outsourcing, 160
    corruption, 99, 102
    poverty, 194

"dilawan", 16
Dinglasan, Katrina, 131, 132, 143n12
Diño, Martin, 73
Diokno, Benjamin, 130, 134
disarmament, 245
Disarmament, Demobilization and Reintegration (DDR), 240, 260n23
    Comprehensive Agreement on the Bangsamoro, 252
    Framework Agreement on the Bangsamoro, 249
    non-state armed actors, 244–46
Disbursement Acceleration Program (DAP), 112
Discipline Office, 115, 116
"District of Visayas", 64
Domínguez, García, 130
Downstream Oil Industry Deregulation Act 1998, 189
drug crackdown, 41, 42, 48, 52
drug criminals, 50
drug war, 41
Dureza, Jesus, 223, 224
Dutertards, 16
Duterte, Rodrigo
    "man of action", 231
    Mindanaoan, 223
"Dutertismo", 13, 27
dynastic democracy, 6
dynastic political structures, 220

E
ease of doing business (EODB), 176–77, 185n29
economic density in Philippines, 80–81
economic governance, 23–24
economic growth
    Filipinos, 128
    growth rate, 127–28
    manufacturing growth, 130–31
    socioeconomic plan, 128

economy
  agricultural growth, 147, 149
  business process outsourcing, 160–65
  economic growth, 147–48
  industrial growth, 147, 150
  institutions, supply side, 176–80
  living standards, 169–75
  macroeconomic management, 153–60
  overseas employment, 165–66
  regional dynamics, 167–69
  services growth, 147, 151
  structural change, 146–53
EDSA. *See Epifanio de los Santos Avenue* (EDSA)
EEZs. *See* exclusive economic zones (EEZs)
employment
  growth, 130
  migrants, 166
  overseas, 165–66
"enabling law", 243
Energy Regulatory Commission (ERC), 189
Enhanced Defence Cooperation Agreement (EDCA), 267, 273, 277
entrepreneurs, 194–95
Epifanio de los Santos Avenue (EDSA), 1, 7, 64, 65, 285
Equalization Fund, 80
Erdoğan, Recep Tayyip, 39
Estados, 67
Estrada, Joseph, 7, 9, 27, 65–67, 106, 109, 112, 286, 288
  civil society resistance, 288–89
  populist challenge, 288–89
Estrada, Joseph E., 48, 49, 56n27, 61n79
European Commission (EC), 109
European Union (EU), 139
Evasco, Leoncio, 300

excise tax, 135
exclusive economic zones (EEZs), 267, 275, 277–79
ex-CPLA, 247
Executive Order (EO), 129
exports, Philippines, 138–39

F
Family Income and Expenditure Surveys (FIES), 132, 175
Family Income Distribution report, 17
"Federal Advocates for a Better Philippines", 72
"Federal State of the Visayas", 64
Federalism and Constitutional Change conference, 73
federalism, in Philippines
  Arroyo, Gloria Macapagal, 65–72
  changing agreement, 69–70
  constitutional change to 2001, 64–65
  Duterte, Rodrigo Roa, 72–79
  economic density, 2007, 80–81
  financing federalism, 79–82
  Mindanao, 84–88
  political dynasties, 82–84
  regional governments agreement, 68–69
Federasyon, 67
Filipinos
  civil society, 283, 287, 294
  economic growth rate, 128
  unemployment rate, 131–33
Final Peace Agreement (FPA), 213, 240
  Moro National Liberation Front, 242, 247
financing federalism, 79–82
fiscal policies, 127
Fisher, Ronald J., 209
Fitch credit rating agencies, 43

Index

Five Principles of Peaceful Coexistence, 270
fly-by-night NGOs (Come N'GOs), 294
food manufacturing, 130
foreign direct investment (FDI), 187, 191
    Philippines, 136–38
    United States, 139
Foreign Policy magazine, 271
fragmentation trade, 152
Framework Agreement on the Bangsamoro (FAB), 210, 211, 240, 243, 248–50
Freedom Constitution 1986, 7
Freedom House, 41
Freedom of Information Act, 114
freedom of navigation, 270–71
Fu Ying, 274
Functional Literacy, Education and Mass Media Survey (FLEMMS), 218
Fund-driven NGOs (FUNDANGOs), 294
funds
    exports, 138–39
    external risks, 139–40
    foreign direct investment, 136–38
    overseas Filipino workers remittances, 139
    taxes, 135–36

G

Garcillano, Virgilio, 68, 107
Generalized System of Preferences Plus (GSP+), 138, 139
"Global Autonomy, Governance, and Federalism Forum", 74
Global Financial Crisis, 2008–9, 127, 137
global production networks, 164
GONGOs (government-owned NGOs), 294
good governance, 102, 107, 110, 113, 115
Good Governance and Anticorruption Cabinet Cluster, 114
governance capacity, 100
Government of the Philippines (GPH), 239, 242–44, 247, 251
government-owned NGOs (GONGOs), 294
government policies, Philippines Competition Commission, 195–96, 200
government-run or -initiated NGOs (GRINGOs), 294
government spending, 133–35
GPH-MILF Joint Normalization Committee, 228
"graft-prone" agencies, 110
grants, 216
GRINGOs (government-run or -initiated NGOs), 294
gross domestic product (GDP), 133, 138, 142, 182n1, 217
    agriculture, 194
    agriculture's share, 147
    economic growth, 45
    employment, 153
    international remittances, 160
    Philippines, 186
    regional country, 167–68
gross regional domestic product, 218
Gross Regional Product (GRP), 167
guardian of public interest, 103, 105, 110
Gutierrez, Merceditas, 9, 108–9

H

Habito, Cielito, 45
Haiyan typhoon, 43, 46

Hashim, Salamat, 241
Hataman, Mujiv, 215
"Hello Garci", 68, 106
Herfindahl index, 220
"high crimes and misdemeanours", 10
historical injustice, 227
Hontiveros, Risa, 113
Hor Namhong 273
House of Representatives, 6, 9–11, 75–76
Human Rights Commission, 28
Human Rights Watch, 41
human security, 209
"Hyatt 10", 68, 107, 113

I

illiberal democracy, 5–8, 22, 39–42
   liberal reformism, 42–47
   right populism, 47–50
   war on drugs, 50–52
illiberal rule, 12
"Imperial Manila", 3, 23
Independent Commission on Policing (ICP), 211, 253
Independent Evaluation Group (IEG), 100, 103
independent government agencies, 40
inequality, 166, 169, 183n15
inflation, 133–35
Information and Communications Technology (ICT), 164
institutional development
   Corruption Perceptions Index, 178, 179
   ease of doing business, 176–77
   Logistics Performance Index, 176, 178–79
   rules of the game, 176
institutions, limited investment in, 217–18
insurrection army, 100, 103

Integrity Development Action Plan (IDAP), 110, 115, 116
Integrity Development Review (IDR), 109, 110, 115
Integrity Development Unit, 115
Integrity Management Program (IMP), 116
Inter-Agency Anti-Graft Coordinating Council, 109
internal management systems, 217
Internal Revenue Allotment (IRA), 82, 167
internally displaced persons (IDPs), 249
International Cooperation Against Corruption, 185n31
International Decommissioning Body (IDB), 251, 253
international environment, 25
international law, 279
International Monitoring Team (IMT), 242
international remittances, 166
interrogating federalism
   financing federalism, 79–82
   political dynasties, 82–84
Islamic State (IS), 208, 224, 225

J

Jee Ick-joo, 52
jobs, 209
Joint Normalization Committee (JNC), 211, 249, 250, 252
Joint Peace and Security Committee (JPSC), 250, 252, 253
Joint Peace and Security Teams (JPST), 250, 254
"judicial docility", 3
justice, 209
justice sector, investment in, 221

Index

K
Kalayaan Island Group, 271
Kilusang Pagbabago (KP), 300–301
Kim, Jim Yong, 99
Klitgaard, Robert, 178, 185n31
Klitgaard's formula, 178
Konrad-Adenauer-Stiftung (KAS) Foundation, 67
Kung walang corrupt, 112
Kusog Mindanaw, 67

L
Labor Force Survey, 132, 175
labour market, 153, 172
Lascanas, Arturo, 137
La Viña, Tony, 224
Le Pen, Marie, 48
"Legislative Track", 86
"lex CEU" legislation, 40
liberal-democratic, 40
liberal oligarchy, 40
Liberal Party (LP), 13, 16, 45, 47, 113, 291
liberal reformism, 41–47
living standard
  education enrolment, 172, 174
  growth with equity, 175
  poverty incidence, 169–70
  and survival rates, 172, 174
  top and bottom income shares, 171
  unemployment rates, 172–73
local governance, 219–21, 228–29
Local Government Act, 183n17
Local Government Code (1991), 63, 65, 80, 82, 84, 219, 220
Local Government Units (LGUs), 219, 220, 229
local normalization, 2575
Logistics Performance Index (LPI), 176, 178–79

Lorenzana, Lito, 70, 71, 73, 83
"low-quality democracy", 6

M
macroeconomic management, 153–60
  current account balances, 158–59
  economic crisis, 153
  exchange rates, 155, 156
  fiscal balances, 162
  government revenue, 158, 160–61
  inflation economy, 153–54
  stock market indices, 155, 157
Maesschalck, Jeroen, 102, 119n19
"majority bloc", 16
"Malacañang diocese", 293
Malolos Congress, 64
Mamasapano incident, 44
managerial capacity, 104
Manila, 51, 167–68, 269, 271, 273, 275, 296
Manila Declaration, 268, 269
Manila Times, 193
manufacturing growth, 130–31
Maoist New People's Army, 246
Marcos, Ferdinand, 3, 9, 43, 241, 242, 285, 298
  burial issue, 298–300
market perceptions, Philippines, 140–41
martial law, 3, 11, 12, 15, 74, 241
Martires, Samuel, 27–28
Masaganang Ani para sa Magsasaka Foundation Inc (MAMFI), 295
Maute group, 244
May 2017 attack on Marawi City, 208
Medium-Term Philippine Development Plan (MTPDP), 107
Memorandum of Agreement on Ancestral Domain (MOA-AD), 212, 242
Mendoza, Ronald, 82

Metro Manila, 76, 80
micro, small and medium-sized enterprises (MSMEs), 187, 194–95
middle class "ABC" voters, 49
migration, brain drain, 166
MILF. *See* Moro Islamic Liberation Front (MILF)
Million People March, 296–97
Mindanao, 3, 24–25, 44, 67, 70, 79, 84–88, 168–69, 209, 297
  complementary track, 210, 213–17
  conflict dynamics, 240–43
  economy and generating jobs, 229–30
  land administration and management agencies, 221
  local governance, 219–21
  Moro National Liberation Front, 248
  peace in, 84–88
  peacebuilding, *see* peacebuilding
  peacemaking, *see* peacemaking
  political Herfindahl index, 220
  political track, 210, 211–13
  political violence, 244
  poverty and insecurity in, 219
  private armed groups, 222
  two-track strategy, 210–11
Mindanao Business Council, 67
Mindanao Coalition of Development NGO Networks (MINCODE), 67
Mindanao Development Authority (MinDA), 229
Mindanao-wide youth employment programme, 230
Mischief Reef, China, 265, 268–70, 276
monetary policies, 127
Moral Renewal Action Plan (MRAP), 110, 115
Moro Islamic Liberation Front (MILF), 8, 24, 25, 84–86, 88, 92n28, 210–13, 216, 222–23, 225, 227–28, 239
  Annex on Normalization, 250–51
  Bangsamoro Islamic Armed Forces, 244
  commanders, 248
  decommissioning in context, 258
  Mindanao conflict dynamics, 240–43
  Muslim Mindanao conflict, 243–44
  normalization, 249
Moro National Liberation Front (MNLF), 65, 84, 85, 88, 90n7, 210, 213, 227, 228, 261n40
  Disarmament, Demobilization and Reintegration, 247
  Final Peace Agreement, 247–48
  "friendly forces", 247–48
  Mindanao conflict dynamics, 240–42
Movement for Change, 300
Muggah, Robert, 246, 256, 260n21
Muller, Jan-Werner, 48, 58n46
Mungiu, Alina, 100, 118n3
Muslim Mindanao, 65, 79
  conflict in, 243–44
  horizontal violence, 243
Mutual Defence Treaty, 278

N

Napoles, Janet Lim, 294–95
Natalegawa, Marty, 273
National Action Plan, 226
national anticorruption, 109
National Anti-Corruption Program of Action (NACPA), 109
National Bureau of Investigation, 109
National Competition Policy, 192
National Competition Review, 187, 192
National Democratic Front (NDF), 15

Index

National Economic and Development Authority (NEDA), 18, 35n65, 128, 130, 135, 192
National Food Authority (NFA), 195, 196
National Price Coordinating Council, 196
National Security Council (NSC), 274, 275
National Telecommunications Commission, 189
neoclassical realists, 266, 267, 280n1
New People's Army (NPA), 137, 299
Newly Industrializing Economies (NIEs), 152
"nine-dash line", 267, 270, 272, 274, 276, 279
non-governmental organizations (NGOs), 13, 39, 248, 253
   civil society, 285, 287, 290–92
   international human rights, 299
   pork-barrel scandal, 294–96
   "shady", 294
normalization
   Annex on, 250–52
   Comprehensive Agreement On the Bangsamoro, 252
   defined, 249
   Framework Agreement on the Bangsamoro, 248–50
   future assessment, 255
   implementation, 252–55
   local normalization, 257
   programme, 227
Nur Misuari, 224, 241, 242
Nye, Joseph, 102, 119n13

O

Obama administration, 53
Obama, Barack, 267, 271
Office of the Ombudsman, 108, 110, 114
Office of the Presidential Adviser on the Peace Process (OPAPP), 210, 216, 217, 232n13
oligopolies, 192–94
Ombudsman, 11, 108–10, 114, 115, 295
opinion polls
   on amendment, 2014 and 2016, 76–77
   federalism in 2009 and 2016, 76, 78
Oplan TokHang, 51
Opportunidades, 175
Orban, Viktor, 39–40
"order over law", 53, 89
Organic Act, 242, 255
Organization of Islamic Cooperation, 213
Organization of Petroleum Exporting Countries (OPEC), 134
organizational capacity, 104
Osmeña, John, 67
overseas employment, 165–66
overseas Filipino workers (OFW) remittances, 139
own-sourced revenue, 219

P

PAMANA (*Payapa at Masaganang Pamayanan*) programme, 210, 213–16
Panatag Shoal, 272–74
Pangkabuhayan Foundation Inc (Pang-FI), 295
Pantawid Pamilya Pilipino Program (4Ps), 26,114, 175
Partido Demokratiko Pilipino-Lakas ng Bayan (PDP-Laban), 13, 15, 16, 73, 75, 76, 79–81, 83, 89, 94n46, 301
peace agreements, 207
Peace Commission, 85
Peace Implementing Panels, 252–53

peace process, 24–25
peacebuilding, 208–9
  challenges to, 227–30
  creating economic opportunity, 229–30
  historical injustice, 227
  local governance, 228–29
  normalization programme, 227
  security, 227–28
peacemaking, 208
  challenges to, 224–26
  rebuild momentum, 224–25
  understanding and addressing extremist threat, 226
penal populism, 49
People Power Coalition, 106
"People Power II", 66, 67
People Power Revolution, 1, 7, 105
People Power Uprising (1986), 285, 287
  see also *Epifanio de los Santos Avenue* (EDSA)
People's Initiative for Reform, Modernization and Action (PIRMA), 65
people's organizations (POs), 287
People's Power Revolution, 64
Pernia, Ernesto, 128
Philippine Army, 247, 253
Philippine Charity Sweepstakes Office, 292
Philippine-China relations, 25
Philippine Competition Act, 24, 187, 189, 196
Philippine Constitution, 9, 115
Philippine democracy, 25
Philippine Development Plan (PDP), 210, 211, 217
  2011–2016, 113–14, 194
  2017–2022, 192
Philippine Export Zone Authority (PEZA), 164

Philippine Government Electronic Procurement System (PhilGEPS), 115
Philippine Institute for Development Studies, 196, 200
Philippine National Police (PNP), 55n10, 219, 250
Philippine National Police Anti-Illegal Drugs Group, 52
Philippine Navy, 272
Philippine peso (PhP), 134–35, 142, 155
Philippine Port Authority, 189
Philippines
  anticorruption governance capacity, 105
  corruption control, 101
  economic density, 80–81
  economic growth rate, 128
  economic record, 1
  exports, 138–39
  foreign direct investment, 136–38
  market perceptions, 140–41
  peso, 134–35
  unemployment rate, 131–33
Philippines Competition Commission (PCC), 24, 186
  business practices, 195
  challenges in the law, 196–97
  competition law, 187–89
  competition policy, 190–91
  economic development, 191–92
  entrepreneurs, 194–95
  GDP growth rate, 186
  government policies, 195–96, 200
  micro, small and medium-sized enterprises, 194–95
  oligopolies, 192–94
  regulatory capture, 198–99
  trade associations role, 195
Philippines Constitution, 188
  Article XII, 188

Index

Philippines—Country Procurement Assessment Report, 200
Philippines Daily Inquirer, 4
Philippines National Competition Policy, 192
Philippines Star, 4
Philippine Statistical Authority (PSA), 130, 131, 138, 182n2
Philippine Stock Exchange Index (PSEI), 158
Phnom Penh, 270, 272, 273
"pivot in Asia", 267, 271
Podemos party, 48
Poe, Fernando, 48, 57n27, 106
police, 249
political butterflies, 47
political capacity, 104
political capital, 224
political clans, 83
political corruption, 102
political dynasties, 13, 82–84
political legitimacy, 104–5, 111, 112, 115, 117
political party, 113, 291
political rhetoric, 107
political track, peacemaking, 210, 211–13
pork-barrel funds, 44
pork-barrel scandal, 294–96
post-Marcos era, 6–7, 11, 12, 43, 286, 291
Potemkin democracy, 40
poverty, 166, 169, 183n15, 210, 218
"power vacuum", 268, 282n16
prelude to 2012, 270–72
"presidentiables", 72
Presidential Anti-Graft Commission (PAGC), 108, 109, 110, 115
Presidential Commission on Values Formation, 108
Presidential Committee on Effective Governance, 108
Presidential Council Against Crime and Corruption, 109
Price Act 1992, 189
principal-agent problem, 100–103
Priority Development Assistance Fund (PDAF), 43
Private Armed Groups (PAGs), 222, 251, 254, 262n54
private sector investment, 218
private sectors, 105
privatization of public policy, 102
Program for International Student Assessment (PISA), 174
project, federalism
   Gloria Macapagal Arroyo, 65–72
   Rodrigo Roa Duterte, 72–79
Project Management Team (PMT), 214
Project of Asia Foundation, 108
public corruption, 99
public enemy number one, 99
public interest, guardian of, 103, 105, 110
public sectors, 105
purchasing power parity (PPP), 171
Putin, Vladimir, 39

Q

quasi "one-party rule", 40
quo warranto, 3, 11, 28

R

Ramos, Fidel V., 7, 27, 65, 71, 105, 112, 269, 274, 275, 277, 283n37, 283n40, 288
Rappler, news outlet, 41
Raquiza, Antoinette R., 44
Raquiza, Maria Victoria R., 45
Reed Bank, 271
"reform constituency", 113
reforming political parties, 83
regional dynamics, 167–69

regulatory capture, 198–99
reintegration, 245
remittances
    and BPO revenues, 160, 163, 164
    economy, 165
    gross domestic product, 160
Reproductive Health (RH) Law, 129, 286, 292–93, 302
Republic Act No. 10963, 160
Republic of the Philippine, 64
Responsible Parenthood and Reproductive Health Law, 129
Revolutionary Proletarian Army–Alex Boncayo Brigade (RPA-ABB), 247
Reyes, Danilo, 50, 59n60
right populism, 47–50
Rizal, Jose, 64
road construction, 218
Robredo, Maria Leonor (Leni), 9, 10, 40, 61n79, 298
Rocamora, Joel, 113, 121n47, 122n74
Roque, Harry, 16
Rose, Gideon, 280n1
Rothstein, Bo, 103, 119n25, 119n26
Roxas, Mar, 45, 113, 122n75
rule of law, 8–12, 29, 49, 103, 113, 114

S
Sajahatra Bangsamoro, 214–15, 216
Sanders, Bernie, 48
satisfaction ratings of presidents, 13–14
Scarborough Shoal, 267, 275
    2012 stand-off in, 272–74
Schacter, Mark, 103, 119n20
Securities and Exchange Commission, 295
security, 209, 227–28
Sereno, Maria Lourdes, 3, 9, 10, 12, 13, 15, 52, 141

services employment, 130
"shady" political entities, 294
Shah, Anwar, 103, 119n20
Sicat, Gerardo P., 152, 182n4
"sick man of Asia", 1, 24, 145, 181
Sidel, John, 50, 59n59
Singh, Ajit, 191, 202n12
Sin, Jaime Cardinal, 45
"Six Point Principles on the South China Sea", 273
small and medium enterprises (SMEs), 194
small arms and light weapons (SALW), 251, 261n46
social democrats, 46
Social Development Program for Farmers Development (SDPFFI), 295
Social Weather Stations (SWS), 17–21, 31n11, 68, 107, 110, 112, 292
socioeconomic agenda, 128–29, 132, 140
socioeconomic plan, 128
socioeconomic status, 17
South China Sea (SCS), 25
    ASEAN, 276–79
    bilateral relations with China, 274–75
    Code of Conduct, 267, 270, 276–79
    "core interest", 271
    external defence capability, 277–79
    "national interest", 271
    overview, 268–70
    prelude to 2012, 270–72
    Scarborough Shoal, 272–74
    Six Point Principles, 273
southern Philippines
    community-centric approach, 257
    Disarmament, Demobilization and Reintegration, 244–46
    local normalization, 257

Index 323

Mindanao conflict, 240–43
Muslim Mindanao conflict, 243–44
non-state armed actors, 244–46
policy coherence, 256–57
State of the Nation Address (SONA), 16, 67, 68, 112, 117
status quo, 24, 63, 220, 292
stock market indices, Philippine, 155, 157, 158
straight path to governance, 101, 112, 116, 117
Subi Reef, 269
subnational dynamics, 167–69
Sulu Archipelago, 242, 244

T
Taliaferro, Jeffrey W., 266, 281n7
"Talibans", 292
taxes, 135–36
    excise oil, 134, 135
Tax Reform for Acceleration and Inclusion (TRAIN), 26–27, 160
tax reform law, 134–35
Teehankee, Julio, 13, 18
telecommunications industry, 193
Teresita Quintos-Deles, 210
Thomas, Vinod, 100
trade associations, 195
Transitional Justice and Reconciliation Commission (TJRC), 211, 221, 228
Transparency International (TI), 28, 99, 178
Transparency International's Corruption Perception Index (TI CPI), 106
Transparent Accountable Governance (TAG), 108, 110
Treaty of Amity and Cooperation in Southeast Asia, 270
Trends in International Mathematics and Science Study (TIMSS), 172, 174
Tripoli Agreement (1976), 65, 90n7
Trump, Donald, 22, 47, 48, 53, 139, 142
Truth Commission, 115, 116, 123n80
turncoatism, 47

U
UN Permanent Court of Arbitration (PCA), 273–74, 276
unemployment
    in Filipinos, 131–33
    rates, 172–73
    welfare effects, 132
Union of Local Authorities of the Philippines (ULAP), 83
United Bangsamoro Justice Party (UBJP), 212
United Nations (UN), 227
United Nations Conference on Trade and Development (UNCTAD), 136, 189, 191, 192
United Nations Convention Against Corruption (UNCAC), 109
United Nations Convention on the Law of the Sea (UNCLOS), 267, 270, 273
United States Agency for International Development (USAID), 109
University of the Philippines (UP), 64, 71
US-China economy, 138
US dollar, 140

V
Value-added Tax (VAT), 135
violent conflict incidents and deaths, Bangsamoro Territory, 222

violent extremism, 224
vocational training, 216
Volume of Production Index (VoPI), 130
Volunteers Against Crime and Corruption (VACC), 10
voting patterns, 221

W
walang mahirap, 112
walang wang-wang, 112, 116
Waltz, Kenneth N., 266, 281n5
Wang Yi, 270, 275
war on drugs, 8, 46, 47, 49–52, 129
West Philippines Sea (WPS), 25
White Movement, 290
Widodo, Joko, 279
World Bank, 33n36, 99, 100, 105, 108, 139, 169, 233n23
  ease of doing business, 176–77
  Logistics Performance Index, 176, 178–79
  Philippines—Country Procurement Assessment Report, 200
  Worldwide Governance Indicators, 178
World Development Report (WDR), 209, 217, 233n25, 234n31
World Justice Project, 9
World Justice Project Rule of Law Index, 141
World Trade Organization (WTO), 140
World Values survey, 49
World War I, 41
Worldwide Governance Indicators, 178
Wu Shicun, 274

Y
Yasay, Perfecto, 274
youth leaders, 226

Z
Zamboanga Siege, 242